Knowledge and Space

Volume 17

Series editor
Johannes Glückler, Department of Geography, University of Heidelberg,
Heidelberg, Germany

Knowledge and Space

This book series entitled "Knowledge and Space" is dedicated to topics dealing with the production, dissemination, spatial distribution, and application of knowledge. Recent work on the spatial dimension of knowledge, education, and science; learning organizations; and creative milieus has underlined the importance of spatial disparities and local contexts in the creation, legitimation, diffusion, and application of new knowledge. These studies have shown that spatial disparities in knowledge and creativity are not short-term transitional events but rather a fundamental structural element of society and the economy.

The volumes in the series on Knowledge and Space cover a broad range of topics relevant to all disciplines in the humanities and social sciences focusing on knowledge, intellectual capital, and human capital: clashes of knowledge; milieus of creativity; geographies of science; cultural memories; knowledge and the economy; learning organizations; knowledge and power; ethnic and cultural dimensions of knowledge; knowledge and action; and mobilities of knowledge. These topics are analyzed and discussed by scholars from a range of disciplines, schools of thought, and academic cultures.

Knowledge and Space is the outcome of an agreement concluded by the Klaus Tschira foundation and Springer in 2006.

More information about this series at https://link.springer.com/bookseries/7568

Johannes Glückler • Heinz-Dieter Meyer
Laura Suarsana

Editors

Knowledge and Civil Society

Editors
Johannes Glückler
Department of Geography
University of Heidelberg
Heidelberg, Germany

Laura Suarsana
Institute Labour and Economy
University of Bremen
Bremen, Germany

Heinz-Dieter Meyer
Professor of Education Governance
and Policy
University at Albany, State University
of New York
Albany, NY, USA

ISSN 1877-9220
Knowledge and Space
ISBN 978-3-030-71146-7   ISBN 978-3-030-71147-4   (eBook)
https://doi.org/10.1007/978-3-030-71147-4

This Springer imprint is published by the registered company Springer Nature Switzerland AG
The registered company address is: Gewerbestrasse 11, 6330 Cham, Switzerland

Acknowledgements

The editors thank the Klaus Tschira Foundation for funding the symposia and the Springer book series on Knowledge and Space. The team of the Klaus Tschira Foundation and the Studio Villa Bosch have been contributing greatly to the success of the symposia for now more than a decade. Together with all the authors in this volume, we are grateful to Katrin Janzen, Leslie Ludwig, and Anna Mateja Punstein for their superb assistance to the editors as well as to the technical editing team for their tireless dedication. Volker Schniepp at the Department of Geography at Heidelberg University has generously helped us to get figures and maps into shape for publication. We also thank all student assistants and colleagues from the Department of Geography who have helped accomplish the symposium as well as this 17th volume in this book series. We are particularly grateful to Tobias Friedlaender, Alaina Marangos, Johannes Nützel, Sandy Placzek, Helen Sandbrink, and Marius Zipf.

Contents

1 The Place of Civil Society in the Creation of Knowledge 1
Laura Suarsana, Heinz-Dieter Meyer, and Johannes Glückler

Part I (Re-)Thinking Civil Society

2 The Dialectic of Civil and Uncivil Society—Fragility, Fault Lines, and Countervailing Forces 19
Heinz-Dieter Meyer

3 Civil Society as an Agent of Change 43
Rupert Graf Strachwitz

4 Undone Science and Smart Cities: Civil Society Perspectives on Risk and Emerging Technologies 57
David J. Hess

Part II Analyzing Civil Society Organizations

5 Specialists for Crumble Cakes? The German LandFrauen Organizations in Social Innovation, and as Educational, Social, and Political Institutions 77
Laura Suarsana

6 Schools of Democracy? Giving Circles and the Civic and Political Participation of Collaborative Philanthropists 109
Angela M. Eikenberry

7 Time Banks as Transient Civic Organizations? Exploring the Dynamics of Decline 131
Johannes Glückler and Jakob Hoffmann

Part III   Spaces, Networks and Fields

**8   Civil Society as Networks of Issues and Associations:
The Case of Food** 149
Mario Diani, Henrik Ernstson, and Lorien Jasny

9   The Geography of Giving in the Philanthropic Field 179
Johannes Glückler and Laura Suarsana

**10   Global Authenticity, Local Authority: Epistemic Power,
Discursive Geographies, and the Creation
of Civil Society Knowledge Networks** 209
E. Fouksman

Part IV   Doing Civil Society

**11   Democracy Movement and Alternative Knowledge
in Hong Kong** 235
Kin-man Chan

**12   Epistemic Activism in the United States:
Examining Meetings Across the Silos of Civil Society** 253
Jen Sandler

**13   Seeding a New World: Lessons from the FeesMustFall
Movement for the Advancement of Social Justice** 275
Adam Habib

**14   Civility, Education, and the Embodied Mind—Three
Approaches** 291
Heinz-Dieter Meyer

The Klaus Tschira Foundation 309

Index 311

Contributors

Kin-man Chan Center for Social Innovation Studies, The Chinese University of Hong Kong, Shatin, New Territories, Hong Kong

Mario Diani Department of Sociology and Social Research, University of Trento, Trento, Italy

Angela M. Eikenberry School of Public Administration, University of Nebraska Omaha, Omaha, NE, USA

Henrik Ernstson Centre for Public Policy Research, School of Education, Communication and Society, King's College London, London, UK

E. Fouksman Centre for Public Policy Research, School of Education, Communication and Society, King's College London, London, UK

Johannes Glückler Department of Geography, University of Heidelberg, Heidelberg, Germany

Adam Habib University of Witwatersrand, Johannesburg, South Africa

David J. Hess Department of Sociology, Vanderbilt University, Nashville, TN, USA

Jakob Hoffmann Department of Geography, University of Heidelberg, Heidelberg, Germany

Lorien Jasny Department of Politics, University of Exeter, Exeter, UK

Heinz-Dieter Meyer Professor of Education Governance and Policy, Department of Educational Policy and Leadership, University at Albany, State University of New York, Albany, NY, USA

Jen Sandler Department of Anthropology, University of Massachusetts Amherst, Amherst, MA, USA

Rupert Graf Strachwitz Maecenata Institute for Philanthropy and Civil Society, Berlin, Germany

Laura Suarsana Institute Labour and Economy, University of Bremen, Bremen, Germany

Chapter 1
The Place of Civil Society in the Creation of Knowledge

Laura Suarsana, Heinz-Dieter Meyer, and Johannes Glückler

This interdisciplinary volume addresses the relations between civil society and knowledge from a social, institutional, and spatial perspective. As knowledge and civil society are co-constitutive (any voluntary civic agency would seem to require a minimum of knowledge and the *kinds* of civic agency shape the production and use of knowledge), we approach their relationship from two viewpoints: (a) what we know and how we think about the civil society shapes our action in it; (b) the particular relations between knowledge and civil society shape how knowledge in civil society becomes actionable. Adhering to the first imperative, we should carefully reflect and occasionally reconsider our assumptions about civil society. In line with the second imperative, we should carefully distinguish the ways in which civil society impacts knowledge. These range from knowledge creation, its interpretation, and its influence on societal and political discourses to its dissemination through civil society.

This book's authors contribute to the discussion on these relations through conceptual reflections on the role and current developments in civil society as well as through empirical research that yields new insights into these relations. Also, they invite readers and researchers to take new and unconventional perspectives on civil

L. Suarsana (✉)
Institute Labour and Economy, University of Bremen, Bremen, Germany
e-mail: laura.suarsana@uni-bremen.de

H.-D. Meyer
Professor of Education Governance and Policy, Department of Educational Policy and Leadership, University at Albany, State University of New York, Albany, NY, USA
e-mail: hmeyer@albany.edu

J. Glückler
Department of Geography, University of Heidelberg, Heidelberg, Germany
e-mail: glueckler@uni-heidelberg.de

J. Glückler et al. (eds.), *Knowledge and Civil Society*, Knowledge and Space 17,
https://doi.org/10.1007/978-3-030-71147-4_1

society and offer some outside-the-box perspectives on how civil society can be conceived and analyzed. Conceptual and empirical approaches go beyond the traditional division of the three sectors—market, state, and civil society—to offer inclusive frameworks, and take a broader and more integrative view on civil society and civic agency. In this introduction to the volume, we review selected strands of the contemporary debate and invite readers to examine the role of and relation between civil society and the creation, interpretation, and reproduction of knowledge, followed by a reflection on contemporary perspectives on the civil society concept. Finally, we will outline the book's structure and sketch out the individual contributions to the questions raised in this volume.

Knowledge and Civil Society

Knowledge has been the focal concept in this book series. Beyond the many conceptualizations of and ascriptions to this term, knowledge denotes the human understanding of concrete and abstract phenomena of the world in which we live. Human understanding differs from data and information in that it is built and rests in people's minds. Whereas bits of data or parcels of commodity can be transferred, knowledge requires comprehension to be translated from one person to the other and from one place to the other. Though being bound to the individual, the creation and interpretation of knowledge remains a relational social process, often collaborative and situated within the confines of symbolic, cultural, and institutional frames (Glückler, Herrigel, & Handke, 2020; Meusburger, 2008). Hence, learning and knowing are geographically situated and contingent social practices (Bathelt & Glückler, 2011).

Similarly to the notion of knowledge, the concept of civil society is also contested (Jensen, 2006) and has received contributions from various disciplines in a broad field of study. Researchers of civil society generally address "the diversity and richness of institutions, organizations and behaviors located between the 'market' and the 'state'" (Anheier, Toepler, & List, 2010, p. V). Civil society encompasses the so-called third or nonprofit sector, which, according to the widely used functional and operational definition of the "Johns Hopkins Third Sector" project, includes organizations that are formal or "institutionalized to some extent," private or "institutionally separate from government," nonprofit-distributing, self-governing, and voluntary, "involving some meaningful degree of voluntary participation" (Salamon & Anheier, 1992, pp. 136–137). Beneath this societal landscape of organizations, practices, and institutions, the concept of civil society is further connected to the public sphere (Calhoun, 2011; Habermas, 1991, 1996), to civic modes of behavior, social movements, or, as an "utopian project," to self-governing democratic coexistence (Adloff, 2005, pp. 8–9).

The relation between civil society and knowledge has several dimensions. Civil society organizations and civic practices are deeply involved in the *creation*, *interpretation*, and *dissemination* of knowledge.

First, civil society has a role in the *creation of knowledge*. Through financial or material support and programming priorities, grant-making foundations and associations as well as further nonprofit-organizations are strongly involved in the funding of higher education institutions and research activities (Warren, Hoyler, & Bell, 2014). Civil society organizations serve as spaces for knowledge production and "democratic innovation" (della Porta & Pavan, 2017, p. 198). Further, civil society organizations and formally and informally organized individuals themselves are active in innovative social practices and in knowledge creation through research activity and the development of new conceptual approaches and solutions for society, addressing societal challenges in the field of social innovation (Domanski, Howaldt, & Kaletka, 2020; Howaldt & Schwarz, 2010; Moulaert, 2016) as well as technology. Researchers increasingly recognize civil society organizations as co-creators of knowledge in regional innovation processes and as elements of innovation systems (Asheim, Grillitsch, & Trippl, 2017). Scholars in regional governance as well as in international development work consider the local embeddedness and knowledge of civil society actors to be key success factors for locally adapted problem-solving (Christmann, Ibert, Jessen, & Walther, 2019; Latulippe & Klenk, 2020; Mistry & Berardi, 2016). This has led to post-colonial debate on issues of legitimization and power structures as well as to discussions on the relations between different forms of knowledge (Antweiler, 1998; Briggs & Sharp, 2004, pp. 661–676; see Chap. 10 by Fouksman). In recent decades, new organizational forms such as innovation communities of interest (Brinks & Ibert, 2015, p. 363), open labs, and makerspaces have emerged as an infrastructure, enabling individuals to independently develop technical solutions, innovations, and prototypes, and to learn through cooperation (Brinks, 2019; Maravilhas & Martins, 2019). In citizen science, individuals are actively engaged in the advancement of empirical research, collectively collecting or analyzing data (Strasser, Baudry, Mahr, Sanchez, & Tancoigne, 2019).

Second, civil society actors actively affect and intervene in the *interpretation of knowledge, sense-making, and political and societal agenda-setting,* hereby influencing public debate and opinion. Civil society as a "locus of political activity" (Cohen & Arato, 1992, p. XVIII) serves "the articulation, aggregation, and representation of interests" (Diamond, 1994, p. 8). In the conception of civil society as the public sphere, a place of deliberation (Calhoun, 2011; Habermas, 1991, 1996) and an "arena in which political ideas are raised, debated, and decided" (Bob, 2011, p. 216), civil society serves "to inform its members, and potentially influence the state and other institutions" (Calhoun, 2011, p. 321). With the globalization of communication and digitalization, the public sphere has increasingly shifted from the national to a global level (Castells, 2008). Associations and lobbies bundle interests as well as they advocate in pre- or non-political contexts and within political process (Cohen & Arato, 1992; Fung, 2003; Hendriks, 2012; Warren, 2011), thereby framing knowledge and (re)interpreting it (Benford & Snow, 2000, see also Chap. 11 by Chan). Hendriks (2006) distinguishes between formalized fora at a micro-level, where deliberation occurs through "participants from civil society who have relatively unformed and flexible preferences," on one hand and the public sphere at the macro-level on the other, as an informal space of "unconstrained communication [. . .] where public opinion is formed, shaped and contested" (Hendriks, 2006, p. 502). Dodge (2010) finds dualistic strategies of deliberation and transmitting ideas both in cooperation with government within deliberative fora as well as staying critical and autonomously outside of these fora. Further, civil society actors can be elements of epistemic communities, with experts on often global geographical scales sharing a common understanding of knowledge and a "common cognitive framework" (Cohendet, Grandadam, Simon, & Capdevila, 2014, p. 929; Haas, 1992). From here, actors interpret and transmit knowledge into policy and distribute it into external local contexts (see Chap. 10 by Fouksman). International nongovernmental actors "directly influence domestic educational policies and as they construct a global interpretation of, and set of responses to, worldwide educational 'needs'" (Meyer & Benavot, 2013; Mundy & Murphy, 2001, p. 85). Further, philanthropists and grant-making civil society organizations exert influence on societal debate with regard to which societal problems they address through their funding, and in their decisions on which topics and selected fields of research they actively support (Clarke, 2019; Frickel et al., 2010; Tompkins-Stange, 2020, see also Chap. 4 by Hess).

Third, civil society organizations are involved in *education and the dissemination of knowledge*. Worldwide, NGOs and other nonprofit educational institutions offer education and training, providing basic and higher education and adult learning (Meyer & Boyd, 2001; Priemer, 2015). Cooperation and networks between the state, market, and civil society in the field of education policy have gained increasing importance in the field of global education policy, where they have also raised critical concerns about an emerging deficit of democratic accountability (Ball, 2012; Meyer & Boyd, 2001; Meyer & Powell, 2020; Meyer & Rowan, 2006). In this way, civil society may play constructive roles as innovator in the field of education, but also faces the risk of educational privatization and filling the gaps left by the governmental education system, with philanthropy towards educational institutions covering an increasingly large share of educational finance and thus sometimes gaining asymmetrical influence on educational structures (Archer, 1994; Ball, 2012; Meyer & Zhou, 2017). Apart from their role in formal education systems, civil society and civic action are expected to provide opportunities to practice, develop, or build civic and citizenship skills, convey democratic values and knowledge of political processes, and to enable and motivate citizens to further political activities (Cohen & Arato, 1992; Dekker, 2009; Eikenberry, 2009; Foley & Edwards, 1998, pp. 11–12; Lichterman & Eliasoph, 2014; Putnam, 2000; Verba, Schlozman, & Brady, 1995). However, the scope and impact of civil society associations as schools of democracy in a Tocquevillian and neo-Tocquevillian sense, emphasizing the "educative, skill-building, and psychological contributions of associations" (Fung, 2003, p. 517), is subject of discussion (Dekker, 2014, see Chap. 2 by Meyer).

Civil engagement has a geographical dimension as well. The numerous types of organizations and activities discussed in this volume range from activities in specific local and regional contexts to organizations that are integrated in global networks and communities. Apart from the spatial scales of actions and their impacts, this volume's authors also illustrate the richness and context-specificity of particular types of civil society, and thus contribute novel insights into civil society's practices and organizations in their relation to knowledge.

Looking for Civil Society in Unexpected Places

Several authors in this volume have utilized unconventional, innovative, and broader perspectives of civil society, addressing its ephemerality, fragility, and intermediality. In a tradition with a two-century-long pedigree, researchers typically conceive civil society as a place of organizations and associations between market and state, characterized by clearly discernible structures and high amounts of persistence and durability. They also often conceive it as unfolding in the agora of the public sphere, that unambiguous social and physical space in which private actors meet to carry out their business of shared interest. This was particularly obvious when civil society reclaimed widespread intellectual attention in the wake of the events associated with the fall of 1989. Thus, it was two large, formal organizations—the Catholic Church and Solidarnosc in Poland—that supplied the crucial infrastructure in which the cracks of the Soviet Union's empire first became obvious. Likewise, the call "Wir sind ein Volk" [We are one people] was first heard in the former GDR's Protestant churches, the only large social space uncontrolled by a dictatorial government. In both cases, it was large-scale formal organizations that provided arenas of civic associations and energy that played a crucial role in the events leading to the fall of the Berlin Wall and, eventually, the Soviet Empire. In a similar vein, researchers often equate the "third sector"—a frequent connate of the civil society—with "non-governmental and nonprofit organizations."

In this volume, we are attempting to expand the optic on the civil society by foregrounding those less expected and unexpected spaces and geographies in which civil society energies unfold, are blocked, and may re-organize and regroup. In particular, several contributors in this volume suggest that an understanding of the full range of civil society action (and its obstacles) should comprise how civil associations and mobilization takes place in spaces of ephemerality, such as:

- networks, fields, and epistemic communities;
- types of knowledge and ways of doing (or not doing) science;
- by means of often unseen small-scale, grass-roots philanthropy, collective action groups, or rural (but quite "unprovincial") women's associations;
- and through social movements that can be harbingers of civility, but can also overshoot their goal and turn violent and uncivil.

The easy fragility and easy reversal of civility into incivility, and hence, the great fragility of civil society are another theme of this collection of papers. While researchers of civil society have previously tended to emphasize its progressive and democratic potential, the last two decades have brought in their tow many social and political reversals that, we may consider today, have grown into spaces of increased inequality and normative and moral heterogeneity that civil society made possible in the first place.

Civil society space, in this perspective, is pre-eminently a social space that may manifest with equal probability as institutional space, virtual space, or physical space. Given the dramatic changes associated with the digital revolution, this is not surprising. Mobilization, organization, and communication—while not limited to the virtual world—are severely hampered if they do not also unfold in cyberspace. Intermediality—both in the sense of multi-mediality (for example, physical and virtual mobilization) and of in-between-ness (e.g., between market and government, or between formal organization and movement) is rapidly becoming a lasting characteristic of civil society. In short, we propose that a useful expansion of our gaze to take in the full range of civil society activities is facilitated by paying greater attention to the ephemeral, fragile, and intermedial nature of civil society processes. Rather than viewing these characteristics as defects or negations of civil society, we may see them as essential aspects and staging grounds of civil society action. In what follows, we flesh out this perspective and offer a brief overview of the chapters included in this book.

The Book's Structure

The authors of Part I of this volume, *(Re-)Thinking Civil Society*, reflect on the role of civil society in contemporary societies. Scholars have formulated a broad range of normative expectations towards civil society's role in democratization and deliberation, with sociologists and political scientists intensively discussing this relation both conceptually and empirically (Cohen & Arato, 1992; Diamond, 1994; Katz, 2006; Walzer, 1995; Warren, 2001). One often finds "the classical liberal, the representative democratic, and the participatory" visions of democratic governance are in contest (Fung, 2003, p. 517). "Contrasting positions highlight that different political theories call on particular kinds of actors within civil society to promote democracy—from individuals, to oppositional groups and social movements, to apolitical associations" (Hendriks, 2006, p. 490). This is accompanied by arguments that civil society's democratic functions are "contingent rather than necessary" (Warren, 2011, p. 378). Undemocratic and uncivil manifestations of civil society are debated (Bob, 2011; Chambers & Kopstein, 2001; Clarke, 2019) as well as possible contradictions between deliberative democracy and civic activism within civil society as a "site for deliberative politics" (Levine & Nierras, 2007; Young, 2001, p. 689), all the way to the suggestion that civil society is "a mere abstraction without substance" (Fine, 1997, pp. 7–28).

Heinz-Dieter Meyer (Chap. 2) contributes to this debate, reflecting on the dialectics of civil and uncivil society. Drawing on Tocqueville, he addresses fragilities and vulnerabilities of the civil society and its inherent risks of tipping towards a "gilded" or "bourgeois" society, tending towards despotism. Meyer suggests that we distinguish more carefully between the *structural and the normative face of civil society,* noticing that the two do not necessarily vary together (a structurally robust third sector of the civil society may coexist with a normatively uncivil society). He concludes with a reflection on the possibility that civil society does not generate the kinds of normative constraints and forces needed to maintain it, and points to relevant parallel concerns in the thought of Tocqueville and contemporary theorists like Böckenförde.

Rupert Graf Strachwitz (Chap. 3) discusses the role of civil society as a change agent in contemporary societies, marked by a crisis of capitalism, democracy, and the nation state, as well as growing inequalities. He outlines potentials and limitations of civil society with regards to its possible role in societal development in a globalized world and examines ways by which the interplay between civil society, the state, and the market may be improved. He supports a value-based approach to civil society and emphasizes the necessity of normative principles when looking at civil society organization, as well as the relevance of trustworthiness of civil society organizations as a prerequisite for their functioning as agents for social change.

David J. Hess (Chap. 4) reflects on the relation between knowledge, technology, and civil society. He explores industrial transition movements in the field of energy as a contemporary form of civil society, and discusses subdivisions in this type of social movement. Hess explores the absence of knowledge as "undone science" in emerging technologies, with regard to research on privacy and health risks for the case of smart cities and smart meters. Regarding civil society's connections with politics of knowledge, he outlines how civil society actors may identify areas of undone science, mobilize resources that allow for research in the identified fields, and enable democratic political processes.

The chapters in the second part of this volume, *Analyzing Civil Society Organizations*, contribute to the knowledge of specific forms of contemporary civil society organizations and offer different approaches to their analysis. Laura Suarsana (Chap. 5) focuses on the LandFrauen organization, a national association of local clubs and associations in Germany. She analyzes the local diversity of civic practices and examines their role in social innovation. Empirically, she illustrates that the LandFrauen make social, cultural and educational offers to address local women's needs in locally specific ways and that they often stimulate social change in the rural areas of Germany. She discusses how the LandFrauen activities are organizationally enabled within vertical and horizontal associational structures and how they are able to adapt to local needs and to initiate social change by interconnecting with the local contexts in which they operate. The deep integration of a large and diverse base of members in rural society empowers the LandFrauen to enact functions as local initiators, catalysts, and multipliers in regional development.

Angela M. Eikenberry (Chap. 6) presents empirically based insights on giving circles as an individualized and informal form of collaborative philanthropic giving and on their influence on their members' civic and political participation. She discusses the role of this emergent form of voluntary associations as schools or pools of democracy, as promoters of civic and political participation, and she discusses how voluntary associations enable their members to develop their skills.

Johannes Glückler and Jakob Hoffmann (Chap. 7) explore the workings of time banks as a new organizational form of exchanging voluntary services within local communities. Whereas researchers of time banks have often focused on their normative aspects and design principles to strengthen democracy or to facilitate co-creation and reciprocity, the authors observe a lack of knowledge about the processes, mechanisms, and dynamics through which the civic practices as well as the organizational form of time banks actually evolve and operate. Previous researchers have observed an empirical puzzle: Why are time banks so often volatile and short-lived organizations? Based on a detailed case study of a time bank in Southern Germany over a period of 11 years, Glückler and Hoffmann illustrate how using dynamic social network analysis helps convey an understanding of the dynamics of organizational life through the lens of the structure and trajectory of individual practices in a time bank.

In Part III of this book, *Spaces, Networks and Fields*, the contributors adopt perspectives on civil society with which they challenge common sector-based conceptualizations of civil society or the third sector (Salamon & Anheier, 1992) as lying between market and state. This perspective has been challenged through empirical observations and conceptualizations that integrate overlaps and hybridization (Anheier & Krlev, 2014; Evers, 2020; Hasenfeld & Gidron, 2005; Lichterman & Eliasoph, 2014), as well as theoretically through approaches such as neo-institutionalism and network perspectives, contributing to a broader understanding of civil society and extended the research field (Adloff, 2016; Brown & Ferris, 2007; Burt, 1983; Diani & McAdam, 2003; Diani & Pilati, 2011; DiMaggio & Powell, 1983; Evers, 1995; Faulk, Lecy, & McGinnis, 2012; Galaskiewicz & Burt, 1991; Guo & Acar, 2005; Johnson, Honnold, & Stevens, 2010; Krashinsky, 1997; Marquis, Glynn, & Davis, 2007; Marshall & Staeheli, 2015, see also Chap. 8 by Diani, Ernstson, and Jasny).

Mario Diani, Henrik Ernstson, and Lorien Jasny (Chap. 8) propose an approach with which they integrate conceptualizations of civil society as a discursive and associational space, combining perspectives on both communicative practices and actors. They provide evidence of civil society as networks of issues and associations for the case of food-related issues in the three urban settings of Cape Town, Bristol, and Glasgow. Firstly, they analyze the structure of networks of issues within three civil society organizations in this field, to gain information on their agenda structures and on how they shape public discourse. Secondly, through empirical exploration of inter-organizational civic networks, they focus on the question if and to what extent the prioritization of food-related issues shapes the structure of alliances within civil society networks, and if this increases the probability of collaboration among two organizations.

Johannes Glückler and Laura Suarsana (Chap. 9) draw on the neo-institutional notion of organizational fields and propose the concept of the philanthropic field to conceptualize the geography of giving and the interrelations of benevolent activities across the domains of private, public, and civic sectors. Empirically, they adopt a multimethod approach including a media analysis of reported acts of giving in the German region of Heilbronn-Franconia and provide evidence on the geography of giving in this region. Based on their analysis, they suggest that the philanthropic field is constituted by diverse actors from all sectors of society who engage in specialization, division of labor, and collaboration. Moreover, practices of giving spread across geographical scales, though the majority of activity concentrates on the local and regional level.

E. Fouksman (Chap. 10) addresses the formation of epistemic communities and the production of knowledge through discursive geographies and identities with two multi-sited case studies in development-focused civil society organizations in Kenya and Kyrgyzstan. She offers insights into how NGOs adapt and use the categories of local and expert knowledge to defend and promote ideas in order to gain both global authenticity and local authority. She demonstrates how these categories provide positions of power for the individuals which are mobile within development networks and within the organizations, and how knowledge and their positions are used to legitimize local project activities as well as to set agenda in global development discourse.

The authors of Part IV of this book, *Doing Civil Society,* provide insights into the practices and challenges of contemporary civil society, utilizing theoretical reflections, scientific analyses, and in-depth ethnographic fieldwork on civil society practices.

Kin-man Chan (Chap. 11) draws on his participant knowledge of the pro-democracy Umbrella movement in Hong Kong to discuss how social movements produce and disseminate alternative knowledge as counter-knowledge to dominant discourses. He analyzes the mobilization period from March 2013 to September 2014 and illustrates how the movement set and changed the public agenda. It mobilized public attention to the issue of constitutional reform through creative actions as well as its ability to provide "repertoires of knowledge practices" (della Porta & Pavan, 2017, p. 300) that allowed for "a common orientation for making claims and acting collectively to produce change" (see Chap. 11 by Chan, p. 237).

Jen Sandler (Chap. 12) offers an approach to broaden the conceptualization of civil society. She argues that civil society is organized and analyzed around silos along lines of organization type, topical focus, and scale, as well as along disciplines. She proposes an integrated perspective of civil society as a set of practices, and hereby focuses on "epistemic activism" projects as cross-field and silo-cutting efforts to produce knowledge and truth and "making it matter." She draws on primary ethnographic fieldwork into civic project meetings of two types of organizations—a civic reform coalition and a social anti-displacement movement—to map epistemic and relational practices and trace the epistemic dimension of civic action.

In his reflection on the #FeesMustFall movement, Adam Habib (Chap. 13) contributes to the understanding of social movements and the lessons to be learnt regarding the effectiveness of protest and social mobilization for social justice. As the Vice-Chancellor and Principal of the University of the Witwatersrand (Wits) in South Africa during the protests, he illustrates the process of violence increasingly becoming an accepted means within the movement, and interrogates the framing and outcomes of the struggle as well as the associated decision-making processes. He raises the importance of ethical conduct by leaders and activists, concluding that social movements must internalize and adapt ethical goals and social justice for sustainable success in social change.

Finally, Heinz-Dieter Meyer (Chap. 14) addresses the question: can there be a civil society without an education that reliably instils norms of civility in the young? What would that education look like? In his chapter on "Civility, Education, and the Embodied Mind—Three Approaches" he argues for a rethinking of education that moves beyond rationalistic conceptions of "head over heart" to one in which head and heart, sentimental and cognitive capacities are in better balance.

Conclusion

This volume reflects the diversity of civil society-knowledge relations—which we have discussed as knowledge creation, interpretation, and dissemination—and the broad variety of knowledge-related civil society practices and organizations within their specific spatial and socio-economic contexts. The authors adopt different angels to reflect on the reframing, analyzing, and doing of civil society, with some offering new conceptualizations and research perspectives.

Beyond that, this book's contributors reveal the reflexivity of this relation: Civil society plays essential roles in the creation of new knowledge, in the invention of innovative social practices, as well as in education and knowledge dissemination. Enactors of civic practices and civil society organizations generate and reinterpret existing knowledge and introduce it into societal debate or larger epistemic networks. At the same time, civil society is highly dependent on knowledge and information in order to perform its functions. Access to knowledge and information, civil society's capability to gain access, acquire, and create knowledge, as well as to process and reinterpret it, are essential for civil society and civic action and to pursue their objectives.

Present developments that affect contemporary civil society open a perspective on new and perhaps unprecedented ambiguities, ranging from rising concerns about incivility, the emergence of new autocratic regimes, increased hurdles for democracy movements (such as in Hong Kong) and shrinking spaces for civil society (Alscher, Priller, Ratka, & Strachwitz, 2017; Anheier, Lang, & Toepler, 2019) to new opportunities through digitalization and new media and the emergence of civil society in unexpected spaces of fields, networks, and communities. There is, also, the still imponderable influence of the coronavirus on everyday life, organizational practice, and civic action: Will our coping with this unprecedented challenge stimulate or chasten and freeze civil society? With regard to what will follow next, we would be glad should this volume contribute to new perspectives and future research on civil society, knowledge, and space.

References

Adloff, F. (2005). *Zivilgesellschaft: Theorie und politische Praxis* [Civil society: Theory and political practice]. Frankfurt: Campus.

Adloff, F. (2016). Approaching philanthropy from a social theory perspective. In T. Jung, S. D. Phillips, & J. Harrow (Eds.), *The Routledge companion to philanthropy* (pp. 56–70). Abingdon: Routledge. https://doi.org/10.4324/9781315740324

Alscher, M., Priller, E., Ratka, S., & Strachwitz, R. G. (2017). The space for civil society: Shrinking? Growing? Changing? *Opusculum, 104*. Retrieved from https://www.maecenata.eu/2017/09/20/the-space-for-civil-society-shrinking-growing-changing/

Anheier, H. K., & Krlev, G. (2014). Welfare regimes, policy reforms, and hybridity. *American Behavioral Scientist, 58*, 1395–1411. https://doi.org/10.1177/0002764214534669

Anheier, H. K., Lang, M., & Toepler, S. (2019). Civil society in times of change: Shrinking, changing and expanding spaces and the need for new regulatory approaches. *Economics: The Open-Access, Open-Assessment E-Journal, 13*, 1–27. https://doi.org/10.5018/economics-ejournal.ja.2019-8

Anheier, H. K., Toepler, S., & List, R. A. (Eds.). (2010). *International encyclopedia of civil society*. New York: Springer. https://doi.org/10.1007/978-0-387-93996-4

Antweiler, C. (1998). Local knowledge and local knowing: An anthropological analysis of contested "cultural products" in the context of development. *Anthropos, 93*, 469–494. Retrieved from https://www.jstor.org/stable/40464844

Archer, D. (1994). The changing roles of non-governmental organizations in the field of education (in the context of changing relationships with the state). *International Journal of Educational Development, 14*, 223–232. https://doi.org/10.1016/0738-0593(94)90036-1

Asheim, B., Grillitsch, M., & Trippl, M. (2017). Introduction: Combinatorial knowledge bases, regional innovation, and development dynamics. *Economic Geography, 93*, 429–435. https://doi.org/10.1080/00130095.2017.1380775

Ball, S. J. (2012). *Global education Inc.: New policy networks and the neo-liberal imaginary*. Abingdon: Routledge. https://doi.org/10.4324/9780203803301

Bathelt, H., & Glückler, J. (2011). *The relational economy: Geographies of knowing and learning*. Oxford, UK: Oxford University Press. https://doi.org/10.1093/acprof:osobl/9780199587384.001.0001

Benford, R. D., & Snow, D. A. (2000). Framing processes and social movements: An overview and assessment. *Annual Review of Sociology, 26*, 611–639. https://doi.org/10.1146/annurev.soc.26.1.611

Bob, C. (2011). Civil and uncivil society. In M. Edwards (Ed.), *The Oxford handbook of civil society* (pp. 209–219). New York, NY: Oxford University Press. https://doi.org/10.1093/oxfordhb/9780195398571.013.0017

Briggs, J., & Sharp, J. (2004). Indigenous knowledges and development: A postcolonial caution. *Third World Quarterly, 25*, 661–676. https://doi.org/10.1080/01436590410001678915

Brinks, V. (2019). 'And since I knew about the possibilities there . . .': The role of open creative labs in user innovation processes. *Tijdschrift voor economische en sociale geografie, 110*, 381–394. https://doi.org/10.1111/tesg.12353

Brinks, V., & Ibert, O. (2015). Mushrooming entrepreneurship: The dynamic geography of enthusiast-driven innovation. *Geoforum, 65*, 363–373. https://doi.org/10.1016/j.geoforum.2015.01.007

Brown, E., & Ferris, J. M. (2007). Social capital and philanthropy: An analysis of the impact of social capital on individual giving and volunteering. *Nonprofit and Voluntary Sector Quarterly, 36*, 85–99. https://doi.org/10.1177/0899764006293178

Burt, R. S. (1983). Corporate philanthropy as a cooptive relation. *Social Forces, 62*, 419–449. https://doi.org/10.1093/sf/62.2.419

Calhoun, C. (2011). Civil society and the public sphere. In M. Edwards (Ed.), *The Oxford handbook of civil society* (pp. 311–323). New York, NY: Oxford University Press. https://doi.org/10.1093/oxfordhb/9780195398571.013.0025

Castells, M. (2008). The new public sphere: Global civil society, communication networks, and global governance. *The ANNALS of the American Academy of Political and Social Science, 616,* 78–93. https://doi.org/10.1177/0002716207311877

Chambers, S., & Kopstein, J. (2001). Bad civil society. *Political Theory, 29,* 837–865. https://doi.org/10.1177/0090591701029006008

Chan, K. (2022). Democracy movement and alternative knowledge in Hong Kong. In J. Glückler, H.-D. Meyer, & L. Suarsana (Eds.), *Knowledge and civil society* (pp. 235–251). Knowledge and Space: Vol. 17. Cham: Springer. https://doi.org/10.1007/978-3-030-71147-4_11

Christmann, G. B., Ibert, O., Jessen, J., & Walther, U.-J. (2019). Innovations in spatial planning as a social process: Phases, actors, conflicts. *European Planning Studies, 28,* 496–520. https://doi.org/10.1080/09654313.2019.1639399

Clarke, G. (2019). The new global governors: Globalization, civil society, and the rise of private philanthropic foundations. *Journal of Civil Society, 15,* 197–213. https://doi.org/10.1080/17448689.2019.1622760

Cohen, J. L., & Arato, A. (1992). *Civil society and political theory.* Cambridge, MA: MIT Press.

Cohendet, P., Grandadam, D., Simon, L., & Capdevila, I. (2014). Epistemic communities, localization and the dynamics of knowledge creation. *Journal of Economic Geography, 14,* 929–954. https://doi.org/10.1093/jeg/lbu018

Dekker, P. (2009). Civicness: From civil society to civic services? *VOLUNTAS: International Journal of Voluntary and Nonprofit Organizations, 20,* 220–238. https://doi.org/10.1007/s11266-009-9089-9

Dekker, P. (2014). Tocqueville did not write about soccer clubs: Participation in voluntary associations and political involvement. In M. Freise & T. Hallmann (Eds.), *Modernizing democracy: Associations and associating in the 21st century* (pp. 45–57). New York: Springer. https://doi.org/10.1007/978-1-4939-0485-3_4

della Porta, D., & Pavan, E. (2017). Repertoires of knowledge practices: Social movements in times of crisis. *Qualitative Research in Organizations and Management, 12,* 297–314. https://doi.org/10.1108/QROM-01-2017-1483

Diamond, L. (1994). Rethinking civil society: Toward democratic consolidation. *Journal of Democracy, 5*(3), 4–17. https://doi.org/10.1353/jod.1994.0041

Diani, M., Ernstson, H., & Jasny, L. (2022). Civil society as networks of issues and associations: The case of food. In J. Glückler, H.-D. Meyer, & L. Suarsana (Eds.), *Knowledge and civil society* (pp. 149–177). Knowledge and Space: Vol. 17. Cham: Springer. https://doi.org/10.1007/978-3-030-71147-4_8

Diani, M., & McAdam, D. (2003). *Social movements and networks: Relational approaches to collective action.* Oxford, NY: Oxford University Press. https://doi.org/10.1093/0199251789.001.0001

Diani, M., & Pilati, K. (2011). Interests, identities, and relations: Drawing boundaries in civic organizational fields. *Mobilization: An International Quarterly, 16,* 265–282. https://doi.org/10.17813/MAIQ.16.3.K301J7N67P472M17

DiMaggio, P. J., & Powell, W. W. (1983). The iron cage revisited: Institutional isomorphism and collective rationality in organizational fields. *American Sociological Review, 48,* 147–160. https://doi.org/10.2307/2095101

Dodge, J. (2010). Tensions in deliberative practice: A view from civil society. *Critical policy studies, 4,* 384–404. https://doi.org/10.1080/19460171.2010.525904

Domanski, D., Howaldt, J., & Kaletka, C. (2020). A comprehensive concept of social innovation and its implications for the local context: On the growing importance of social innovation ecosystems and infrastructures. *European Planning Studies, 28,* 454–474. https://doi.org/10.1080/09654313.2019.1639397

Eikenberry, A. M. (2009). *Giving circles: Philanthropy, voluntary association, and democracy.* Bloomington, IN: Indiana University Press. Retrieved from https://muse.jhu.edu/book/3882

Eikenberry, A. M. (2022). Schools of democracy? Giving circles and the civic and political participation of collaborative philanthropists. In J. Glückler, H.-D. Meyer, & L. Suarsana (Eds.), *Knowledge and civil society* (pp. 109–130). Knowledge and Space: Vol. 17. Cham: Springer. https://doi.org/10.1007/978-3-030-71147-4_6

Evers, A. (1995). Part of the welfare mix: The third sector as an intermediate area. *VOLUNTAS: International Journal of Voluntary and Nonprofit Organizations, 6,* 159–182. https://doi.org/10.1007/BF02353995

Evers, A. (2020). Third sector hybrid organisations: Two different approaches. In D. Billis & C. Rochester (Eds.), *Handbook on hybrid organisations* (pp. 294–310). Cheltenham: Edward Elgar. https://doi.org/10.4337/9781785366116

Faulk, L., Lecy, J. D., & McGinnis, J. (2012). Nonprofit competitive advantage in grant markets: Implications of network embeddedness. *Andrew Young School of Policy Studies Research Paper Series, 13–07.* https://doi.org/10.2139/ssrn.2247783

Fine, R. (1997). Civil society theory, enlightenment and critique. *Democratization, 4,* 7–28. https://doi.org/10.1080/13510349708403499

Foley, M. W., & Edwards, B. (1998). Beyond Tocqueville: Civil society and social capital in comparative perspective: Editors' introduction. *American Behavioral Scientist, 42,* 5–20. https://doi.org/10.1177/0002764298042001002

Fouksman, E. (2022). Global authenticity, local authority: Epistemic power, discursive geographies and the creation of civil society knowledge networks. In J. Glückler, H.-D. Meyer, & L. Suarsana (Eds.), *Knowledge and civil society* (pp. 209–232). Knowledge and Space: Vol. 17. Cham: Springer. https://doi.org/10.1007/978-3-030-71147-4_10

Frickel, S., Gibbon, S., Howard, J., Kempner, J., Ottinger, G., & Hess, D. J. (2010). Undone science: Charting social movement and civil society challenges to research agenda setting. *Science, Technology, & Human Values, 35,* 444–473. https://doi.org/10.1177/0162243909345836

Fung, A. (2003). Associations and democracy: Between theories, hopes, and realities. *Annual Review of Sociology, 29,* 515–539. https://doi.org/10.1146/annurev.soc.29.010202.100134

Galaskiewicz, J., & Burt, R. S. (1991). Interorganization contagion in corporate philanthropy. *Administrative Science Quarterly, 36,* 88–105. https://doi.org/10.2307/2393431

Glückler, J., Herrigel, G., & Handke, M. (2020). On the reflexive relations between knowledge, governance, and space. In J. Glückler, G. Herrigel, & M. Handke (Eds.), *Knowledge for governance* (pp. 1–21). Knowledge and Space: Vol. 15. Cham: Springer. https://doi.org/10.1007/978-3-030-47150-7_1

Glückler, J., & Hoffman, J. (2022). Time banks as transient civic organizations? Exploring the dynamics of decline. In J. Glückler, H.-D. Meyer, & L. Suarsana (Eds.), *Knowledge and civil society* (pp. 131–146). Knowledge and Space: Vol. 17. Cham: Springer. https://doi.org/10.1007/978-3-030-71147-4_7

Glückler, J., & Suarsana, L. (2022). The geography of giving in the philanthropic field. In J. Glückler, H.-D. Meyer, & L. Suarsana (Eds.), *Knowledge and civil society* (pp. 179–208). Knowledge and Space: Vol. 17. Cham: Springer. https://doi.org/10.1007/978-3-030-71147-4_9

Guo, C., & Acar, M. (2005). Understanding collaboration among nonprofit organizations: Combining resource dependency, institutional, and network perspectives. *Nonprofit and Voluntary Sector Quarterly, 34,* 340–361. https://doi.org/10.1177/0899764005275411

Haas, P. M. (1992). Introduction: Epistemic communities and international policy coordination. *International Organization, 46,* 1–35. https://doi.org/10.1017/S0020818300001442

Habermas, J. (1991). *The structural transformation of the public sphere: An inquiry into a category of bourgeois society.* Cambridge, MA: MIT Press.

Habermas, J. (1996). *Between facts and norms: Contributions to a discourse theory of law and democracy.* Cambridge: Polity.

Habib, A. (2022). Seeding a new world: Lessons from the #FeesMustFall movement for the advancement of social justice. In J. Glückler, H.-D. Meyer, & L. Suarsana (Eds.), *Knowledge and civil society* (pp. 275–290). Knowledge and Space: Vol. 17. Cham: Springer. https://doi.org/10.1007/978-3-030-71147-4_13

Hasenfeld, Y., & Gidron, B. (2005). Understanding multi-purpose hybrid voluntary organizations: The contributions of theories on civil society, social movements and non-profit organizations. *Journal of Civil Society, 1,* 97-112. https://doi.org/10.1080/17448680500337350

Hendriks, C. M. (2006). Integrated deliberation: Reconciling civil society's dual role in deliberative democracy. *Political Studies, 54,* 486–508. https://doi.org/10.1111/j.1467-9248.2006.00612.x

Hendriks, C. M. (2012). *The politics of public deliberation: Citizen engagement and interest advocacy.* London: Palgrave Macmillan. https://doi.org/10.1057/9780230347564

Hess, D. J. (2022). Undone science and smart cities: Civil society perspectives on risk and emerging technologies. In J. Glückler, H.-D. Meyer, & L. Suarsana (Eds.), *Knowledge and civil society* (pp. 57–73). Knowledge and Space: Vol. 17. Cham: Springer. https://doi.org/10.1007/978-3-030-71147-4_4

Howaldt, J., & Schwarz, M. (2010). *Social innovation: Concepts, research fields and international trends.* Dortmund: Sozialforschungsstelle Dortmund.

Jensen, M. N. (2006). Concepts and conceptions of civil society. *Journal of Civil Society, 2,* 39–56. https://doi.org/10.1080/17448680600730934

Johnson, J. A., Honnold, J. A., & Stevens, F. P. (2010). Using social network analysis to enhance nonprofit organizational research capacity: A case study. *Journal of Community Practice, 18,* 493–512. https://doi.org/10.1080/10705422.2010.519683

Katz, H. (2006). Gramsci, hegemony, and global civil society networks. *VOLUNTAS: International Journal of Voluntary and Nonprofit Organizations, 17,* 332–347. https://doi.org/10.1007/s11266-006-9022-4

Krashinsky, M. (1997). Stakeholder theories of the non-profit sector: One cut at the economic literature. *VOLUNTAS: International Journal of Voluntary and Nonprofit Organizations, 8,* 149–161. https://doi.org/10.1007/BF02354192

Latulippe, N., & Klenk, N. (2020). Making room and moving over: Knowledge co-production, indigenous knowledge sovereignty and the politics of global environmental change decision-making. *Current Opinion in Environmental Sustainability, 42,* 7–14. https://doi.org/10.1016/j.cosust.2019.10.010

Levine, P., & Nierras, R. M. (2007). Activists' views of deliberation. *Journal of Public Deliberation, 3,* 4. https://doi.org/10.16997/jdd.48

Lichterman, P., & Eliasoph, N. (2014). Civic action. *American Journal of Sociology, 120,* 798–863. https://doi.org/10.1086/679189

Maravilhas, S., & Martins, J. (2019). Strategic knowledge management in a digital environment: Tacit and explicit knowledge in Fab Labs. *Journal of Business Research, 94,* 353–359. https://doi.org/10.1016/j.jbusres.2018.01.061

Marquis, C., Glynn, M. A., & Davis, G. F. (2007). Community isomorphism and corporate social action. *Academy of Management Review, 32,* 925–945. https://doi.org/10.5465/amr.2007.25275683

Marshall, D. J., & Staeheli, L. (2015). Mapping civil society with social network analysis: Methodological possibilities and limitations. *Geoforum, 61,* 56–66. https://doi.org/10.1016/j.geoforum.2015.02.015

Meusburger, P. (2008). The nexus of knowledge and space. In P. Meusburger, M. Welker, & E. Wunder (Eds.), *Clashes of knowledge: Orthodoxies and heterodoxies in science and religion* (pp. 35–90). Knowledge and Space: Vol. 1. Dordrecht: Springer.

Meyer, H.-D. (2022a). The dialectic of civil and uncivil society—Fragility, fault lines, and countervailing forces. In J. Glückler, H.-D. Meyer, & L. Suarsana (Eds.), *Knowledge and civil society* (pp. 19–42). Knowledge and Space: Vol. 17. Cham: Springer. https://doi.org/10.1007/978-3-030-71147-4_2

Meyer, H.-D. (2022b). Civility, education, and the embodied mind—Three approaches. In J. Glückler, H.-D. Meyer, & L. Suarsana (Eds.), *Knowledge and civil society* (pp. 291–308). Knowledge and Space: Vol. 17. Cham: Springer. https://doi.org/10.1007/978-3-030-71147-4_14

Meyer, H.-D., & Benavot, A. (Eds.). (2013). *Pisa, power, and policy: The emergence of global educational governance.* Oxford Studies in Comparative Education: Vol. 23. Didcot: Symposium. https://doi.org/10.15730/books.85

Meyer, H.-D., & Boyd, W. L. (2001). *Education between state, markets, and civil society: Comparative perspectives*. Mahwah: Lawrence Erlbaum Associates. https://doi.org/10.4324/9781410602114

Meyer, H.-D., & Powell, J. J. (2020). New institutionalism in higher education. In M. E. David & M. J. Amey (Eds.), *The SAGE encyclopedia of higher education* (pp. 1084–1089). Vol. 3. Thousend Oaks: Sage. https://doi.org/10.4135/9781529714395.n405

Meyer, H.-D., & Rowan, B. (2006). *The new institutionalism in education*. New York, NY: SUNY Press.

Meyer, H.-D., & Zhou, K. (2017). Autonomy or oligarchy? The changing effects of university endowments in winner-take-all markets. *Higher Education, 73*, 833–851. https://doi.org/10.1007/s10734-017-0109-1

Mistry, J., & Berardi, A. (2016). Bridging indigenous and scientific knowledge. *Science, 352*, 1274–1275. https://doi.org/10.1126/science.aaf1160

Moulaert, F. (2016). Social innovation: Institutionally embedded, territorially (re)produced. In D. MacCallum, F. Moulaert, J. Hillier, & S. V. Haddock (Eds.), *Social innovation and territorial development* (pp. 11–24). Abingdon: Routledge. https://doi.org/10.4324/9781315609478

Mundy, K., & Murphy, L. (2001). Transnational advocacy, global civil society? Emerging evidence from the field of education. *Comparative Education Review, 45*, 85–126. https://doi.org/10.1086/447646

Priemer, J. (2015). *Zivilgesellschaftliches Engagement für Bildung* [Civil societal engagement for education]. Essen: SV Wissenschaftsstatistik gGmbH im Stifterverband für die Deutsche Wissenschaft. Retrieved from http://ziviz.de/publikationen/bildungsstudie_2015

Putnam, R. D. (2000). Bowling alone: America's declining social capital. In L. Crothers & C. Lockhart (Eds.), *Culture and politics: A reader* (pp. 223–234). New York: Palgrave Macmillan. https://doi.org/10.1007/978-1-349-62965-7_12

Salamon, L. M., & Anheier, H. K. (1992). In search of the non-profit sector. I: The question of definitions. *VOLUNTAS: International Journal of Voluntary and Nonprofit Organizations, 3*, 125–151. https://doi.org/10.1007/BF01397770

Sandler, J. (2022). Epistemic activism in the United States: Examining meetings across the silos of civil society. In J. Glückler, H.-D. Meyer, & L. Suarsana (Eds.), *Knowledge and civil society* (pp. 253–273). Knowledge and Space: Vol. 17. Cham: Springer. https://doi.org/10.1007/978-3-030-71147-4_12

Strachwitz, R. G. (2022). Civil society as an agent of change. In J. Glückler, H.-D. Meyer, & L. Suarsana (Eds.), *Knowledge and civil society* (pp. 43–56). Knowledge and Space: Vol. 17. Cham: Springer. https://doi.org/10.1007/978-3-030-71147-4_3

Strasser, B. J., Baudry, J., Mahr, D., Sanchez, G., & Tancoigne, E. (2019). "Citizen science"? Rethinking science and public participation. *Science & Technology Studies, 32*(2), 52–76. https://doi.org/10.23987/sts.60425

Suarsana, L. (2022). Specialists for crumble cakes? The German LandFrauen organizations in social innovation and as educational, social, and political institutions. In J. Glückler, H.-D. Meyer, & L. Suarsana (Eds.), *Knowledge and civil society* (pp. 77–107). Knowledge and Space: Vol. 17. Cham: Springer. https://doi.org/10.1007/978-3-030-71147-4_5

Tompkins-Stange, M. E. (2020). *Policy patrons: Philanthropy, education reform, and the politics of influence*. Cambridge, MA: Harvard Education.

Verba, S., Schlozman, K. L., & Brady, H. E. (1995). *Voice and equality: Civic voluntarism in american politics*. Cambridge, MA: Harvard University Press.

Walzer, M. (1995). The concept of civil society. In M. Walzer (Ed.), *Toward a global civil society* (pp. 7–28). Providence: Berghahn.

Warren, A., Hoyler, M., & Bell, M. (2014). Strategic cultures of philanthropy: English universities and the changing geographies of giving. *Geoforum, 55*, 133–142. https://doi.org/10.1016/j.geoforum.2014.06.006

Warren, M. E. (2001). *Democracy and association*. Princeton, NJ: Princeton University Press.

Warren, M. E. (2011). Civil society and democracy. In M. Edwards (Ed.), *The Oxford handbook of civil society* (pp. 377–390). New York, NY: Oxford University Press. https://doi.org/10.1093/oxfordhb/9780195398571.013.0030

Young, I. M. (2001). Activist challenges to deliberative democracy. *Political Theory, 29,* 670–690. https://doi.org/10.1177/0090591701029005004

Part I
(Re-)Thinking Civil Society

Chapter 2
The Dialectic of Civil and Uncivil Society—Fragility, Fault Lines, and Countervailing Forces

Heinz-Dieter Meyer

Fragility: The Civil and Uncivil Society

Since its inception at the pen of Locke, Montesquieu, Ferguson, Tocqueville, and J. S. Mill, and notably since its revival during the Eastern European anti-totalitarian uprising of the late 1980s and early 1990s, the idea of the civil society has raised hopes, excited social reforms, energized social movements, and inspired writers and activists for whom the term conjures up free association, self-organization, and non-coercive governance. It has been an idea that empowered the overthrow of dictators, the resistance to totalitarian rule, and the protection of minorities. Yet, time and again, and especially in the past several decades, the civil society has also been an arena which has dashed hopes, and disappointed expectations, a sphere where old dictators were overthrown, but new ones were readily installed; where xenophobic rallies replaced the celebration of crumbling walls of repression; where indicators showing that social inequality was being ameliorated turned sharply to signal the reemergence of the gilded society; and where arenas that had witnessed the emergence of independent institutions of educational excellence began to bear witness to the reemergence of oligarchic structures of exclusivity and privilege.

In this paper, I submit that the dialectics reflected in the above zig-zag of the civil society invites us to rethink the civil society in two ways:

- first it requires that we come to terms with the civil society as an *inherently fragile* institution;

I am grateful for helpful comments from Alan Kahan and the members of the SUNY Political Theory Workshop, especially Peter Breiner, Mort Schoolman, and Nathaniel Williams.

H.-D. Meyer (✉)
Professor of Education Governance and Policy, Department of Educational Policy and Leadership, University at Albany, State University of New York, Albany, NY, USA
e-mail: hmeyer@albany.edu

J. Glückler et al. (eds.), *Knowledge and Civil Society*, Knowledge and Space 17,
https://doi.org/10.1007/978-3-030-71147-4_2

- secondly, it demands that we engage more squarely and deliberately the moral *countervailing forces* capable of arresting the slide into incivility.

I address the first task in the first part of the essay, where I plead for an appraisal of the civil society that acknowledges its potentials as well as its pitfalls, ambivalences and tipping points. We need to better understand the features that can make the two superficially homologous and the tipping points at which one morphs into the other. For example, both, *civil society* and *gilded society* are open for the public role of philanthropy and independent associations. They both harness, in their fashion, the energy of people's particularistic attachments. They both encourage bottom-up self-government through foundations, endowments and charitable giving. Both allow for private citizens to shape public life beyond the casting of ballots on election day, and for decentralized private-public partnerships to assume important roles in public life. Both exalt the benign effects of private initiative and self-organization, the important role of self-regulating markets, and their potential to assume some of the governance functions of bureaucratic states.

But against a backdrop of steep socio-economic inequalities and with nation states rocked by the challenges of globalization and mass migrations, these similarities and affinities may also obscure distinctions where *differences of degree* morph into *differences of kind*: where, for example, moderate inequality that often acts as a spur to diligence, entrepreneurialism and a scaffolding for upward mobility tips into extreme inequality that dashes, discourages and demoralizes hopes of collective advancement and breeds distrust and resentment; where the freedom to form associations and create foundations may empower the many under one condition, but also disempower them when a few of these associations become astronomically well-financed and influential. As the civil society gives way to the gilded or bourgeois society it may not only pass tipping points where markets turn from agents of empowering choice to arenas of corrosive inequality. It may also facilitate the morphing of cultural pluralism in a religiously neutral public sphere into normative indifference in a morally anesthetized public square. Or it may see the change of philanthropic giving from cultivating generosity and benevolence to a tool that allows a handful of mega-rich foundations to pursue their policy utopias as they bypass democratic accountability (see, e.g., Collins & Flannery, 2020). As individuals loose sight of the moral foundations of democratic civility, there may be no amount of self-organized associations or philanthropically funded projects to save the civil society.

We can appreciate these ambivalences more thoroughly if we explore the possibility that these changes are not mere aberrations from the default of the civil society, to be repaired by smarter social policy. Rather, we might see the civil society as an inherently *fragile, vulnerable* and corruptible institution that easily morphs into its opposite. Such a dialectical view is aware of democratic civility's association-strengthening effects as well as its community eroding and *dis*sociative potential, its power to energize and as well as to corrode civility. This view may ultimately be more realistic than views that are either one-sidedly optimistic or one-sidedly pessimistic.

But this dialectical view gives rise to a crucial question that is at the center of Part II of this paper: What, if any, are the *countervailing forces* that exist or can be mobilized to keep the civil society from wildly oscillating between strong bottom-up associative impulses and equally strong top-down oligarchic impulses? The view that sees both faces of the civil society—its association-strengthening and its association undermining, its bowling together and bowling alone (Putnam, 1995), its community-building and its "lonely-in-the-crowd" (Riesman, 1969) potential—finds precedent in established social theory. I draw here mainly on Tocqueville who had a keen sense of these ambivalences, and who believed in *the need for countervailing moral and spiritual forces* capable of checking the corruption of the civil society.

Ultimately, this is an essay to restore faith in the civil society by better understanding its vulnerabilities and fragility and by placing the question about countervailing forces more squarely on our intellectual and political agenda.

The essay thus cuts against several rival conceptions:

- *The civil society is in reality "nothing but" a bourgeois society,* a cosmetic and ultimately ineffective dressing of the wounds systemically cut by capitalism. This, the Marxist position, has gained a lot of face-validity in the past 20 years and David Harvey is one of its most effective contemporary proponents: "NGOs have grown and proliferated under neo-liberalism, giving rise to the illusion that opposition mobilized outside of the state apparatus and within some separate entity called 'civil society' is the powerhouse of oppositional politics and social transformation" (Harvey, 2005, p. 21; see also Hunt, 1987). This is the view of the civil society as a thin veil of bourgeois society. Although I believe that the civil society can indeed morph into its uncivil, bourgeois antipode, I believe the reductionist view of it as "nothing but" a veil on capitalism to be ultimately misguided. I also believe that pinning the blame for the most recent failures of the civil society on the new oligarchy (Krugman, 2011; Picketty, 2014; Rosen, 2014) is correct, but not sufficient. For while it seems that the civil society is being upstaged by the untamed market as the righteous heir of self-organized social activity—Piketty: "the risk of a drift towards oligarchy is real and gives little reason for optimism about where the United States is headed" (2014, p. 28)—we ought not ignore that for the civil society to trade places with the gilded society, the idea of virtue-civility and moral restraint more broadly first had to be abandoned *en masse*.

- The second view that this essay challenges is that *the civil society can do no wrong.* This, the romantic conception of the civil society, assumes that the more self-organized associations, the more and the wealthier the philanthropy, and the less state intervention, the better. This, too, is a one-sided view of things that ignores the many ways in which incivility, illiberality, and despotism can grow in the cracks between self-organized associations and in the gaps between classes of formally equal but politically or economically unequal citizens. It also ignores the by now patently obvious fact that a strong associational life *per se* is no guarantee for civility. I'll return to this below.

- Thirdly, and perhaps most importantly: if it is true that the civil society is inherently fragile, we need to reengage the crucial problem of what kinds of *countervailing forces* can be mobilized to keep the project on track? As Alan Kahan (2015) recently reminded us, Tocqueville believed that countervailing forces capable of doing that are necessarily *moral and spiritual*. Although he was a master-analyst of the providential institutional design features that the nascent American democracy inherited, and although these design features were important and necessary to keep the project of liberal democracy on track, they were not sufficient.[1] Institutional design alone cannot save the civil society. But how can moral and spiritual forces be effective given our experience with the civic divisiveness of religion and our decision to coral it into the sphere of private choice carried out behind high walls of separation? I'll suggest that any practicable answer today must include a more effective navigation of the three-fold fault lines of the civil society.

The Inherent Fragility of the Civil Society

The Liberal Account

At the heart of the civil society tradition is the idea of an intermediate social space lodged between citizens and government, and state and market. For John Locke, one of the earliest exponents of the idea, society is both morally and politically prior to the state. For his "Two Treatises on Government" (1689/1988) to effectively reject the Hobbesian Leviathan Locke needed effective instruments of self-government in addition to and beyond the control of the central government. A half century later (1748), Montesquieu emphasized the role of the *corps intermédiaires* to maintain liberty in the face of centralized power (Montesquieu, 1989, pp. 17–18). He did so in response to the rise of centralized monarchical governments of proportions unthinkable for the city-states of antiquity. Montesquieu, like Locke, was concerned that a society squashed between central government on the one hand and an unorganized mass of atomized individuals on the other would inevitably fall victim to the rulers' untrammeled despotism. Intermediate social bodies could check this danger. The author of the "Spirit of the Laws" derived his remedy for government despotism from the experience of pre-monarchical France, where the power of the king's house had once been limited and counterbalanced by the power of rivaling

---

[1] Peter Breiner, in an instructive recent essay (2019), considers how both Rousseau and Tocqueville seek to identify the kinds of *virtuous cycles* that can be engendered by good institutional design to prevent the corruption of democratic government. He demonstrates the affinity in their thought and Tocqueville's largely unacknowledged debt to Rousseau. But to this reader he leaves open the question whether the virtuous cycles thus engendered can carry the full weight of keeping liberal democracy on track. I'll suggest below that neither of the two authors believed that virtuous cycles could succeed without important moral supports.

aristocratic families and municipalities. One of his most famous followers, Alexis de Tocqueville, was later to reconceive this idea based on the new realities of life in modern democracies.

The distrust that Montesquieu expressed vis-a-vis the illiberal tendencies of centralized government was shared by many other European writers. One of the earliest was Wilhelm von Humboldt. His essay on "Die Grenzen der Wirksamkeit des Staates" ["On the Limits of the Effectiveness of the State"][2] still stands as one of the earliest manifestos of civil society thinking. In the essay, von Humboldt limits legitimate state action to a very few necessary domains such as national defense and internal security. Education, in particular, was off limits. Two decades before he became Prussia's chief architect of education, von Humboldt rejected the idea of "national education," which he believed to lie "wholly beyond the limits within which the State's activity should properly be confined" (von Humboldt, 1851/1969, p. 54; see also Meyer, 2016, Chapter 4).

In the hands of these writers, the civil society idea is shot through with an abiding *distrust* in the unfailing benevolence of central government, a rejection of the feasibility of the philosopher-king or the Leviathan model, and an understanding that "even under the best forms, those entrusted with power have, in time, and by slow operations, perverted it into tyranny . . ." (Jefferson, 1779/1984, p. 365). Rather than placing their trust in the reason and benevolence of an exalted few at the helm of the machinery of government, the civil society thinkers place their trust in the ability of an associated citizenry to govern themselves.

Alexis de Tocqueville

Alexis de Tocqueville is the writer who has, more than any other author, developed and elaborated that idea for the new condition of democratic equality. In "Democracy in America", Tocqueville famously observes that "nothing . . . more deserves attention than the intellectual and moral associations in America" (1835 & 1840/1969, p. 517). Voluntary associations were key institutions for democratic vitality (Villa, 2006). "In every case, at the head of any new undertaking, where in France you would find the government or in England some territorial magnate, in the United States you are sure to find an association" (1835 & 1840/1969, p. 513). According to Tocqueville, civil society represents a tradeoff between the benefits of top-down administrative organization and the benefits of vigorous bottom-up participation:

> In America the force behind the state is much less well regulated, less enlightened, and less wise, but it is a hundred times more powerful than in Europe. . . . I know of no other people who have founded so many schools or such efficient ones, or churches more in touch with the religious needs of the inhabitants, or municipal roads better maintained. So it is no good looking in the United States for uniformity and permanence of outlook, minute care of

---

[2] von Humboldt's clunky but exacting title "Ideen zu einem Versuch, die Grenzen der Wirksamkeit des Staates zu bestimmen" ["Ideas to an Essay to Determine the Limits of the Effectiveness of the State"] has typically been shortened to "On the Limits of State Action" in English translations.

> details, or perfection of administrative procedures; what one does find is a picture of power, somewhat wild perhaps, but robust, and a life liable to mishaps but full of striving and animation. (1835 & 1840/1969, pp. 92–93)

The American civil society experience and especially the ubiquity of voluntary associations inspired Tocqueville to adapt Montesquieu's idea of intermediate organizations to the conditions of modern democracy. In Tocqueville's view, liberty was threatened not only by centralized monarchies, but also by rule of the majority in democratic societies, which conceivably could produce a similarly unmediated juxtaposition of centralized power and unorganized masses. The mere fact that democratic government was elected by the majority did little to alleviate this problem. Tocqueville's lasting discovery was that, under democratic conditions, the role of intermediate bodies could be played by *civic associations* that could be at once independent of government and provide great numbers of people with an opportunity to learn and practice the art of self-government.

> One of the happiest consequences of the absence of government (when a people is happy enough to be able to do without it, a rare event) is the ripening of individual strength which never fails to follow from it. Each man learns to think and to act for himself without counting on the support of any outside power which, however watchful it be, can never answer all the needs of man in society . . . . (Tocqueville, 1831–1832/1971, p. XI)

But Tocqueville famously warns:

> But one must say it again, there are but few peoples who can manage like that without a government. Such a state of affairs can only exist at the two extremes of civilization. The savage with nought but his physical needs to satisfy, he too relies on himself. For the civilized man to be able to do the same, he must have reached that state of society in which knowledge allows a man to see clearly what is useful for him *and his passions do not prevent him from carrying it out* (emphasis added). The most important concern for a good government should be to get people used little by little to managing without it. (Tocqueville, 1831–1832/1971, p. XI)

The post-1989 revival

Although highly influential in the United States, in continental Europe the civil society has long been eclipsed by a different narrative, that of the *welfare state*. For many decades the public seemed more deeply preoccupied with socio-economic equality to be ameliorated by the welfare state than by self-government facilitated by self-organized initiative and associations. This trend, if it was one, seems to have been broken by the fall of the Soviet empire and the events of 1989.

In the wake of these events, the idea of the civil society (or any of its synonyms, such as civic associationism or third sector), generated much intellectual and political excitement (see, e.g., Anheier, Lang, & Toepler, 2019; Berger & Neuhaus, 1996; Dahrendorf, 1990; Diamond, 1994; Dionne, 1998; Ehrenberg, 1999; Glendon, 1991; Keane, 1998; Putnam, 1995; Shils, 1991; Walzer, 1995). It promised to be useful not only in resisting the Soviet Union's totalitarianism but also in reframing and reconceptualizing some vexing problems of social reform which often pitted pro-government against pro-market advocates, sometimes superimposing another long-standing controversy between communitarians and libertarians (Walzer, 1995).

That the fall of the Berlin Wall and the implosion of communist collectivism in 1989 should have re-energized the civil society, is, in retrospect, not surprising. For Eastern European dissidents, who had lived their lives under a regime that routinely and zealously squashed all social action independent of the state, the collapse of communism left the public square for the first time free for individual citizens to associate voluntarily. A further spur of excitement came from a newfound skepticism with the bureaucratic bloat of the welfare state and excitement over market-based alternatives. At about the time that the Soviet Empire began its terminal decline, the Western capitalist economies were swept up in a trend toward deregulation and privatization prompted by a reaction against "big government" and a widespread reexamination of the proper responsibilities of government spurred by hopes in a "new public management" that would borrow management ideas from the private sector and adapt them for public sector use (Osborne & Gaebler, 1993).

A further impetus for the resurgence of the idea of civil society was the opening to an ethnic and cultural *pluralism* that characterized societies changed by globalization and immigration. The notion of civic pluralism was revived by writers like Isaiah Berlin (2013), Nathan Glazer (1997), Charles Taylor (1992, 1996) and Michael Walzer (1983; 1995). They argued that the earlier idea of a dominant culture or ethnicity organized around a core of shared values and surrounded by a few dissenting voices on the fringe (duly tolerated by the majority), was and should be giving way to the idea of a *thick* pluralism that sees divergent creeds, beliefs, and worldviews as matters of first importance in a group's self-understanding. Isaiah Berlin saw the new pluralism as a long overdue correction of a rationalist view of humans as creatures of reason and reason only, a view in which shared feelings and beliefs—the stuff of culture—are relegated to a marginal corner in the life of communities. In the new pluralism, the cultural commitments of groups and communities are viewed not as obstacles to be overcome, or as residual remains of an obsolete past, but as durable attachments from which different groups weave their tapestry of collective understanding.

By the mid-1990s, and as a result of these confluences of deep political, ideological, and cultural shifts, the civil society had been re-established as a vital energizing force of liberal democracy (Dionne, 1998; Taylor, 1996; Walzer, 1995).

Democratic Despotism

Near the end of "Democracy in America", Tocqueville (1835 & 1840/1969, p. 690) asks a critical question that has received a far fainter echo from interpreters and advocates of democracy and civil society than his positive and optimistic espousal of the civil society's liberal potential in the earlier parts: "What Sort of Despotism Democratic Nations Have to Fear".

In this section, Tocqueville returns to an idea that had already occupied him in his thinking about the tyranny of the majority: that the equality of conditions may also contain the seeds of despotism. For Tocqueville, the condition of democratic equality, while it may spur civic cooperation and the development of the skill of self-government, also engenders a love for egalitarian conditions and for material comfort and convenience. As a result, people withdraw from the public sphere and into the small circle of family and friends in the spirit of "individualism" which he famously defines as "a calm and considered feeling which disposes each citizen to isolate himself from the mass of his fellows and withdraw into the circle of family and friends" (1835 & 1840/1969, p. 506).

As their self-governing energies weaken, an expanded central government and/ or a few oligarchs that untamed markets have thrown up the Nasdaq, move in to pick up the slack. This opens the door for *democratic despotism*, a new political condition, a kind of tyranny different from the one ubiquitous in the ancient world. The burdens of ancient tyranny "fell most heavily on some," but "never spread over a great number." Democratic despotism, by contrast, is "more widespread" but "milder." It "degrades" rather than "torments."

The slide into despotism can be surprisingly smooth. "[A]n innumerable multitude of men, circling around in pursuit of the petty and banal pleasures" (pp. 691–692) facing each other in a society whose power is "absolute, thoughtful of detail, orderly, provident, and gentle" (p. 692). The individual becomes a self-centered person who exists only "in and for himself, and though he still may have a family, one can at least say he has not got a fatherland" (p. 692).

Democratic despotism is administered by officials who rule more like "schoolmasters" than "tyrants." They preside over a regime which "gladly works for the happiness of its people" so that subjects enjoy themselves, if only because they think "of nothing but enjoyment." Under such a condition the "vices of those who govern" may combine with the "weaknesses of the governed" to bring the American experiment to "ruin." While free choice is still possible, "it daily makes the exercise of free choice less useful and rarer, restricts the activity of free will within a narrower compass, and little by little robs each citizen of the proper use of his own faculties." The result is a description of a new kind of servitude that even Kafka would have found it hard to improve upon:

> Having thus taken each citizen in turn in its powerful grasp and shaped men to its will, government then extends its embrace to include the whole of society. It covers the whole of social life with a network of petty, complicated rules that are both minute and uniform, through which even men of the greatest originality and the most vigorous temperament cannot force their heads above the crowd. It does not break men's will, but softens, bends, and guides it; it seldom enjoins, but often inhibits, action; it does not destroy anything, but prevents much being born; it is not at all tyrannical, but it hinders, restrains, enervates, stifles, and stultifies so much that in the end each nation is no more than a flock of timid and hardworking animals with the government as its shepherd. (p. 692)

The state thus turns into an institution that could not more fully deserve the "iron cage of servitude" moniker that Max Weber was later to pin on it.

Tocqueville's fear regarding the soft despotism face of democracy echoes a similar ambivalence expressed by other writers who saw capitalism capable of engendering both, greater degrees of civility and greater self-centered individualism and, as in Marx, despotism. A case in point is A. O. Hirschman's (1992) analysis of this two-faced nature of capitalist-commercial society, that showed up as early as in Montesquieu's *doux commerce* thesis, as well as in Marx' bourgeois society's *self-destruction* thesis. (Hunt, 1987)[3]

Individualism and untamed markets

Tocqueville thus sees democratic equality harboring two opposing tendencies or potentialities: the tendency for democratic self-government and the tendency for a new form of despotism. One reason for this seeming paradox is that the decentralization that is associated with strong civil society can also provide a protective shield for rising inequality. As individuals withdraw from the public sphere, the pursuit of private wealth becomes all consuming.

> In democratic countries, no matter how rich a man is, he is almost always dissatisfied with his fortune, because he finds that he is less wealthy than his father was and he is afraid that his son will be less wealthy than he. So most wealthy men in democracies are dreaming of ways to increase their riches, and naturally their eyes turn to trade and industry, for these seem the quickest and best means of getting rich. In this respect, they share the poor man's instincts without his necessities, or rather they are driven by the most imperious of all necessities, that of not sinking. (Tocqueville, 1835 & 1840/1969, p. 552)

As the few winners and the many losers of the economic game engage in dissonance reduction, resentment grows on both sides of the divide. The more numerous middle and lower classes resent the upper classes for the inordinate, out-of-proportion gap that separates them from one another. And the super-rich resent and fear those on the other side of their gated communities for engaging in "class warfare." As Wilkinson and Pickett (2009) impressively demonstrated, the result is an epidemic of distrust that leaves *both* groups worse off as corrosive effects wreak havoc on the mental and physical health of all.

Inequality is thus a key switchman determining whether the aggregate effects of associative self-organization are positive or negative. Under conditions where a country's socio-economic and moral center rests in a flourishing middle class, characterized by high degrees of social mobility, and easy interaction across dividing

---

[3] Tocqueville's contemporary Marx, for all the divergences in their diagnosis of capitalism and democracy, saw some forms of despotism in ways Tocqueville might have recognized. Here is Marx describing the 1851 dictatorial coup of Louis Bonaparte in language which a contemporary of the year 2020 reads with wondrous recognition:

"Driven by the conflicting demands of the situation to keep the public's eye as on a sleight-of-hand conjurer through constant surprises on himself as Napoleon's substitute, hence to carry out daily coup d'etats en minitiature, [Louis] Napoleon throws the whole civil economy into chaos, violates everything that seemed inviolable to the revolution of 1848, renders some tolerant of revolution and others lusting for it, creates anarchy in the name of order, while at the same time stripping the entire machinery of the state off its halo, profaning it and making it at once loathsome and ridiculous" (Marx, 1852/1960, p. 207; own translation).

lines of status and wealth, the associative effect may trump the withdrawal effect. Under conditions of high socio-economic inequality, the withdrawal effect trumps the associative effect. The rich become fearful; the poor hopeless.

The withdrawal from public life that Tocqueville observed earlier is further hastened by the rise of an *"industrial aristocracy"*—one of the few places where Tocqueville's commentary veers into the sphere of economics. He observes that ordinary people's withdrawal from the public sphere is not only a result of the growing illusion of mutual independence as their material prosperity grows. It is also the result of a growing class of people degraded by the conditions of work in the factories of the owners of gigantic enterprises who lack the resources and energy for engaging in public life. While democracy makes "men grow more alike," the newly emerging industry spurs the development of separate classes: "inequality increases in the less numerous class in the same ratio in which it decreases in the community." Therefore:

> [T]he friends of democracy should keep their eyes anxiously fixed in this direction; for if ever a permanent inequality of conditions and aristocracy again penetrates into the world, it may be predicted that this is the gate by which they will enter. (Tocqueville, 1835 & 1840/1969, p. 558)

Paradoxically, as Smith (2010) points out, government attempts to combat inequality or injustice can add a further source of corrosion in that it leads to increased political *centralization*. In the United States, for example, the fight against slavery and for civil rights engendered a vast expansion of the machinery of central government and paved the way for similar expansions in other spheres, notably education.

Inequality and tyranny

At this point it is helpful to recall that Tocqueville's view of the importance of relative equality and a civic virtue minded middle class has deep roots in the moral and political thought of the Greek founders. Aristotle, in particularly, firmly believes that self-government flourishes best with a strong middle class. To him it was evident that gross inequality obstructs self-government:

> . . . in the case of the goods of fortune . . . a middling possession is the best of all. [A person of moderate wealth] is readiest to obey reason, while for one who is [very wealthy or very poor] it is difficult to follow reason. The former sort tend to become arrogant and base on a grand scale, the latter malicious and base in petty ways; and acts of injustice are committed either through arrogance or through malice. (Aristotle, 1941, p. 1222, Politics 1295b4)

A political community that has extremes of wealth and poverty "is a city not of free persons but of slaves and masters, the ones consumed by envy, the others by contempt. Nothing is further removed from affection and from a political partnership" (Aristotle, Politics 1295b22).

Aristotle's teachers had weighed in on this point as well. In "The Republic" (Book VIII) Plato describes how, the love of lucre creates a class system in which both the wealthy and the poor lose interest in virtue. The rich "care only for making money, and are as indifferent as the pauper to the cultivation of virtue". "One, seeing another grow rich, seeks to rival him, and thus the great mass of the citizens become lovers of money" (Plato, 1968, p. 317).

> And so they grow richer and richer, and the more they think of making a fortune the less they think of virtue; for when riches and virtue are placed together in the scales of the balance, the one always rises as the other falls. [...] And in proportion as riches and rich men are honoured in the State, virtue and the virtuous are dishonoured. [...] And what is honoured is cultivated, and that which has no honour is neglected. (Plato, 1968, p. 317)

The ruling laws and ruling individuals are bound to fall victim to the love of money:

> . . . men become lovers of trade and money; they honour and look up to the rich man, and make a ruler of him, and dishonor the poor man. (Plato, 1968, p. 318)

Clearly, both Tocquevillian (e.g., Smith, 2010) and contemporary criticism of oligarchy and untamed market policies (i.e., Krugman, 2011; Piketty, 2014; Rosen, 2014; Stiglitz 2015; see also Meyer & Zhou, 2017 for oligarchic tendencies in US higher education), are standing on the tall shoulders of the Greek founders.

Summary: Associative and Dissociative Effects in the Civil Society

Under conditions of democracy as described by Tocqueville, civil society is an arena of two opposing effects, an associative and a dissociative effect. The former strengthens participation and engagement. The latter triggers civic disengagement and withdrawal from the public sphere. The former energizes and invigorates the public sphere; the latter creates apathy and indifference. We can expect the dissociative effect to be particularly strong when great economic growth in untamed markets causes inequality to rise and all are pre-occupied with safeguarding their economic status in a winner-take-all competition. Under those conditions, the moral bonds and moral obligations are weakening; the confidence, will, and skill for self-government wanes, and the readiness to abandon public affairs and self-government to a strong central authority grows (see Table 2.1).

Table 2.1 Strengthening and corrosive effects in the civil society effects

Strengthening versus Corrosive Effects in the Civil Society	
Strengthening (Associative) Effects	**Corrosive (Dissociative) Effects**
→ ripening of individual strengths → flourishing of decentralized networks of associations which do real work of governance → ordinary citizens develop the 'skill to be free' and realize the potential benefits of self-organized cooperation→ stronger self-interest *properly* understood → invigorating civil society → effective checks on central government	→ increasing affluence and well-being → nourishing the illusion of individual independence → withdrawal from public life → "lonely crowd" / "bowling alone"→ inviting greater role for central government → greater self-interest *im*properly understood → weakening willingness to participate in checks on central government

Note. Source: Design by author

In sum, the *civil society is not self-sustaining*. The skill of associative self-government and public sphere participation does not, in and of itself, generate the full set of skills needed for democratic civility. Moreover, as we'll see presently, even where associational life is strengthened, it may not be the kind that sustains a *civil* society.

The structural and normative dimension of the civil society

Based on the above discussion, it is useful to distinguish two dimensions or "faces" of the civil society: the structural and the normative. In the *structural dimension* we would register the strength of a given society's associational life, the degree to which the sector between state and markets is replete with bottom-up energy of associations, foundations, charities, partnerships, and "third sector" organizations, facilitative of independent participation of individuals and groups in the public sphere. This dimension of the civil society may empirically be weakly or strongly developed. As we saw above, the liberal account takes its strong development to be a hallmark of the civil society.

In the *normative dimension* we would register the strength of a given society's civil and moral life, the degree to which groups and individuals conduct themselves peacefully, with a measure of self-restraint, a measure of empathetic caring for and about the other, and an abhorrence of and rejection of violence. In this dimension, we again may observe weak and strong states of public life.

It suffices to make this distinction to observe that these two dimensions of the civil society need not vary together (see Table 2.2, below). Put differently: *a strong associational life is not the only worry of those interested in a vigorous civil society.* We can have strong associational life, along with rather weak normative restraints on how and for what ends those associations operate. The failings here may be of two kinds: on the one hand there may be a significant portion of associations espousing (or silently tolerating) violence and hatred. This is the case importantly discussed by Chambers and Kopstein (2001). On the other there may be a significant number of organizations which, thanks to an extraordinary degree of wealth and resources, are able to command an inordinately strong voice in the public square to a point where they overshadow and discourage public involvement and debate.

We may also encounter the reverse condition: a society with limited or weakly developed associational life, in which a few large private or semi-public organizations play a key role in a society's moral and spiritual life (cell 3, Table 2.2). Such

Table 2.2 The structural and normative dimension of the civil society

Normative Dimension	Structural Dimension	
	Weak	Strong
Weak	Anomie	Oligarchy
Strong	Corporatism	Civil Society

Note. Source: Design by author

moral corporatism may effectively shape civic life through an array of charitable, educational, and social welfare-oriented organizations and activities. Germany, with its long tradition of harnessing Christian charity for public ends, may be a case in point. In fact, Germany has, in many ways, cultivated a tradition that harnesses and encourages cooperation between governmental or quasi-governmental and religiously rooted organizations in sectors from health-care, education, to social welfare and disability services (see Glenn, 2002; Meyer, Minkenberg, & Ostner, 2000).

While these kinds of organizations may well leave an imprint of charity and virtue on public life, they are doing so in a way that does not require widespread associational participation. In fact, these organizations, although technically independent of government, are often perceived as part and parcel of a large state-controlled bureaucratic welfare structure.

Finally, the case where neither associational life nor civic morality are strong, might be best described by Durkheim's condition of "anomie," a state where order is either non-existent or merely the result of a state's coercive power.

The purpose of distinguishing the two faces of the civil society is to emphasize that civic and moral vitality does not automatically follow from a strong associational life; it can, especially under conditions of stark socio-economic inequality, even be defeated by it. As Chambers and Kopstein (2001) point out, we may well be joining and bowling together, but our thoughts and discussions might be dominated by prejudice, hatred, and resentment.

The Need for Countervailing Moral Forces

When seen in the context of its inherent fragility in general and the inevitable ups and downs of a market economy in particular, the civil society looks more like a roller coast with its peaks of civic renewal and valleys of incivility, than like the pre-ordained progression towards self-government and civility as which it has often been portrayed (including by this author[4]). This more sober view of civil society does not mean we give up on it and its potential to buttress democratic political forms with civic energy of self-government. But it would seem that we need to work harder in seeking to understand which, if any, *countervailing forces* can help stay the corrosive tendencies that seem to grow so easily in the heart of the civil society.

---

[4] See, for example, my "The Return of the Civil Society" (in Meyer & Boyd, 2001) which expounds a one-sidedly optimistic view of the civil society.

The Tocqueville-Kahan Thesis

Alan S. Kahan's (2015) recent masterful and compelling reconstruction of Tocqueville's ideas on this point goes a long way to do that. From Kahan's analysis we can infer that Tocqueville—although he was a master-analyst of institutional design (Elster, 2009; Meyer, 2003)—was convinced that institutional design alone would not save liberal democracy. Rather, he (Tocqueville) insisted on the vital role of a moral and spiritual foundation for democracy and the civil society. Kahan shows that Tocqueville's reference to the fundamental role of moral and spiritual forces in general and Christianity in particular cannot be dismissed as an idiosyncratic (and architecturally inessential) attempt to reconcile his private beliefs as a practicing (albeit often reluctant) Catholic with his hopes for a liberal democracy. Rather, for Tocqueville a liberal democracy without moral and spiritual checks and balances was an impossibility. *Liberal democracy needs not only political, but also moral and spiritual checks and balances.* This part of Tocqueville's meditation on democracy has, indeed, been the least acknowledged (but see Fradkin, 2000). This may be because, as Kahan suggests, it clashes with the rationalist and secular disposition of much of Western academia. Another reason may be that in our collective experience with religion's civic role the potential for organized religion to unite and uplift seems not securely dissociated from its potential to divide and separate.

Kahan's careful reconstruction makes it clear that Tocqueville the practicing Catholic never forces the hand of Tocqueville the social scientist. His analysis is nuanced enough to demonstrate the vital role of a moral and spiritual tradition that is capable of checking what Tocqueville sees as the inevitable moral entropic tendencies of democratic equality. According to Tocqueville it is essential that there are forces to help people realize the limitations and ultimate unsatisfactoriness of the pursuit of happiness understood as a pursuit of wealth and pleasure and the need to tap into sources of inner peace and well-being that are independent of the fluctuating fortunes of the market place or the iron-caged certainties of the rational state. One might say, that while Tocqueville's personal horizon was limited in this regard to Christianity (him having only limited, selective and rather distorted awareness of non-Christian religious traditions like Islam and Hinduism), his intellectual penetration of the problems of civil society leaves us with an open invitation to probe *any* kind of spiritual tradition or practice that can arrest the relentless but ultimately hollow pull of commerce and upward mobility as main source of meaning and success in democratic society.

Tocqueville arrives thus at what Kahan calls his "spiritual checks and balances thesis" because of an assumption about *basic human dispositions* that most modern social scientists are loath to make. Tocqueville believes that for humans, freedom is unattainable lest we transcend the strictures of materialism and the shallow pursuits of sense pleasure that many of his contemporaries deemed a sufficient basis for social civility and peace. As Kahan shows, his view of human nature is anchored in two principles:

– humans will not be relieved of the great causes of human suffering—uncertainty and doubt, illness and death—by means of knowledge or material well-being alone;
– for that reason humans are propelled to act from a need for both material *and* non-material satisfactions (Kahan, 2015, pp. 50–51).

With the first principle Tocqueville cuts against Descartes' rationalism and casts his lot with Pascal who knows that there is an element of belief and wisdom that transcends rational knowledge. With the second principle Tocqueville cuts against the utilitarian idea that satisfying material desires alone can lead to lasting satisfaction and happiness.

These two basic assessments of human nature—the impossibility to arrive at inner peace by means of rational knowledge alone and the impossibility to limit our aspirations to the satisfaction of material desires—imply that people under conditions of democratic equality face two possible fates: the first, resulting from abandoning democracy "to its wild instincts" is a degrading path leading to tyranny and servitude where men come to "know society only by its vices and miseries" (Tocqueville, quoted in Kahan, 2015, p. 13).[5]

The second is a path where our attachment to material well-being is kept in check by the need for non-material growth. Spirituality and religion are universal cultural forces uniquely helpful in this regard:

> Man's instincts constantly push his soul toward the contemplation of another world, and it is religion that leads him there. So religion is only a particular form of hope, and it is as natural to the human heart as hope itself. [. . .] [T]o believe that democratic societies are naturally hostile to religion is to commit a great mistake. (Tocqueville, quoted in Kahan, 2015, p. 69)

In contrast to some of his contemporaries, who believed in the possibility of building a stable civil society on nothing more than the orientation toward the satisfaction of material desires, Tocqueville sees an insuppressible spiritual need in humans and wants to harness it for the project of liberal democracy.

Kahan summarizes Tocqueville's assessment thus: "Religion instills loftiness and spiritualism in the democratic soul, rescuing it from the materialism, pettiness, and individualism that threaten to monopolize it. Religion is the spiritual antidote to democracy's flaws." As to the type of religion, Kahan describes Tocqueville's ecumenical stance thus: "Almost any religion (provided it is sufficiently democratic to maintain its hold on democratic people) will do" (Kahan, 2015, p 72).

There is thus little hope for a stable civil society unless non-violence in our external affairs is coupled with and buttressed by non-violence internally—in the hearts and minds of people.

---

[5] Since Kahan relies on the new Nolla/Schleifer translation/edition of Tocqueville's Democracy (Alexis de Tocqueville, Democracy in America. Editor: Eduardo Nolla; translator: James T. Schleifer. Indianapolis: Liberty, 2012) and since this translation sometimes differs noticeably from the G. Lawrence translation I use, I provide the Nolla / Schleifer page quotations in this section.

Böckenförde and Habermas

Ironically, Tocqueville's understanding of the need for countervailing moral and spiritual forces is witnessing a recent comeback, if from a somewhat unlikely (and, as far as I can tell, unconnected) source. In 1967, the German federal judge Ernst Wolfgang Böckenförde published a lecture containing what since has become known as the Böckenförde "dictum:"

"The liberal, secularized state is nourished by presuppositions that it cannot itself guarantee." [Der freiheitliche, säkularisierte Staat lebt von Voraussetzungen, die er selbst nicht garantieren kann.] (Böckenförde, 2006, p. 112).

Böckenförde describes this as "the great risk into which the [secular] state has entered for the sake of liberty. As a liberal state, it can be sustained only if the freedom that the state grants the citizens regulates itself from the inside, from the moral substance of the individual and the homogeneity of society"[6] (ibd).

Böckenförde's main question is our ability to reconcile the political imperative of a secular, religiously non-aligned "state" (the German "Staat" is often encompassing of both "government" and "society" and hence only imperfectly translated by either "government" or "state") with the sociological truism of society's social integration through shared moral bonds that keep particularistic tendencies from over-boarding. Without such moral bonds, he suggests, government and society are likely to disintegrate into what Durkheim would have called social anomy. Yet, the secular state, while depending on these bonds and utilizing them, is unable to guarantee and reproduce them, in part because of its obligation to secularism and religious neutrality. Thus, Böckenförde offers a diagnosis of the secular state in modern society as operating under (and contributing to) a condition of *moral entropy*. The center is unlikely to hold and reinforcements seem nowhere in sight. Or are they?

Here Böckenförde (like Tocqueville a Catholic) offers a thesis with strong affinity to Tocqueville. Aware that religious (and that means to him initially Judeo-Christian) forces cannot and should not expect official state support, he holds that they nonetheless deserve space in the modern civil society because of their positive civic role and their contribution to civil cohesion. But, again, like Tocqueville, Böckenförde argues that there is no need to limit the compass of those forces to Judeo-Christian ones, given, for example, the potential of Islam to similarly serve in such a role. Even further: there is no need to limit the compass to religious forces, in general. As he suggested in a 2009 interview: moral bonds can be generated through social practices other than distinctly religious ones, including through social movements like those for ecological or social justice (Böckenförde, 2009).[7]

---

[6] „Das ist das große Wagnis, das er, um der Freiheit willen, eingegangen ist. Als freiheitlicher Staat kann er einerseits nur bestehen, wenn sich die Freiheit, die er seinen Bürgern gewährt, von innen her, aus der moralischen Substanz des Einzelnen und der Homogenität der Gesellschaft, reguliert."

[7] Böckenförde, Ernst W., „Freiheit ist ansteckend". TAZ (Tageszeitung), 23.9.2009

In addition, government policy, while it cannot guarantee moral bonds, can facilitate their cultivation where they spring up spontaneously in society, in a variety of other ways. Instruments of such policy include:

- education;
- an open stance towards *all* religion and religious movements (as long as they are willing to operate within constitutional legal bounds);
- community-oriented social movements like ecological and labor unions;
- social policy that supports and facilitates bottom-up movements and institutions that contribute to the common welfare.

In general, while the state cannot be pro-religious, it need not be anti-religious. In this way, Böckenförde seems to hope that from this diverse interaction of spontaneous forces protected and encouraged by proper policy, a kind of shared understanding (he calls it "homogeneity"—a more fraught term) that emerges to bond the diverse members of a community and encourages their maintaining their "inner moral substance." Referencing Ralf Dahrendorf, he calls this a "sense of belonging" that can be generated by means of a sense of shared language, history, and traditions up to and including those bonds generated by having a national soccer league.

But are these forces strong enough to reliably counteract the morally corrosive forces of individualism and narrow self-interest *im*properly understood? There is reason to doubt that. Not only would a truly pluralistic conception of society allow for multiple languages and traditions. The problem here is that in a secular and pluralistic society the only truly binding shared conceptions are largely or exclusively *procedural*: recognizing the other's *right* to practice and conduct themselves according to beliefs and rules that are foreign to me. This is clearly necessary. But the problem here is that such a principle, while supporting the individual's consent to leave the other alone, does not, in itself, provide a positive desire to cooperate and bond with the other, let alone to help and learn from her. Tolerance, if it is merely born from a reciprocally self-interested will to be left alone, is not compassion. It does not involve the heart.[8] Hence, it is not clear whence the "state-supporting" (*staatstragendes*) ethos may reliably come. We are back to the start: the liberal state needs a degree of voluntary moral bonding that it cannot generate.[9]

---

[8] There is a peculiar "Continental" (as opposed to Anglo-American) way in which Böckenförde, unlike Tocqueville poses the problem. Rather than beginning with individuals in society, he begins with "the state". The problem then becomes how *the state* can contribute to creating moral citizens. By contrast, in Tocqueville we begin with the social individual and the notion that humans cannot long ignore the fact of their mortality. This individual, aware of their "sickness onto death" and the impossibility of rising above that fatal condition through rational knowledge is inherently inclined to seek moral and spiritual counsel and to develop forms of moral and spiritual cultivation *before* the state ever gets to worry about society's cohesion. In Böckenförde, by contrast, the problem is from the first framed as a problem of social order: "the state" needs to recruit moral citizens.

[9] „Der Staat ist darauf angewiesen, dass die Bürger gewisse Grundeinstellungen, ein staatstragendes Ethos haben, sonst hat er es schwer, eine am Gemeinwohl orientierte Politik zu verwirklichen. Wenn alle seine Ziele nur mit Zwang durchgesetzt werden müssten, wäre der Staat bald kein freiheitlicher Staat mehr" (Böckenförde, 2009).

Conservative and Liberal Readings of the "Dictum"

The sense of the limited power of procedural norms of constitutionally guaranteed
rights and liberty has given rise, in some quarters, to a call—sometimes in reference
to Böckenförde—for a "guiding culture" (in Germany, a *Leitkultur*) that, it is argued,
should recognize and give a privileged role to those particular moral forces that have
historically carried much of the burden of moral integration in a given place and
geography. For Europe in general and Germany in particular, this would be represented by the religions of Judeo-Christian heritage. Representatives of this view
have, thus, argued (to give one example) for the constitutionality of displaying the
Christian cross in public schoolrooms. Some have, on similar grounds, called for a
ban to the Hijab, the female head covering that is part of Islamic belief and culture
considered to be foreign to the guiding culture (see Gordon, 2013).

But such a narrow, traditionalist reading of the idea of countervailing forces is
not required by Tocqueville nor Böckenförde. Jürgen Habermas, for example,
rejects the idea of a *Leitkultur* in terms that indicate his embracing of the
Böckenförde dictum:

> [T]he democratic state should not overhastily reduce the polyphonic complexity of the
> range of public voices, for it cannot be sure whether in doing so it would not cut society off
> from scarce resources for generating meanings and shaping identities. Especially regarding
> vulnerable domains of social life, religious traditions have the power to provide convincing
> articulations of moral sensitivities and solidaristic intuitions. (Habermas, 2009, in Gordon,
> 2013, p. 192)

Böckenförde's dictum is explicitly invoked by Habermas in his historical exchange
with then Cardinal Joseph Ratzinger (the later Pope Benedict XVI) at the outset of
his statement on the "pre-political moral foundations of the liberal state" in January
2004.[10] Habermas agrees that the liberal state requires a political integration of citizens that goes beyond a mere *modus vivendi* (Habermas & Ratzinger, 2018, p. 34).
Habermas argues that it's not necessary to decide whether the secular state is, *in
principle*, incapable to generate the solidaristic value-based bonding that is required
for its peaceful operation. It is, he suggests, in any case evident that our historical-
empirical condition, where expansionist markets and large, rational-administrative
states are marginalizing value-based action, pre-political moral forces, including
religious ones, can and should be allowed to play a cohesion-strengthening role:
"markets and administrative powers are increasingly crowding out societal solidarity—understood as coordination of action by way of values, norms and communicative action—of ever more domains of the lifeworld" (Habermas, in Habermas &
Ratzinger, 2018, p. 32).

---

[10] Following an invitation by the Catholic Academy of Bavaria (Germany), the "philosopher and
the pope" famously engaged in a discussion on the "pre-political moral foundations of the liberal
state" in January 2004. In their respective statements, both writers agree that "reason" and "religiously founded faith" (Vernunft und Glaube) can beneficially interact, enrich, and check and
balance each other.

Under such conditions, religiously motivated solidaristic action can play an important corrective and constructive role. Given this potentially constructive role of religion (and the simple fact that a significant number of citizens interpret their role in the community in religious terms) the secular citizen can legitimately be expected to practice (*einüben*) a self-reflexive awareness regarding the limits of enlightenment (Habermas & Ratzinger, 2018, p. 35).[11] Secularists can concede to religious conviction a status that is not simply irrational. (p. 35). Similarly, secular citizens cannot deny their religiously oriented co-citizen the right to couch their contributions to public debate in religious language (Habermas & Ratzinger, 2018, p. 36).[12]

The above discussion easily articulates with Tocqueville's notion of moral and spiritual countervailing forces. The ultimate conclusion is that government cannot be more moral than the citizens in their un-coerced voluntary inclinations. Here, we seem to return to the starting point: does a civil society that fosters materialistic success and the illusion of independence not inevitably corrode citizens' moral intuitions? Does it not inevitably lead from self-interest properly understood to self-interest *im*properly understood? From solidarity and compassion to egotism and indifference? In other words: if all that bonds us is a reciprocal will to be left alone in our myriad private ways, then nothing of much force would seem to bond us; community would seem fragile, and civility mere politesse.

Alasdair MacIntyre has expanded the scope of reflection on this condition:

> [U]nless there is a telos which transcends the limited goods of practices by constituting the good of a whole human life, the good of a human life conceived as a unity, it will both be the case that a certain subversive arbitrariness will invade the moral life and that we shall be unable to specify the context of certain virtues adequately. (MacIntyre, 1981, p. 203)

Reaching past the tradition of organized religion that figures so prominently in Tocquevillian and post-Tocquevillian thought on countervailing forces, MacIntyre suggests that we tap *Aristotelian ethics* as a source of countervailing moral development. His "After Virtue" (1981) has become the springboard for a renewal of interest in the virtue ethics around the central thesis "that the Aristotelian moral tradition is the best example we possess of a tradition whose adherents are rationally entitled to a high measure of confidence in its epistemological and moral resources"

---

[11] As Gordon (2013) notes, Habermas' embracing of Böckenförde's dictum, implies a noticeable distancing from Habermas' earlier view that posited that "an ambivalent modern age will stabilize itself exclusively on the basis of the secular forces of a communicative reason." (Habermas, in Habermas & Ratzinger, 2018, p. 38).

[12] Ratzinger, in his parallel statement, suggests that there are pathologies of organized religion that benefit from the checks and balances of secular reason (for example the experience of religiously motivated terror). Likewise, there are also pathologies of reason (the hubris that deems everything doable worth doing, including the building of nuclear bombs or the artificial cloning of human beings) that benefit from the checks and balances of religiously founded belief. Reason and religion are co-relationally called upon to engage in a "process of mutual cleansing and healing" ("Korrelationalität von Vernunft und Glaube, Vernunft und Religion, die zu gegenseitiger Reinigung und Heilung berufen sind)" (Habermas & Ratzinger, 2018, p. 57).

(MacIntyre, 1981, p. 277). He also reminds us that virtues are not merely about external conduct:

> "Virtues are dispositions not only to act in particular ways, but also to feel in particular ways. To act virtuously is not, as Kant was later to think, to act against inclination; it is to act from inclination formed by the cultivation of the virtues" (MacIntyre, 1981, p. 149).

The above discussions of the moral and religious supports of democratic civility, point not only to the societal and external but also to the social-psychological and internal roots of the fragility of the civil society. We can learn from them that our thinking about the civil society is often hampered by an externalist focus, a perspective that sees civility only as a problem of external order and neglects the necessary inner dimension of civility. This line of thought suggests a richer sense of civility that comprises external and internal dimensions. In fact, I believe that the question of civility as an *embodied virtue* holds the key to some of the most pressing problems of the civility—incivility dialectic we face today. To heed the lessons this holds requires that we move past a conception of civility as mere outer non-violence and reflect seriously on how peace becomes *embodied* and obtains a foothold in the human heart. [13]

Arresting the Slide to Incivility: Recovering the Politics of the Mean

To conclude, I'll submit that the civil society is an institutional artifice erected over three fault-lines. The first two of these have long been recognized and discussed in the work of classic social theorists. These are

- the *socio-economic fault-line* demarcated by untamed markets on one end and various forms of coercive collectivism on the other;
- the *political fault-line* of an iron cage bureaucracy on one end, and of oligarchic despotism on the other.
- The less well reflected *moral fault line* of untrammeled individualism on end and of moral and religious fundamentalism on the other. [14]

For politics to steer a course through this landscape of rocks and hard places remains perhaps the key governance challenge our time, rivaled only by the ecological sustainability challenge. Both of these would seem to have all the ease of keeping a tractor trailer on a tightrope. But difficult or not: civil society politics would seem to be best understood as the politics of moderation, a mean between extremes, cultivating the center around tamed markets by means of social democracy, civil-minded

---

[13] For one interpretation of an emerging confluence of relevant ideas and their compatibility with early Greek thought see Chap. 14 by Meyer.

[14] An important exception is Jonathan Haidt's extraordinary "The Righteous Mind: Why Good People are Divided" by Politics and Religion. New York: Vintage, 2012.

self-organization, and facilitative of moral toleration, inclusion, and flourishing. Above all, they must be the politics of non-violence.

But here it is worth pointing to a new development, something that might assist in a renewed effort to cultivate the mean between extremes:

One result of the rapid cultural globalization going on before our eyes has large numbers of people in the West now encountering traditions of moral cultivation that, while not original to Western culture, are compatible with longstanding Western predilections for rational-secular forms of moral thinking, a reality not available to writers of Tocqueville's time. This, the West's intellectual and social opening to non-theistic moral practices and traditions, notably those of Confucianism and Buddhism, may offer what Kahan called "alternative forms of spirituality" and moral cultivation. "Twenty-first century democracies may find alternative forms of spirituality useful as well—as Tocqueville did—and they may well take forms unfamiliar to Tocqueville" (Kahan, 2015, p. 211). This may prove significant. For whereas Western democracies have a good deal of experience with centrist politics of moderation regarding the socio-economic and political fault lines (especially in the form of European social democracy and American limited government), the cultivation of moral and spiritual community that is safe from tipping into religious fundamentalism is much less developed.

I began this essay by considering the civil society's inherent fragility—a fragility that can result from some of its very successes, some of which foster material well-being, but also encourage individualistic withdrawal, breed the illusion of independence and hold moral and spiritual cultivation to be the optional pursuits of private citizens. These changes may not only give rise to dramatic gaps in wealth and income among classes. They also readily start a slide down the slippery slope of callous indifference to one's fellow citizen and, ultimately, open the space in which distrust, suspicion, incivility and the longing for benign despots grows. To check these tendencies, the remedies that have traditionally been proposed are necessary but not sufficient. Rather, there seems reason to take seriously the idea of the cultivation of moral and spiritual forces as a necessary, but independent countervailing factor that take us out of the narrow orbit of our mundane concern for material well-being and keep alive the care for our better angels.

References

Anheier, H. K., Lang, M., & Toepler, S. (2019). Civil society in times of change: Shrinking, changing and expanding spaces and the need for new regulatory approaches. *Economics, 13*(2019-8), 1–27. https://doi.org/10.5018/economics-ejournal.ja.2019-8

Aristotle. (1941). Politics. In R. McKeon (Ed.), *The basic works of Aristotle* (pp. 1127–1324). New York: Random House.

Berger, P. L., & Neuhaus, R. J. (1996). *To empower people: From state to civil society* (2nd ed.) (M. Novak, Ed.). Washington, D.C.: AEI.

Berlin, I. (2013). *The crooked timber of humanity: Chapters in the history of ideas* (2nd ed.). Princeton, NJ: Princeton University Press.

Böckenförde, E.-W. (2006). Die Entstehung des Staates als Vorgang der Säkularisation [The genesis of the state as a process of secularization]. In E.-W. Böckenförde (Ed.), *Recht, Staat, Freiheit: Studien zur Rechtsphilosophie, Staatstheorie und Verfassungsgeschichte* (pp. 92–114). Frankfurt: Suhrkamp.

Böckenförde, E.-W. (2009, September 23). Freiheit ist ansteckend [Freedom is contagious]. *Die Tageszeitung* (Berlin), p. 4. Retrieved from https://taz.de/Freiheit-ist-ansteckend/!576006/

Breiner, P. (2019). The dynamics of political equality in Rousseau, Tocqueville, and beyond. In D. Gordon (Ed.), *The Anthem companion to Alexis de Tocqueville* (pp. 169–186). New York: Anthem.

Chambers, S., & Kopstein, J. (2001). Bad civil society. *Political Theory, 29,* 837–865. https://doi.org/10.1177/0090591701029006008

Collins, C., & Flannery, H. (2020). Gilded giving 2020: How wealth inequality distorts philanthropy and imperils democracy. Retrieved from https://inequality.org/wp-content/uploads/2020/07/Gilded-Giving-2020-July28-2020.pdf

Dahrendorf, R. (1990). *The modern social conflict: An essay on the politics of liberty.* Berkeley, CA: University of California Press.

Diamond, L. (1994). Rethinking civil society: Toward democratic consolidation. *Journal of Democracy, 5*(3), 4–17. https://doi.org/10.1353/jod.1994.0041

Dionne, E. J. (1998). *Community works: The revival of civil society in America.* Washington, D.C.: The Brookings Institution.

Ehrenberg, J. (1999). *Civil society: The critical history of an idea.* New York, NY: New York University Press.

Elster, J. (2009). *Alexis de Tocqueville, the first social scientist.* Cambridge, UK: Cambridge University Press.

Fradkin, H. (2000). Does democracy need religion? *Journal of Democracy, 11*(1), 87–94. https://doi.org/10.1353/jod.2000.0008

Fukuyama, F. (1999). *The great disruption: Human nature and the reconstitution of social order.* New York: Free.

Glazer, N. (1997). *We are all multiculturalists now.* Cambridge, MA: Harvard University Press.

Glendon, M. A. (1991). *Rights talk: The impoverishment of political discourse.* New York: Free.

Glenn, C. L. (2002). *The ambiguous embrace: Government and faith-based schools and social agencies.* Princeton, NJ: Princeton University Press.

Gordon, P. E. (2013). Between christian democracy and critical theory: Habermas, Böckenförde, and the dialectics of secularization in postwar Germany. *Social Research, 80,* 173–202. https://doi.org/10.1353/sor.2013.0026

Habermas, J., & Ratzinger, J. (2018). *Dialektik der Säkularisierung: Über Vernunft und Religion* [Dialectics of secularization: About reason and religion]. Freiburg: Herder.

Haidt, J. (2012). *The righteous mind: Why good people are divided by politics and religion.* New York: Vintage.

Harvey, D. (Ed.). (2005). *Spaces of neoliberalization: Towards a theory of uneven geographical development.* Hettner Lectures: Vol. 8. Stuttgart: Franz Steiner.

Hirschman, A. O. (1992). *Rival views of market society and other recent essays.* Cambridge, MA: Harvard University Press.

Hunt, G. (1987). The development of the concept of civil society in Marx. *History of Political Thought, 8,* 263–276.

Jefferson, T. (1984). A bill for the more general diffusion of knowledge. In M. Peterson (Ed.), *Thomas Jefferson: Writings* (pp. 365–373). New York: Library of America.

Kahan, A. S. (2015). *Tocqueville, democracy, and religion: Checks and balances for democratic souls*. Oxford, UK: Oxford University Press.

Keane, J. (1998). *Civil society: Old images, new visions*. Cambridge: Polity.

Krugman, P. (2011, November 3). Oligarchy, American style. *New York Times*. Retrieved from https://www.nytimes.com/2011/11/04/opinion/oligarchy-american-style.html

Locke, J. (1988). *Two treatises on government* (P. Laslett, Ed.). Cambridge, UK: Cambridge University Press. (Original work published 1689). https://doi.org/10.1017/CBO9780511810268

MacIntyre, A. (1981). *After virtue: A study in moral theory*. Notre Dame, IN: University of Notre Dame Press.

Marx, K. (1852/1960). Der achtzehnte Brumaire des Louis Bonaparte [The 18th Brumaire of Louis Bonaparte]. In K. Marx & F. Engels (Eds.), Werke: Vol. 8 (pp. 194–207). Berlin: Dietz.

Meyer, H.-D. (2003). Tocqueville's cultural institutionalism: Reconciling collective culture and methodological individualism. *Journal of Classical Sociology, 3*, 197–220. https://doi.org/10.1177/1468795X030032005

Meyer, H.-D. (2016). *The design of the university: German, American, and "world class."* New York: Routledge. https://doi.org/10.4324/9781315754161

Meyer, H.-D., & Boyd, W. L. (2001). *Education between state, markets, and civil society: Comparative perspectives*. Mahwah: LEA.

Meyer, H.-D., Minkenberg, M., & Ostner, I. (2000). *Religion und Politik: Zwischen Universalismus und Partikularismus* [Religion and policy: Between universalism and particularism]. Jahrbuch für Europa- und Nordamerika-Studien: Vol. 2. Opladen: Leske & Buderich.

Meyer, H.-D., & Zhou, K. (2017). Autonomy or oligarchy? The changing effects of university endowments in winner-take-all markets. *Higher Education, 73*, 833–851. https://doi.org/10.1007/s10734-017-0109-1

Mill, J. S. (1982). *On liberty*. (G. Himmelfarb, Ed.). London: Penguin. (Original work published 1859)

Montesquieu. (1989). *The spirit of the laws* (A. M. Cohler, B. C. Miller, & H. S. Stone, Trans. and Ed.). Cambridge, UK: Cambridge University Press.

Osborne, D., & Gaebler, T. (1993). *Reinventing government: How the entrepreneurial spirit is transforming the public sector*. New York: Plume.

Piketty, T. (2014). *Capital in the twenty-first century* (A. Goldhammer, Trans.). Boston, MA: Harvard University Press.

Plato. (1968). *Republic* (B. Jowett, Trans.). New York: Airmount.

Putnam, R. D. (1995). Bowling alone: America's declining social capital. *Journal of Democracy, 6*(1), 65–78.

Riesman, D. (1969). *The lonely crowd: A study of the changing American character* (19th ed.). New Haven, CT: Yale University Press.

Rosen, R. J. (2014, April 25). Nobel Prize-winning economist: We're headed for oligarchy. *The Atlantic* (Washington, D.C.). Retrieved from https://www.theatlantic.com/business/archive/2014/04/nobel-prize-winning-economist-were-heading-for-oligarchy/361200/

Shils, E. (1991). The virtue of civil society. *Government and Opposition, 26*, 3–20. https://doi.org/10.1111/j.1477-7053.1991.tb01120.x

Smith, R. M. (2010). Oligarchies in America: Reflections on Tocqueville's fears. *Journal of Classical Sociology, 10*, 189–200. https://doi.org/10.1177/1468795X10371711

Stiglitz, J. E. (2015). *The great divide: Unequal societies and what we can do about them*. New York: Norton.

Taylor, C. (1992). *Multiculturalism and 'the politics of recognition.'* Princeton, NJ: Princeton University Press.

Taylor, C. (1996). Two theories of modernity. *The Responsive Community, 6*(3), 16–25.

Tocqueville, A. (1969). *Democracy in America* (G. Lawrence, Trans.; J. P. Mayer, Ed.). New York: Doubleday. (Original work published 1835 & 1840)

Tocqueville, A. (1971). *Journey to America* (G. Lawrence, Trans.; J. P. Mayer, Ed.). New York: Anchor. (Original work published 1831–1832)

Tocqueville, A. (2012). *Democracy in America* (J. T. Schleifer, Trans; E. Nolla, Ed.). Indianapolis: Liberty. (Original work published 1835 & 1840)

Villa, D. (2006). Tocqueville and civil society. In C. B. Welch (Ed.), *The Cambridge companion to Tocqueville* (pp. 216–244). Cambridge, UK: Cambridge University Press. https://doi.org/10.1017/CCOL0521840643

von Humboldt, W. (1969). *The limits of state action* (J. W. Burrow, Ed.). Cambridge, UK: Cambridge University Press. (Original work published 1851). https://doi.org/10.1017/CBO9781316036372

Walzer, M. (1983). *Spheres of justice: A defense of pluralism and equality.* New York: Basic.

Walzer, M. (Ed.). (1995). *Toward a global civil society.* Providence: Berghahn.

Wilkinson, R., & Pickett, K. (2009). *The spirit level: Why greater equality makes societies stronger.* New York: Bloomsbury.

Chapter 3
Civil Society as an Agent of Change

Rupert Graf Strachwitz

A random choice of indicators may provide ample evidence that the 21st century is marked by exceptional and substantial societal change:

- the revolution in communication,
- the supposed takeover by secret and artificial powers beyond our control,
- the shift of political and economic power away from Europe and North America,
- the surging worldwide interdependence of the human race,
- population growth,
- the fact that our planet might become uninhabitable,
- the resurrection of the individual, not least in a gender context, and
- the reintroduction of religion into public discourse.

These indicators are not necessarily coherent with each other; on the contrary, they appear to represent a mounting uncertainty regarding all our traditions of living, learning, and governing. To add to this, the 2020 COVID-19 crisis will most certainly lead to a fundamental reassessment of the very fabric of society. Our social order is crumbling. Yet, those creating models and plans for innovation tend to focus on technical issues, hoping that the fabric will remain the same. However, a realistic assessment of the world will necessarily produce the result that social change without a change of fabric cannot be sustainable. We should be addressing three issues that determine the public sphere:

(1) the crisis of capitalism,
(2) the crisis of democracy,
(3) the crisis of the nation state.

R. G. Strachwitz (✉)
Maecenata Institute for Philanthropy and Civil Society, Berlin, Germany
e-mail: rs@maecenata.eu

© The Author(s) 2022
J. Glückler et al. (eds.), *Knowledge and Civil Society*, Knowledge and Space 17,
https://doi.org/10.1007/978-3-030-71147-4_3

And if this were not enough, a growing divide between privileged and underprivileged members of society at large and of nearly every national and regional community leaves these communities with insurmountable problems of social unrest and indeed of survival. The legitimacy of any form of governance is at stake (Aziz, 2020, p. 60), and preserving this legitimacy and reinstating trust is certainly not made easier by the COVID-19 crisis and the way some governments have been handling it.

Most recently, the majority of the British and American people and increasingly substantial minorities in France, Germany, Italy, and many other European countries have demonstrated that all this is not really true. They lament the disappearence of the way of life of a bygone age, wish to hang on to customs of old, and fail to realize that preserving essentials will require a number of fundamental changes. Most people would be at a loss to say what merits saving and what must undergo a change so substantial that one cannot even imagine the outcome. What is certain is that political leaders are failing to face the real issues, resorting instead to mistrust and control mechanisms—although they should be aware that no society can be based on mistrust, and that more controls precede going under. The demise of East Germany in 1989/90 is a case in point.

Although Western theorists in the 1990s were quick to proclaim "the end of history" (Fukuyama, 1992), representative democracy and statehood of the type developed over the past 300 years seem to have had their day. The combined overbearing power of state bureaucracies and multinational corporations needs to be replaced by some kind of post-democracy, as some would argue, or by a more participative, citizen-orientated system. The dignity and uniqueness of the individual is endangered by menacing collectivities; encouraging and nudging these individuals to think in categories of *we* rather than of *I*, to put some brakes on excessive competitiveness, might provide a sensible way forward. The snag is that a market economy that relies on competition has proven to be more successful in supplying the citizens with goods and services than a government-organized non-competitive economy. Nevertheless, and despite the fact that governments are regularly underperforming,

> today many scholars still hold that political boundaries are the most fundamental man-made lines on the map due to a bias toward territory as the basis of power, the state as the unit of political organization, an assumption that only governments can order life within those states, and a belief that national identity is the primary source of people's loyalty. (Khanna, 2011, p. 46)

Even in the inner circle of governmental responsibilities, supra-, trans-, and international governance structures have taken over as decisive players in a global governance system, as have regional and local communities, international corporations that are seemingly more and more successful in evading government supervision—and communities of choice, which are attracting more loyalty and are seemingly crowding out communities of fate in determining people's more-often-than-not multiple identities.

Thus, village squares, debating networks of the metropoles, parliaments, and assemblies seem old-fashioned in an age where communication works by very different rules. Raghuram Rajan, who argues in favour of "a devolvement in power from federal government through the regional government to the community" (Rajan, 2019, p. 325), is wrong in supposing that shifting executive powers from one level of government to another could solve the problem of how to remodel the public sphere. It seems highly doubtful whether any of this can prevent the fundamentals of society, democracy, human and civil rights, the rule of law, and cultural traditions being destroyed. The "Twilight of Democracy" (Applebaum, 2020) seems all too apparent.

All this could be seen as a gloomy picture. While we seem to know so much, we apparently do not know how to effect social change. Our governors firmly believe technical innovation will solve our problems and refuse to recognize the need for societal change. Think tanks abound—which in itself is a clear indicator that something must be wrong—and yet, although some of them aspire to tell us what to do, none seem to come up with *the* solution. And what is more: As Charles de Gaulle famously quiopped, politics have become too serious a business to allow us to leave them to politicians—let alone to government officials!

While many ideas have been put forward over the past two generations, nothing substantial has been achieved in providing a practical solution to this fundamental dilemma. Habermas' model of discursive democracy that connects democratic political processes to a normative concept of institutionalising the interplay between diverse societal arenas, has been widely received in academic circles, but seems to have had little impact on societal development, the crisis of democracy in recent years, and the slow erosion of traditional political processes (Habermas, 1994, pp. 361–363).

In reviewing this set-up, I will look at societal forces that for the last few centuries have been crowded out by domineering nation states, and that are now reasserting their right to be actively involved in shaping society. In particular, I will focus on the role of civil society, and discuss to what extent civil society players may be instrumental or at least helpful in developing a new world order. In so doing, I will need to sum up the knowledge base regarding the potentials and limitations inherent to civil society, and examine the ways by which interplay between civil society, the state, and the market may be improved.

The Domain of Civil Society

Over the past generation or so, the existence of civil society as an arena of collective action in the public sphere that will cooperate or compete with players in the state and market arenas has become blatantly apparent (Dahrendorf, 1995). The civic space, on occasion but not always used as a synonym of the space for civil society, has seemingly grown considerably since Arato and Cohen argued that "the concept of civil society is more than a mere slogan" (Arato & Cohen, 1988, p. 40). Clearly, the notion of a civic space touches on the human and civil rights of individual citizens as much as it does on those of associative bodies and philanthropic institutions.

But the unclear definition also shows how much nearer the citizen is to civil society than to the modern state, notwithstanding the fact that political theory defines liberal democracies as ruled by the people. It is therefore reasonable to assume that civil society is in many ways the civic space, provided spontaneous civic action and individual public-mindedness are counted.

Civil society has existed in one form or another at least since the time of "The Great Transformation" (Polanyi, 1944), the "Axial Age," elaborated by the German philosopher Karl Jaspers in 1949 (Jaspers, 1953) to mean a period between the eighth and the second century B.C., when a worldwide, nearly simultaneous transformation of thought and subsequently of society took place. However, over the past two generations or so, a novel concept of civil society has emerged that differs from previous concepts, including the one put forward by Adam Ferguson (1767/1995). It may be seen today as an arena of collective movements and organisations, which are in many ways hugely diverse, but do bear some common traits that allow us to distinguish them from organisations and institutions that form part of the state or the private business sector. If, contrary to Margaret Thatcher's famous quip (Keay, 1987), society is something that exists and is not synonymous with the state or the nation, relevant collective action takes place in all three of these arenas, the term "arena" being preferable to "pillar" as it denominates areas of movement, action, and change.

Civil society may be described as the place where citizens engage by their own free will, participate directly in affairs to do with the common good, and voice their concerns, ideas, criticism, and agreement. For the purposes of the Johns Hopkins Comparative Nonprofit Sector Project, Lester Salamon and his colleagues defined a number of principles by which one may decide whether an activity, a movement, an organization, or an institution should be considered part of this particular arena (Salamon, Anheier, List, Toepler, & Sokolowski, 1999, pp. 26–28)[1]:

- Access should be voluntary.
- The organisation should not be engaged in core government business.
- Profit should not be a prime objective.
- The governance structure should be autonomous.
- Any profits accruing may not be distributed to members or owners.

Though civil society organisations (CSOs) command a considerable full-time and part-time workforce, the arena as such is based and relies heavily on volunteerism, and thus on philanthropy in its widest sense. Philanthropy in the true sense of the word is not just what donors of funds are practising, let alone what foundations do; philanthropy is the spirit in which gifts of empathy, time, ideas, know-how, reputation, and financial resources are put at the disposal either of individuals in need, or of organisations deemed able to use these gifts to perform their self-allotted tasks. In philosophy, the first mention of philanthropy is most probably found in

---

[1] Salamon and Anheier offered a definition to be used more or less internationally throughout the Johns Hopkins Comparative Nonprofit Sector project. This has since been expanded and undergone certain variations, but may still serve as an acceptable working base.

Plato, who, in his dialogue "Euthyphron" (1924), lets Socrates call himself a philanthropist because he lets others partake of his wisdom free of charge. In 1960, the French political economist Francois Perroux (1960) described giving as the attribute of what we call civil society, whereas force is associated with the state, and exchanges are associated with the market.

The division between civil society, the state, and the market is necessarily conceptual (Anheier & Seibel, 1993), and overlaps and unclear edges exist in reality. In 1999, Salamon et al. concluded there was a

> vital need to improve the general awareness of . . . [the nonprofit sector] in virtually every part of the world, and to monitor the trends affecting it on a more pervasive, and more sustained, basis. The existence of a vibrant nonprofit sector is increasingly being viewed not as a luxury, but as a necessity, for peoples throughout the world. Such institutions can give expression to citizen concerns, hold governments accountable, promote community, address unmet needs, and generally improve the quality of life. Putting this sector firmly on the mental map of the world is therefore a matter of some urgency. (1999, p. 38)

While many people believe civil society can achieve what the public and the private sector cannot, that they are destined to be agents of change, this proposition will be refuted by others—particularly those in government and business. They will receive academic backing from traditional economists who firmly believe in the power of the market, and will rely on the state's superior power and vastly superior financial resources to demonstrate its ongoing position in the driver's seat. However, Amitai Etzioni, one of the forefathers of civil society research, was certainly right in saying: "Actually, this third sector may well be the most important alternative for the next few decades, not by replacing the other two, but by matching and balancing their important roles" (Etzioni, 1973, p. 318).

Both academia and public opinion, and not least the agents of civil society in the field, have continued to engage in a discussion over definition. This is decidedly unfortunate, as it renders it more difficult to make a conclusive case for civil society as an arena and most particularly for the involvement of this arena in discussions over societal development and change. Even the pioneering work undertaken by Salamon and his many associates since the 1990s in mapping the empirical evidence in a comparative fashion worldwide, while highlighting the sheer size of civil society, has not achieved one of its purposes—that is, presenting a standardized and universally accepted notion of what civil society is, and who is part of it.

Since the American economist Richard Cornuelle first spoke of an independent sector beyond the state and the market in 1965, the discussion about the overall function of this sector or arena has never stopped. Cornuelle (1965) argued that associations of volunteers could effectively solve social problems without recourse to heavy-handed bureaucracy, whereas governments would commonly prefer to see these associations and foundations support their own work in a subservient fashion and neither question government decisions nor adopt any degree of independence. Little wonder that service-providing and intermediary organisations are popular with governments, while the self-help, self-fulfilment, and community-building roles are habitually overlooked and advocacy, watchdog, and political discourse roles are viewed with suspicion. Responding to pressure from the citizens, advocacy has found its way into tax exemption, and the watchdog role has gained acceptance for watching over excess market behavior. But Colin Crouch's (2011) insistence that given the parliaments' failure in fulfilling that role, civil society's main task is to act as watchdog in public affairs, has not to date made government theorists and practitioners rethink the interplay between the various contributors to the development and execution of policy. On the contrary, the public sector, and, somewhat strangely, the media, tend to belittle the role of civil society and use arguments to do with the rank of representative democracy to enhance their own role, at the same time accepting the private sector—business—as a driving and quite regularly decisive force in determining policy.

In the eyes of those caught up in the present system of government, the most obnoxious role models of civil society are those demanding to be heard as contributors to public discourse—with one notable exception: In countries whose governments are seen as undemocratic in the sense that they have not taken on and/or said goodbye to principles Western democracies uphold, civil society that opposes the government is hailed as the expression of the people's will. We have seen this happen in the past, not least in the Central and Eastern Europe transformation process in the late 1980s. To put it very bluntly: Civil rights fighters in China are considered heroes, while civil rights protests in Hamburg at a G20 conference are seen as a criminal disruption of public order, and civil liberties activists in Catalunia are quickly labelled as terrorists (Strachwitz, 2018, pp. 17–30).

Though philanthropic giving is by no means the prime source of civil society funding, it is most certainly a major driving force in empowering its agents. Empowered in this way, as Albert Hirschman rightly established (1970), CSOs may engage in tasks that support existing societal systems ("loyal"), may distance themselves from mainstream society ("exit"), or become an opposing force ("voice"). Under all three of these headings, we may see eight distinct role models; many organizations are active in more than one (Strachwitz, Priller, & Triebe, 2020, p. 4 et passim):

- service provision,
- advocacy,
- watchdog,
- intermediary,
- self-help,
- community building,
- political discourse, and
- self-fulfilment (personal growth).

The last two are perhaps the most interesting. Whereas Europeans have long argued that enabling personal growth, self-fulfilment, and a fulfilled and happy life is arguably the prime obligation of any community to its members, Asian political theorists would challenge this view, contending that society takes precedence over the individual. Yet, even then, civil society is probably the arena where personal growth through voluntary involvement may be achieved. That civil society should have a permanent and undisputed seat at the table when matters of society at large are debated is far from universally accepted, notwithstanding the lip service those in power pay to the importance of civil society when it so pleases them—most commonly when these debates take place far from home. Habermas and others have argued the necessity of a "deliberative democracy" to explain the existence of an arena beyond the state and the market (Habermas, 1994, p. 363). These role models have developed over the past thirty years or so, both in practice and in theory, and obviously, many civil society players follow several role models simultaneously. This entails not only having a problem of defining civil society itself, but also one of defining its activities—a fairly academic debate when it comes to deciding whether a hospital managed by a not-for-profit organization is part of civil society or not, but a very real issue when talking about terrorism, civil liberties, and indeed social change.

The resources in volunteer work and donations that civil society can command are near to nothing compared to what governments obtain from the citizens by way of taxes, and what the business community makes by selling goods and services. In this respect, civil society, while being responsible for a considerable portion of any country's gross domestic product, is yet the smallest of the three arenas; this will not change in the foreseeable future. What, then, can civil society bring to the table?

The Unique Contribution

Beyond any doubt, a sizeable number of CSOs today have an important public function. Sports clubs, welfare and health organisations, protest movements, and watchdogs are part of societal life, and their members have learnt to voice opinions in the public sphere. They can on occasion be extraordinarily powerful in setting the agenda, moving issues, nudging lawmakers, or restraining them. Some find this easier than others. Traditional CSOs tend to be caught up in a neo-corporatist arrangement with the state and depend on public money to perform their services. They find it more difficult to shed their subservient attitude than do the younger advocacy organisations that rely on the support of their members and donors. The power of example is nudging more and more citizens everywhere in the world to actively contribute to public affairs and to do so in more ways than just by going to vote for a political party or leader once every few years. "Much of what Tocqueville saw as the reasons for modern democracies being lively and diverse and having the potential to integrate (the importance of associative life, of a community culture, and of religion) is just as important in 21st century society as it was then" (Kronenberg, 2013, p. 6).

This is because empathy, friendship, and engagement with emotional needs are at the very core of what constitutes a healthy societal arrangement. Communities depend on emotions, which modern governments horribly fail to convey. The sentiment of compassion, as described by Adam Smith (1759), is often connected to the solidarity deemed to be essential to keep a community together. Be this as it may, the failure of the state is not restricted to the examples chosen from serious deficiencies in pursuing the day-to-day business of government, but should be seen as a general systemic phenomenon that requires corrective action.

In some instances, the growth in coherence, power, and strength that civil society has accomplished over the past generation or two, its ability to post societal needs and drive the issues, has been decisive. Care for the environment, gender issues, individual liberties, and indeed the fall of the Berlin Wall and the process of transition in Central and Eastern Europe in 1989/1990, were driven by civil-society action, by determined activists and philanthropists. This will most certainly happen again. The Fridays for Future movement, started by a single teenage Swedish girl, is a case in point. The heterogenous, heterarchical, and more often than not overtly chaotic structure of a CSO may on occasion be better suited to become a hotbed of new ideas and both creative and potentially disruptive innovation than an orderly government agency and/or corporation.

Beyond these narratives, civil society's impact and legitimacy rest on a normative theory. Evaluators need normative principles to decide whether or not an organisation may be considered "good" or, in other words, acceptable to society. Among them, one may determine some very general ones, such as

- a basic belief in the human being as the supreme principal of society,
- respect for other human beings, their distinct and possibly very different ways of life and convictions,
- adherence to basic societal principles such as human and civil rights, the rule of law, and government by the people for the people, and
- a belief in a pluralist society that allows for each and every individual to lead the life she or he wishes, provided this does not infringe on the life of others.

Furthermore, some principles are specific to civil society, for example:

- a fundamental empathy for fellow men and women,
- a strict priority for ideals and ideas rather than for personal material gains,
- a commitment to accounability to the citizenry at large,
- an acknowledgement of everyone's right to assemble and associate, and
- an endorsement of a political role for civil society.

Civil society is by no means inherently good. Just as there are good and bad governments, and honest traders and crooks in business, there exist, of course, CSOs we do not approve of, be this in a fundamental sense or simply because they have differing views. The Ku Klux Klan, the National Rifle Association of America, and, to name a German example, Pegida, are examples of the first, whereas a plethora of associations and foundations whose goals do not correspond to other people's may be among the second. This will not allow us to simply disregard or disqualify organisations the views or goals of which we do not approve of. On the contrary, respect for others carries the obligation to listen most carefully to opposing statements and to consider positions we do not embrace. Furthermore, this respect will make us exercise caution and restraint when it comes to playing the power game. Large foundations and other CSOs face a particular challenge here. But in doing so, they will join an ever-growing number of smaller, very often minute CSOs and become what in other arenas is proving to be virtually impossible: agents of change. Agents of change—and indeed all CSOs—are never legitimized by size, nor by election procedures. They are legitimate by the quality of their proposals. A fairly novel and increasingly important and attractive subsector of civil society has proven to be particularly well suited. It is what may be termed informal civil society, movements without much—or even any—structure. They convene around one issue, one thought, one philanthropic impulse. During the refugee wave that hit Germany in 2015 and 2016, it was individuals who assembled their friends, small groups of volunteers called up over social media, responsible citizens who, in the light of a failing government bureaucracy, lived up to Angela Merkel's famous "Wir schaffen das [We can do this]."[2] It was they who enabled Germany to cope with one million refugees in less than six months. It is they who will most probably be the most influential agents of change.

It seems that governments are losing their monopoly of the public sphere, are trying to save what they can, and are leaving the possible outcome to providence. They profess to be set on innovation, and refuse to take into account that innovation in technical matters implies an innovative solution to the dilemma of an antiquated political order. Whether this solution can be disruptive and at the same time evolutionary rather than repeating the mistakes of the 20th century and attempting to create a *new man* by way of revolution, remains an open question. It will depend on how widespread a readiness for change may be, and on how many centres actively develop models and ideas for a new order. It is a total misconception that new orders have come about as a result of a singular revolutionary act and an ensuing one-off brainstorming session. In each and every case, new arrangements had a longish history of preparation, of civil society at its very best designing and discarding competing ideas to a point where consensus could be achieved over a compromise. In this sense, more than in any other, civil society may truly be considered an agent of change. Taking to the streets can be extraordinarily effective, and is a civil right as much as it is a civil society prerogative. But moving issues by convening and debating is arguably the more sustainable contribution that civil society can bring to the table.

The Trust Issue

All this said, there exists a highly relevant caveat to be considered. For social change to be sustainable, it seems all-important that it should be underpinned by trust. This alone presents the present Western political order with a considerable dilemma. In Europe and North America, the majority of citizens do not trust political parties, the government, the state as such, business corporations, or large institutions in general.

---

[2] German Federal Chancellor Angela Merkel first used this phrase on August 31st, 2015, at a press conference following a visit to a refugee camp near Dresden where local opponents of her refugee policy booed and heckled her.

This has much to do with the fact that "the system" has actively engaged in a growing mistrust of its citizens. Rules and controls have crowded out all previously entertained conventions of interaction between citizens and public bodies. For many, the logic is clear: If they are not trusted, why should they trust others? The downside of this is that "findings suggest that individuals who distrust and fear to be exploited show self-serving, and hence untrustworthy, moral cognition themselves" (Weiss, Burgmer, & Mussweiler, 2018). The 19th Annual Edelman Trust Barometer (2019), while reporting an overall modest rise in the level of trust, shows it still to be far removed from satisfactory. In the "general population" bracket, 56% trust business and nongovernmental organizations (NGOs) and 47% trust government and the media. In the "informed public" bracket, the figures are 69% for NGOs, 68% for business, and 58% for government and media (Edelman, 2019, p. 5). One cannot envisage the roughly 50% of citizens who do not trust business, nor NGOs, nor the state becoming more trustful if these three arenas were to cooperate on a more level playing field. On the contrary, civil society in particular will have to be careful not be seen as part of the system, or as having finally succumbed to government (and potentially business) pressure. Its reputation as the civic or citizens' arena is at stake. If the idea of a new public sphere is to catch on, all concerned, and most specifically civil society, urgently need to improve on the trust placed in them.

Rebuilding trust may be seen as a prime goal to restabilize society. Society cannot possibly exist on the basis of control mechanisms, but needs to contain a core of mutual trust. Mechanisms to restore this trust have been put on the table; they need to be discussed and adopted (viz., Alter, Strachwitz, & Unger, 2019). The criteria were assembled in answering the question what value-added philanthropic institutions can bring to the table.

Strengthening the value-based approach of civil society implies respecting common societal principles such as the rule of law, human and civil rights, and democracy, as well as specific civil-society principles, such as respect for the individual, refraining from using force, accepting plurality, and others. Along with my colleagues Alter and Unger, I have developed a set of criteria that may act as guidelines in determining whether a civil society actor may be deemed to be trustworthy:

a) Commitment: to address the question whether a CSO is living up to the essentials of the eco-system of civil society. Its underpinning qualities are compassion, understanding, and respect.
b) Public purpose: to specify that action has to be tailored to principles of benefit to society. Its supporting qualities are goals, responsiveness, and integrity.
c) Relevance: to underline the necessity that action is conducted to make a difference and leave a mark. Its underpinning qualities are sustainability, effectiveness, and impact.
d) Performance: to refer to internal stakeholders acting in a professional manner. Its underpinning qualities are state-of-the-art practice, leadership, and stakeholder relationships.

e) Accountability: to accentuate the existent consciousness of a responsibility to society. Its supporting qualities are transparency, responsibility, and compliance. (Alter et al., 2019, pp. 4–6)

If civil society is to perform as an agent of change, obeying these standards of a trustworthy movement, organization, or institution in a satisfactory manner is an obligatory prerequisite. If civil society is to make a difference, its behavior must be above reproach. The disruption affecting civil society, civic action, and philanthropy as much as other sectors of society is largely due to failing in this respect. Institutions of social interaction and participation, religious communities, trade unions, political parties, and other traditional membership organisations have lost critical ground.

The Iconic Turn

Disruptive dynamics have been accelerating since the end of the 20th century, producing significant transformations of social, economic, and political structures. Globalization, new communities of choice, and high-speed technological innovation are reducing the role of previously dominant actors, notably the state, whereas the private sector has become a major player in many sectors, from infrastructure and transport to pensions and health-care systems. Technological inventions have transformed the pace of communication, revolutionized the way one works, and individualized how one spends one's leisure time. Disruption as the new normal is here to stay.

In order to render a contribution of civil society to social change a viable and sustainable proposition, an "open government partnership," citizen participation, and corporatist models of civil society involvement in public affairs most certainly will not suffice. To achieve a paradigm shift, "raising citizens" (Mounk, 2018, p. 245) rather than specialists is the essential first step. Adapting educational curricula to include the knowledge base for performing well in the public sphere is a precondition to changing attitudes. However, education alone is not enough—participation and finally responsibility must also evolve (D'Ambrosio, 2018, p. 44).

The survival of the fittest is as little suited to governing the market's contribution to society as are Friedman's notions of stakeholder value. Reining in extreme capitalism requires refocussing it towards stakeholder value, sustainable and responsible development, and measures to bridge rather than widen the divide between the rich and the rest of society. The expectation that the very rich "will transform the character of governments, shrinking the realm of compulsion, and widening the scope of private control over resources" (Davidson & Rees-Mogg, 1999, p. 256) cannot—and should not—persist.

Given the crisis of democracy, the failures of constitutional arrangements and procedures after long periods of seemingly good or at least adequate functioning, some are looking with interest at systems that combine a market economy with an authoritarian government. Little do they realize that a China-type political order will not favor those who believe they can exert more influence in such a system. But to avoid democracy drifting in that direction, it must acquire a new licence to operate, a new lease of life.

The notion of three arenas into which the individual may move at his or her free will, to be part of whichever collectivity he and she wishes to belong for a certain task or time, is worth taking up for this reason if for no other. With it, one underpins the supremacy and unique dignity of the individual human being, while not forgetting each human being's responsibility for the community he or she happens to belong to by fate or chose to belong to by choice, and for society as a whole. According civil society adequate and permanent representation therefore seems to be a logical step, all the more so as civil society actors bring presents of empathy, ideas, know-how, reputation, time, and resources to the table. The state may well be expected to relinquish powers in favor of a level playing field that embraces non-governmental and non-business players.

Given the elements of a contemporary paradigm, it seems that a global world order is not to be avoided, even if many citizens feel terrified at the thought. However: "Globalization is almost always written about in terms of how it operates within the existing order, rather than how it creates a new order" (Khanna, 2011, p. 48). In order to be acceptable and indeed workable, the new global world order will have to contain a massive measure of subsidiarity, to read a very careful assessment of cultural differences and traditions, and a clear view as to which problem needs to be discussed, decided upon, and solved at which level of a multi-tier and multi-arena societal order.

All this said, there is a bright side to disruptive innovation. Civil society can and indeed should never be reponsible for setting rules that affect every citizen. This is the government's core business, and in a liberal democracy, these decisions should exclusively be taken by those elected by the people as a whole. Indeed, this is what we pay our governments to do. The famous battle cry of "no taxation without representation" still stands today as it did in 18th-century North America. But if we can achieve a situation in which everyone realizes that taking the final decision is not the equivalent to preparing for them by offering analyses, ideas, arguments, and solutions, this would indeed be an iconic turn. There is no reason to assume that government officials—or indeed business executives—are any wiser than other citizens. If they could be made to realize that, on the contrary, social change emerges from chaos rather than from order, society could develop in a fascinating way.

We are seeing that some governments and most international governmental organisations are developing a taste for citizen participation, open government partnerships, and otherwise labelled formats of direct contact between rulers and the ruled. While this may be a good way of overcoming the increasing divide between a political class and increasingly frustrated citizens, it should not be overlooked that it may easily be manipulated in order to project openness and dialogue in public, yet using events with uninformed citizens to keep those who have real knowledge on particular issues out of the debate. It remains to be seen whether this policy will ultimately succeed or whether the citizens concerned will undergo a gradual educational process and become an informal civil society movement and eventually a formalized CSO.

Issues of legitimacy and relevance are still being discussed—by professional politicians who continue to cherish the notion that they are in the drivers' seats, by mainstream academia, by the media who still prefer to report on the occasional scandal or local events rather than offering civil society full participation in the debate on public affairs. If, however, we can consistently demonstrate that we will only reach striven-for goals by adopting principles embraced by civil society, it will become clear that, as Parag Khanna (2011) put it, the "dotgov-, dotcom-, and dotorg-worlds" will interact on a level playing field.

References

Alter, R., Strachwitz, R. G., & Unger, T. (2019). Philanthropy. Insight: Work in progress. Maecenata Observatorium: Vol. 31. Berlin: Maecenata. Retrieved from https://cdn.ymaws.com/www.istr.org/resource/resmgr/calls/mo-31_philanthropy.insight.pdf

Anheier, H. K., & Seibel, W. (1993). Defining the nonprofit sector: Germany. (The Johns Hopkins Nonprofit Sector Project, Working Paper 6). Retrieved from https://www.ess-europe.eu/sites/default/files/publications/files/defining-the-nonprofit-sector-germany.pdf

Applebaum, A. (2020). *Twilight of democracy: The failure of politics and the parting of friends.* London: Penguin.

Arato, A., & Cohen, J. (1988). Civil society and social theory. *Thesis Eleven, 21,* 40–64. https://doi.org/10.1177/072551368802100104

Aziz, M. H. (2020). *Future world order.* n.p.: Amazon KDP.

Cornuelle, R. C. (1965). *Reclaiming the American Dream: The role of private individuals and voluntary associations.* New York: Random House.

Crouch, C. (2011). *The strange non-death of neoliberalism.* Cambridge: Polity.

Dahrendorf, R. (1995). Economic opportunity, civil society and political liberty. (United Nations Research Institute for Social Development, Discussion Paper 58). Retrieved from http://www.unrisd.org/80256B3C005BCCF9/httpNetITFramePDF?ReadForm&parentunid=AF2130DF646281DD80256B67005B66F9&parentdoctype=paper&netitpath=80256B3C005BCCF9/(httpAuxPages)/AF2130DF646281DD80256B67005B66F9/$file/DP58.pdf

D'Ambrosio, R. (2018). Democrazia e politica: Risvolti etici [Democracy and politics: Ethical implications]. In R. D'Ambrosio & C. Venturi (Eds.), *La democrazia: Voci a confronto.* Rome: Gregorian and Biblical Press.

Davidson, J. D., & Rees-Mogg, L. W. (1999). *The sovereign individual: Mastering the transition to the information age.* New York: Touchstone.

Edelman. (2019). 2019 Edelman trust barometer: Global report. Retrieved from https://www.edelman.com/sites/g/files/aatuss191/files/2019-03/2019_Edelman_Trust_Barometer_Global_Report.pdf?utm_source=website&utm_medium=global_report&utm_campaign=downloads

Etzioni, A. (1973). The third sector and domestic missions. *Public Administration Review, 33,* 314–323. https://doi.org/10.2307/975110

Ferguson, A. (1995). *An essay on the history of civil society* (F. Oz-Salzberger, Ed.). Cambridge, UK: Cambridge University Press. (Original work published 1767)

Fukuyama, F. (1992). *The end of history and the last man.* New York: Free.

Habermas, J. (1994). *Faktizität und Geltung: Beiträge zur Diskurstheorie des Rechts und des demokratischen Rechtsstaats* (4th ed.) [Facticity and validity: Contributions to the discourse theory of law and the democratic constitutional state]. Frankfurt: Suhrkamp.

Hirschman, A. O. (1970). *Exit, voice, and loyalty: Responses to decline in firms, organizations, and states.* Cambridge, MA: Harvard University Press.

Jaspers, K. (1953). *The origin and goal of history.* New Haven, CT: Yale University Press.

Keay, D. (1987, October 31). Aids, education and the year 2000! *Woman's Own* (London), pp. 8–10.

Khanna, P. (2011). *How to run the world: Charting a course to the next renaissance.* New York: Random House.

Kronenberg, V. (2013). Was hält die Gesellschaft zusammen? Ein Blick zurück nach vorn [What holds society together? A look back forward]. *Aus Politik und Zeitgeschichte, 63*(13–14), 3–6.

Mounk, Y. (2018). *The people vs. democracy: Why our freedom is in danger and how to save it.* Cambridge, MA: Harvard University Press.

Perroux, F. (1960). *Économie et société: Contrainte, échange, don* [Economy and society: Constraint, exchange, gift]. Paris, France: Presses Universitaires de France.

Plato. (1924). *Euthyphro, apology of Socrates, and Crito* (J. Burnet, Ed. and Notes). Oxford, UK: Oxford University Press. https://doi.org/10.1093/actrade/9780198140153.book.1

Polanyi, K. (1944). *The great transformation.* Boston: Beacon.

Rajan, R. (2019). *The third pillar: How markets and the state leave the community behind.* New York: Penguin.

Salamon, L. M., Anheier, H. K., List, R., Toepler, S., & Sokolowski, S. W. (1999). Global civil society: Dimensions of the nonprofit sector. Baltimore: Johns Hopkins Center for Civil Society Studies. Retrieved from http://ccss.jhu.edu/wp-content/uploads/downloads/2011/08/Global-Civil-Society-I.pdf

Strachwitz, R. G. (2018). Chancen und Herausforderungen der Zivilgesellschaft heute [Opportunities and challenges of civil society today]. In R. M. Kordesch, J. Wieland, & M. N. Ebertz (Eds.), *Die Arbeit der Zivilgesellschaft* (pp. 17–30). Weilerswist: Velbrück Wissenschaft. https://doi.org/10.5771/9783748901617-17

Strachwitz, R. G., Priller, E., & Triebe, B. (2020). *Handbuch Zivilgesellschaft* [Civil society handbook]. Maecenata Schriften: Vol. 18. Berlin: de Gruyter.

Weiss, A. Burgmer, P., & Mussweiler, T. (2018). Two-faced morality: Distrust promotes divergent moral standards for the self versus others. *Personality and Social Psychology Bulletin, 44,* 1712–1724. https://doi.org/10.1177/0146167218775693

Chapter 4
Undone Science and Smart Cities: Civil Society Perspectives on Risk and Emerging Technologies

David J. Hess

Planning is currently underway for the development of a new urban infrastructure that will underlie the smart city. The envisioned future includes developing a smart grid, transforming buildings with the "internet of things," monitoring transportation remotely, commercializing air space for drones, and connecting vehicles to each other and the digital "cloud." The development of this digitized urban space is based on wireless communications that will increasingly connect and integrate the urban technological systems of electricity, transportation, and buildings. The smart city will require new research fields in engineering, computer science, and the social and behavioral sciences to guide technological innovation, regulatory policy, management strategies, and consumer interfaces that accompany the transition. Yet, this future smart city will be no different from past cities in at least one respect: it will be a contested space with different views about the design of the new technological systems and different knowledge claims that accompany controversies over design.

Because the world of connected and automated vehicles, digitized energy, and the "internet of things" has not yet arrived in full force, the contestation that will accompany its arrival has not yet crystallized, and the new urban space has not yet gained sustained attention from public-interest civil society organizations. One exception is the smart grid, which is already partially implemented in many parts of the world and has been accompanied by an emergent politics of knowledge and design. The smart grid is understood here as the application of digital technologies and computer software to a previously largely analog electricity system. Of special interest for the present discussion is the smart meter, which is the consumer interface of the smart grid. The smart meter is a digital electricity meter that enables the remote reading of a building's electricity consumption. In many countries, these digital meters have replaced the older analog meters. The new technology often makes it possible for the utility to engage in the direct management of internal

D. J. Hess (✉)
Department of Sociology, Vanderbilt University, Nashville, TN, USA
e-mail: david.j.hess@Vanderbilt.Edu

© The Author(s) 2022

J. Glückler et al. (eds.), *Knowledge and Civil Society*, Knowledge and Space 17,
https://doi.org/10.1007/978-3-030-71147-4_4

appliances such as air conditioning and heating systems. With the building owner's permission, the utility can send a signal to alter the setting on the heating and air conditioning system in order to control daily changes in the electricity load. The smart meter can also be used to provide time-of-use and real-time pricing to help manage peak load, to pinpoint power outages, to provide more effective responses, and to facilitate the adoption of distributed energy resources.

By studying how civil society organizations have reacted to the advent of the smart meter, one can begin to get a picture of the role of civil society in the broader transition to the future smart city. In this sense, the smart meter may be treated as a "harbinger technology" (that, is, a technology that serves as a forerunner of much greater levels of cyberphysical infrastructure) and used to foreshadow the as-yet unknown and emerging politics of the smart city. At the same time, the study of civil society and smart meters can also contribute to general social science knowledge about publics, science, and technology.

Background Concepts

In the study of knowledge, technology, and civil society, it is useful to begin with a distinction between social movements and civil society. The term *civil society* is understood here as a broad category of social organization and social relationship that is distinct from the family, the government, and the private sector. It is based on associational activity and can include clubs, religious groups, churches, charities, and political civil society; frequently, civil society organizations also have a special nonprofit tax status. In contrast, a *social movement* is a sustained mobilization of "challengers" (individuals and organizations) that are located in the subordinate positions of a social field (such as the electricity industry or the political field), that seek fundamental changes in the social field, and that encounter resistance to those changes from the "incumbents" located in the dominant positions of the field. Frequently, the leading organizations and individuals in a social movement are non-governmental organizations that can be characterized as political civil society, but movements often include coalitions with elected and appointed political officials, scientists, religious groups, and segments of the private sector.

Researchers who study social movements have tended to build theory based on empirical research on mobilizations in the political field. Many such movements can be characterized as having a universalistic goal of achieving justice for disadvantaged groups based on race, ethnicity, class, gender, sexuality, age, and other dimensions of structural inequality. Many also have the universalistic goal of enhanced democratic governance, especially in conditions of dictatorship and corruption of governments. In contrast, the industrial transition movement can include these societal change goals, but it also has the goal of bringing about a fundamental change in an industry and/or an associated technological system (Hess, 2016). Adding this type of movement to the field of social movement studies reveals new areas of research for a general theory of social movements, most notably the relationship between movements and science and technology.

The industrial transition movement can be further subdivided into a set of four ideal types, of which actual movements frequently represent an amalgam (see Fig. 4.1). The central distinction is between aspirations that involve societal change and those focused more narrowly on technological systems and industrial change. If the primary goal is societal change, there are two main subtypes: enhancing democracy, such as transforming governance processes for the industrial system (e.g., more democratic regulatory processes) or developing new ownership patterns and organizational forms in the industry (e.g., municipalization, cooperatives, or community solar); and remediating situations of inequality, unfairness, and lack of access, such as mobilizations in favor of low-income energy assistance, price containment, and green job development. Likewise, if the goal is a sociotechnical transition, one can distinguish between the industrial opposition subtype—which has the goal of ending a technology, such as coal, or remediating its harmful effects, such as coal-ash spills—and the subtype of alternative industrial development, which has the goal of helping to bring to scale desirable innovations, such as renewable energy or energy efficiency.

The concept of an industrial transition movement, with these four subtypes, can be applied across a range of spatial scales and with a topical scope that suits the researcher's needs. For example, a researcher might examine opposition to natural-gas fracturing technologies at the continental scale or in a much smaller geographical region within a country. Likewise, the scope may include a range of subtypes of industrial transition movements in a demarcated spatial area. For example, a study of New York State electricity politics and policy since 2000 compared four mobilizations that mapped roughly onto the four subtypes to show how the mobilizations are networked through distinct coalitions of civil society and other organizations that exist in silos with relatively low overlap and communication among them (Hess, 2018). The project also showed a trend toward integration, and with the

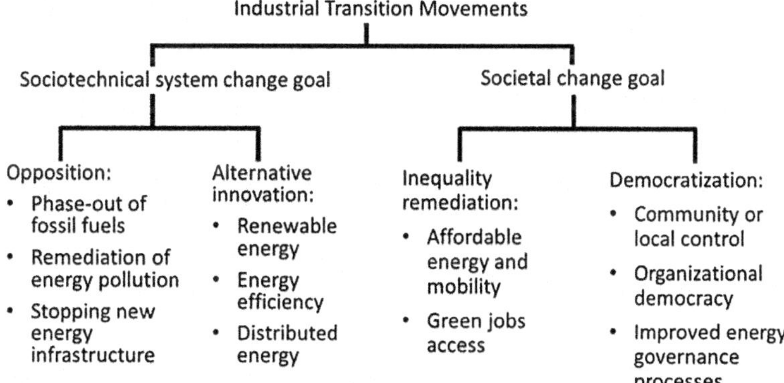

Fig. 4.1 Types of industrial transition movements (energy). Source: Design by author

integration, the development of new organizations and frames, especially the broad frame of energy democracy.

This study will examine the emergence of the industrial transition movement associated with smart meter development in the US. As a constituent element of the smart grid, the smart meter has received attention because it represents the interface between the increasingly digitized electricity system and the customer-citizen. To a large extent private-sector actors developed the technology with little democratic deliberation and participation in its design and implementation. Members of the utility and the information-technology industries have assumed that the technology is beneficial because it will increase energy efficiency, reduce costs to the utilities and potentially to consumers, improve resilience in the event of power outages, and enable the integration of distributed energy resources such as rooftop solar. Yet, the implementation of the technological change raises a wide range of questions that are likely to become emblematic of challenges that will occur with the broader transition to smart cities.

The analysis that follows will focus on civil society, smart meters, and mobilizations in the United States and especially in California, where the mobilizations were the most intense and widespread. Public mobilizations and participation in smart-meter policy will be approached through the lens of industrial transition movements. Using this lens, one can discern all four subtypes:

1. Anti-smart-meter networks have emerged in some countries, and their members frequently criticize the lack of democratic process in the decision-making that led to the adoption of smart meters. These criticisms come from both the political left and right (Hess, 2014). In North America, smart-meter opponents sometimes link their action to the democratic goal of community or public control over energy generation, a goal that has appeared throughout the history of the electricity industry and that currently appears in movements to municipalize utilities or to shift to a form of local control known as community choice (Hess, 2019).

2. Members of anti-smart-meter networks have also expressed concern about the equity dimension, based largely on the unequal distribution of expenses that emerges with time-of-use pricing (Hess, 2014). The digital technology of smart meters can enable options for consumers to save on energy costs if appliances such as clothes dryers are used during off-peak hours. But such advantages are more readily available to households with time flexibility and with advanced technologies, and the technological change consequently becomes associated with an affordability and price-equity problem. Another example of an affordability problem occurs when regulators or utilities have allowed opt-out provisions to wireless smart meters, but they have charged prohibitively high monthly fees for consumers who wish to exercise the option (e.g., The Utility Reform Network, 2012).

3. Members of smart-meter mobilizations also show concern about technical and design issues such as the possible health effects of smart meters and about privacy and security. The former concern is rooted in health risks claimed to be

associated with low-level microwave radiation, and the latter with the potential to know what people are doing inside the home because of the unique signature of appliances and even movies.

4. The mobilizations can involve support for a wide range of technological innovations, such as support for design innovation that ensures privacy for the new technologies or support for an emerging industry that has produced a wide range of products and services that provide shielding from non-ionizing electromagnetic radiation.

This study will focus on the third and fourth types of industrial transition movement subtypes, that is, efforts to address the sociotechnical change goals of health and privacy-security, both in the oppositional and pro-alternative variants. In the US for each of these issues, there is a moderately developed network of civil society organizations that can provide a basis for the exploration of knowledge, technology, civil society, and undone science.

In addition to bringing to the study of knowledge and civil society the lens of industrial transition movements, this study also draws attention to the diversity of goals among civil society organizations. Three basic types of organizations will be discussed here. First, anti-smart meter groups tend to be informal, grassroots organizations that emerge during the installation period. There is not enough research yet to understand the conditions for their mobilization and demobilization, but it is possible that achieving an opt-out rule at an affordable cost may be the condition that leads the groups to go into abeyance. These groups raise a wide range of concerns with respect to smart meters, including democracy and equity goals, but frequently in North America the groups focus especially on risks to health, privacy, and security. Second, privacy organizations have a broad range of concerns about privacy and are generally more formal and well-established organizations. They may be considered as a subset of the broader movement of consumer organizations, and they occasionally become active in the field of smart-meter politics. Third, EMF risk organizations are sometimes formal nonprofit organizations, but in some cases, they are only information-providing web sites that are linked to EMF remediation businesses. Thus, these organizations can represent a combination of civil society and entrepreneurial business organizations. The three sections that follow will discuss each of these three types of civil society and their responses to smart meters.

With respect to the question of knowledge and ignorance, these three types of civil society actors draw attention to the need for different types of knowledge. Some of the knowledge is future knowledge that utilities and other industrial organizations accept as necessary, such as the computer science and engineering knowledge needed to provide assurances of privacy that are necessary for consumer acceptance. However, some of the knowledge is also what I and others have termed *undone science.* The concept of undone science is situated in the broader field of research on knowledge and ignorance as one of the many forms of ignorance (Gross & McGoey, 2015; Hess, 2020). Among the different types of nonknowledge, undone science has two main elements. First, it is a specified absence or low quantity of scientific research; in other words, it is a possible future knowledge that can be identified as needed or wanted. Many actors in the state, industry, science, and civil society frequently identify future research agendas of desired but as yet incomplete knowledge. However, undone science is more specific than simply a formulation of desired future knowledge. The second aspect of undone science is that it is a situated knowledge that is identified by reformers who claim to speak for a broad public interest, such as members of public-interest civil society organizations, who think that the public would benefit from knowing more about a topic. In the context of emerging technologies, undone science often refers to research on health, environmental, privacy, safety, or other kinds of risk. Industrial actors and allied groups that are supporting the new technologies have rejected research that documents risk, safety, or other public interest concerns as unwanted, and, in some cases, they have worked to suppress or defund the research.

When this situation occurs, some researchers may still take up the challenge, but they often do so in marginalized settings such as unfunded work by independent scientists. Thus, undone science refers to a specification of what is unknown but potentially knowable and that if known, might help advocates of the public interest to defend better regulation, innovation, and public protections. It is knowledge that can be positioned to have potential effects in the political field.

Grassroots Anti-Smart-Meter Mobilizations

Grassroots anti-smart-meter networks emerged throughout North America, but the most concentrated mobilizations were on the West Coast from California to British Columbia (Hess, 2014; Hess & Coley, 2014). These networks generally were not comprised of formal, nonprofit organizations, but they sometimes included participation from formal organizations, including the EMF organizations to be described below. The reasons given for opposition varied substantially. Analyses of testimony and media reports indicate that health concerns from wireless microwave transmission were paramount (Hess, 2014; Hess & Coley, 2014). The mobilizations tended to attract a wide range of political perspectives, from conservatives who were concerned about "big brother" to progressives concerned about democracy, process, and precautionary politics.

The grassroots mobilizations resulted in many local government resolutions and ordinances as well as extensive public testimony and some protest. Although the anti-smart meter advocates were unable to stop the smart-meter deployment or to gain a design shift to wired meters, in 2012 the California Public Utilities Commission approved an opt-out program that allowed customers to retain an analog meter for a fee, and other states and provinces offered similar concessions. In the case of California, anti-smart-meter advocates supported the measure in general terms, but some program issues remained controversial. An investor-owned utility argued that in addition to the option to switch back to an analog system, customers could also opt-out by accepting a modified smart meter with the radio turned off. The utility maintained that the radiofrequency emissions from the "radio off" smart meters were well within the federal government's safety standard and that leaving the already installed smart meters would allow greater flexibility for future customers. However, opponents as well as a number of local governments continued to be concerned about the health effects of the meters even with the radiofrequency turned off, and they fought for the right to remove the meters rather than rely on modification of the already installed smart meters (California Public Utilities Commission, 2011). The anti-smart-meter groups also advocated against opt-out fees because the charges for customers far outweighed the costs for utilities to reinstall the analog meters. In 2014, the Public Utilities Commission agreed to cap the monthly opt-out fees.

The grassroots anti-smart-meter networks did not generate new scientific knowledge. Some proponents created citizen science in the form of YouTube videos that measured radiofrequency emissions from smart meters and provided testimonials from people who claimed to have experienced health effects. The main relationship with scientific knowledge was the circulation of knowledge, that is, explaining to the public and to local governments why a moratorium was needed while more safety research was conducted or why an opt-out policy should be required in the absence of a moratorium. The arguments included references to scientific research on potential health effects of living in proximity to constant wireless emissions from smart meters.

Privacy Organizations

An important reason why the advent of the smart meter has raised concerns from consumers and public-interest civil society organizations is that each appliance has a unique electronic signature. Thus, it is possible to know when people are home and what they are doing there, a prospect that conjures up images of Orwell's *1984* (1949). As with other internet-based technologies, privacy standards are vital to guide what kind of information will be collected, the degree of granularity of the information, how the information will be used, when it will be deleted, and who has access to it. Furthermore, there are closely connected security issues based on the risk of breaches of private information or the possibility of assembling information into detailed pictures of each person. Criminals could use records to determine when people are at home or away from home, and they could potentially also cause fires by hacking into heating units. Thus, privacy and security issues are closely interwoven.

Whereas governments and industry tend to dismiss health concerns, they are much more willing to entertain the need to develop good privacy and security standards. Industry recognizes that without public confidence, resistance will rapidly mount and lead to the discrediting of smart meters and the "internet of things." In the United States, recognition of the importance of the problem has grown with each new major privacy breach, and the European Union's General Data Protection Regulation also affected privacy practices on the North American continent. Thus, the relationship between civil society organizations that advocate for privacy and industrial incumbents such as the utilities is much less oppositional than for the goal of opt-outs or moratoria. Nevertheless, in the US there is considerable public awareness that government legislators and regulators are captured by industrial interests. In response, privacy advocacy organizations have played a public-interest role by pressuring the federal and state governments to adopt better privacy standards and implementation.

As for many issues involving energy and new technologies, California has been a leader in the United States. The state government's constitution includes a privacy provision, and a state law (Senate Bill 17 of 2009) authorized the California Public Utilities Commission to enact privacy provisions. Two civil society organizations, the Electronic Privacy Frontier Foundation and the Center for Democracy and Technology, provided comments in the regulatory process for privacy and smart meters in the state (Lynch & Tien, 2010). The organizations carefully opened their comments by discussing the benefits of smart meters; hence, the position of these civil society organizations was not in opposition to smart-meter installations.

In contrast with the grassroots anti-smart-meter mobilizations, the privacy organizations did not argue that smart-meter deployment should be halted or that affordable opt-out provisions should be immediately implemented. Rather, they asserted that the California Public Utilities Commission should adopt regulatory policy that follows the general fair information practices principles (Lynch & Tien, 2010). These principles exist in various versions, and the organizations' testimony included the following: transparency of data management practices, individual participation with consent, purpose specification for data use, data minimization, use limitation, data quality and integrity (accurate, timely, complete), data security, and accountability and auditing. (These principles also appear in the European Union's General Data Protection Regulation.) The organizations also advocated for a prohibition on nondisclosed use by third parties and for a requirement of data destruction when the specified use is no longer operational.

In 2011, the privacy organizations claimed that the California Public Utilities Commission had accepted their recommendations (Jeschke, 2011). Senate Bill 1476, which legislators enacted that year, prohibited utilities from sharing, disclosing, selling, or otherwise making accessible to third parties a customer's data, which includes information about electrical and gas consumption, without the consent of the customer. The measure also required utilities to use "reasonable security procedures and practices" to protect these data (Senate Bill 1476 of 2010). In 2014, the state government approved Assembly Bill 1274, which expanded the earlier smart meter privacy law by putting the same restrictions on businesses that work with smart meter data, such as internet service providers and financial institutions.

The approval of privacy principles and regulations is only part of the story; with the advent of these regulations, there must be effective implementation. The effectiveness of privacy implementation depends in part on the willingness of utilities to follow through with the legislators' and regulators' intent, but it also requires new knowledges and technologies to ensure privacy. Privacy technology assurances need to be developed. For example, how frequently should a customer's electricity consumption be sampled? Does a less frequent rate of sampling, such as once per day, ensure privacy, or is it still possible to figure out home activities? Should customer data be aggregated, and if so, what rules of aggregation should be followed? The utilities can bring together readings from multiple smart meters to reach a total energy reading but without obtaining any data on a specific household's energy consumption (Cavoukian & Polonetsky, 2013). Researchers are still developing privacy aggregation protocols for smart meters that are tolerant of communication failures or smart-meter malfunctioning in order to avoid privacy breaches (e.g., Hoepman, 2017; Won, Ma, Yau, & Rao, 2016). However, aggregation may also make it difficult to use real-time pricing programs, and other ways of protecting privacy may be preferable. These questions and problems help to motivate the development of a new knowledge associated with the management of privacy for the smart grid. In turn, this area of privacy research is a subfield of the emerging field of "privacy engineering," for which graduate education is now becoming available.

In summary, the mobilization of privacy organizations has generally operated within the framework of acceptance of the technological transition. Civil society organizations have articulated privacy principles and privacy guidance, and the push for good privacy practices has helped to stimulate the development of new knowledges and technologies (even a new research field) in privacy engineering. Many questions remain unanswered, and many problems remain unsolved, but the development of privacy science and technology for the smart grid is a developing scientific research field rather than undone science. The utilities and related companies recognize the need to implement the technology in order to ensure the overall public acceptance of the technological transition, and the implementation of the General Data Protection Regulation in Europe in 2018 is having significant spillover effects on North American policies and practices. In other words, resources are already forthcoming to develop the science and technology needed to meet policy goals and guidelines for privacy standards, and the field of privacy research is untroubled by industry-based attacks on its credibility. Such is not the case for the third type of civil society mobilization.

EMF Risk Organizations

EMF risk (or safety) organizations include informational web sites run by individuals, small businesses, and formal nonprofit organizations. They have existed for decades, and they have been involved in a wide range of public controversies involving risk from non-ionizing EMF. This category of EMF includes high-voltage power lines and electricity transformer sites near homes and schools, faulty wiring and dirty electricity inside buildings, the use of radar on military bases near civilian residences, the safety of radar for military and police workers, microwave ovens, computers, cell phone towers (mobile phone masts), wi-fi, cell phones, and cordless phones. In North America, the primary intersection of the EMF risk organizations with the politics of smart meters involves the potential health risks from exposure to wireless transmission.

An informal survey by a smart-meter organization indicated that common complaints include sleep disturbances, stress and anxiety, headaches, and tinnitus (Halteman, 2011). The peer-reviewed research tends to come from the related field of research on the effects of microwave radiation associated with cell phones and towers (mobile phones and masts). In other words, there is very little direct research on the health effects associated with wireless smart meters. However, the research on wi-fi and cellular phones is relevant because it involves a similar frequency of EMF radiation to the one used for wireless smart-meter transmissions.

Because the power density of the EMF radiation declines rapidly with distance, a person's exposure is affected by the location of the meter installation on the outside wall of the building, the size of the building, and how much time the person spends in the room near the meter. A meter bank in an apartment complex where the inside space is a bedroom or office would expose occupants to much higher EMF emissions than a single meter located on the outside of a garage and away from sleeping areas. (High levels of exposure may also apply to people who sleep with their wi-fi routers next to their beds and cell phones under their pillows).

Researchers who study health effects of EMF radiation have recommended precautionary standards, and some areas of the world have enacted standards close to these recommendations. Whereas the US standard is set at a non-precautionary level of 10,000 μW/cm^2, which is based on thermal or tissue-heating effects, other areas of the world recognize standards based on nonthermal biological effects. The Council of Europe (2011) has recommended a maximum indoor exposure level of .6 V/m (.1 μW/cm^2) and a medium-term goal of .2 V/m (.01 μW/cm^2). A group of experts in Norway recommended a whole-body exposure limit of .17 μW/cm^2, with a potential precautionary limit of .017 μW/cm^2 (Fragopoulou et al., 2010). In Germany, the Institut für Baubiologie + Ökologie (2008; Institute for Building Biology and Ecology) designated .001 μW/cm^2 as the boundary between slight and severe concern. The BioInitiative Report (BioInitiative Working Group, Sage, & Carpenter, 2012), which was written by an international network of EMF health experts, recommended a precautionary indoor exposure limit equivalent to .0003–.0006 μW/cm^2.

Although the standards are helpful guidelines, they can be confusing in practice. For example, using the relatively accurate Acoustimeter, a smart meter installed on the outside wall of the garage of the house of the author generates an average inside power density of .0001–.0005 μW/cm^2 at three meters with one layer of aluminum foil shielding on the inside wall, and it has spikes or peak frequencies of .01–.06 μW/cm^2. The evaluation of safety or risk depends partly on which standard is used, whether one uses average or peak power densities, and how far one is from the smart meter. Moreover, the health effects literature, which includes hundreds of studies, is not always calibrated to the power density units used in measurement devices.

Nevertheless, by the twenty-first century, radiofrequency meters have become widely available and marketed through the network of EMF safety and remediation companies. In addition, an industry of EMF consultants and businesses, with certification and training, has emerged to help building owners to evaluate and remediate high emissions. Thus, it is possible to have a building evaluated and to measure exposure, as well as to remediate exposure just as is done for radon risk. But doing so requires some knowledge and financial resources, a problem that leads to intersections with the equity goal that sometimes emerges in the EMF health-risk organizations.

Although the level of risk associated with microwave transmissions remains unknown, every year the public health and subclinical peer-reviewed research continues to document more health effects. This situation is an example of undone science, whereby the incumbent actors of an industrial regime view additional research as potentially threatening to the current configuration of the technological system, a view that is backed by systematic underfunding and a history of some attacks on scientists who have documented risk. In the case of research on the health effects of wireless technologies, there is little government-sponsored research in the US, and scientists who engage in research in this field risk their careers. Journalists and scientists have documented the systematic reduction of funding from the government to independent scientists that began to be evident by the early 1980s, and they have also documented the campaigns by the military and industry to discredit or bury independent research that demonstrates health effects (e.g., Becker & Selden, 1985; Brodeur, 1977; Marino, 2010). Rather than seek answers to these questions and develop low-emissions technologies and shielding, industry members have instead sought to reassure consumers about the safety of EMF radiation and to support a view of the research field on health effects of EMF radiation as in a permanent state of inconclusive knowledge. This approach to the research field is similar to the one that industry members have adopted toward research on climate change, some chemicals, and tobacco, where the goal is to prevent regulatory intervention by arguing that the science is unsettled and that there is no basis for the regulation based on an industry definition of "sound science" (Oreskes & Conway, 2010; Rampton & Stauber, 2001).

The other side of undone science is the generation of incumbent science. A systematic review of research has documented how industry-funded science tends to produce negative findings about health risk from EMF at a significantly higher rate than independent science (Huss, Egger, Hug, Huwiler-Müntener, & Röösli, 2007). Incorrect information about health risks then circulates through public relations campaigns. An example of the utilities' approach to safety concerns appears on the web site of the Smart Energy Consumer Collaborative, an industry group that educates consumers about the benefits of smart meters. With respect to health concerns, the website had the following quote: "It would take 375 years of direct contact with a smart meter to equal the same amount of radio frequency exposure from a daily, 15-minute cell phone call over the course of one year" (Smart Energy Consumer Collaborative, 2020). This quotation appears on other websites used to reduce the concerns of customers about health effects. The authority for the quotation is a study by the California Council on Science and Technology (2011), which various independent EMF researchers have criticized for accuracy (Carpenter, 2011; Hirsch, 2011; Maret, 2011). Civil society organizations generally do not enter directly into the scientific controversy, which is best left to researchers, but EMF risk organizations such as the Center for Electrosmog Prevention (2011a) have publicized the flaws of the study. Moreover, smart-meter groups have raised additional questions about the credibility of other experts employed by industry (Burke, 2015).

In addition to challenging industry assertions that there is no scientific basis for health risks that customers and smart-meter groups raise, EMF risk organizations also participate in government regulatory proceedings by providing knowledge and information. For example, the Center for Electrosmog Prevention participated in the California Public Utilities Commission rule-making, and the EMF Policy Institute participated in federal rule-making procedures. The organizations defended opt-out provisions and pointed to the need to provide protection for persons with health conditions and disabilities that may require special consideration with respect to exposure to EMF fields. Without invoking the disputed category of electrosensitives, these organizations cited studies that medical implants may malfunction with exposure to wireless smart-meter emissions (Singer, n.d.). They argue that current safety policies fail to protect these groups of people and that policies such as opt-out fees violate the Americans with Disabilities Act, a connection that links the sociotechnical goal of emissions reduction with the equity goal of remediation of rights. The Center for Electrosmog Prevention (2011b) stated that to charge these vulnerable populations for opt-out rights is "similar to denying a person in a wheelchair any access to services, with the exception of a 'for-fee ramp.'"

As in the case of privacy-related mobilization, health concerns can also be the basis for the development of new technologies. In this case, the most obvious alternative technology is wired technology that would connect the meter to the utility through fiber-optic cables. This feasible technological substitution makes it possible to avoid the entire question of the health effects of wireless transmission, but it would require cooperation with the cable or land-line industries, and it could mean cost increases for the utilities. (Wired technology also does not eliminate health-risk concerns, which have occurred in some parts of Europe even for wired technology). In the absence of wired technology, there is an industry of companies that offer a wide range of products designed to reduce exposure: fabrics, clothing, and paints that reduce EMF exposure; shielding devices for smart meters, cell phones, routers, automobile cabins, and computers; books and videos; and a wide range of devices that can measure exposure.

Some countries and subnational regions have wired systems, and some countries have also restricted wi-fi for the most vulnerable segments of the population. For example, in France wi-fi has been banned in nursery schools and minimized in elementary schools. But the main way of achieving the goal of reduced exposure to microwave radiation is to develop and use wireless technology at levels of power density below which health effects have not been demonstrated. Numerous technical design solutions could be developed to reduce emissions, just as has been done for emissions from power plants and vehicles, but unlike privacy research, this topic is largely one of undone science and industrial non-innovation.

On the whole, EMF risk organizations face an uphill battle. People are unlikely to give up the convenience of wireless technology, especially for cell phones, and the primary way to resolve public health concerns is likely going to be through the design of a next generation of technologies that has lower microwave emissions. At this point, it is not possible to say with assurance what the acceptable minimum level of exposure to wireless microwave radiation should be because researchers have not yet found a threshold minimum dose. Whereas this question is one for the natural and health sciences, a social science perspective can point to another type of conclusion: there is a policy collision looming ahead. On the one hand, public-health researchers continue to generate knowledge about health risks at low exposures, and the lowest observed effect level at which health effects are evident continues to decline. On the other hand, the wireless industry continues to push new technologies in the home, the workplace, the transportation system, and even on lamp posts, which is generating more, not less, cumulative exposure. It is possible that future research and policy will establish a minimum threshold level below which biological effects are not detected, and it is possible that this level will still allow a next generation of wireless technology to function adequately. But no one will know if the research is not being done.

One example of the potential collision course ahead is the fate of California's Senate Bill 649 of 2017. Had it been approved, the bill would have required local governments to lease out public property, such as streetlights and traffic signal poles, to the wireless industry for the installation of "small cell" telecommunications facilities. The bill would have also capped the fees local governments can charge these companies, and it would have restricted cities' ability to gather public input and negotiate leases. Proponents of the bill argued that the measure would expand the state's connectivity, bring it closer towards the 5 GHz future of telecommunication, and boost the economy. Unsurprisingly, local governments opposed the bill because it would have eliminated their discretion over how to use public property. Activists and scientists also argued that the radiation and electromagnetic frequencies emitted by cellular towers in public buildings and utility poles would create a public health risk. Governor Edmund "Jerry" Brown vetoed the bill in October 2017.

Conclusions

Several general implications emerge from this review of different aspects of one industrial transition movement in one country. First, with respect to the general social science problem of understanding the connections between civil society and the politics of knowledge, this analysis points to the value of tracking differences across civil society organizations and coalitions even where they may have mostly consistent objectives (Hess, 2018). Grassroots networks were focused mostly on gaining moratoria and opt-out provisions; electronic privacy organizations drew attention to the implementation of good privacy principles; and EMF safety organizations underlined health-related risks, potential violations of disability law, and the value of remediation technologies.

Second, although some connections with the equity goal were flagged, this study has focused more on the sociotechnical side of industrial transition movements than on the societal change goals that sometimes emerge in the context of the smart grid. The advantage of a broad typology is that it enables questions about what other types of politics might have been left out of the analysis. Examples of societal transition goals that sometimes emerge in the context of smart grid politics include democracy goals (e.g., improved democratic participation in rule-making and standards and the broader question of public ownership of electricity systems) and equity goals (e.g., the cost of opt outs and the effects of wireless exposure on persons with chronic health conditions and pacemakers). But even within the category of sociotechnical change goals, this study shows how goals often overlap in practice. For example, oppositional goals—such as a moratorium or opt-out policy—will tend to coincide with generative goals—such as support for the remediation industry. The mobilizations help to create the conditions that favor the generation of new types of knowledges and technologies, such as privacy engineering and EMF remediation. Older technologies, such as wired transmission systems, receive new valuation from a safety perspective.

Third, these movements draw attention to the politics of research priorities and agendas. Although mobilizations of civil society organizations can help to motivate the generation of new research fields and associated technological innovation, the position of these research fields with respect to the incumbents of the industrial fields can vary dramatically. The utilities seem willing to swallow the pill of privacy restrictions in order to reap the gains of time-of-use pricing, grid resilience, load stability, and reduced labor costs. But the prospect of a return to analog meters is a much more fundamental threat to the future electricity grid, and the shift to a wired system may entail competitive risks from the telecommunications industry. Moreover, although wired systems are feasible for smart meters and for computer connections in buildings, they pose an existential threat to the future world of connected transportation and mobile connections. Thus, one type of knowledge—privacy engineering—is merely part of the terrain of a complex digital world in which almost anything about individuals is potentially knowable, whereas the other type of knowledge—health risks from wireless communications—poses a potentially deeper set of challenges. One type of knowledge is merely a future and emergent research field, whereas the other suffers from loss of government funding, industry-funded counter studies, and other mechanisms that create a situation of undone science and non-innovation. Social movements can play a vital role in the democratic politics of technology by helping to identify undone science, to mobilize resources to help get the science done, and to open up policy decisions to democratic political processes that include industry perspectives but are also insulated from industry pressure.

Acknowledgements　This project was partially supported by the US National Science Foundation, OISE-1743772, Partnerships for International Science and Engineering (PIRE) Program: "Science of Design for Societal-Scale Cyber-Physical Systems." Any opinions, findings, conclusions, or recommendations expressed here do not necessarily reflect the views of the National Science Foundation. I thank Magdalena Sudibjo for research assistance on portions of the paper.

References

Becker, R. O., & Selden, G. (1985). *The body electric: Electromagnetism and the foundation of life*. New York: William Morrow and Company.

BioInitiative Working Group, Sage, C., & Carpenter, D. O. (Eds.). (2012). *The BioInitiative report: A rationale for a biologically-based public exposure standard for electromagnetic fields (ELF and RF)*. Retrieved from http://www.bioinitiative.org

Brodeur, P. (1977). *The zapping of America: Microwaves, their deadly risk, and the coverup*. New York: W. W. Norton & Company.

Burke, P. (2015). Ethics complaint. Retrieved from www.stopsmartmetersbc.com/wp-content/uploads/2015/10/hirsch-sept-2015-finaL-2.doc

California Council on Science and Technology. (2011). Health impacts of radio frequency exposure from smart meters: April 2011—Final report. Retrieved from https://ccst.us/publications/2011/2011smart-final.pdf

California Public Utilities Commission. (2011). Decision modifying Pacific Gas and Electric Company's smartmeter program to include an opt-out option. Retrieved from http://docs.cpuc.ca.gov/PUBLISHED/AGENDA_DECISION/158309.htm

Carpenter, D. O. (2011). Sage reports: Expert letters to CCST: David O. Carpenter, M. D. Retrieved from http://sagereports.com/smart-meter-rf/?p=297

Cavoukian, A., & Polonetsky, J. (2013). Privacy by design and third-party access to customer energy usage data. Retrieved from https://www.ipc.on.ca/wp-content/uploads/Resources/pbd-thirdparty-CEUD.pdf

Center for Electrosmog Prevention. (2011a). Smart meters radiation exposure up to 160 times more than cell phones (Hirsch). Retrieved from http://www.electrosmogprevention.org/public-health-alert/smart-meters-radiation-exposure-up-to-160-times-more-than-cell-phones-hirsch/

Center for Electrosmog Prevention. (2011b). Opening brief of Center for Electrosmog Prevention on smart meter opt out restrictions imposed by Americans with Disabilities Act or California Public Utilities Code 453(B). Retrieved from http://docs.cpuc.ca.gov/publisheddocs/efile/brief/170230.pdf

Council of Europe. (2011). The potential dangers of electromagnetic fields and their effects on the environment. Resolution 1815. Retrieved from http://assembly.coe.int/nw/xml/XRef/Xref-XML2HTML-en.asp?fileid=17994&

Fragopoulou, A., Grigoriev, Y., Johansson, O., Margaritis, L. H., Morgan, L., Richter, E., & Sage, C. (2010). Scientific panel on electromagnetic field health risks: Consensus points, recommendations, and rationales. *Reviews on Environmental Health, 25*, 307–317. https://doi.org/10.1515/REVEH.2010.25.4.307

Gross, M., & McGoey, L. (2015). *Routledge international handbook of ignorance studies*. Abingdon: Routledge.

Halteman, E. (2011). Wireless utilities meter safety impacts survey: Final results summary September 13, 2011. Retrieved from http://emfsafetynetwork.org/wp-content/uploads/2011/09/Wireless-Utility-Meter-Safety-Impacts-Survey-Results-Final.pdf

Hess, D. J. (2014). Smart meters and public acceptance: Comparative analysis and governance implications. *Health, Risk & Society, 16*, 243–258. https://doi.org/10.1080/13698575.2014.911821

Hess, D. J. (2016). *Undone science: Social movements, mobilized publics, and industrial transitions*. Cambridge, MA: MIT Press.

Hess, D. J. (2018). Energy democracy and social movements: A multi-coalition perspective on the politics of sustainability transitions. *Energy Research & Social Science, 40*, 177–189. https://doi.org/10.1016/j.erss.2018.01.003

Hess, D. J. (2019). Coalitions, framing, and the politics of energy transitions: Local democracy and community choice in California. *Energy Research & Social Science, 50*, 38–50. https://doi.org/10.1016/j.erss.2018.11.013

Hess, D. J. (2020). The sociology of ignorance and post-truth politics. *Sociological Forum, 35,* 241–249. https://doi.org/10.1111/socf.12577

Hess, D. J., & Coley, J. S. (2014). Wireless smart meters and public acceptance: The environment, limited choices, and precautionary politics. *Public Understanding of Science, 23,* 688–702. https://doi.org/10.1177/0963662512464936

Hirsch, D. (2011). Comments on the draft report by the California Council on Science and Technology "Health impacts of radio frequency from smart meters." Retrieved from http://www.ccst.us/projects/smart2/documents/letter8hirsch.pdf

Hoepman, J.-H. (2017). Privacy friendly aggregation of smart meter readings, even when meters crash. In R. Bilof (Ed.), *CPSR-SG'17: Proceedings of the 2nd Workshop on Cyber-Physical Security and Resilience in Smart Grids* (pp. 3–7). New York: Association for Computing Machinery. https://doi.org/10.1145/3055386.3055389

Huss, A., Egger, M., Hug, K., Huwiler-Müntener, K., & Röösli, M. (2007). Source of funding and results of studies of health effects of mobile phone use: Systematic review of experimental studies. *Environmental Health Perspectives, 115,* 1–4. https://doi.org/10.1289/ehp.9149

Institut für Baubiologie + Ökologie. (2008). Building biology evaluation guidelines: For sleeping areas (K. Gustavs, Trans.). Retrieved from https://www.home-biology.com/images/emfsafety-limits/BuidlingBiologyLimits.pdf

Jeschke, R. (2011). California proposes strong privacy protections for smart meters. Electronic Frontier Foundation. Retrieved from https://www.eff.org/deeplinks/2011/05/california-proposes-strong-privacy-protections

Lynch, J., & Tien, L. (2010). Joint comments of the Center for Democracy & Technology and the Electronic Frontier Foundation on proposed policies and findings pertaining to the smart grid: California Public Utilities Commission, Rulemaking 08-12-009. Retrieved from https://www.eff.org/files/cdteffjointcomment030910.pdf

Maret, K. (2011). Commentary on the California Council on Science and Technology Report "Health impacts of radio frequency from smart meters." Retrieved from http://sagereports.com/smart-meter-rf/?p=368

Marino, A. A. (2010). *Going somewhere: Truth about a life in science.* Belcher: Cassandra.

Oreskes, N., & Conway, E. M. (2010). *Merchants of doubt: How a handful of scientists obscured the truth on issues from tobacco smoke to global warming.* New York: Bloomsbury.

Orwell, G. (1949). *1984.* London: Secker & Warburg.

Rampton, S., & Stauber, J. (2001). *Trust us, we're experts! How industry manipulates science and gambles with your future.* New York: Jeremy P. Tarcher/Putnam.

Senate Bill No. 17 (2009). California, USA.

Senate Bill No. 1476 (2010). California, USA.

Senate Bill No. 649 (2017). California, USA.

Singer, K. (n.d.). Medical implants: The effects of electromagnetic signals from wireless devices on medical implants and medical equipment. Retrieved from http://www.electronicsilentspring.com/primers/medical-implants/

Smart Energy Consumer Collaborative. (2020). Smart grid facts. Retrieved from https://smartenergycc.org/smartgrid101/

The Utility Reform Network. (2012). SM opt out costs should come profits, not rates. Retrieved from http://www.turn.org/press-release/sm-opt-out-costs-should-come-from-profits-not-rates/

Won, J., Ma, C. Y. T., Yau, D. K. Y., Rao, N. S. V. (2016). Privacy-assured aggregation protocol for smart metering: A proactive fault-tolerant approach. *IEEE/ACM Transactions on Networking, 24,* 1661–1674. https://doi.org/10.1109/TNET.2015.2425422

Part II
Analyzing Civil Society Organizations

Chapter 5
Specialists for Crumble Cakes?
The German LandFrauen Organizations
in Social Innovation, and as Educational,
Social, and Political Institutions

Laura Suarsana

The LandFrauen clubs and associations[1] as contemporary civil society organizations are spread widely across Germany, with a focus on the rural areas. Strongly locally embedded and interconnected nationwide, they address local needs and the interests of women and women in agriculture, and contribute to social and cultural infrastructure and the development of rural regions. They engage in education, knowledge transfer, and political interest representation, and address societal challenges. Despite these activities and their size of about 500,000 members in more than 10,000 local clubs, 22 state associations, and one federal association (DLV e.V., 2020a), the German LandFrauen are to a large part neglected by social sciences and often reduced to "specialists for crumble cakes" (Int. 02, see also Icken, 2002, p. 9; Sawahn 2009, 2012).

In this chapter, I present empirical results on the LandFrauen and illustrate that their activities go far beyond baking, as they, in manifold dimensions, contribute to societal change and the development of rural areas. This case study contributes to the debate on civil society's role in societal change and social innovation: I will discuss how the LandFrauen organizations as an institutional frame enable these activities, which are highly reliant on their diverse and strongly locally rooted base of members. I analyze the diverse practices from the conceptual perspective of social innovation as an approach whose practical dimension is expected to hold particularly high potential for rural areas, which are often affected by infrastructural and socioeconomic deficits and structural weaknesses. The empirical results on the German LandFrauen clubs and associations show that LandFrauen are highly

---

[1] Throughout this chapter, I use *clubs* for the very local organizations with individual members. I use *associations* for the higher organizational levels with—regularly—organizational members (apart from exceptions with individual memberships also on higher associational levels).

L. Suarsana (✉)
Institute Labour and Economy, University of Bremen, Bremen, Germany
e-mail: laura.suarsana@uni-bremen.de

J. Glückler et al. (eds.), *Knowledge and Civil Society*, Knowledge and Space 17,
https://doi.org/10.1007/978-3-030-71147-4_5

engaged in initiating change and development in rural Germany by uniquely addressing women's needs through social, cultural, and educational offers: The members' social interactions thereby function as a ground and starting point for further activities that set impulses in local development.

Based on the empirical research, I argue that the LandFrauen activities are, on one hand, integrated into specific local fields and highly adaptive to local needs and interests through the deep integration of the large and diverse base of members in their local villages and rural society. In parallel, they receive support from higher associational levels, providing them with knowledge, ideas, and institutional support. The interwoven local and interregional activities, cooperation, and the exchange of knowledge and ideas, and a broad internal and external network—across horizontal and vertical levels as well as across geographies—can be highlighted as a key feature of the LandFrauen associations, and as the base of their societal engagement.

This chapter is structured as follows: I will first discuss social innovation as conceptual background and underlying research perspective, followed by a discussion of the LandFrauen as an object of research and an element of associational life in Germany. On this basis, I will derive my research questions and provide an overview on methods, in order to then elaborate my empirical findings on the LandFrauen practices related to societal change, and how they are organized within the associational structure. I reflect upon these results in a discussion of how the discussed practices relate to the concept of social innovation, and of prerequisites that facilitate the explored practices. The chapter closes with a conclusion.

Social Innovation as a Research Perspective

New Solutions for Society, Unfolding in Practices

The notion of *social innovation* is diffuse and contested (Domanski, Howaldt, & Kaletka, 2020, p. 458; Howaldt & Schwarz, 2010, pp. 2–3) with regard to its analytical status as well as its use in policy practices (Moulaert, MacCallum, & Hillier, 2013, p. 13). Key commonality in the variety of understandings of the term is the connection to societal change and the meeting of social problems and needs through new societal solutions (Domanski et al., 2020, pp. 460–462; Howaldt & Schwarz, 2010; Moulaert & MacCallum, 2019, p. 31; Mulgan, Tucker, Ali, & Sanders, 2007, pp. 1, 8; Wendt, 2016, pp. 10–12; Zapf, 1989). Social innovation is related to novelty and innovation as conceptualized by Schumpeter (1912, 1942), with processes of diffusion and implementation as relevant criteria (Wendt, 2016, p. 11)[2] that "a novel idea was put into practice and became institutionalized," or that existing

---

[2]Authors further refer to the process of "creative destruction" as "disruption of existing institutions" (Howaldt & Schwarz, 2016, p. 58).

elements have been innovatively recombined (Christmann, Ibert, Jessen, & Walther, 2020, p. 4), or transferred into new contexts or spatial settings (Christmann, 2020a, p. 426).

Moulaert and MacCallum (2019, pp. 32–37) identify two, partly contrasting, paradigms in the research field on social innovation: One they refer to as "Anglo-American," instrumental and technocratic and related to business and organizational management sciences, its proponents often considering social innovation as complementary to market activity (p. 32). As a second thought line they identify the more interdisciplinary "Euro-Canadian social economy literature," connected to regional development literature and to normative and emancipatory expectations, its proponents relating social innovation to "empowerment, solidarity, socio-political renewal and institutional transformation" (p. 34): They argue that it improves social relations on the micro-level between individuals as well as on the macro-level "between classes and other social groups" (Moulaert et al., 2013, p. 16). Further, it is expected to "collectively [empower] people (especially marginalized people) to act" (Moulaert & MacCallum, 2019, p. 4). In this view, social innovation unfolds in processes and practices and in joint action from different societal actors "beyond business and government routines" (Brandsen, Evers, Cattacin, & Zimmer, 2016b, pp. 6–7). It relates to social transformation (Wendt, 2016, p. 13) and includes citizens and larger parts of society as agents of innovation (Domanski et al., 2020).

Social Innovation as Embedded and Contextualized Phenomenon

Relational conceptualizations of innovation processes discuss the relevance of social interaction, embeddedness, proximity, and institutional context for the creation and transmission of knowledge, understanding the latter as "embodied social practice" (Amin & Cohendet, 2004, p. 11; Bathelt & Glückler, 2011; Boschma & Frenken, 2010; Glückler & Bathelt, 2017; Rutten, 2017)—which unfolds locally (Asheim & Gertler, 2005, p. 293), as well as independent of locality, for example, within virtual or temporal knowledge communities (Bathelt, Feldman, & Kogler, 2011; Bathelt, Malmberg, & Maskell, 2004; Grabher & Ibert, 2014; Growe & Henn, 2020; Lambooy, 2010; Rutten, 2017, p. 159). Researchers have raised communities of practice and epistemic communities as contexts and grounds for learning, knowledge creation, and innovation among groups and collectives (Amin & Roberts, 2008; Lave & Wenger, 1991; Müller & Ibert, 2015, p. 339; Punstein & Glückler, 2020, pp. 546–548; Wenger, 1998). Accordingly, social innovation is perceived as contextualized "territorial phenomena, embedded in spaces, social relations and institutions that are defined by particular cross-scalar and cross-sectoral dynamics" (Moulaert & MacCallum, 2019, p. 77) and integrated into "socio-economic structures, institutions and practices" (p. 35).

> Social innovation is always related to collective social action aiming at social change. The institutional perspective sees social innovation as a result of the exchanges and application of knowledge and resources by agents mobilized through legitimization activities. (Cajaiba-Santana, 2014, p. 43)

Global economic dynamics result in particular localized and spatially concentrated needs, which are addressed within communities through solutions and innovative practices beyond economic concepts. Whereas the addressed problems are place-based, the developed solutions also require and mobilize non-local and trans-local actors, networks, and relations (Moulaert & MacCallum, 2019, pp. 79–80). Researchers have increasingly discussed social innovation's relevance for local and regional development, its potential for rural areas, often in reference to its local and institutional contextualization (Christmann, 2019, 2020a, 2020b; Christmann et al., 2020; Domanski et al., 2020, p. 455; Füg & Ibert, 2020; Howaldt & Schwarz, 2018, pp. 6–7; Richter, 2019; Schermer & Kroismayr, 2020). Here, local contexts are spaces in which "societal challenges become obvious as concrete social demands and in which problems are tackled by new social practices, often in unlikely collaborations" (Domanski et al., 2020, p. 468), while "institutional embedding—including taking to scale" is perceived as essential factors of success for "socially innovative policies and collective strategies" (Moulaert et al., 2013, p. 18).

The LandFrauen Organizations in German Civil Society and as Object of Research

By examining the German LandFrauen organizations, I am investigating a rather traditional form of associational life in Germany, with a long history and predecessors stretching to the end of the 19th century (Sawahn, 2009), and a spatial focus in Germany's rural regions. The spectrum of members is nearly entirely female—apart from sponsorship and honorary memberships, and some regional exceptions.[3] The largest share of members is above 60 (Suarsana, 2017; Int. 01-18). The general organizational goal is

> . . . more justice and equal opportunities for women who are at home in rural areas. This includes the perception and recognition of achievements and equal participation of rural women in work and family, in society and politics, in education, economy, and culture. (DLV e.V., 2020b, own transl.)

In this context, the LandFrauen are involved in diverse activities on all geographic and associational levels, which are linked horizontally and vertically through exchange and cooperation, such as in committees, cooperation, and common events (DLV e.V., 2020a, pp. 23–36; Suarsana, 2017; see Fig. 5.1). More than 10,000 local clubs and the 437 district and 22 state associations are an active

---

[3] Such as in Brandenburg, where also men can become regular members (own research).

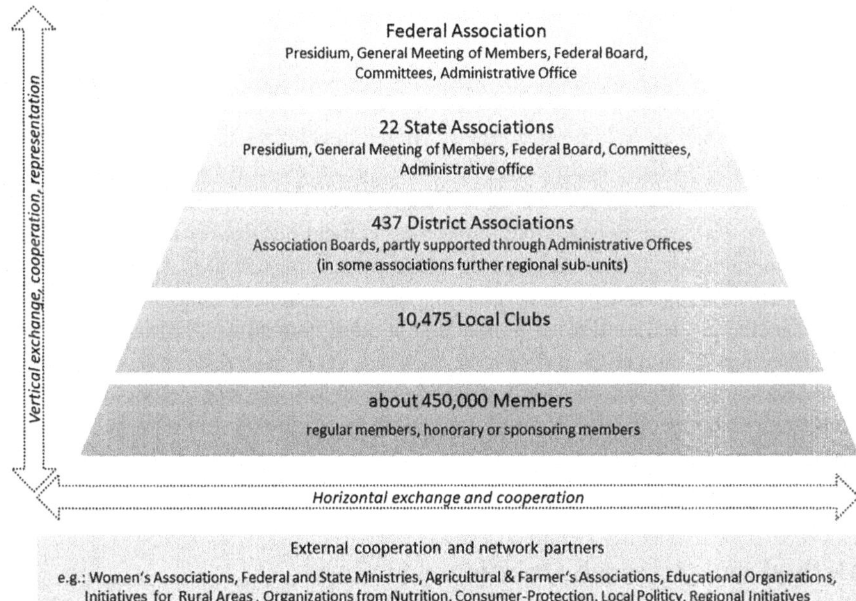

Fig. 5.1 The German LandFrauen associations' organizational structure. Based upon Suarsana (2017, p. 532). Organizational Data and information on cooperation and network partners: DLV 2020a, pp. 24–28

element of associational life in Germany, which since 2016 in total comprise more than 600,000 registered associations as the "dominant legal form" of German civil society—that structures, as well as it is based on, civic engagement (Priemer, Krimmer, & Labigne, 2017, p. 5). The organizations are broadly represented in external boards, directorates, and committees, such as the German Women's Council and Agricultural Associations, and in various ways cooperate with partners from politics or the fields of education, agriculture, nutrition, and consumer protection, as well as within local or regional policy or regional development initiatives (DLV e.V., 2020a, pp. 24–26, Suarsana, 2017).

Research on the German LandFrauen has so far mostly focussed on their roots and history (Bridenthal, 1994; Helmle, 2009; Krieg, 1999; Sawahn, 2009, 2012; Schwarz, 1990). As contemporary organizations of German civil society, they can be considered as somehow "hidden figures" that only to a small degree are subject of discussion in the social sciences. Scholars have included them in broader analyses of the German associational landscape, women's and agricultural networks, and lobby organizations (e.g., Biegler, 2001; Icken, 2002, p. 9; Rudolph & Schirmer, 2004, p. 145). As associations, they can be expected to play essential roles in building social capital and contributing to social cohesion (Putnam, 2000), serving as spaces of political socialization and schools of democracy, a "link between micro- and macro-levels and an integrative element for state and society" (Zimmer, 2007, p. 88, own transl.). In this, they "promise other ways of getting things done, from supporting pub[l]ic spheres and providing representation to cultivating the virtues of citizens and providing alternative forms of governance" (Warren, 2001, p. 3). Suarsana (2017) highlights the relevance of the German LandFrauen organizations as an element of rural civil society and regional development. Their role in rural areas is discussed as a "driving force of village development" (Rosa-Luxemburg-Stiftung, 2005) in their addressing of "basic questions of rural development", in their spectrum of members and broad representation of women in rural areas (Krambach, 2005, pp. 5–6), in their functions as local multipliers as a potential for "the economic, social, and cultural development in the country" (pp. 6–8), or as participants of LEADER-projects (Ebeling, 2017). Further, scholars have to a lesser degree included the LandFrauen in studies on adult education (Ambos & Greubel, 2012; Baumgart, Becker, Borsch, Merre, & Maas, 2004; Beetz, Bender, & Haubold, 2018; Kaschuba, 1996), and with regards to their project work in fields such as health (Jackisch et al., 2020), employment (Putzing, 2003), tourism (Kistemann, 2003), and biodiversity (Lütt, 2007).

Method and Research Questions: Analysis of the LandFrauen's Role in Social Change and Innovation

Based on the above, I perceive social innovation as societal solutions—new concepts or recombinations—that have a procedural component, are related to implementation in practice and collective agency, are based on exchange of knowledge,[4] occur institutionally, are socially embedded, and are related to processes of transformation, empowerment and mobilization.

My central research focus in this chapter is to explore how the LandFrauen in their activities and engagement contribute to societal development and serve as carriers of social innovation, and how these activities unfold locally and are influenced by the institutional and organizational structure: To what extent do LandFrauen practices and organizations relate to societal change and promote social innovation? To what extent do they relate to processes of empowerment and "reconfigured social relations"? Which organizational and infrastructural prerequisites enable/further the development of societal solutions and social innovation through LandFrauen? In what follows I will illustrate the results of this empirical assessment of the LandFrauen activities and analyze their societal functions in (rural) society.

The empirical basis of this chapter are 18 qualitative interviews, 17 with leading representatives of 22 LandFrauen Associations in total on the federal-state and national level in Germany, as well as with the president of the national LandFrauen association. I conducted interviews with the German LandFrauen Associations in

---

[4]Knowledge thereby understood as in the introductory chapter of the *Knowledge and Space* volume "Knowledge for Governance" as "human understanding of concrete and abstract phenomena of the world in which we live"; see Glückler, Herrigel, and Handke (2020, p. 4). For a more detailed reflection on knowledge in its relation to space, see Meusburger (2008).

Brandenburg, Bremen, Hamburg, Lower Saxony (Hanover), Lower Saxony (Weser-Ems), Hesse, Mecklenburg-Western Pomerania, Rhineland, Rhineland-Nassau, Saarland, Saxony, Saxony-Anhalt, Westphalia-Lippe, Thuringia, Schleswig-Holstein, Württemberg-Hohenzollern, and with the LandFrauen Group in the Bavarian Farmers' Association.

Most interview partners were, and mostly still are, in parallel to their voluntary or vocational associational work, integrated as active members into their local home club/association. Some are further engaged within the intermediary regional associations, or are elected members of the board of the national association (see Table 5.1). Thus, the interview partners could provide deep insights not only on the higher aggregated associational activities, but also on local clubs' activities. Interviews were conducted between June and September 2020 via phone with members of the president boards and with managing directors of the associations all over Germany, with an average length of 50 minutes.

All interviews were recorded and fully transcribed using the digital transcription service F4x and the qualitative text analytical software MAXQDA. Further, all interviews were analyzed following qualitative content analysis (Mayring, 2015). The results of this analysis are presented in the following chapter on findings, and they form the base of argumentation if not stated otherwise. All direct citations were translated from German into English and linguistically smoothed regarding dialect, colloquial language, and non-thematic fillers.

Table 5.1 Interview details

Total number of Interviews:	18
Organizational structure:	
Registered federal association:	1
Registered federal state associations:[a]	14 (of 19)
Federal state associations incorporated into the state's farmer's association:	3 (of 3)
Interview partners:	
President/Chairwoman of the board (honorary):	11
Managing director (vocational):	5
Board member/Vice president:	2
Interview partners represented in the board of the national federal association:	5 (of 8)
Regional distribution of the interviewed associations (state level):	
Associations in Western Germany:	12 (of 17)
Associations in Eastern Germany:	5 (of 5)
Representation of members through interviewed associations:	
Total of (paying) members represented:[b]	314,814 (76.3%)
Total of (paying) members represented (Eastern Germany)	5,979 (100%)
Total of (paying) members represented (Western Germany):	308,835 (76.0%)

[a]For historical reasons (see Sawahn, 2009), there are 22 federal associations in the 16 German federal states
[b]Membership data from DLV e.V. (2019, p. 42)
Note. Source: Design by author

Further, I conducted participatory observation during the nationwide *LandFrauen Days* that took place in Erfurt in 2016 and in Ludwigshafen in 2018 with 5,000 and 3,000 participants, events that are organized by the German association for all members of the LandFrauen clubs and associations in Germany. I also draw on primary sources, such as the websites and annual reports of the LandFrauen associations.

Findings: LandFrauen Organizations and Practices in Societal Change and Social Innovation

Diversity, Geography, and Local Contextualization of the LandFrauen Organizations and Activities

The associations and clubs differ highly across Germany.[5] The interviews revealed large differences and different foci of activities, although I could identify a number of core activities throughout all interviews that relate to the general goals of addressing and representing the interests of women, families in rural areas, and specifically women in agriculture, engaging for good conditions of living in rural areas.

As key characteristics of the LandFrauen organizations, several interviewees highlighted the wide range of members, which includes women across all professions, generations, confessions, political affiliations, and social classes, which they attributed to bridging societal functions. They thereby named the overall diversity across regions and members as a quality of the organizational structure. Each club[6] develops an annual program following the interests and perceived local needs of the local members. Local social activities and regularly organized meetings thereby form the ground for a broad range of further educational and also political activities on local as well as higher associational levels. Vice versa, higher associational levels influence local club activities through setting lead or annual topics, suggesting topics or referents for the education programs, or through central and nation- or statewide projects, or further offers addressed to all associational levels.

The breadth of activities across the clubs and associations is reflected in Table 5.2, which lists all activities by number and subject for 2017 (last data available). The largest share of activities relates to the everyday life and interests of the members in fields of health, sports, arts and culture, consumer policy, home economics, and nutrition. Further activities form a smaller proportion of the overall spectrum, but nevertheless the yearly numbers range into several thousands. These include work for the common good and social work, activities related to agriculture, societal and economic policy, as well as competence-related activities in the fields of communication, association management, media competence, and IT.

---

[5]Accordingly, the activities and examples illustrated below surely do not apply to all clubs or associations.

[6]As well as the district and federal state associations.

Table 5.2 LandFrauen activities (all associational levels) by subject area in 2017

Events at local, district, state, and federal level by subject area	Number of Activities[a]	Share of Activities (%)
Health, sports	44,239	37.4
Art, culture, creativity	24,418	20.6
Consumer policy, home economics, nutrition	11,206	9.5
Activities for the common good, social work	8,060	6.8
Family, social issues	6,958	5.9
Agriculture, rural area, environment	5,674	4.8
Communication, association management	5,233	4.4
Societal and social policy	3,714	3.1
Media competence, IT	1,009	0.9
Economic policy	891	0.8
Other	7,009	5.9
Total	**118,411**	**100.0**

[a]Data for Bremen not included. No data available in the category *Activities for the Common Good, Social Work* for Bavaria and Rhine-Hesse. No data available in the category *Other* for Hamburg, Mecklenburg-Western Pomerania, Rhine-Hesse
Note. Source: Design by author. Data from DLV e.V. (2018, p. 42)

Regarding associational structure and activities, broad differences exist horizontally—across the state and district associations and the local clubs—as well as vertically: The higher associational levels fulfil broader and more political functions than the community-oriented local clubs. Horizontally, differences exist in internal organization as well as with regard to the activities, foci, and goals. The variety of clubs reflects the variety of members (see Table 5.3), and interviewees illustrated the influence of local institutional context and structure (see Cajaiba-Santana, 2014) on the clubs and associations. They referred to the associations' differing statutes and the local clubs' strong autonomy, as well as to the specific local conditions, including social infrastructure—local population, identity of the local members, further associations in the villages, and support from politics and potential partners—and material and public service infrastructure, such as the existence of publicly open space, or premises that can be used for meetings and events. Interviewees raised varying political support across the federal states. They especially described the eastern associations as highly regarded and supported, perceived as "important players," by politicians (Int. 04). In urban settings in which the LandFrauen are also represented, interviewees stated less need for social infrastructure in comparison to peripheral regions. All interview partners considered the identity of local individuals who are board members and/or engaged in coordinating their local club, define topics and set the annual programs, to be highly influential on the local activities.

East and West German LandFrauen organizations differ regarding member structure and their historical background. The eastern associations were founded after German reunification, "more top-down" (Int. 13), with crises and growing unemployment especially in agriculture in the eastern states. The newly founded associations offered support and exchange, and partly functioned as an institutional frame

Table 5.3 Educational activities of the German LandFrauen organizations in 2019

Educational Format	LandFrauen Organizations (state and federal level)	LandFrauen Associations (state level)	LandFrauen Associations (federal level)	German Adult Education Centers[a]
Courses/ Seminars:	**51,521**	**51,512**	**9**	**523,611**
Teaching hours:	125,444	125,252	192	15,646,263
Participants/ Enrollments:	689,719	689,563	156	5,912,896
Lectures/ Discussion Events:	**19,448**	**19,441**	**7**	n.d.
Teaching hours:	66,038	66,001	37	n.d.
Participants:	564,077	563,599	478	n.d.
Study Trips/ Excursions:	**10,763**	**10,762**	**1**	**8,204**
Days:	27,519	27,518	1	n.d.
Participants:	302,234	302,177	57	174,319
Exhibitions/ Markets:	**3,991**	**3,990**	**1**	**n.d.**
Days:	7,681	7,671	10	n.d.
Total of Educational Events:	**85,723**	**85,705**	**18**	**637,701**[b]
Total of Participants/ Enrollments:	1,556,030	1,555,339	691	8,162,146

[a]Latest data available for 873 of total 894 in 2018
[b]Includes contractual measures and individual events not listed above
Note. Source: Data on the LandFrauen organizations (totals re-calculated) from DLV e.V. (2020a, pp. 28–32), adult education center statistics (2018) from Lux (2020, p. 1)

for measures of public employment. In addition, the share of women in agriculture varies, so the extent associations address agricultural issues in their offers accordingly does as well. Institutional structure differs with regard to cooperation with the state farmer's association, ranging from the clubs' and associations' complete independence to close cooperation and organizational integration of the associations as sub-organizations into the farmer's associations.[7] In Bavaria, LandFrauen membership results exclusively from company-related affiliation to a farm with membership in the farmers' association. In the further state and regional associations, the proportion of women from agriculture was estimated to range between about 10% to 20%.[8]

---

[7]This is the case in Bavaria, Rhineland-Nassau, and South Baden.
[8]These numbers could only be estimated by the interviewees, as data is not available.

Despite these regional specifics, "goals and interests are similar" (Int. 15), and intense exchange and cooperation occurs within the LandFrauen's broad personal and organizational network.

Community-Building, Togetherness, and Local Social Embeddedness as a Ground for Further Activities

Community is what women look for and find with us. And our large network that we have throughout Germany is something that really sets us apart. (President, German LandFrauen Association)

Interviewees named classic associational activity, the building of social capital (Putnam, 2000) and functions as "social glue" (Int. 12) through social activity, togetherness, community building, and contributions to local village life as core activities on the very local level. According to them, creating opportunities to come together and meet within the community on a regular basis and to exchange about personal as well as local and societal problems[9] are the very element and heart of the LandFrauen. Through their programs and activities, the LandFrauen create conditions and a context for women and local people to meet, engage in social, creative, or educational activities, and to come together, exchange, and interact socially—for example in choirs, reading clubs, sports courses, or seasonal festivities. In this, they contribute to local social and cultural infrastructure in the villages and to social integration, for example, of elders suffering social isolation or newly moved residents. Further, the institutionalized and formally organized activities are broadly accompanied by informal togetherness and interaction, supporting and "appreciating" (Int. 08) each other, and the provision of neighborhood assistance (Int. 13) and "taking care of each other" in the villages (Int. 09). The individual members' social integration thereby creates a basis for the local club's activities.

This sense of community and togetherness and belonging among LandFrauen on the local level is continued inter-regionally and state- and nationwide, and seems to exist across all geographical and associational levels. This is reflected in wide interaction and formal as well as informal exchange among clubs and associations (see Section 5.4.5). A strong sense of togetherness was also a key observation during the national LandFrauen Days in which I participated: I noted a cheerful and open atmosphere and willingness to communicate, interact, and exchange between the women's groups who arrived from all over Germany. Many of the women I spoke to during the events expressed how much they appreciated the event character and visiting the event together with their local group, as well as meeting further LandFrauen from across the country. In Erfurt, for example, the day ended with the

---

[9] They include infrastructural problems regarding childcare, internet connections, and right-wing populism in peripheral rural regions.

thousands of participating women standing and singing together with the band on stage.

Local Engagement, and Functions as Initiators, Catalysts, or Multipliers in Rural Areas

Integrated into their social contributions, the LandFrauen address further issues related to the quality of life in rural areas through practical local engagement and project activities with which they handle deficiencies in public service provision and rural infrastructure (Suarsana, 2017). Infrastructure, provision of healthcare, internet, and mobility were named as essential issues necessary to "provide perspectives for families in the rural area" (Int. 14). Hereby, I could identify different functions in their regional activity:

Firstly, as *local initiators,* LandFrauen often spring into action when local infrastructure is to be shut down. "It starts with a petition and ends with 'we'll run your house in,' or we'll be very pragmatic and tackle the problem on site" (Int. 16). In Lower Saxony, LandFrauen initiated a public mobility bus project (Bürgerbusverein Badbergen e.V., n.d.). In Saxony and Mecklenburg-Western Pomerania, they provide a local kindergarten (LFV Mecklenburg-Vorpommern e.V., 2020). Federal associations, such as in Bavaria, Hesse, and North Rhine-Westphalia, initiated support hotlines for women or people from agriculture as a solution to provide anonymous exchange and support, addressing issues of social isolation in rural areas. In Saxony, for example, the ministers of education and the arts as well as regional television were invited to take part in a bus ride for a second-grade elementary school student from a small rural village in order to highlight the consequence of planned school closings that would lead to very long bus rides for primary school pupils. Secondly, interviewees stated that LandFrauen, with their broad base of female members deeply rooted in the rural society, often function as *multipliers* in rural areas (Int. 04). Several associations engage for democracy—in Saxony, for example, they educate local *democracy consultants*. Through campaigns and informational activities, the women mobilize others within the villages/regions. Several interviewees highlighted a sense for practical solutions and life management skills as a capability of the LandFrauen in their local engagement, which they stated makes them "very well recognized, by politics, by the mayors and district administrators" (Int. 09). Interviewees described that local clubs build local partnerships and support the establishment of new connections among further actors within the villages, and as a connecting local institution bring together various groups. Thirdly, LandFrauen can be attributed *catalyst or supporting functions* in external projects or in joint activities—with further partners, such as from local civil society, administration, or politics—that meet local needs and problems or help shape the local public space. In Schleswig-Holstein, for example, LandFrauen support *Market Meeting Places*, initiated by the federal state of Schleswig-Holstein (Markt-Treff

Schleswig-Holstein, n.d.). Cooperative projects are partly publicly funded, and activities are often integrated into regional development initiatives such as LEADER[10] (Ebeling, 2017).

LandFrauen as Institutional Frame and Social Spaces for Learning, Education, and Knowledge Diffusion in Rural Areas

Central and de-central coordinated education activities

Activities of knowledge dissemination occur on every associational level. The local clubs, district associations, as well as federal associations pursue manifold de-central as well as joint or centrally organized educational activities. They offer courses, lectures, workshops, and informational events, in order to "bring knowledge and education into the country"—with course education as a "key activity for the state association," as well as through the local associations on site, which "have this educational mandate in addition to their social issues and being involved in the village structures" (Int. 07). In this, education is brought into peripheral areas where further structures and offers in adult education do not exist. While "in cities, women visit adult education centers to further educate themselves", they "stay in the village structures" (Int. 07) and thus provide locally specific offers.

In total, in 2019 more than 50,000 courses and seminars were conducted, 19,500 discussion events, and more than 10,000 educational trips or excursions (Table 5.3), with altogether 1.5 million enrolled participants.[11] In comparison, the 873 adult education centers in Germany offered a total of 637,701 educational events in 2018, with 532,611 courses and 8,204 study trips (Lux, 2020, p. 1).

In their local offers and their annual programs, the local clubs can rely on offerings and inspiration from higher associational levels: State associations offer topics and internal and external speakers that the local clubs can draw on—partly financially supported through the state association. Many activities, selected educational fields, activities, and course offerings are highly locally specific and organized by the local clubs autonomously and independently from higher associational levels. On higher association levels, the selection of programs and topics is based on decision processes within the boards and committees, including the feedback, expressions of interest, and perceived needs and problems from lower associational levels. Joint projects across the associational levels are partly financed by federal and state ministries or/and supported through further partners. In some federal states, such as Baden-Württemberg and Bavaria, educational activity is carried out through specially set up educational facilities (*Bildungswerke*), which

---

[10] "In two-thirds of all 15 regional action groups in [federal state], a LandFrau has a seat" (Int. 06).

[11] Participants counted by enrollment, not by participant identity—thus double counting may occur.

as organizational entities receive governmental funding. In part, educational activity is integrated into nationwide programs or projects, coordinated by the federal association.

Educational activities are often based on the training of multipliers who then share their knowledge on the lower associational levels, in the respective regions, or within local clubs. Regional or local specialists are trained as multipliers in central levels and then "disseminate knowledge" (Int. 16) or offer coaching and support in their respective regions, for topics such as digitalization, nutrition, consumer protection, and agriculture-related issues.

Many educational activities relate to "everyday skills" (Int. 02): "[n]ew knowledge . . . relevant for everyday life" (Int. 07). This includes informing on issues like powers of attorney, care, criminal prevention, insurance, law, pension notices, and rent, as well as nutrition, cooking, or gardening. Educational and societal topics are addressed in a way suited to the target group of women in rural areas. Complementary to their local, regional, and national engagement, the federal association as well as the state associations of Baden-Württemberg and Bavaria also disseminate knowledge in international development work, for example, providing agricultural training and support as well as female empowerment in Kenya and Ghana.

Addressing contemporary societal challenges

Educational offers, informational events, and campaigns, especially of the federal and state associations, address broader contemporary societal problems and "promote such new topics" (Int. 07) as sustainability and avoidance of food and plastic waste. "We try to take up socially relevant topics and deal with them in such a way that they are transported down to the local clubs and the members" (Int. 07). From there, issues are spread further within the rural population and through the members' personal networks.

In cooperation with state medical associations, health insurances, or universities, LandFrauen disseminate knowledge on new medical developments and engage to prevent myocardial infarction, breast cancer, hearing problems amongst the elderly and children, or injuries through falls. Digitalization, the usage of modern digital media and communication technology and how to communicate via the new media, is broadly addressed in many associations and also within projects of the national association. LandFrauen have implemented several projects that provide training and seminars, especially for elderly women, in topics such as the use of tablets, smartphones, and new media. In Baden-Württemberg, for example, *Senior Technology Ambassadors* are trained (LFV Württemberg-Baden e.V., 2020b). In Schleswig-Holstein, the project *e-LandFrauen* provides computer education. Associations have set digitalization as leading themes for several years, through initiatives such as Baden-Württemberg's *Digital without limits!?* (LFV Württemberg-Baden e.V., 2020a) and Württemberg-Hohenzollern's *LandFrauen 4.0*, in which the associations bring digitalization-related knowledge to its members and inform them about the potentials, as well as risks, of digital technology. Reacting to the Corona pandemic, many associations have offered courses for the local boards on how to hold online seminars and organize online meetings. Several clubs further engage in the external nationwide project *digital neighborhoods*, which "came from the federal level" and has been "very well accepted" on the district level (Int. 03).

> This image, the LandFrauen always bake cakes and knit and crochet and sew. Yes, because we can. But we are also open to topics such as dealing with PCs, dealing with tablets, dealing with telemedicine. We have just started a new qualification of digital mentors. In cooperation with a Department of the Ministry of Energy and Agriculture. . . . And these LandFrauen, six to eight, are trained to use smartphones and tablets over several days. And they then go back as multipliers to the LandFrauen associations, to their clubs, to make their older women fit in this. (Int. 07)

Further, central activity on the federal, state, and also district and local levels centers around education in the field of nutrition and the origins of food, and in consumer education and engaging in consumer-producer dialogue. Apart from external activities, such as in schools or kindergartens, this also includes internal activities to build understanding and appreciation among the members (Int. 04).

Preservation, dissemination, and recombination of "traditional" knowledge

LandFrauen engage in, disseminate, and contribute to the preservation of local, historical,[12] and traditional knowledge and pass it within their institutional and social structure. They engage in activities related to regional customs such as knotting carpets, spinning wool, crocheting, and speaking in dialect, such as *Plattdeutsch* (Low German)—"many things from harvest festivals to traditional costume groups, folk dance groups to Easter fountain festivals" (Int. 16). Members disseminate related knowledge in the course and event program, partly coordinated on the state associational level, but also intensively carried out autonomously by members at the local level: "The women want that and organize it for themselves" (Int. 18). This partly entails recombinations of traditional knowledge. For example, LandFrauen in several, especially eastern, federal states, pursue binding of harvest crowns as a local custom. The necessary knowledge is taught in commonality and transferred in practice as non-codified knowledge, as well as taught explicit in workshops. Thereby, LandFrauen developed new modes of tying as "freestyle harvest crowns" (Int. 02), innovatively reinterpreting traditional practice. Further, LandFrauen utilize tradition-related events to address contemporary issues: "They can bring across political demands wonderfully at such a harvest festival, and the women have understood that you can combine it well to keep the traditional, but to make demands at that point" (President, German LandFrauen Association).

---

[12] LandFrauen archive historical knowledge, such as by "writing down life stories" (Int. 05). In Schleswig-Holstein, the state association established, in cooperation with a museum, an historical archive to document former rural life from a women's perspective (LFV Schleswig-Holstein e.V., 2020). Further, they author or publish books on regional traditions and specialities.

Learning and exchange among the diverse base of members and reaching different societal groups as a source for societal change

Several interviewees perceived bridging functions through including and addressing the interests of women of all ages, professions, confessions, and political affiliations, and described processes of exchange and relation-building between the individual members. Apart from social integration and creating an understanding of the respective life situations, this leads to learning and transfer of knowledge and experiences. During educational trips and excursions across Germany, LandFrauen organizations create new personal connections among the LandFrauen interregionally, as these often include exchange visits of the district association within the target region.

According to the interview partners, the elder generations above the age of 60 form the major share of members. Aspirations to institutionally integrate a larger number of young women have in recent years proven successful in many associations. Interviewees reported that younger women explicitly address and highly value the elder generation's practical and traditional knowledge, such as crafting, cooking and baking skills, while further highlighting the relevance of the young LandFrauen learning about the life problems of elderly women in rural areas. Vice versa, younger women bring "new and innovative ideas" (Int. 01) into the clubs, provide insights into their generation, and introduce elders, in an informal and open manner, to contemporary societal and technical topics—a development that is as well supported through institutionalized educational offers, such as "combined courses, knitting and computer courses. One teaches using the mouse, and the other teaches how to use the knitting needle" (Int. 16).

Exchange and diffusion of ideas across regions and throughout the associational structure

Intensive exchange that allows for the diffusion of ideas between the individual members and across regions and associational levels can be highlighted a general characteristic of the LandFrauen organizations. Between all organizational levels, intensive horizontal and vertical communication occurs, as well as cooperation and exchange on the respective ideas, activities, and projects. Several interviewees reported having taken over "sparkling ideas" (Int. 02) from other clubs or associations, and that they actively seek information, knowledge, and ideas from other regions, following a "pragmatic approach. We don't need to reinvent the wheel" (Int. 05).

Exchange occurs, firstly, formally organized within the associational structure. This includes representation in boards, working together in expert groups, committees, and planning days, as well as conferences and meetings on specific topics. At the delegate assembly on the federal level, delegates report positive and successful activities from the respective regions. In addition, at the state level, the local and district associations send representatives to committees for exchange. Activities allow for the physical or—especially since the beginning of the Corona pandemic—increasingly digital co-presence of representatives or members from the different regions or districts. Neighbor associations are also often invited to events like the LandFrauen Days on the regional or district level. District associations organize visiting tours to each other across regions in Germany, and local clubs organize meetings or share events or courses together. Secondly, this formal exchange is accompanied by informal exchange. Personal contacts overlap formal organizational structures and support the interassociational exchange across regions. Several interviewees reported informal activities of exchange and interaction, based on personal and social relations that have emerged in the course of organized exchange or joint activities.

Organized and informal exchange is supported through several communication channels that allow for further sharing of ideas, good practices, innovative projects, ideas for events and speakers, new concepts, and developed solutions. Associations, clubs, and members receive information on each other's activities through annual programs and reports, newsletters, websites, and further means of digital communication. During the Corona pandemic, internal communication has become increasingly digitalized, and members have developed and spread among the associations new organizational practices and formats to bring women together, such as digital wine tastings, in which women from different regions digitally met and got to know each other (Int. 01).

Several interviewees described an example for the diffusion of ideas within the organizational structure with regards to the Corona pandemic. One association, during lockdown, started sending postcards to the members in order to "keep contact and say, hold on, we are with you" (Int. 17). Across several interviews, I could reconstruct how this idea was started within one association and from there diffused among regions and was copied by several further associations, who, through formal or informal contact channels, had learned about it and took over the concept, as well as partly extended it through further elements.

> We had a very spontaneous idea to design this postcard during the Corona period. And we had to reorder them three times. And then a friend from Westphalia wrote to me: Man, that is a great idea. I said, just imitate it. And then they copied it in their own way. And now they're doing it in Nassau too, and they want to do it in Saxony too. I say it's wonderful. So of course, you can spread that and join in. (Int. 01)

Although this is just a small example, it illustrates the close contact among the LandFrauen representatives, as well as the permeability for idea transmission among the organizations. Further, apart from the internal network as a source of ideas, interviewees named the dense network to other associations and partners as inspiration for ideas and sources of knowledge.

Advocacy work, Interest Representation, and Setting Public and Political Agenda

Interest representation, raising topics to the societal and political agenda, and influencing public debate is pursued in different qualities and quantities. "The core task is to demand attractive living conditions in rural areas from politics" (Int. 18). Topics range from equal pay and further gender equality issues to services of general interest, such as digitalization in rural areas. LandFrauen associations can be considered highly relevant in their function to give voice to and represent females in the field of agriculture, as women are strongly underrepresented: In the presidential boards of the farmer's associations, women have a total share of 11.9%[13] (18 of in total 151 seats). In the federal association and in five of the 18 state/regional associations, women are not represented on presidential boards at all.

On the local level, interest representation occurs partly and often in a smaller dimension, frequently relating to specific local problems and as reactions to infrastructural deficits or cutbacks regarding topics such as offers of childcare, broadband coverage, or provision of health- and midwifery care. The described activities are oriented towards current problems within the villages. Members identify and name these problems and look for ways to solve them. Interviewees brought up that these activities are often not considered political or "classically feminist" (Int. 16) activities, and that regular club members rather have an "everyday understanding" (Int. 12) of politics. Local communication activity differs highly, as it depends on the voluntary engagement and identity of local board members (Int. 11).

Higher associational levels address broader societal issues in their political work. Activities include communicating LandFrauen demands to politics and range from information campaigns, public relations work and press releases, entering into dialogue with political actors or further nonprofit actors in national and federal ministries, to demonstrations and collection of signatures for petitions, taking positions and communicating political demands to federal and state ministries before elections or legal initiatives, and organizing informational events on women and agricultural issues. For this, the federal association, as well as the state associations, offer support and training to their members (see Section 5.6). The higher associational levels, and increasingly the district and local organizations, engage in social media activity and allow for low-threshold information on their activities and positions. The associations are broadly represented and engaged in external committees and networks, especially in the fields of education, gender equality, nutrition, and agriculture, and are represented in the German Women's Council.

---

[13] Own survey, as per 27.10.2020. Included were the presidents or presidential board of the member associations of the federal farmer's associations as published on the association's websites. For Bavaria, the presidential conference was included.

Mobilization and Empowerment for Politics, Associational Work, and Entrepreneurial Activities

The LandFrauen's[14] political engagement—for example, in their city or district councils or as mayors—is supported and promoted throughout the associational structure, for example, through informational events and initiating local discussion rounds or inviting successful female politicians as role models. The federal association and several state associations offer training and qualification in skills such as rhetoric and communication for political and associational work. Apart from motivating women to take up institutionalized functions in political processes, clubs inform and gather LandFrauen in "classic" associational functions as "a pre-political space,", "mobilize at a very low threshold and motivate women to get involved" (Int. 3).

Several associations promote democracy and empower women to engage towards preventing racism and right-wing extremism, to address populism and to engage in politics, for example, in eastern Germany, and in two state associations of Lower-Saxony in a joint project *Democracy means you!—Are women fairly represented in rural areas?* (own transl.).

Further, federal associations and several national associations focus on mobilizing and supporting women with regard to entrepreneurial activities. Offers include vocational training to provide women with knowledge and capabilities to become self-employed or to set up their own businesses. State associations, partly, offer coaching and education, or provide further support through their network, e.g. training women as local guides or *ambassadors* for regional products. In a nationwide project *Selbst ist die Frau* [Women do it themselves, own transl.], the federal association initiates networks to support and encourage female founders. Women with start-up experience are trained as start-up coaches and offer workshops on self-employment (Int. 04). To improve working condition for women in the country, in Lower-Saxony, Hanover, co-working spaces are tested as a means for women to better balance work and family life (Niedersächsischer LandFrauenverband Hannover, 2020). In addition, qualification and vocational training is offered for women in agriculture, and "that they can get their voice heard in local politics, also in the public space" (Int. 16). Moreover, during the national LandFrauen Days in Erfurt (2016) and Ludwigshafen (2018), political mobilization, as well as the support of women, and promoting female entrepreneurship, especially in agriculture, were central elements.

---

[14]One interviewee stated that she knew villages where the combination of political activity and LandFrauen engagement was institutionalized in such a way that the LandFrauen board members were in principle engaged into regional politics (Int. 12).

Discussion: LandFrauen as a Case Example for the Promotion of Social Change Through Civil Society—Practices and Prerequisites

Practices—The LandFrauen's Role in Social Innovation

The LandFrauen in their manifold activities are a case example of how civil society contributes to social innovation and can function as an agent of societal change—with new ideas and concepts, political involvement, as well as through practical engagement as initiators, catalysts, or local multipliers. They relate to criteria and expectations towards social innovation as discussed in Section 2:

(1) Firstly, LandFrauen pursue activities related to "satisfaction of needs" as an element of social innovation as stated by Moulaert and MacCallum (2019, p. 4.). Interviewees named various innovative projects and solutions for the improvement of rural areas, or to support women and women in agriculture. They bring together women of all ages, professions, and generations with specific insights into local needs. The large number of women and creative ideas coming together was raised as a ground and "important pool" (Int. 03), to quickly find and implement simple, pragmatic, and often unconventional solutions to challenges and infrastructural deficits in rural areas—for example, "converting a residential property, . . . or enabling a daycare center to be set up temporarily on one's farm, when the local kindergarten closes" (Int. 03).

Thereby, some interviewees did not consider the development of new societal solutions and new knowledge and ideas as key activities or general primary goal of their organizations. They stressed, though, that—as elaborated above—the LandFrauen organizations often contribute to societal or local solutions through identifying and naming problems and societal needs quite early, and in bringing them into political processes and societal debate: "What defines us is that we pass on information and network with experts" (Int. 18).

(2) Secondly, the LandFrauen have bridging functions in their villages and rural areas and build new relations among actors in their local and political work, and thus contribute to social innovation as "reconfigured social relations" (Moulaert & MacCallum, 2019, p. 50). Several interviewees stated that LandFrauen function as a "motor" (Int. 02) in the country and take initiative for joint local activities and projects. The interviewees hereby raised the relevance of the LandFrauen as politically neutral intermediates, gathering further partners together through "an associational structure that networks well with others. They are very creative in getting women who have often moved here to be involved" (Int. 05). The federal-state and national LandFrauen associations are integrated into broad networks and cooperation with external partners, as well as they are represented in external political committees, working groups, and in boards of further organizations related to their fields of expertise. Several interviewees named good relations to project partners—locally, as well as on the federal state

level, such as educational organizations, saving banks, health insurances, as well as further associations and clubs or actors from the philanthropic field (see Chap. 9 by Glückler and Suarsana), ministries, or politicians:

> The State Secretary for Digitalization just said he brings digitalization to [the federal state] together with the LandFrauen. Because he also knows what kind of network we have and how many we are. (Int. 01)

(3) Thirdly, in their educational and political activities, as well as in their encouragement and mobilization of women to "speak up" (Int. 11) and engage in local politics or societal debate, LandFrauen (in the local clubs as well as on higher associational and geographical levels) relate to social innovation in the dimension of "empowerment or political mobilization" (Moulaert & MacCallum, 2019, p. 4)—be it in single organized events, such as demonstrations for equal pay or for mother's rents, in long-term projects, or in encouraging direct involvement of women in political processes. Their raising awareness on topics like gender equality and the structural disadvantages women face, racism, or ecological issues among elderly and rural women (Int. 02, 04, 11, 18) can be especially highlighted, as these women may be expected to only sparsely involve into the related societal discourses.

Prerequisites—What Facilitates LandFrauen Practices Towards Social Innovation?

In this second part of the discussion, I address the question *how* these civil society organizations achieve the illustrated—planned, and unplanned—societal benefits as valuable outcomes, especially for rural areas. I argue that activities mainly depend on two key prerequisites that enable LandFrauen to their activities and creates a ground for the promotion of societal change: Firstly, local contextualization—LandFrauen adapt to local conditions and needs, and activities are shaped and influenced by local and regional conditions and the collective agency of contextualized individuals in the understanding of Cajaiba-Santana (2014, see also Subsection 2). Secondly, in parallel, the clubs and associations as an institutional frame have enabling and structuring functions, with informal, as well as formal cooperation and networks across the horizontal and vertical structure. This institutional embeddedness has been raised as a success factor for social innovation by Moulaert et al. (2013, p. 18).

(1) *Local contextualization, the diverse and broad membership base, and the organizational network is a capacity and a ground for local engagement and political work.*

The LandFrauen members and representatives and their local voluntary engagement are context-specific, deeply rooted in their local village contexts, and integrated into local fields of actors. A large share of activities unfolds at the very local level, with actors adapting the specific needs identified by individual local boards and members. Interviewees named the broad network and the high number of represented women, which the associations reach in their activities, as a strength that makes the associations and clubs multipliers and relevant partners for political and non-state actors, as well as a basis for the diffusion of innovative practices into rural societies. The LandFrauen represent the full diversity of women in rural areas, they are politically neutral, and inter-confessional. Due to their broad and diverse base of members, they have the capacity to jointly develop quick, creative, and pragmatic solutions to local challenges and mobilize local individuals and resources for their implementation. Therefore, interviewees stated, external partners perceive and appreciate LandFrauen as reliable, pragmatic, and influential. Further, the large base of members can function as a source of legitimacy for the associations in their political demands and their taking position in public debate.

The interaction within and across the local clubs and groups of LandFrauen can be considered as "local buzz"—an "information and communication ecology created by face-to-face-contacts, copresence, and colocation" with "intended and unanticipated learning processes in organizational and accidental meetings" supporting the "development of shared values, attitudes and interactive schemes typical for communities of practice" (Bathelt, Malmberg, & Maskell, 2004 p. 38). As discussed above, these enable the LandFrauen to engage in interactive learning and problem solving (p. 45)—supported through the common goals and interests.

Further, interviewees stated that LandFrauen have a strong and noticed position in political processes—a statement that can be backed by the fact that on the LandFrauen Days I participated, several high-ranking politicians—from Chancellor Angela Merkel to the Federal Minister of Agriculture—personally spoke to the women and stressed their role and importance for rural areas and society. Regarding local activities, interviewees illustrated close relations and good cooperation with various local organizations and partners, for example from politics and administration or the philanthropic field (see Chap. 9 by Glückler and Suarsana).

Interviewees illustrated the relevance of the LandFrauen network as a source of institutionalized support, as well as its quick reaction to societal problems, by the example of voluntary production of face masks during the beginning of the Corona pandemic in places all over Germany, on large scales of often hundreds or thousands. The clubs' and members' local networks organized the distribution in cooperation "with other organizations . . . You've seen it spread like a spider's web" (Int. 15).

(2) *Institutional embeddedness allows for vertical and horizontal cooperation, exchange, and access to resources across the associational levels and "beyond geography"* (Bathelt, Cohendet, Henn, & Simon, 2017, p. 11).

A broad range of diverse perspectives and individuals are joined through a sense of community and common understandings and practices. In this, the Land Frauen can be considered as institutions, "ongoing and stable patterns of repeated social interaction, based on mutual expectations that owe their existence to purposeful constitution or unintentional emergence" (Glückler & Bathelt, 2017, p. 121).

The clubs and associations "stabilize interaction and correlated patterns of behaviour" (Setterfield, 1993, as cited in Bathelt, Cohendet, Henn, & Simon, 2017, p. 4), and "as collective actors . . . align resources and interests in pursuit of a common goal" (Glückler & Bathelt, 2017, p. 122).

Despite differences and high heterogeneity, the LandFrauen clubs and associations form a stable organizational context that pre-structures the local, regional, and national common activities and create frameworks for the practices and joint activities of their members and representatives, as well as the cooperation with external partners. The members and representatives are deeply rooted in their local as well as specific associational contexts. In parallel, an often-stated feeling of community, belonging, and social proximity creates the basis for further activities and is also felt on higher geographical/associational levels. This sense of community and the underlying social relations and activities support institutionalized exchange and form the basis for societal engagement and for educational and political work.

The local clubs, socially rooted in the villages and rural society, are integrated into an inter-regional organizational network where ideas, concepts, and knowledge, as well as resources and institutional support are exchanged and diffuse across geographical and associational levels. The underlying and permeable vertical and horizontal organizational structure allows for the quick dissemination of ideas, practices, and knowledge, and to spread information into the rural area. This is supported and supplemented by underlying social ties and informal exchange.

Further, the higher aggregated associational levels, their broad network, allows for the implementation of larger projects, partly government-funded or co-funded by external partners. They create access to external resources and support and provide opportunities for funding, educational offers, as well as they train multipliers that reach out to the specific regions.

Not only the local clubs, but also associations on higher organizational levels benefit from institutional embeddedness and horizontal and vertical connectivity: Through inner-associational representation, formal and informal exchange, and connections among the associational levels, issues and topics are transported from the bottom up into the higher associational levels. From there, "good connections into state politics as well as federal politics" (Int. 16) are used to set agenda in political processes.

In their activities and the local and societal functions, LandFrauen—as well as their clubs and associations as collective actors—can be conceptualized as "key players of socio-spatial change" in the dimensions identified by Gailing and Ibert (2016, p. 391): (1) On the micro-level, as "leaders", they may create a "mood of optimism" among local followers and generate or "initiate demonstration projects" (p. 400). This applies to engaged individual and board members in the local clubs that—as learnt from the interviews—are highly influential on the local activities and offerings. Further, this can be related to the manifold context-specific activities individual LandFrauen conduct to improve their local villages. (2) As intermediaries or "boundary spanners" on a meso-level[15] (pp. 393–394), they mobilize "external, territorial rooted knowledge as well as institutional and cultural resources in favor of a space" (p. 400). Throughout the inner-associational structure, knowledge, ideas, and institutional support are accessible from the higher associational levels as well as from further partners from other regions on the same horizontal level. (3) Further, on a macro-level, "governance-pioneers" are stated to "prepare ways or modes of governance, collective arenas for action, and in changing policy content" (p. 400). This may hold for the LandFrauen associations as collective actors in their interest representation, political work, and lobby activity on the federal-state and national level. In this combination of activities, they may—intentionally or unintentionally—contribute to "transition, creativity, innovation, [and] path creation" (p. 400) and to societal change.

Conclusion

By the example of the LandFrauen clubs and associations, this chapter has illustrated how civil society practices can relate to social change in rural areas of Germany, and how relational connections to many other partners at local and above local level enable civil society organizations to further social change and social innovation. The results indicate that agents of social innovation need to adapt to local needs, while in parallel, this presents associations with the challenge to align their often centralized structures and goals with the diversity of local challenges and local partners.

The empirics have shown that, although the 10,000 local clubs and regional and federal state associations are highly individual and heterogeneous, they can be attributed relevant roles in social change and social innovation and as educational, social, and political institutions. This case study revealed manifold practices through which the LandFrauen, as an element of German associational life and rural society, contribute to social change and social innovation—as initiators, as supporters, as catalysts in external or joint activities with partners, or as regional multipliers in the diffusion of knowledge, debates, or practices directed towards contemporary societal challenges. Through interest representation, mobilization, and intensively local, as well as nationwide exchange, LandFrauen identify and call attention to problems of rural communities, and jointly develop and implement related ideas and solutions.

Apart from their traditional associational and social functions (Putnam, 2000; Warren, 2001; Zimmer, 2007), the LandFrauen are unique in their spectrum of activities and their engagement for women and the rural spaces in Germany. They provide social, cultural, and educational infrastructure. They bring issues into societal debate and into political process through advocacy and identifying and naming

---

[15] Richter (2019) has identified similar functions for rurally embedded social enterprises, for which he, among further aspects, identifies the re-contextualization of ideas as "embedded intermediaries" and information brokers (pp. 185–186) as key functions.

challenges and problems of women and in rural areas. In this, they contribute to the public sphere (Calhoun, 2011; Habermas, 1962/1989) and set societal and political agenda. They promote societal change as they diffuse contemporary societal debates and solutions, and related knowledge, into rural areas. Through practical local engagement, clubs and associations actively engage to improve rural areas and the situation of women, and through respective projects and activities they implement creative and innovative solutions for rural areas. On higher associational (as well as geographical) levels, representation of interests is a focal activity, whereas the clubs, associations, and their local activities serve as a pre-political space of debate and discussion. They mobilize and empower women as well as represent their interests locally, throughout the federal states, and nationwide. They create awareness in the rural periphery of broader societal and political issues concerning women and the rural areas, and they support female engagement in politics through support and coaching in the field of political and associational work. LandFrauen connect, empower, and mobilize women for political and associational engagement, and they support female (self-)employment.

As prerequisites enabling LandFrauen to pursue their activities, I identified two key characteristics: Firstly, the institutional frame of clubs and associations allows for support, cooperation, and exchange across the vertical and horizontal structure, and provides access to resources and a broad network to external partners. LandFrauen organizations create institutional environments that allow for processes and practices of joint learning, interaction, and the diffusion of knowledge and ideas, as well as providing institutionalized support and encouraging debate and joint activities among the organizations, the local members, and its representatives. The associations thereby fulfil transmitting functions between the local members and higher associational (and geographical levels), as well as representing the members in broader political and societal contexts. The stable organizational structure of clubs and associations—as social and political institutions—are based on the broad representation of their diverse membership base, especially in rural areas, and on the specific horizontal and vertical interwoven organizational structure. They create temporary as well as timely stable and ongoing spaces for learning and exchange, and enable women to engage in practices of social, educational, and political activity, as well as in activity to improve the living conditions in their rural (or urban) surrounding. Secondly, the activities towards social change, especially on the very local level of villages and communities, unfold contextualized on the ground of the broad, diverse, and deeply locally rooted membership base in the rural areas. The local LandFrauen, the individual members and their clubs, are strongly integrated and embedded into local fields of actors and rural society.

In this, the LandFrauen as "key players in socio-spatial change" (Gailing & Ibert, 2016, p. 391) connect the local rural villages and their female members with women, internal and external partners, and societal developments from outside the local context. On a meso- and macro-level, they enter into political debate and put LandFrauen positions and problems on societal and political agenda. Potential for further research on the LandFrauen may lie in the debate on criteria of success for the implementation of social innovation practices against the background of their external relations from a field-oriented perspective (DiMaggio & Powell, 1983; see also Chap. 9 by Glückler and Suarsana).

Brandsen, Evers, Cattacin, and Zimmer (2016a) stress that social innovations are precarious in that "they are often timely limited and do to a large part not further diffuse out of their local context" (p. 307). This study is limited to the LandFrauen practices towards social change, and their prerequisites. A deeper analysis of the LandFrauen's external relations, and how their ideas, solutions, and practices unfold further among the actors throughout organizational fields, might shed further light on the conditions for the successful implementation of social innovation in (rural) society.

References

Ambos, I., & Greubel, S. (2012). Ökonomische Grundbildung für Erwachsene: Themenfeld „Akteurs- und Angebotsanalyse": Abschlussbericht [Basic economic education for adults: Subject field "Analysis of actors and offers"]. Retrieved from www.die-bonn.de/doks/2012-oekonomische-grundbildung-akteurs-und-angebotsanalyse-01.pdf

Amin, A., & Cohendet, P. (2004). *Architectures of knowledge: Firms, capabilities, and communities*. Oxford, UK: Oxford University Press.

Amin, A., & Roberts, J. (2008). Knowing in action: Beyond communities of practice. *Research Policy, 37*, 353–369. https://doi.org/10.1016/j.respol.2007.11.003

Asheim, B. T., & Gertler, M. S. (2005). The geography of innovation: Regional innovation systems. In J. Fagerberg, D. C. Mowery, & R. R. Nelson (Eds.), *The Oxford handbook of innovation* (pp. 291–317). Oxford, UK: Oxford University Press. https://doi.org/10.1093/oxfordhb/9780199286805.003.0011

Bathelt, H., Cohendet, P., Henn, S., & Simon, L. (2017). Innovation and knowledge creation: Challenges to the field. In H. Bathelt, P. Cohendet, S. Henn, & L. Simon (Eds.), *The Elgar companion to innovation and knowledge creation* (pp. 1–25). Cheltenham: Edward Elgar. https://doi.org/10.4337/9781782548522.00006

Bathelt, H., Feldman, M. P., & Kogler, D. F. (2011). *Beyond territory: Dynamic geographies of knowledge creation, diffusion, and innovation*. Regions and Cities: Vol. 47. Abingdon: Routledge.

Bathelt, H., & Glückler, J. (2011). *The relational economy: Geographies of knowing and learning*. Oxford, UK: Oxford University Press. https://doi.org/10.1093/acprof:oso bl/9780199587384.001.0001

Bathelt, H., Malmberg, A., & Maskell, P. (2004). Clusters and knowledge: Local buzz, global pipelines and the process of knowledge creation. *Progress in Human Geography, 28*(1), 31–56. https://doi.org/10.1191/0309132504ph469oa

Baumgart, E., Becker, U., Borsch, K., Merre, J., & Maas, I. (2004). Professionalisierung im Ehrenamt und zielgruppenorientierte Weiterbildung: Das Projekt „Lebenslanges Lernen" im Landfrauenverband Bernkastel-Wittlich [Professionalization in voluntary work and target group-oriented further training: The "Lifelong Learning" project in the Rural Women's association in Bernkastel-Wittlich]. In D. Behrmann, B. Schwarz, & K. Götz (Eds.), *Professionalisierung und Organisationsentwicklung: Optimierung der Rahmenbedingungen des lebenslangen Lernens in der Weiterbildung*. Bielefeld: Deutsches Institut für Erwachsenenbildung—Leibniz-Zentrum für Lebenslanges Lernen.

Beetz, S., Bender, P., & Haubold, F. (2018). Erwachsenenbildung im ländlichen Raum: Ergebnisse der qualitativen Studie „Weiterbildungsbedarf in ländlichen Regionen im Freistaat Sachsen" [Adult education in rural areas: Results of the qualitative study "Needs for further training in rural regions in the Free State of Saxony"]. Edition VHS Aktuell—Beiträge zur Weiterbildung: Vol. 7. Retrieved from https://www.vhs-sachsen.de/fileadmin/user_upload/Dokumente/Projektdoku_Land_web.pdf

Biegler, D. (2001). *Frauenverbände in Deutschland: Entwicklung—Strukturen—politische Einbindung* [Women's associations in Germany: Development—structures—political involvement]. Forschung Politikwissenschaft: Vol. 139. Opladen: Leske + Budrich. https://doi.org/10.1007/978-3-322-97540-9

Boschma, R., & Frenken, K. (2010). The spatial evolution of innovation networks: A proximity perspective. In R. Boschma & R. Martin (Eds.), *The handbook of evolutionary economic geography* (pp. 120–135). Cheltenham: Edward Elgar. https://doi.org/10.4337/9781849806497.00012

Brandsen, T., Evers, A., Cattacin, S., & Zimmer, A. (2016a). The good, the bad and the ugly in social innovation. In T. Brandsen, S. Cattacin, A. Evers, & A. Zimmer (Eds.), *Social innovations in the urban context* (pp. 303–310). Cham: Springer. https://doi.org/10.1007/978-3-319-21551-8_25

Brandsen, T., Evers, A., Cattacin, S., & Zimmer, A. (2016b). Social innovation: A sympathetic and critical interpretation. In T. Brandsen, S. Cattacin, A. Evers, & A. Zimmer (Eds.), *Social innovations in the urban context* (pp. 3–18). Cham: Springer. https://doi.org/10.1007/978-3-319-21551-8_1

Bridenthal, R. (1994). Die Rolle der organisierten Landfrauen bei der konservativen Mobilmachung in der Weimarer Republik [The role of organized rural women in conservative mobilization in the Weimar Republic]. *Feministische Studien, 12*(1), 110–121. https://doi.org/10.1515/fs-1994-0112

Bürgerbusverein Badbergen e.V. (n.d.). Über uns—Entstehung [About us—Formation]. Retrieved from https://www.buergerbus-badbergen.de/ueber-uns-entstehung/

Cajaiba-Santana, G. (2014). Social innovation: Moving the field forward: A conceptual framework. *Technological Forecasting and Social Change, 82,* 42–51. https://doi.org/10.1016/j.techfore.2013.05.008

Calhoun, C. (2011). Civil society and the public sphere. In M. Edwards (Ed.), *The Oxford handbook of civil society* (pp. 311–323). Oxford, UK: Oxford University Press. https://doi.org/10.1093/oxfordhb/9780195398571.013.0025

Christmann, G. B. (2019). Innovationen in ländlichen Gemeinden [Innovations in rural communities]. In W. Nell & M. Weiland (Eds.), *Dorf: Ein interdisziplinäres Handbuch* (pp. 235–240). Berlin: J.B. Metzler. https://doi.org/10.1007/978-3-476-05449-4

Christmann, G. B. (2020a). Introduction: Struggling with innovations: Social innovations and conflicts in urban development and planning. *European Planning Studies, 28,* 423–433. https://doi.org/10.1080/09654313.2019.1639396

Christmann, G. B. (2020b). Soziale Innovationen in ländlichen Räumen [Social innovations in rural areas]. In C. Krajewski & C.-C. Wiegandt (Eds.), *Land in Sicht: Ländliche Räume in Deutschland: zwischen Prosperität und Peripherisierung* (pp. 228–239). Bonn: Bundeszentrale für Politische Bildung.

Christmann, G. B., Ibert, O., Jessen, J., & Walther, U.-J. (2020). Innovations in spatial planning as a social process—phases, actors, conflicts. *European Planning Studies, 28,* 496–520. https://doi.org/10.1080/09654313.2019.1639399

DiMaggio, P. J., & Powell, W. W. (1983). The iron cage revisited: Institutional isomorphism and collective rationality in organizational fields. *American Sociological Review, 48,* 147–160. https://doi.org/10.2307/2095101

DLV e.V. (2018). Jahresbericht 2017: Stimmgewaltig. Mitbestimmend. Mittendrin [Annual Report 2017: Loud voiced. Participating. In the middle]. Retrieved from https://www.landfrauen.info/fileadmin/Redaktion/PDF/Publikationen/2018_dlv_Jahresbericht_2017_web.pdf

DLV e.V. (2019). Jahresbericht 2018: Vertrauen festigen: Veränderung wagen [Annual Report 2018: Build trust: Dare to change]. Retrieved from https://www.landfrauen.info/fileadmin/Redaktion/PDF/Publikationen/2018_LandFrauen_dlv_Jahresbericht_Webversion.pdf

DLV e.V. (2020a). Jahresbericht 2019: Landfrauen zeigen Flagge [Annual Report 2019: LandFrauen plant their flag]. Retrieved from https://www.landfrauen.info/fileadmin/Redaktion/ PDF/Publikationen/Jahresbericht_dlv_2019.pdf

DLV e.V. (2020b). Aus Liebe zum Land: Wofür aktive LandFrauen stehen: Ziele und Botschaften [What active LandFrauen stand for: Goals and messages]. Retrieved from https://www.land-frauen.info/verband/ziele-botschaften

Domanski, D., Howaldt, J., & Kaletka, C. (2020). A comprehensive concept of social innovation and its implications for the local context—on the growing importance of social innovation ecosystems and infrastructures. *European Planning Studies, 28,* 454–474. https://doi.org/10.108 0/09654313.2019.1639397

Ebeling, B. (2017). Akteure der Landwirtschaft in Leader-Aktionsgruppen: Untersuchungen zur Teilnahmemotivation vor dem Hintergrund sozio-kultureller Fragmentierung [Agricultural actors in Leader action groups: Studies on the motivation to participate against the background of socio-cultural fragmentation] (Doctoral dissertation). Georg-August-Universität Göttingen, Germany. Retrieved from https://alr-hochschulpreis.de/sites/default/ files/publikationen2020-04/2017-A-Ebeling_Akteure-der-Landwirtschaft-in-Leader-Aktionsgruppen.pdf

Füg, F., & Ibert, O. (2020). Assembling social innovations in emergent professional communities: The case of learning region policies in Germany. *European Planning Studies, 28,* 541–562. https://doi.org/10.1080/09654313.2019.1639402

Gailing, L., & Ibert, O. (2016). Schlüsselfiguren: Raum als Gegenstand und Ressource des Wandels [Key figures: Space as an object and resource of change]. *Raumforschung und Raumordnung, 74,* 391–403. https://doi.org/10.1007/s13147-016-0426-3

Glückler, J., & Bathelt, H. (2017). Institutional context and innovation. In H. Bathelt, P. Cohendet, S. Henn, & L. Simon (Eds.), *The Elgar companion to innovation and knowledge creation* (pp. 121–137). Cheltenham: Edward Elgar. https://doi.org/10.4337/9781782548522.00015

Glückler, J., Herrigel, G., & Handke, M. (2020). On the reflexive relations between knowledge, governance, and space. In J. Glückler, G. Herrigel, & M. Handke (Eds.), *Knowledge for governance* (pp. 1–21). Knowledge and Space: Vol. 15. Cham: Springer. https://doi. org/10.1007/978-3-030-47150-7_1

Grabher, G., & Ibert, O. (2014). Distance as asset? Knowledge collaboration in hybrid virtual communities. *Journal of Economic Geography, 14*(1), 97–123. https://doi.org/10.1093/jeg/lbt014

Growe, A., & Henn, S. (2020). Temporäre räumliche Nähe—Akteure, Orte und Interaktionen [Temporary proximity—actors, places, and interactions]. *Raumforschung und Raumordnung, 78*(1), 1–3. https://doi.org/10.2478/rara-2020-0004

Habermas, J. (1989). *The structural transformation of the public sphere: An inquiry into a category of bourgeois society* [Strukturwandel der Öffentlichkeit: Untersuchungen zu einer Kategorie der bürgerlichen Gesellschaft] (T. Burger & F. Lawrence, Trans.). Cambridge, MA: The MIT Press. (Original work published 1962)

Helmle, S. (2009). „Wie man sich durchbeißen kann"—Landfrauenarbeit in Bayern nach 1945 ["How to break through"—Farm women and their organization in Bavaria after 1945]. In T. Oedl-Wieser & I. Darnhofer (Eds.), *Gender Issues in der Landwirtschaft* (pp. 27–42). Jahrbuch der Österreichischen Gesellschaft für Agrarökonomie: Vol. 18(2). Vienna: Facultas.

Howaldt, J., & Schwarz, M. (2010). *Social innovation: Concepts, research fields and international trends.* Studies for Innovation in a Modern Working Environment: Vol. 5. Aachen, Germany: RWTH Aachen University.

Howaldt, J., & Schwarz, M. (2016). Social innovation and its relationship to social change: Verifying existing social theories in reference to social innovation and its relationship to social change. TU Dortmund University. Retrieved from https://eldorado.tu-dortmund.de/bit-stream/2003/35207/1/SI-DRIVE-D1-3-Social-Change-final-260416.pdf

Howaldt, J., & Schwarz, M. (2018). Soziale Innovation [Social innovation]. In B. Blättel-Mink, I. Schulz-Schaeffer, & A. Windeler (Eds.), *Handbuch Innovationsforschung* (pp. 1–17). Wiesbaden: Springer.

Icken, A. (2002). *Der deutsche Frauenrat: Etablierte Frauenverbandsarbeit im gesellschaftlichen Wandel* [The German Women's Council: Established women's association work in social change]. Opladen: Leske & Budrich.

Jackisch, C., Berg, C., Bohnenkamp, H., Seifart, U., Serve, H., & Maulbecker-Armstrong, C. (2020). Präventionsprogramme der Landeskrebsgesellschaften [Prevention programs of the regional cancer societies]. *Forum, 35*(1), 24–30. https://doi.org/10.1007/s12312-020-00747-6

Kaschuba, G. (1996). Bildungsprozesse in den Biographien von Frauen in ländlichen Regionen. *REPORT Literatur- und Forschungsreport Weiterbildung, 37/1996,* 53–66. Retrieved from http://www.die-bonn.de/id/1674

Kistemann, E. (2003). Landfrauen in Nordrhein-Westfalen als Gästeführerinnen. Kulturlandschaftliche Aspekte in der Ausbildung [LandFrauen in North Rhine-Westphalia as tour guides. Cultural landscape aspects in training]. *Kulturlandschaft, 13*(1/2), 29–32. Retrieved from https://www.kulturlandschaft.org/publikationen/kulturlandschaft-1/2003_01-02.pdf

Krambach, K. (2005). Vorwort [Preface]. In Rosa-Luxemburg-Stiftung (Ed.), *Landfrauen— treibende Kraft der Dorfentwicklung: Dokumentation einer Tagung* (pp. 4–8). Retrieved from http://www.rosalux.de/fileadmin/rls_uploads/pdfs/Themen/Wirtschaft/Landfrauen-3. Juni05.pdf

Krieg, B. (1999). Landfrauenbewegung im Wandel: Ziele, Inhalte, Herausforderungen und Perspektiven [The changing LandFrauen movement: Goals, content, challenges and perspectives]. In H. Heidrich (Ed.), *Frauenwelten: Arbeit, Leben, Politik und Perspektiven auf dem Land* (pp. 79–98). Bad Windsheim: Fränkisches Freilandmuseum.

Lambooy, J. G. (2010). Knowledge transfers, spillovers and actors: The role of context and social capital. *European Planning Studies, 18*(6), 873–891. https://doi.org/10.1080/09654311003701407

Lave, J., & Wenger, E. (1991). *Situated learning: Legitimate peripheral participation.* Learning in Doing: Social, Cognitive, and Computational Perspectives: Vol. 3. Cambridge, UK: Cambridge University Press.

LFV Mecklenburg-Vorpommern e.V. (2020). Trägerschaft der Kita Kinderland in Friedland [Trusteeship of the Kinderland day care center in Friedland]. Retrieved from https://landfrauen-mv.de/der-verband/unsere-kita

LFV Schleswig-Holstein e.V. (2020). LandFrauen-Archiv Molfsee: Die Geschichte der Frauen sichtbar machen [LandFrauen-Archiv Molfsee: Making the history of women visible]. Retrieved from https://landfrauen-sh.de/wir/landfrauen-archiv-molfsee/

LFV Württemberg-Baden e.V. (2020a). Leitthema 2020–2023—Grenzen-los digital!? [Leading theme 2020–2023—Digital without limits!?]. Retrieved from https://landfrauen-bw.de/bildung/leitthema-2020-2023/

LFV Württemberg-Baden e.V. (2020b). Seniorenbotschafterinnen für neue Medien [Senior ambassadors for new media]. Retrieved from https://landfrauen-bw.de/projekte/senioren-technik-botschafterin/

Lütt, S. (2007). Wiederansiedlung von 60 Wildpflanzenarten in Schleswig-Holstein: Das Jubiläumsprojekt des LandFrauen Verbandes [Resettlement of 60 wild plant species in Schleswig-Holstein: The anniversary project of the LandFrauen association]. *Kieler Notizen zur Pflanzenkunde, 35,* 60–71. Retrieved from https://www.zobodat.at/pdf/Kieler-Notizen-zur-Pflanzenkunde_35_0060-0071.pdf

Lux, T. (2020). Volkshochschulen in der Bundesrepublik Deutschland 2018 in Zahlen: Zahlen in Kürze [Adult education centers in the Federal Republic of Germany 2018 in figures: Numbers in brief]. Retrieved from http://www.die-bonn.de/doks/2020-volkshochschule-statistik-02.pdf

Markt-Treff Schleswig-Holstein. (n.d.). MarktTreff: Viele Angebote unter einem Dach [MarktTreff: Many offers under one roof]. Retrieved from https://markttreff-sh.de/de/markttreff-angebot

Mayring, P. (2015). *Qualitative Inhaltsanalyse: Grundlagen und Techniken* [Qualitative content analysis: Theoretical background and procedures] (12th ed.). Weinheim: Beltz.

Meusburger, P. (2008). The nexus between knowledge and space. In P. Meusburger, M. Welker, & E. Wunder (Eds.), *Clashes of knowledge: Orthodoxies and heterodoxies in science and religion* (pp. 35–90). Knowledge and Space: Vol. 1. Dordrecht: Springer. https://doi.org/10.1007/978-1-4020-5555-3

Moulaert, F., & MacCallum, D. (2019). *Advanced introduction to social innovation.* Cheltenham: Edward Elgar.

Moulaert, F., MacCallum, D., & Hillier, J. (2013). Social innovation: Intuition, precept, concept, theory and practice. In F. Moulaert, D. MacCallum, A. Mehmood, & A. Hamdouch (Eds.), *The international handbook on social innovation: Collective action, social learning and transdisciplinary research* (pp. 13–25). Cheltenham: Edward Elgar. https://doi.org/10.4337/9781849809993.00011

Mulgan, G., Tucker, S., Ali, R., & Sanders, B. (2007). Social innovation: What it is, why it matters and how it can be accelerated. Skoll Centre for Social Entrepreneurship. Retrieved from https://wayback.archive-it.org/org-467/20190705170110/http://eureka.sbs.ox.ac.uk/761/1/Social_Innovation.pdf

Müller, F. C., & Ibert, O. (2015). (Re-)sources of innovation: Understanding and comparing time-spatial innovation dynamics through the lens of communities of practice. *Geoforum, 65,* 338–350. https://doi.org/10.1016/j.geoforum.2014.10.007

Niedersächsischer LandFrauenverband Hannover. (2020). *Pressemitteilung: „CoWork: für dich—fürs Land!"* [Press release: "CoWork: for you—for the country!"]. Retrieved from https://landfrauen-nlv.de/news/detail/news/pressemitteilung-cowork-fuer-dich-fuers-land.html

Priemer, J., Krimmer, H., & Labigne, A. (2017). *ZiviZ-Survey 2017: Vielfalt verstehen: Zusammenhalt stärken [Understand diversity: Strengthen cohesion: ZiviZ survey 2017].* Essen: Edition Stifterverband. Retrieved from https://www.ziviz.info/ziviz-survey-2017

Punstein, A. M., & Glückler, J. (2020). In the mood for learning? How the thought collectives of designers and engineers co-create innovations. *Journal of Economic Geography, 20*(2), 543–570. https://doi.org/10.1093/jeg/lbz019

Putnam, R. D. (2000). Bowling alone: America's declining social capital. In L. Crothers & C. Lockhart (Eds.), *Culture and politics: A reader* (pp. 223–234). New York: Palgrave Macmillan. https://doi.org/10.1007/978-1-349-62965-7_12

Putzing, M. (2003). Neue Erwerbsperspektiven für Frauen auf dem Lande: Ergebnisse eines innovativen Modellprojektes. *Der Kritische Agrarbericht, 2003,* 58–62. Retrieved from http://make-sense.org/fileadmin/Daten-KAB/KAB-2003/Putzing.pdf

Richter, R. (2019). Rural social enterprises as embedded intermediaries: The innovative power of connecting rural communities with supra-regional networks. *Journal of Rural Studies, 70,* 179–187. https://doi.org/10.1016/j.jrurstud.2017.12.005

Rosa-Luxemburg-Stiftung. (2005). Landfrauen—treibende Kraft der Dorfentwicklung: Dokumentation einer Tagung [Rural women—driving force in village development: Documentation of a conference]. Retrieved from http://www.rosalux.de/fileadmin/rls_uploads/pdfs/Themen/Wirtschaft/Landfrauen-3.Juni05.pdf

Rudolph, C., & Schirmer, U. (2004). *Gestalten oder verwalten? Kommunale Frauenpolitik zwischen Verrechtlichung, Modernisierung und Frauenbewegung* [Design or manage? Local women's politics between juridification, modernization and women's movement]. Wiesbaden: VS Verlag für Sozialwissenschaften. https://doi.org/10.1007/978-3-663-01245-0

Rutten, R. (2017). Beyond proximities: The socio-spatial dynamics of knowledge creation. *Progress in Human Geography, 41*(2), 159–177. https://doi.org/10.1177/0309132516629003

Sawahn, A. (2009). *Die Frauenlobby vom Land: Die Landfrauenbewegung in Deutschland und ihre Funktionärinnen 1898 bis 1948 [The women's lobby from the country: Landfrauen movement in Germany and its functionaries from 1898 to 1948].* Frankfurt: DLG.

Sawahn, A. (2012). „Tradition mit frischem Wind": Weibliches Selbstbildnis als Machtfaktor der Landfrauenvereine ["Tradition with a breath of fresh air": Female self-portrait as a power factor in LandFrauen associations]. In D. Münkel & F. Uekötter (Eds.), *Das Bild des Bauern:*

Selbst- und Fremdwahrnehmungen vom Mittelalter bis ins 21. Jahrhundert (pp. 147–178). Göttingen: Vandenhoeck & Ruprecht.

Schermer, M., & Kroismayr, S. (2020). Social innovation in rural areas. *Österreichische Zeitschrift für Soziologie, 45*(1), 1–6. https://doi.org/10.1007/s11614-020-00398-w

Schumpeter, J. (1912). *Theorie der wirtschaftlichen Entwicklung: Eine Untersuchung über Unternehmergewinn, Kapital, Kredit, Zins und den Konjunkturzyklus* [The theory of economic development: An inquiry into profits, capital, credit, interest, and the business cycle]. Leipzig: Duncker & Humblot.

Schumpeter, J. (1942). *Capitalism, socialism, and democracy*. New York: Harper & Brothers.

Schwarz, C. (1990). *Die Landfrauenbewegung in Deutschland: Zur Geschichte einer Frauenorganisation unter besonderer Berücksichtigung der Jahre 1898 bis 1933* [The Landfrauen movement in Germany: On the history of a women's organization with special consideration of the years 1898 to 1933]. Studien zur Volkskultur in Rheinland-Pfalz: Vol. 9. Mainz: Gesellschaft für Volkskunde in Rheinland-Pfalz.

Suarsana, L. (2017). Die LandFrauenorganisationen und ihr lokales Engagement im Spiegel der Regionalentwicklung [The German Country Women's Associations and their civic engagement in the light of regional development]. *Raumforschung und Raumordnung, 75*(6), 527–542. https://doi.org/10.1007/s13147-017-0502-3

Warren, M. E. (2001). *Democracy and association*. Princeton, NJ: Princeton University Press.

Wendt, W. R. (2016). Soziale Innovationen—Innovation des Sozialen: Begriff und Geschäft der Neuerung im Kontext der Sozialwirtschaft [Social innovations—innovation of the social: Concept and business of innovation in the context of the social economy]. *Sozialer Fortschritt, 65*(1/2), 10–16. http://www.jstor.org/stable/45018150

Wenger, E. (1998). *Communities of practice: Learning, meaning, and identity*. Cambridge, UK: Cambridge University Press.

Zapf, W. (1989). Über soziale Innovationen [On social innovations]. *Soziale Welt, 40*(1/2), 170–183. http://www.jstor.org/stable/40878048

Zimmer, A. E. (2007). *Vereine—Zivilgesellschaft konkret* [Associations—civil society concrete] (2nd ed.). Grundwissen Politik: Vol. 16. Wiesbaden: VS Verlag für Sozialwissenschaften. https://doi.org/10.1007/978-3-531-90626-3

Chapter 6
Schools of Democracy? Giving Circles and the Civic and Political Participation of Collaborative Philanthropists

Angela M. Eikenberry

The New River Valley Change Network, a group of about 12 individuals with varying backgrounds and experiences, meets once a month in members' homes and offices in Blacksburg, Virginia, to give away money they contribute to a fund held at the local community foundation. Each member donates about $10 a month or $100 a year. Members decide together, through a consensus decision-making process, where to give their money. The group occasionally invites community experts and activists to their meetings to learn about projects or organizations in need of funding. They prefer to fund small organizations and endeavors that might lead to social change.

Washington Womenade holds volunteer-organized potluck dinners where attendees donate $35 to a fund that provides financial assistance to individuals who need help paying for prescriptions, utility bills, rent, and so on. "Members" show up when they choose, and the focus of time together is highly social. In 2002, a *Real Simple* magazine story on Washington Womenade led to the creation of dozens of unaffiliated Womenade groups across the country. This article also inspired Marsha Wallace to launch Dining for Women, now a US-based national network of more than 400 chapters across the country in which women meet for dinner monthly and pool funds they would have spent eating out, to support internationally based grassroots programs helping women around the world.

BeyondMe is an expanding network of small teams made up of young professionals. Members of each team select a charity or social enterprise to support for one year after reviewing brief proposals, often requiring a "Dragon's Den" or "Shark's Tank" pitch by the charity or social enterprise as part of the selection process. Members, on average, donate £4,000 and 150 volunteer hours to the chosen

A. M. Eikenberry (✉)
School of Public Administration, University of Nebraska Omaha, Omaha, NE, USA
e-mail: aeikenberry@unomaha.ed

© The Author(s) 2022
J. Glückler et al. (eds.), *Knowledge and Civil Society*, Knowledge and Space 17,
https://doi.org/10.1007/978-3-030-71147-4_6

"

organization. Teams support a variety of causes, including jobless young offenders, homeless youth, and women who have experienced abuse and sexual exploitation. BeyondMe's staff and most teams are based in London, UK.

The groups described above—called giving circles—are examples of a growing movement emerging across the US, the UK, and elsewhere. They are philanthropic voluntary associations[1] that involve individuals pooling resources to support organizations and individuals of mutual interest. They also include social, educational, and engagement opportunities for volunteer members, connecting participants to charities, communities, and one another. Although giving circles come in a range of sizes and foci, these groups' key and defining attributes are that they involve individuals who together decide on support for organizations (and sometimes individuals) through giving money (and sometimes time). They also informally or formally educate members about philanthropy, charities, and issues in the community; include a social dimension; engage members in grant making and running the group; and typically maintain independence from any one charity or social enterprise (Eikenberry, 2007, 2009). Hundreds of giving circles have been identified across the US, and a growing number have formed in the UK and elsewhere (Bearman, 2007a, 2007b; Bearman, Carboni, Eikenberry, & Franklin, 2017; Eikenberry, 2009; Eikenberry & Bearman, 2009; Eikenberry & Breeze, 2015; John, Tan, & Ito, 2013; Rockefeller Philanthropy Advisors, 2009; Rutnik & Bearman, 2005).

Giving circles are much like the voluntary groups—where individuals voluntarily come together to accomplish a purpose—that have been a staple of the American and British landscape for some time; one can see similarities in Women's Clubs and Kiwanis, Rotary, or book club or church groups. However, what makes giving circles different is their express philanthropic purpose (i.e., they are created to give money or other resources to organizations or causes), the environment in

---

[1] Philanthropy's meaning and manifestations have changed a good deal throughout history, as Merle Curti (1968/1973) articulates. Scholars today have come to broadly define it as the act of giving money and other resources, including time, to aid individuals, causes, and organizations. Payton and Moody (2008) define it as "voluntary action for the public good." Philanthropy is a term distinct from nonprofit and tax-exempt organizations, charities, and voluntary associations, though all are interrelated. Voluntary associations predate (as those described by Alexis de Tocqueville (1835/2000) in Democracy in America), continue to exist alongside, or sometimes become nonprofit and charitable organizations. They are made up of individuals who voluntarily come together to accomplish a purpose and range from informal self-help or study groups to more formal organized groups such as the Kiwanis or League of Women Voters. A main characteristic of a voluntary association is that it is run by volunteers (Driskell & Wise, 2017). Nonprofit organizations are those organizations designated in the United States by a state as a nonprofit corporation and often by the US Internal Revenue Service as tax-exempt. The term nonprofit, then, is used to designate a legal and regulatory status for an organization that typically does work related to the arts, education, health care, and social welfare. Nonprofit organizations can be quite diverse, ranging from small, human service organizations, such as homeless shelters or arts centers, to large, federated organizations, such as the American Red Cross or Salvation Army, to substantially endowed universities, hospitals, and foundations. Charity is a legal term used in the UK to define organizations established for charitable purposes only and is subject to the control of the High Court's charity law jurisdiction.

which they have emerged and in which they operate, and their typically informal and independent structures. Giving circles represent a transformation in the way less affluent people are attempting to address community problems through giving and volunteering manifested in the "new philanthropy" environment. They demystify the philanthropic process and enable individuals to do something charitable, in their own way (Eikenberry, 2009). This is a response to and reflection of larger changes taking place in a society that is increasingly individualized and where traditional federated associations are losing their grassroots natures (Hustinx, 2010; Lorentzen & Hustinx, 2007; Painter & Paxton, 2014).

As the authors of the literature below describe, much has been written or speculated about traditional voluntary associations as "schools of democracy," teaching people civic skills and virtues and serving as avenues for civic and political participation. Many scholars have questioned and tested the validity of these claims and the degree of cause and effect between voluntary association membership and civic and political participation, generally finding positive relationships, but with some variations by level and length of participation and type of association. Debate continues about the degree to which voluntary associations *cause* greater civic and political engagement or attract people already prone to such engagement. However, the authors of existing research mainly focus on traditional associations and large-scale data sets that make it difficult to unpack the "conditions needed to encourage people… to develop civic virtues and skills and get involved in politics" (Dekker, 2014, p. 56); they also tend to put little focus on philanthropy, which is inherently a political act but not often acknowledged as such (Nickel & Eikenberry, 2013). This is important because policy actors have increasingly looked to philanthropy and nongovernmental institutions to address community problems, including supporting areas of basic needs and education (Giridharadas, 2018; Henriksen, Smith, & Zimmer, 2012; Pharoah, 2011).

Studying giving circles enables addressing some of these issues by asking the question: Does participation in these new forms of philanthropic voluntary association lead members to increase their civic and political participation? That is, do giving circles serve as schools of democracy by providing educational or other features that lead participants to become more civically or politically engaged? Indicators of civic participation include: giving, volunteering, and participation in efforts to address community problems. Indicators of political participation include participation in efforts to change government policy and participation in other political activities such as voting and contacting public officials (Keeter, Zukin, Andolina, & Jenkins, 2002; van der Meer & van Ingen, 2009). To examine the research question, I draw on data gathered in the US and the UK through surveys of current and past members of various types of giving circles and control groups of donors not in giving circles, as well as semi-structured interviews with giving circle members. I focused my data collection on the US and the UK because they have the longest established and largest number of giving circles globally. Although the two countries' philanthropic cultures differ in important ways, as described below, both have promoted philanthropy and voluntary association as policy alternatives to public social welfare and as a response to public sector austerity.

The rest of the chapter is organized as follows: First, I provide an overview of the relevant literature pertaining to the research focus, starting with a discussion of voluntary associations and their relationship to civic and political participation as schools of democracy, moving on to the changing social and philanthropic environment, and finally discussing giving circles. Second, I outline an overview of my methodology. Thirdly, I present my findings. I finish the paper with discussion and conclusions.

Voluntary Associations, the Changing Environment and Giving Circles

Voluntary associations have long been viewed as important mechanisms for promoting democracy, an idea often attributed to Alexis de Tocqueville's (1835/2000) observations during his tour of America in the early 19th century. Tocqueville believed that through engagement in voluntary associations, citizens learned civic virtues and skills, participated directly in governance, and improved the quality and equality of representation in governance—they served as schools of democracy (Fung, 2003; Lichterman, 2006). Building on Tocqueville's observations, scholars see voluntary associations as a means for citizens to achieve the virtues necessary for democratic citizenship: trust, moderation, compromise, reciprocity, and skills of democratic discussion and organization (Newton, 1997; Warren, 2001). Almond and Verba (1963/1989), in their comparative analysis of political culture in five countries, showed that voluntary association membership had a positive impact on civic and political competence. Putnam (1993, 2000) also suggested members of voluntary associations display more political sophistication, social trust, and civic and political participation than others. Further, Verba, Schlozman, and Brady (1995) found voluntary associations of all types provide opportunities for "the acquisition of politically relevant resources and the enhancement of a sense of psychological engagement with politics" (p. 4). They note that even when individuals pursue activities with no direct political content, such as chairing a committee to arrange a fundraising event, they have opportunities to develop organizational and communication skills that are relevant for politics and learn to tolerate and to deal with diverging opinions. McLeod et al. (1996) contend voluntary associations can provide exposure to political cues, social contact, and recruitment networks that facilitate civic and political participation; Musick and Wilson (2008) write that engagement in voluntary associations can make people more aware of what is happening in their community and the structural nature of social problems and the need for political solutions.

Many have questioned and tested the validity of these claims and the degree of cause and effect between voluntary association membership and civic and political participation in numerous countries and contexts (e.g., Dekker, 2014; Dekker & van den Broek, 1998; Howard & Gilbert, 2008; Jeong, 2013; Newton & Montero, 2007;

Parry, Moyser, & Day, 1992; Schulz & Bailer, 2012; van der Meer & van Ingen, 2009; van Deth, 1997), generally finding positive relationships with some exceptions and variations by level and length of participation and type of association. In particular, scholars disagree on the importance of "intensity" of participation and connection to civic and political participation. Putnam (1993, 2000) highlighted the importance of active (face-to-face) versus passive (check-writing) involvement in associations' impact on social capital and participation. Others have found intensity to have little or no significant effect (Almond & Verba, 1989; van der Meer & van Ingen, 2009; Verba, Schlozman, & Brady, 1995; Wollebæk & Selle, 2003). However, Wollebæk and Selle (2003) found in relation to social capital a cumulative effect of participation when the member belongs to several associations simultaneously.

There is also debate about the *socialization* effect of voluntary associations—that associations make citizens civically and politically active—versus a *selection* effect—that certain personality traits stimulate citizens to join voluntary associations and engage in political activities at the same time, without a causal relation between the two (Armingeon, 2007). Through their study of 17 European countries, van der Meer and van Ingen (2009) found the additional effects of "active" participation were marginal and the correlation between associational involvement and political action was not explained by the accumulation of civic skills and civic mindedness through the association. They concluded that "voluntary associations are not the schools of democracy they are proclaimed to be, but rather pools of democracy" (p. 281); that is, "voluntary associations do not make citizens politically active, but bring politically active citizens together" (p. 303). Dekker (2014) also surmised based on his analyses of more than a dozen countries' voluntary association participation data that for some people, involvement in voluntary associations and voluntary work are stepping stones towards politics, whereas for others it offers an opportunity of doing something for the community without getting involved in politics. In other words, participation in associations has different effects depending on the person. Thus, within the literature on the connection between voluntary associations and civic and political participation, there is need for more work to "unpack the conditions" that lead people to get involved in community affairs and politics (Dekker, 2014, p. 56). Researchers looking at the connections between voluntary association and civic and political participation have so far done little to account for societal shifts and changes in participation in traditional social structures.

Scholars suggest that societies are in the midst of a social transformation from "collectivistic" to "individualistic" and "institutionalized" to "self-organized" (Hustinx & Lammertyn, 2003, p. 168). Social relations have changed from being close to loose, permanent to provisional, and thorough to superficial (Gundelach & Torpe, 1996, p. 12). Beck describes society as increasingly characterized by the dissolution of traditional parameters and "variation and differentiation of lifestyles and forms of life, opposing the thinking behind the traditional categories of large-group societies…" (as cited in Ellison, 1997, pp. 711–712). In this context, traditional "voluntary associations have become optional" (Gundelach & Torpe, 1996, p. 13) and indeed, active membership in such associations, at least in the US, appears to be in decline (Painter & Paxton, 2014; Putnam, 2000; Skocpol, 2002).

Scholars have documented the growing use of informal, self-organized, and decentralized initiatives. The emergence of small, self-help support groups and peer-to-peer sharing (e.g., Archibald, 2007; Borkman, Karlsson, Munn-Giddings, & Smith, 2005; Wuthnow, 1994) as well as "network associations"—looser, more informal, and personal forms of association (Fung, 2003; Gundelach & Torpe, 1996; Wuthnow, 1998)—are, according to Wuthnow (1994), rooted in both a breakdown of traditional support structures—neighborhoods and family—and a continuing desire for community; they have "emerged as a serious effort to combat forces of fragmentation and anonymity in our society" (p. 40). Within these types of small and informal associations, engagement is often directed toward concrete problem solving in everyday life. Individuals want (or have) to cope with day-to-day problems on their own terms and in their own way; unlike previous generations, they are uninterested in engagement that is full-time and life-long (Bang & Sørensen, 1999; Macduff, 2005; van der Pennen & Schreuders, 2014). Wuthnow (1998) writes that "instead of cultivating lifelong ties with their neighbors, or joining organizations that reward faithful long-term service, people come together around specific needs and to work on projects that have definite objectives" (p. 8).

Giving circles are indicative of this trend in shifting organizational structures and desire for more hands-on engagement. Studies of the landscape of giving circles in the US and the UK (Eikenberry, 2009; Eikenberry & Breeze, 2015) show that many are formed of small groups and networks, and that participants view giving through the giving circle as a much more proactive approach to philanthropy than has traditionally been the case. One of the most often cited reasons people say they join giving circles is the chance to become more engaged in the giving process—to be doing more than just writing a check and also interacting directly with nonprofit organizations. Some also say they appreciate the simple, nonbureaucratic nature of the giving circle—it's fun, and a chance to be social "while doing good" (Eikenberry, 2007).

But what do these new forms of association mean for engaging individuals in civic and political areas? Based on interviews and document analysis, Eikenberry (2009) found giving circles generally provide opportunities for democratic participation within the group—they provide opportunities for agenda setting, decision making and face-to-face deliberative discourse—and they also build members' capacities through education about voluntary organizations, community issues, and philanthropy. Many groups in the US emphasize formal donor education (Bearman, 2007b; Eikenberry, 2009; Moody, 2008). Do giving circles—as new and emerging forms of philanthropic voluntary associations— increase civic and political participation for members? In the next section, I describe the methodology I use to address this question.

Methodology

In this section, I provide an overview of the methodology I used to address the research question. I gathered data primarily through surveys of giving circle members and control groups of people not in giving circles, supplemented by interviews with giving circle members in the US and UK. I describe these methods in more detail below.

I focused my data collection on the US and UK because these countries have the longest established and largest number of giving circles globally and because both countries have in recent years promoted philanthropy and voluntary association as policy alternatives to public social welfare and as a response to public sector austerity. However, the UK has a very different philanthropic culture than the US—where the US has long touted itself as the most philanthropic of nations and philanthropy enjoys historical popularity, in the UK, as Wright (2001) notes, "while it has enjoyed a very recent renewal of interest . . . for many in Britain it still carries disparaging connotations of Victorian 'do-gooderism' and is often seen as elitist, patronizing, morally judgmental, and ineffective, as well as old-fashioned and out-of-date. . . . It is perceived as an idea whose time came, was proved unworkable, and went—to be replaced by a universal, fair, and more efficient welfare-state" (p. 400). This has been changing in recent years as there have been a number of efforts to promote charitable giving and strengthen the culture of philanthropy in the UK (Pharoah, 2011; The Philanthropy Review, 2011; Sargeant & Breeze, 2004; Walker, 2014), with the emergence of giving circles due in part to these efforts.

Eikenberry and Breeze (2015) outline similarities and differences between giving circles in the US and UK. Structurally, both countries have similar types of groups, including some that are focused on specific demographic groups such as young professionals. The UK also has some types of giving circles, such as the live crowd-funding model, that are unique to it. In both countries, giving circles are typically initiated by someone who heard about or had the idea themselves; they are seen as an alternative to "mainstream" philanthropy, partially focus on developing philanthropy, and many emphasize networking/socializing. In the UK, there is additional focus on "normalizing" giving in a context that lacks widespread cultural affirmation for philanthropy. There is also a larger focus on the pursuit of solidarity and social change. In both countries, giving circles mainly give money (and time) and feature various decision-making processes and types of events. Those in the UK generally appear to place less emphasis on grant-making due diligence and instead rely on trust in fellow members and beneficiaries. UK groups also appear more staff driven and put less emphasis on formal educational programming. Although members in both countries come from a mixture of backgrounds, the total percentage of race/ethnicity, women, or other identity-based groups is lower in the UK.

Surveys

My colleagues and I administered surveys of giving circle members and control groups of people not in giving circles in the US and the UK. We originally administered a survey in the US to understand if and how participation in a giving circle has changed members' behavior related to giving, volunteering, and civic and political engagement. In addition, we asked if and how participation in a giving circle changed members' awareness or knowledge about philanthropy, nonprofit organizations, and community issues. Finally, we wanted to know if and how participation in a giving circle changed members' perceptions or attitudes about philanthropy, community issues, government and nonprofit roles and responsibilities, and political and social values. With our UK survey, we updated and revised the US version to address some cultural differences as well as to improve its usefulness for the giving circles that participated in the survey, while also trying to maintain questions that could be used for comparison across countries. In presenting the data reported below, I focus on the findings related to civic and political behaviors.[2]

We constructed and administered the US survey via paper and internet between November 2007 and April 2008. The sample included 26 giving circles, drawn from the Forum of Regional Association of Grantmakers' giving circle database, consisting of giving circles that represented various types and sizes and identity groups (e.g., women, African-American, young professionals) in order to get a broad cross-section of data. The giving circles in the sample also represented a range in terms of years of existence and geographic locations. In choosing this sample, we also took into consideration earlier studies that had been published on particular giving circles. We recruited giving circle members and past members through giving circle leadership in each giving circle in the sample. The control group included a random sample of donors to a University Foundation supplemented with a nonrandom sample of public administration graduate students and alumni.

We administered the UK survey online between April 2014 and February 2015. Seven giving circles or networks of circles participated in the study, including those representing a diversity of types of giving circles in the UK, with an oversampling of young philanthropist groups. It was fairly reflective of the broader landscape of giving circles in the UK, as young philanthropist groups account for the largest number of circles and participants. The control group was made up of a UK university's donors and of people who said they were just starting with a giving circle (had been members for less than one month).

For the US, we sent surveys to approximately 890 giving circle members and 938 individuals in the control group—a total of 1,828 people. We estimated the overall response rate at 37%. The response rate was 48% for giving circle members and 23% for the control group. Giving circle respondents in the US sample were

---

²See a copy of the US survey here: https://www.academia.edu/12175637/The_Impact_of_Giving_Together_Full_Report. For a copy of the UK survey, go to: https://drive.google.com/file/d/0B0D7zXPukqEQbHliY2EzNkRjNjQ/view?usp=sharing.

significantly more likely to be female, from diverse racial/ethnic groups, and older on average than the control group. In addition, giving circle members attended religious services significantly less frequently than the control group. Regarding political orientation, giving circle members were more significantly likely to describe themselves as liberal or middle-of-the-road compared to the control group. Finally, there was a large difference between giving circle members and the control group in the amount they say their households donated to charity over the past year. The mean for giving circle members was $7,682 compared to $4,945 for the control group. This difference was statistically significant. However, the average annual family income of giving circle members was also significantly higher than the control group: around $106,500 compared to around $90,000. There was no significant difference between giving circle members and the control group for educational level, years living in current community, marital status, and number of children.

For the UK survey, we emailed about 4,184 people the survey link (through contacts at each giving circle or network) and 507 people answered part or all of the survey—an overall response rate of 12.1%. Ultimately, there were 359 useable responses—201 giving group respondents and 158 control group respondents. The demographic characteristics of the UK giving circle and control group respondents were largely similar except for a few areas: Giving circle respondents were significantly more likely to be 30 to 39 years old, say they found it "difficult to get by on present income," and to be married. They were significantly less likely to be male, from an Asian ethnicity, retired, living in the Southeast of England, living in their community less than one year, and single. There were no significant differences for mean age, ranges in income, education, or religious attendance. The UK survey did not include a question about political orientation.

Dependent variables included in the survey to measure civic and political participation featured the following (drawing on Keeter et al., 2002; van der Meer & van Ingen, 2009):

- **Giving**: measured by asking all respondents for their best estimate of the total amount they contributed during the past 12 months (US) or month (UK). Giving circle members were also asked about the degree to which their giving had changed due to the giving circle.
- **Volunteering**: measured by asking all respondents for their best estimate of the total number of hours they had volunteered during the past month (asked in the UK only). Giving circle members in the US and UK were also asked about the degree to which the amount of time they volunteer changed due to the giving circle.
- **Efforts to address problems in the community**: measured by asking giving circle members in both countries about the degree to which their participation in efforts to address problems in the community changed due to the giving circle.
- **Efforts to change government policy**: measured by asking giving circle members in both countries about the degree to which their participation in efforts to change government policies at the local, national, or international levels changed due to the giving circle.

- **Participation in civic and political activities**: measured by asking all respondents in both countries if they had participated in certain activities during the past year such as: working with others to solve a problem in the community; voting; talking to others about an election or campaign; signing a petition about a social or political issue; and other items noted in more detail below.

The above dependent variables were examined in relation to four independent variables:

- **Participation in a giving circle**: measured by asking all respondents if they belonged to a giving circle or giving group, defined in the US survey as "a group of individuals who pool money and other resources and decide together where to give these away. This does not include donor recognition programs that nonprofit organizations use to honor donors." It was defined in the UK survey as: "A giving group involves individuals collectively donating money and/or time to support charitable organizations, projects or individuals. Participants in the group typically have input on how funding or other support is spent and often participate in discussions and social and educational events about philanthropy and the charitable sector."
- **Level of participation within a giving circle**: measured by asking giving circle members about the degree to which they had participated in certain activities within a giving circle in the past 12 months (US) or had participated in as a member of the giving group (UK), such as taking part in deciding who received funding, going on site visits, volunteering with a funding recipient, doing research, or holding leadership position(s).
- **Length of time participating in a giving circle**: measured by asking giving circle members how long they had been a member of a giving circle (US) or had participated in the giving group (UK). If a respondent indicated being in more than one giving circle, they were asked to answer based on the giving circle they had participated in the longest.
- **Participation in multiple giving circles**: measured by asking giving circle members how many giving circles they currently belong to (US) or number of giving groups in which they had participated in the past five years (UK).

These four independent variables can provide some indication of the degree to which giving circles may serve as "schools" increasing civic and political participation. If giving circles serve as schools increasing civic and political participation, we would see not only that people in a giving circle would have higher participation than to those not in giving circles, but this participation would rise with more engagement (in one or more giving circles) and length of engagement.

To analyze the survey data, we calculated frequencies and percentages for all items and means when applicable. We created descriptive statistics based on all respondents, comparing giving group respondents to control group respondents, and comparing across giving groups. We then created crosstabs using SPSS Custom Tables for questions that contained at least one nominal response field. We performed T-tests to determine whether means were statistically significantly different between the giving circle and control group response, and calculated the Pearson Correlation to measure the strength of the relationship between level of engagement and dependent variables. We utilized the one-way analysis of variance (ANOVA) to determine whether there were any statistically significant differences between continuous numeric variables, as was the case with length of engagement and number of giving circles, and dependent variables.

Interviews

In the US, we conducted 30 interviews with a purposively selected sample of members from 11 giving circles. Giving circle leaders helped make contact with members. We interviewed giving circle members with varying levels of involvement in the group, length of membership, gender and gender orientation, profession, and racial/ethnic identity. They were also members of different types of giving circles. Interviews were conducted on the telephone, recorded, and transcribed. They took place between December 26th, 2007, and May 23rd, 2008, and ranged from 22 minutes to 55 minutes, with the average length 36 minutes.

In the UK, we conducted 26 interviews with a sample of members from 14 giving circles. We selected a sample of giving circles that included a range of characteristics based on size, structure, geographic location, and demographic make-up, and mostly engaged with the lead contact in the group; however, in some groups we talked to more than one member. There were three group interviews and in two giving groups geared to young professionals, we talked to multiple members individually (three in one group; six in another). Interviews took place between April 10 to September 9th, 2013, and February 24th to April 21st, 2015, across the UK.

We analyzed transcripts using MAX QDA qualitative data analysis software and followed an iterative process of contextualizing and categorizing strategies (Maxwell, 1998, p. 90). This process included: listening to the entire interview and reading transcripts and other documents completely through to get a sense of the whole, rereading and coding segments, and recoding and grouping codes into broad clusters of similar topics or nodes, primarily around the research questions though allowing for emergent topics. We then iteratively recoded these clusters into more specific and simplified codes, creating "trees" (Coffey & Atkinson, 1996, p. 29).

Findings

I have drawn the findings described from data from surveys and interviews to examine the impact of giving circles on members' civic and political participation in relation to each of the dependent variables: giving, volunteering, participation in efforts to address problems in the community, participation in efforts to change government policy, and participation in other activities such as voting and contacting public officials. See a summary of the results in Table 6.1.

Giving

People in giving circles in the US donated more on an annual basis than people who were not in giving circles. The mean for giving circle members was $7,681, compared to $4,944 for the control group. This difference was statistically significant. However, because the average annual family income of giving circle members was also higher than the control group, there was no statistically significant difference for average household contributions between these two groups when controlling for income. Nonetheless, two-thirds (67%) of giving circle members indicated the total amount they contributed each year had increased due to giving circle participation. Kahn (2007) and Moody (2008) had similar findings with their studies of Social

Table 6.1 Giving circle impact on civic and political participation—US & UK

	Giving Circle Members Compared to Control Group		Level of Engagement in Giving Circle		Length of Engagement in Giving Circle		Number of Participating Giving Circles	
	t	p-value	r	p-value	F	p-value	F	p-value
Giving								
US – per year	2.52	.006*	0.0381	.490	0.186	.028*	0.205	.0002**
UK – per month	2.374	.018*	0.059	.442	2.109	.067	1.272	.283
Volunteering								
US – per year	NA	NA	0.360	.000*	0.1701	.0022*	0.1093	.0504
UK – per month	1.619	.107	0.276	.001**	7.243	.000*	1.114	.331
Participation to Address Problems in the Community								
US	NA	NA	0.251	.000*	0.1323	.0168*	0.0443	.4259
UK	NA	NA	0.220	.008**	1.114	.356	0.163	.850
Involvement in Changing Government Policy								
US	NA	NA	0.281	.000*	0.0644	.2480	0.1605	.0038*
UK	NA	NA	0.041	.626	0.642	.668	0.350	.705
Civic & Political Activities								
US	5.78	.000*	0.2505	.000*	0.3316	.000*	0.0783	.1707
UK	1.954	.052	0.172	.022*	4.872	.000*	7.160	.001*

*Correlation is significant at the 0.05 level (2-tailed)
**Correlation is significant at the 0.01 level (2-tailed)
Note. Source: Design by author

Venture Partners. This may mean, then, that giving circle members said giving increased when it did not, the increased amount was not big enough to make a statistically significant difference, or they gave less before and are now more like the control group. At least one-third of those interviewed in the US said their personal giving had increased since joining a giving circle. In addition, a handful of interviewees indicated their giving had shifted from elsewhere to the giving circle or had decreased due to retirement and job loss since joining the giving circle.

In the UK, giving circle respondents gave significantly more per month on average than the control group (£253 vs. £108 per month), even when controlling for income. This difference, however, is largely due to giving by those with household incomes of £75,001 or above, where giving group respondents gave significantly more than control group respondents, on average £353 compared to £103 per month. Nonetheless, three-quarters (77%) of giving circle participants said the giving group caused them to increase or substantially increase the amount they give each year. Similarly, reports on impact done by UK-based The Funding Network (TFN) in 2012 found that 66% of TFN members said they give more to charity as a result of their participation in TFN. A perceived increase or expansion in giving was also brought up frequently in interviews with members.

We further examined the effect of giving circle participation on members' giving by looking at association with level and length of engagement in the group, and number of groups in which members engaged. The findings for the US show levels of engagement within the giving circle were not significantly associated with total amount contributed. However, total contributions rose significantly as the length of time in the giving circle increased, even when accounting for income. In addition, people in more than one giving circle donated significantly more than other members, with an average of $13,400 compared to $6,834 for members in one giving circle and $4,945 for people in no giving circles. The association between number of giving circle memberships and the total amount given was highly significant and remained so when controlling for income. This suggests, then, that given enough time or participation in several groups, giving circles influence members to give more. However, in the UK, the amount given per month was not significantly associated with level or length of engagement, nor number of giving groups in which a member participated.

Volunteering

In the US, a little less than half (46%) of giving circle members reported that participation in a giving circle increased the amount of time they volunteered. In addition, at least half of interviewees said that when they joined a giving circle, they already had a long history of volunteering, dating back to high school and through pro bono neighborhood work, volunteering with the United Way, a church, or elsewhere. Thus, it may be that for some, there is an impact on increasing volunteering but for many they were already active before joining the group. Studies of SVP found that

63% to 68% of respondents noted an increase in their volunteerism after joining SVP (Kahn, 2007; Moody, 2008). This higher amount might be explained by the fact that SVP focuses much more on member volunteering than many other giving circles. It may also be that volunteering increases with engagement level and over time.

In the UK, although giving circle members did on average volunteer at a higher rate per month than the control group respondents (7.15 vs. 6.30 hours per month), there was no significant difference between giving circle members and the control group. In addition, only 43% of giving circle respondents said the giving group helped to increase or substantially increase the amount of time they volunteer each year. The impact report on TFN done in 2012 also found that 29% of respondents said they volunteered more or had become a trustee to an organization they had met through TFN. A few members also said in interviews that they got involved volunteering with charities beyond their giving group.

The US and UK data show members were more likely to say their total time volunteering significantly increased as their level of engagement and length of participation in a giving circle increased. They also said their volunteer time increased as participation in the number of giving circles increased, but the association was not significant in either country. Thus, overall, although people may already come to the giving circle having been active as a volunteer, as they are more involved in the giving circle and for a longer period of time, they increase their rate of volunteering.

Participation in Efforts to Address Problems in the Community

Two-thirds (64%) of US giving circle members said the giving circle led them to increase their participation in efforts to address problems in the community. In the UK, 53% said the giving group caused them to increase or substantially increase their participation in efforts to address problems in the community, whereas 47% said participation had not changed in this area. As level of engagement and length of engagement increased, US giving circle respondents were significantly more likely to say they increased their participation in efforts to address problems in the community. This increased for the number of giving circles as well, but it was not significant. In the UK, giving circle respondents were significantly more likely to say they increased their participation in efforts to address problems in the community as their level of engagement in the giving circle increased. There was no significant association when it came to length of engagement or number of giving groups. It seems in this area, then, level of engagement in both countries, and length of engagement in the US, have some kind of effect on increasing members' participation in addressing problems in the community.

Involvement in Efforts to Change Government Policy

Only one-third (34%) of US giving circle respondents said they increased their involvement in changing government policy due to the giving circle; however, as both the level of engagement within the giving circle increased and the number of these circles increased, respondents were significantly more likely to say they increased their participation in efforts to address problems in the community. There was also a positive but not significant association between length of participation and involvement in changing government policy. In the UK, only 14% of giving group respondents said the giving group caused them to increase or substantially increase their involvement in changing government policies. There was no significant association when it came to level or length of engagement, nor number of giving groups. In this area, giving circles seem to have little effect in members' participation in changing government policy; in the US, however, these efforts do seem to increase with level of engagement in the giving circle and when participating in multiple giving circles.

Civic and Political Activities

In both surveys, we created an index to show the degree of overall civic and political engagement based on a number of activities in which people might participate (there were a total of 14 activities in the US survey and a total of 9 in the UK survey).[3] The index average for US giving circle members was 8.8 compared with 7.3 for the control group. This difference was statistically significant. However, further analysis showed that only some income groups showed a statistically significant difference between giving circle and control group respondents: incomes of $25,000 to $34,999 and $50,000 to $149,999. SVPI also found in their survey of partners that

---

[3] Civic engagement indicators were created based on the index used by CIRCLE: Center for Information and Research on Civic Learning and Engagement: http://www.civicyouth.org/practitioners/Core_Indicators_Page.htm#1. These include: working with others to solve a problem in the community; volunteering; belonging to a group or association; donating money; voting; talking to others about an election or campaign; contacting public officials; contacting a media outlet to express an opinion on a social or political issue; protesting, marching, or demonstrating; signing a petition about a social or political issue; and either buying or not buying something because of a company's social or political values. For the UK survey, we used a revised and trimmed down version that included: took part in a protest, march, or demonstration; contacted a newspaper or other media to express your opinion about a political or social issue; helped raise money for a charitable cause; contacted or visited a public or elected official to express your opinion; belonged to a voluntary group or association, either locally or nationally (such as a trade union, professional association, political or social group, sports or youth group); signed a petition about a political or social issue; voted in a local, national, or European election; worked together with someone or a group to discuss or address a problem in the community; bought or did not buy something because of the social or political values of the company that produces or provides it.

70% of respondents indicated SVP had some, significant, or a primary impact on their community involvement as well (Kahn, 2007). In the UK, the index average was 4.2 for giving circle members and 3.8 for the control group. The difference was not significant. The only significant difference was that a higher portion of giving group respondents indicated they had worked together with someone or a group to discuss or address a problem in the community.

Furthermore, in the US, as level of engagement in the giving circle increased, the civic and political engagement index significantly increased. It was also evident from the survey that length of time in a giving circle and number of giving groups were positively but insignificantly associated with the index of civic and political engagement. In the UK, civic and political activities were significantly higher as the level and length of engagement in the giving circle as well as the number of giving groups increased.

According to US interviews, the number of members who said they were more civically and politically active because of the giving circle was small. However, those who did think they had become more active due to the giving circle included those who had become motivated by a growing awareness of community problems through the giving circle and thus become more involved in local elections, writing elected officials, or supporting various groups and paying closer attention to social issues, and those who were inclined to be active but were not because they did not feel they had previously had a good avenue for such action. For example, since join-ing her giving circle, one respondent began identifying other ways to effect change, including joining the Committee for World Outreach. Another interviewee dis-cussed how the giving circle meetings enabled her to learn about local issues and then take action. Three people talked about how their experience in a giving circle inspired them to talk more about political issues with their friends and family and helped them figure out where to go to get something done.

Even if civic and political activities did not increase, some indicated giving greater thought to the relationship between what they learned through the giving circle and their behaviors. For example, one interviewee said the giving circle made her question whether she was doing enough. Others saw the giving circle as another way to be active. Interviewees in the UK indicated that politics were not a focus of the group, although they could come up indirectly. One person in a mentor group noted:

> In [giving group] everyone's very polite so you probably won't get much about politics. I guess it doesn't have a political agenda either. . . . I mean [giving group] is very much kind of work out what kind of charity you want to invest in and invest in it. A debate might come up like during an initial discussion session when you're trying to think about different inter-ests and where needs, what kind of part of the NGO sector needs funding. Maybe that might lead to politics. Otherwise, I don't think, it's not really that into political discussion basically.

Discussion and Conclusions

In this study, I have sought to understand whether giving circles—as new and emerging forms of philanthropic voluntary associations in the US and the UK—increase civic and political participation. That is, do giving circles serve as schools of democracy? From my findings, I conclude that:

- Amount of **giving** increases significantly with being in a giving circle in both countries, and length of engagement and number of giving circles in the US.
- Amount of **volunteering** increases significantly with level of engagement and length of engagement in both countries.
- Participation in **addressing problems in the community** due to the giving circle increases significantly with level of engagement in both countries and length of engagement in the US.
- Involvement in **changing government policy** due to the giving circle increases significantly with level of engagement and number of giving circles in the US.
- Participation in various **civic and political activities** are positively associated with being in a giving circle (significant only in the US), and these increase significantly with level and length of engagement in both countries and with number of giving groups in the UK.

Overall, then, I find:

- **Participating in a giving circle** seems to matter for increasing giving in both countries, and civic and political activities in the US Membership does not appear to affect the amount of volunteering.
- The **level of engagement** in a giving circle is associated with more volunteering, participation in addressing problems in the community, and civic and political activities in both countries, as well as more involvement in changing government policy in the US. Level of engagement does not seem to have a significant impact on giving.
- The **length of engagement** in a giving circle is associated with more volunteering and civic and political activities in both countries, and more giving and participation in addressing problems in the community in the US. Length of engagement does not seem to have a significant impact on involvement in changing government policy.
- The **number of giving circles** in which someone participates is associated with more giving and involvement in changing government policy in the US, and civic and political activities in the UK.

From the data I then conclude that, generally, giving circles do seem to serve as schools in several areas, particularly related to volunteering, participation in efforts to address problems in the community, and other civic and political activities as level and length of engagement increase. However, for some civic and political activities, particularly giving and involvement in changing government policy, giving circles have less of a schooling effect. The findings on the relationship between participation in these voluntary associations and civic and political participation seem to align with previous studies' findings that this relationship is generally positive for giving circles. On their basis, I also conclude that impact varies by areas and country, and the interviews indicate it varies by participant as well (Dekker, 2014).

In this study, I also provide insight into the effect of newer types of voluntary associations emerging in today's environment. As opposed to traditional, bureaucratic voluntary associations, giving circles tend to be less formal smaller groups and looser networks. The findings indicate that these structures lead to a positive impact on civic and political engagement—perhaps more so for volunteering and participation in efforts to address problems in the community, and various civic and political activities; less so for giving or changing government policy. Thus, although giving circles represent more informal, self-organized, and decentralized forms of association emerging in a less institutionalized environment, they still seem to have a similar effect to more traditional associations. In future, researchers will need to examine more closely what particular aspects of participation in the giving circle might lead to increased civic and political participation. Through my analysis of different models of giving circles in the UK, I have found that different activities lead to different outcomes related to giving, volunteering, and learning about philanthropy and charities (Eikenberry, 2015).

Finally, what do the findings reveal related to the debate about voluntary associations as schools or pools of democracy? In general, in line with Putnam (1993, 2000) and Wollebæk and Selle (2003), the findings indicate that more active engagement (measured in this study by level and length of engagement in the giving circle and number of giving circles) can make a difference in impact on level of civic and political engagement. That is, active and sustained participation in the association seem to have greatest impact on civic and political engagement, generally supporting a schools thesis. However, the data also show that impact varies for some areas and by member—some people interviewed indicated they are already highly engaged civically and politically in various activities and the giving circle provides another opportunity for them to extend this engagement, supporting the "pools" or "selection" thesis (Armingeon, 2007; van der Meer & van Ingen, 2009). One conclusion then is that giving circles, as well as other types of voluntary association, may serve as both schools and pools of democracy.

References

Almond, G. A., & Verba, S. (1989). *The civic culture: Political attitudes and democracy in five nations*. Princeton, NJ: Princeton University Press. (Original work published 1963)

Archibald, M. E. (2007). *The evolution of self-help: How a health movement became an institution*. New York: Palgrave Macmillan.

Armingeon, K. (2007). Political participation and associational involvement. In J. W. van Deth, J. R. Montero, & A. Westholm (Eds.), *Citizenship and involvement in European democracies: A comparative analysis* (pp. 358–383). Routledge Research in Comparative Politics: Vol. 17. Abingdon: Routledge.

Bang, H. P., & Sørensen, E. (1999). The everyday maker: A new challenge to democratic governance. *Administrative Theory & Praxis, 21,* 325–341. https://doi.org/10.1080/10841806.199 9.11643381

Bearman, J. E. (2007a). Hosting a giving circle: The benefits and challenges of giving together. Washington, D.C.: Forum of Regional Associations of Grantmakers. Retrieved from https://www.unitedphilforum.org/system/files/resources/Hosting%20 a%20Giving%20Circle%20-%20The%20Benefits%20and%20Challenges%20of%20 Giving%20Together.PDF

Bearman, J. E. (2007b). More giving together: The growth and impact of giving circles and shared giving. Washington, D.C.: Forum of Regional Associations of Grantmakers. Retrieved from https://www.unitedphilforum.org/system/files/resources/More%20Giving%20 Together%20-%20The%20Growth%20and%20Impact%20of%20Giving%20Circles%20 and%20Shared%20Giving.PDF

Bearman, J. E., Carboni, J., Eikenberry, A. M., & Franklin, J. (2017). The landscape of giving circles/collective giving groups in the U.S., 2016. Giving Circles Research Group. Retrieved from https://scholarworks.iupui.edu/bitstream/handle/1805/14527/giving-circles2017-2.pdf

Borkman, T., Karlsson, M., Munn-Giddings, C., & Smith, L. (2005). *Self-help and mental health: Case studies of mental health self-help organizations in US, England, and Sweden.* Sköndal, Sweden: Sköndalsinstitutet. Retrieved from http://urn.kb.se/ resolve?urn=urn:nbn:se:esh:diva-681

Coffey, A. J., & Atkinson, P. A. (1996). *Making sense of qualitative data: Complementary research strategies.* Thousand Oaks: Sage.

Curti, M. (1973). Philanthropy. In P. P. Wiener (Ed.), *Dictionary of the history of ideas: Studies of selected pivotal ideas: Law, concept of to protest movements* (Vol. III, pp. 486–493). New York: Charles Scribner's Sons. (Original work published 1968)

Dekker, P. (2014). Tocqueville did not write about soccer clubs: Participation in voluntary associations and political involvement. In M. Freise & T. Hallmann (Eds.), *Modernizing democracy: Associations and associating in the 21st century* (pp. 45–57). New York: Springer. https://doi. org/10.1007/978-1-4939-0485-3_4

Dekker, P., & van den Broek, A. (1998). Civil society in comparative perspective: Involvement in voluntary associations in North America and Western Europe. *Voluntas: International Journal of Voluntary and Nonprofit Organizations, 9,* 11–38. https://doi.org/10.1023/A:1021450828183

de Tocqueville, A. (2000). *Democracy in America* (H. C. Mansfield & D. Winthrop, Eds. and Trans., with an introduction by H. C. Mansfield & D. Winthrop). Chicago, IL: University of Chicago Press. (Original work published 1835)

Driskell, R., & Wise, J. (2017). Voluntary associations. In B. S. Turner, C. Kyung-Sup, C. F. Epstein, P. Kivisto, W. Outhwaite, & J. M. Ryan (Eds.), *The Wiley-Blackwell encyclopedia of social theory.* New York: John Wiley & Sons. https://doi.org/10.1002/9781118430873.est0400

Eikenberry, A. M. (2007). Giving circles: Self-help/mutual aid, community philanthropy, or both? *International Journal of Self Help and Self Care, 5,* 249–278. https://doi.org/10.2190/SH.5.3.d

Eikenberry, A. M. (2009). *Giving circles: Philanthropy, voluntary association, and democracy.* Bloomington, IN: Indiana University Press.

Eikenberry, A. M. (2015). *A study of the impact of participation in UK giving circles* (Unpublished report). Retrieved from https://www.academia.edu/15260901/A_Study_of_the_Impact_of_ Participation_in_UK_Giving_Circles_Full_Report

Eikenberry, A. M., & Bearman, J. E. (2009, May). The impact of giving together: Giving circles' influence on members' philanthropic and civic behaviors, knowledge and attitudes. Retrieved from https://www.unitedphilforum.org/system/files/resources/The%20Impact%20of%20 Giving%20Together.PDF

Eikenberry, A. M., & Breeze, B. (2015). Growing philanthropy through collaboration: The landscape of giving circles in the United Kingdom and Ireland. *Voluntary Sector Review, 6,* 41–59. https://doi.org/10.1332/204080515X14241771107299

Ellison, N. (1997). Towards a new social politics: Citizenship and reflexivity in late modernity. *Sociology, 31,* 697–717. https://doi.org/10.1177/0038038597031004004

Fung, A. (2003). Associations and democracy: Between theories, hopes, and realities. *Annual Review of Sociology, 29,* 515–539. https://doi.org/10.1146/annurev.soc.29.010202.100134

Giridharadas, A. (2018). *Winners take all: The elite charade of changing the world.* New York: Knopf.

Gundelach, P., & Torpe, L. (1996). *Voluntary associations: New types of involvement and democracy.* Paper presented at the ECPR workshop on "Social involvement, voluntary associations and democratic politics," Oslo, Norway. Retrieved from https://vbn.aau.dk/files/95864/35031996_2.pdf

Henriksen, L. S., Smith, S. R., & Zimmer, A. (2012). At the eve of convergence? Transformations of social service provision in Denmark, Germany, and the United States. *Voluntas: International Journal of Voluntary and Nonprofit Organizations, 23,* 458–501. https://doi.org/10.1007/s11266-011-9221-5

Howard, M. M., & Gilbert, L. (2008). A cross-national comparison of the internal effects of participation in voluntary organizations. *Political Studies, 56,* 12–32. https://doi.org/10.1111/j.1467-9248.2007.00715.x

Hustinx, L. (2010). I quit, therefore I am? Volunteer turnover and the politics of self-actualization. *Nonprofit and Voluntary Sector Quarterly, 39,* 236–255. https://doi.org/10.1177/0899764008328183

Hustinx, L., & Lammertyn, F. (2003). Collective and reflexive styles of volunteering: A sociological modernization perspective. *Voluntas: International Journal of Voluntary and Nonprofit Organizations, 14,* 167–187. https://doi.org/10.1023/A:1023948027200

Jeong, H. O. (2013). From civic participation to political participation. *Voluntas: International Journal of Voluntary and Nonprofit Organizations, 24,* 1138–1158. https://doi.org/10.1007/s11266-012-9316-7

John, R., Tan, P., & Ito, K. (2013). Innovation in Asian philanthropy: Entrepreneurial social finance in Asia. (Working Paper No. 2). Singapore: Asia Centre for Social Entrepreneurship and Philanthropy, National University of Singapore. Retrieved from https://www.philanthropy-impact.org/sites/default/files/downloads/innovation_in_asian_philanthropy_april2013.pdf

Kahn, E. H. (2007, September 10). *Demonstrating social venture partners' impact: 2007 philanthropy development report.* Seattle: Social Venture Partners International. Retrieved from http://www.socialventurepartners.org/network-office/wp-content/uploads/sites/37/2013/12/2007-Summary-Report-on-Philanthropy-Development.pdf

Keeter, S., Zukin, C., Andolina, M., & Jenkins K. (2002). The civic and political health of the nation: A generational portrait. Center for Information and Research on Civic Learning and Engagement (CIRCLE). Retrieved from http://files.eric.ed.gov/fulltext/ED498892.pdf

Lichterman, P. (2006). Social capital or group style? Rescuing Tocqueville's insights on civic engagement. *Theory & Society, 35,* 529–563. https://doi.org/10.1007/s11186-006-9017-6

Lorentzen, H., & Hustinx, L. (2007). Civic involvement and modernization. *Journal of Civil Society, 3,* 101–118. https://doi.org/10.1080/17448680701554282

Macduff, N. (2005). Societal changes and the rise of the episodic volunteer. In J. L. Brudney (Ed.), *Emerging areas of volunteering* (pp. 51–64). ARNOVA Occasional Paper Series: Vol. 1, No. 2. Indianapolis: Association for Research on Nonprofit Organizations and Voluntary Action. Retrieved from https://cdn.ymaws.com/www.arnova.org/resource/resmgr/Publications/ARNOVA_Emerging_Areas_of_Vol.pdf

Maxwell, J. A. (1998). Designing a qualitative study. In L. Bickman & D. J. Rog (Eds.), *Handbook of applied social research methods* (pp. 69–100). Thousand Oaks: Sage.

McLeod, J. M., Daily, K., Guo, Z., Eveland Jr., W. P., Bayer, J., Yang, S., & Wang, H. (1996). Community integration, local media use and democratic processes. *Communication Research, 23,* 179–209. https://doi.org/10.1177/009365096023002002

Moody, M. P. (2008). "Building a culture": The construction and evolution of venture philanthropy as a new organizational field. *Nonprofit and Voluntary Sector Quarterly, 37,* 324–352. https://doi.org/10.1177/0899764007310419

Musick, M. A., & Wilson, J. (2008). *Volunteers: A social profile.* Bloomington, IN: Indiana University Press.

Newton, K. (1997). Social capital and democracy. *American Behavioral Scientist, 40,* 575–586. https://doi.org/10.1177/0002764297040005004

Newton, K., & Montero, J. R. (2007). Patterns of political and social participation in Europe. In R. Jowell, C. Roberts, R. Fitzgerald, & G. Eva (Eds.), *Measuring attitudes cross-nationally: Lessons from the European social survey* (pp. 205–238). London: Sage.

Nickel, P. M., & Eikenberry, A. M. (2013). Gastrophilanthropy: Utopian aspiration and aspirational consumption as political retreat. *Reconstruction, 12.* Retrieved from http://digitalcommons.unomaha.edu/pubadfacpub/33

Painter, M. A., & Paxton, P. (2014). Checkbooks in the heartland: Change over time in voluntary association membership. *Sociological Forum, 29,* 408–428. https://doi.org/10.1111/socf.12090

Parry, G., Moyser, G., & Day, N. (1992). *Political participation and democracy in Britain.* Cambridge, UK: Cambridge University Press. https://doi.org/10.1017/CBO9780511558726

Payton, R. L., & Moody, M. P. (2008). *Understanding philanthropy: Its meaning and mission.* Bloomington, IN: Indiana University Press.

Pharoah, C. (2011). Private giving and philanthropy: Their place in the Big Society. *People, Place & Policy Online, 5,* 65–75. https://doi.org/10.3351/ppp.0005.0002.0003

The Philanthropy Review. (2011). A call to action to encourage more people to give and people to give more: Recommendations from the Philanthropy Review, June 2011. Retrieved from https://www.philanthropy-impact.org/sites/default/files/downloads/A%20Call%20to%20Action%20-%20June%202011_0.pdf

Putnam, R. D. (1993). *Making democracy work: Civic traditions in modern Italy.* Princeton, NJ: Princeton University Press.

Putnam, R. D. (2000). *Bowling alone: The collapse and revival of American community.* New York: Simon & Schuster.

Rockefeller Philanthropy Advisors. (2009, August). *Diversity funds inventory.* New York: Rockefeller Philanthropy Advisors.

Rutnik, T. A., & Bearman, J. E. (2005). Giving together: A national scan of giving circles and shared giving. Washington, D.C.: Forum of Regional Associations of Grantmakers. Retrieved from https://www.unitedphilforum.org/system/files/resources/Giving%20Together%20-%20A%20National%20Scan%20of%20Giving%20Circles%20and%20Shared%20Giving.PDF

Sargeant, A., & Breeze, B. (2004). A blueprint for giving: The final report of the giving campaign. London: The Giving Campaign. Retrieved from https://pdfs.semanticscholar.org/4010/5bec52876541b726742f5525bf62f20f733e.pdf

Schulz, T., & Bailer, S. (2012). The impact of organisational attributes on political participation: Results of a multi-level survey from Switzerland. *SPSR Swiss Political Science Review, 18,* 1–27. https://doi.org/10.1111/j.1662-6370.2012.02052.x

Skocpol, T. (2002). The United States: From membership to advocacy. In R. D. Putnam (Ed.), *Democracies in flux: The evolution of social capital in contemporary society* (pp. 103–136). Oxford, UK: Oxford University Press. https://doi.org/10.1093/0195150899.003.0004

van der Meer, T. W. G., & van Ingen, E. J. (2009). Schools of democracy? Disentangling the relationship between civic participation and political action in 17 European countries. *European Journal of Political Research, 48,* 281–308. https://doi.org/10.1111/j.1475-6765.2008.00836.x

van der Pennen, T., & Schreuders, H. (2014). The fourth way of active citizenship: Case studies from the Netherlands. In N. Gallent & D. Ciaffi (Eds.), *Community action and planning: Context, drivers and outcomes* (pp. 135–156). Bristol, UK: Bristol University Press. https://doi.org/10.2307/j.ctt1t89cwg.15

van Deth, J. W. (Ed.). (1997). *Private groups and public life: Social participation, voluntary associations and political involvement in representative democracies.* London: Routledge.

Verba, S., Schlozman, K. L., & Brady, H. E. (1995). *Voice and equality: Civic voluntarism in American politics*. Cambridge, MA: Harvard University Press.

Walker, C. (2014). *Give more campaign review and evaluation*. London: Directory of Social Change.

Warren, M. E. (2001). *Democracy and association*. Princeton, NJ: Princeton University Press.

Wollebæk, D. & Selle, P. (2003). Participation and social capital formation: Norway in a comparative perspective. *Scandinavian Political Studies, 26,* 67–91. https://doi.org/10.1111/1467-9477.00080

Wright, K. (2001). Generosity vs. altruism: Philanthropy and charity in the United States and United Kingdom. *Voluntas: International Journal of Voluntary and Nonprofit Organizations, 12,* 399–416. https://doi.org/10.1023/A:1013974700175

Wuthnow, R. (1994). *Sharing the journey: Support groups and America's new quest for community*. New York: Free.

Wuthnow, R. (1998). *Loose connections: Joining together in America's fragmented communities*. Cambridge, MA: Harvard University Press.

Chapter 7
Time Banks as Transient Civic Organizations? Exploring the Dynamics of Decline

Johannes Glückler and Jakob Hoffmann

After the outbreak of the financial and economic crisis in the US and many European countries in 2007, alternative economic practices have become celebrated responses to cope with unemployment, precarity, and austerity policies. Yet although the economic recession triggered this new call for an "alternative," diverse (Gibson-Graham, 2008) or community (Gibson-Graham, 2014) practices are neither new nor are exclusively a response to phases of economic downturns. The relative nature of the denominator "alternative" has let its utilizers to conflate a vast variety of attitudes and approaches, ranging from claims to oppose (anti-capitalist), transform (neo-capitalist) or overcome (post-capitalist) the conventional market economy (Sánchez, 2017). Despite these strong normative claims, empirical knowledge about the many forms of alternative practices and their ways of working is still limited, especially because a new multiplicity of practices has only started to emerge. Therefore, social and geographical research on new civic forms of organizing is a timely and valuable contribution to explore the contemporary flourishing of alternative economic practices.

The contemporary surge in these practices also marks a period of social and organizational innovation. The trend of building new forms of organizing coproduction, local trade, and economic solidarity reinforces the notion of the organizational society. Contemporary societies are increasingly configured around (often multiple) memberships of individuals in organizations, such as corporations, associations, clubs, parties, charities, and other civil society organizations (Perrow, 1991). Hence, individual agency hardly occurs without touching upon organizational concerns, such as vested interests, normative positions, and the corresponding interdependencies (Lazega, 2016, 2018). Time banks are one organizational expression of the wide variety of alternative economic practices. Although their number has grown globally (Cahn & Gray, 2015), and especially strongly in Spain in recent years

J. Glückler (✉) · J. Hoffmann
Department of Geography, University of Heidelberg, Heidelberg, Germany
e-mail: glueckler@uni-heidelberg.de; j.hoffmann@uni-heidelberg.de

J. Glückler et al. (eds.), *Knowledge and Civil Society*, Knowledge and Space 17,
https://doi.org/10.1007/978-3-030-71147-4_7

(Valor & Papaoikonomou, 2016), the broader phenomenon of community currencies was already widely discussed before the 2007 economic crisis, for example, in the UK (Batchelor, 2003; Boyle, 2003; Gregory, 2009; Seyfang, 2003a, 2003b; Stuart, 2003; Thrift, 2002), the USA (Collom, Lasker, & Kyriacou, 2012), and in other countries such as New Zealand (Diprose, 2016), Germany (Meier, 2001), Italy (del Moral-Espín, 2017), or Japan (Hayashi, 2012).

Researchers have often focused on time banks' normative dimension and design principles to strengthen democracy (Thrift, 2002), or to enhance cocreation and reciprocity (Clement et al., 2016). Despite growing empirical research, there is still a lack of understanding of the processes, mechanisms, and dynamics through which time banks evolve and operate. One empirical puzzle researchers have observed is the question why time banks have often been vulnerable and short-lived organizations. Some suggest that community currencies tend to fall short of their ambitious economic goals (Dittmer, 2013; Williams et al., 2001) and struggle with psychological barriers towards participation (Ozanne, 2010). Others find that time banks fail to achieve and retain the critical mass of people to show continuous commitment and long-term engagement (Seyfang & Longhurst, 2013). After the beginning of the economic crisis in 2007, time banks have blossomed in many Spanish and other European cities and regions (Sánchez-Hernández & Glückler, 2019), yet frequently, they began to wither after a few years. How, then, do time banks really work and what are the processes through which they grow and decline?

To answer this question, it is necessary to look behind the normative surface of these organizations and study the empirical practices that define local exchange: its (alternative) economic transactions. It is here that methods of social network analysis are especially helpful (see Chap. 8 by Diani, Ernstson, and Jasny and Chap. 9 by Glückler and Suarsana). They facilitate observing not only individual relations or transactions, but also enable one to map and analyze the overall network structure as well as to trace this structure through time. We argue that the question of how this activity is structured through time is essential for understanding the dynamics of emergence, reproduction, and demise. In this chapter, we offer a brief introduction into relational thinking and the characteristics of social network research, especially in human geography. To illustrate the potential of social network analysis for the study of alternative practices, we present parts of a more comprehensive case study of a time bank in Germany (Hoffmann & Glückler, 2021). Specifically, we illustrate how formal network analysis may help one to understand the dynamics of organizational life through the lens of the structure and trajectory of individual alternative economic practices in a time bank.

Relational Thinking and Social Networks

The analysis of social networks is inspired by a relational view of the social world. *Relational thinking* departs from the notion that social actors are not isolated beings who carry out atomistic behavioral scripts. Instead, they are embedded in a social context that constitutes meaning through interaction and institutions: "Relational thinking has become an overarching perspective in social theory that shifts the analytical focus from attributes and categories to context, process, and emergence" (Bathelt & Glückler, 2011, p. 240). In geography, for example, a relational view is opposed to traditional approaches, whose proponents use spatial structures or spatial variables as a starting point for analyses. Instead, adopters of relational geography focus on the actors most relevant to the problem or question under investigation. Researchers thus need to study the positioning of actors and agency within broader contexts of social and institutional relations. Social action is assumed both to be constrained by networks of social relations and at the same time to transform these structures in dynamic ways (Bathelt & Glückler, 2018).

The concept of the *network* denotes a set of nodes that are connected by a certain number of ties. Social science researchers focus on *social* networks, in other words, the way in which individuals or organizations are related to one another (Wasserman & Faust, 1994). Beyond this formal definition, social network researchers proceed from the assumption that the structure of relationships as a whole conditions the opportunities and constraints for individual action in the network (Mitchell, 1969, p. 2). In other words, although individuals are embedded into a structure of social relations, the network structure itself also has an effect on individual action.

Researchers use the concept of the network on different analytical levels: as theory, as method, and as empirical object (Glückler, 2013). The starting point of a *theory of social networks* is the axiom of the anti-categorical imperative mentioned earlier. With it, one postulates that explanations of social phenomena—such as power, cooperation, development, or innovation—should not only include the actors' categorical characteristics but also their embedding in manifold social relations. This relational perspective benefits from both interpretative theories, for example, actor-network theory, and formal network theories, whose proponents focus on explaining the specific characteristics and effects of networks. Both approaches are necessary because network effects depend on the specific meaning of the relationships in a social context. Network structures thus do not have universal, but contingent, social meanings and consequences (Pachucki & Breiger, 2010). Depending on the research interest, three classes of theories can be distinguished (Borgatti & Halgin, 2011).

First, *network theories* explain the social consequences of structural network properties. The theories of weak ties (Granovetter, 1973), structural holes (Burt, 1992), structural equivalence (Burt, 1988), or the theory of small worlds (Uzzi & Spiro, 2005) are well-known approaches used, for example, to link individual advantages such as access to information, negotiation potential, or career opportunities with the increasing centrality of actors. However, specific network structures have differential rather than universal advantages. For example, proponents of the theory of structural folds (Vedres & Stark, 2010) postulate that it is precisely actors' cohesion that promotes successful innovation cooperation, which stands in opposition to those theorists focusing on networked resource-access such as structural hole theory. Second, and in contrast to relational theories, adopters of *theories of networks* are devoted to explaining structural properties of networks from categorical initial conditions. They show that relationships arise, for example, as a function of spatial proximity, similar social status, or common organizational affiliation. Third, proponents of *network theories of networks* attempt to explain network consequences from structural network properties. Those adopting dynamic approaches to network evolution, for instance, aim to identify geographically and historically specific development paths, in which the formation and dissolution of relationships is dependent on earlier relationships and in which the change of a development path can thus be explained endogenously from the knowledge of earlier structures (Glückler, 2007). Due to the low availability of longitudinal network data on social or corporate relationships, however, network analytical research on the geographical evolution of networks is still in its infancy (ter Wal & Boschma, 2009).

Researchers can conduct their analysis of social networks with a wide variety of *methods*, ranging from formal network analysis (Borgatti, Everett, & Johnson, 2013; Wasserman & Faust, 1994) or qualitative to mixed methods of network analysis (Domínguez & Hollstein, 2014). In any case, the unit of observation is relational data, that is, information about the existence and quality of relationships between actors. In practice, researchers often use already existing (so-called secondary) data, such as official statistics of patent applications or research cooperation. They offer the advantage of relative completeness of information, depending on the quality of the source. On the other hand, primary data collection such as interviews or surveys enables researchers to observe otherwise inaccessible relationships such as the exchange of information, advice-seeking and recommendations, or mutual support and solidarity between persons. With good planning, they also achieve high response rates.

The procedures of social network analysis start at different levels. They enable the description and analysis of positions of individual actors at the micro level (e.g., centrality), of subgroups of actors at the meso level (e.g., coherent clusters or functional roles), and of structural characteristics at the macro level of the whole network (e.g., centralization, fragmentation, role structures). Building on relational data and the three scales of analysis (actor, substructure, entire network), there is a continuous advance in methodologies and a growing interest in geography to use these methods (Glückler & Doreian, 2016; Glückler, Lazega, & Hammer, 2017). Three recent examples of interest for geographers are methods for positional (Glückler & Panitz, 2016a, 2016b; Prota, 2016), evolutionary (Nomaler & Verspagen, 2016), and multi-level (Brailly, 2016; Lazega & Snijders, 2016) network analysis. In the context of this chapter, we would like to portray a case study of the exchange network of a time bank that is geographically situated in a city in Southern Germany.

A Network Perspective on Time Banks

The inception of time banking in its current form is most often attributed to Edgar Cahn, an American law professor, who conceptualized time banks as a community-based measure against poverty in the 1980s (Cahn & Gray, 2015; Cahn & Rowe, 1992). Time banks respond to a desire for egalitarian economic exchange, which is facilitated by providing a locally limited and community-specific currency. The value of a community currency is equivalent to the time spent on the provision of a service. Participants can valorize their own time through provision of services to other members, and, in turn, spend their income on services provided by others. Of course, the notion of organizing local exchange through a community currency has much older historical roots. Early concepts of community-based economic practices are found in the works of John Bellers (1654 to 1725), Robert Owen (1771 to 1858), or Silvio Gesell (1862 to 1930) (Polanyi, 1944).

In the relatively sparse academic literature, time banks have been associated with community development, social inclusion, and active citizenship (Gregory, 2009; Seyfang, 2004). As such, they have become a tool for local policymaking, aimed especially at the support of disadvantaged neighbourhoods. Despite a rising number of empirical studies on time banks, relatively little is known about the structure and dynamics of exchanges in time banks. Taking a relational view of this type of organization, we conceive a time bank as an evolving network of social exchange (Whitham & Clarke, 2016). As time banks increasingly use digital accounting systems (Cahn & Gray, 2015), transaction records enable us to track each individual transaction and to reconstruct the entire network's process of formation and change.

Although some empirical researchers have partially used transaction data (Carnero, Martinez, & Sánchez-Mangas, 2015; Lasker et al., 2011; Seyfang, 2001), they have rarely exploited it for the analysis of the entire network structure. As an exception, Collom (2008) and Collom et al. (2012) collected egocentric data on the relational patterns of focal individual members (so-called ego networks). To take the potential of network analysis a step further, we aim to overcome the limitations of dyadic atomism (Granovetter, 1992) by using the connectivity of the entire network in a dynamic framework. Such an approach offers a unique opportunity to study the process of emergence and demise as well as aspects of systemic stability, which have been identified as a research frontier in previous studies (Valor & Papaoikonomou, 2016).

An Urban Time Bank in Southern Germany

We focus our research on a time bank (TB) located in Southern Germany (SG), called TBSG hereafter to comply with our agreement not to disclose its true name. Founded in the late 1990s as a loose coalition of citizens in southern Germany, TBSG was established as a mature legal entity of a charitable association by 2008.

The main goal of the time bank is to develop a sustainable network for facilitating neighbourly help. TBSG facilitates the exchange of all goods and services unless prohibited by law or contrary to ethical principles. Offerings are broad and depend on the skills and abilities of the individual members. Services, such as massages, hair cutting, advice, repairs, gardening or teaching, are mainly exchanged directly among members, although the trade of goods, most often self-grown or self-made food, is also common at monthly meetings or celebrations. Members may exchange within the whole region, and some members live in the surrounding towns and villages.

The community currency (so-called 'talents') enables members to trade without cash and within a closed economic cycle. One 'talent' corresponds to 15 minutes of work; the time value of each trade can be negotiated among the trading partners. Every member registers an account at the beginning of their membership. New members must first earn an initial amount of talents through service or goods before being allowed to use their account. By statute, the account balance is constrained to a lower limit of −20, and to an upper limit of 200 talents (50 hours) to avoid both opportunism and accumulation. Furthermore, a monthly membership fee is collected to cover administrative costs, including a semi-annual magazine, which members use to advertise offerings and requests.

Today, TBSG counts about 100 registered members, not all of whom are necessarily active. The members' demographic composition has changed remarkably over the last 20 years. Although the average age was 43 years, with only 28% of the members being older than 50 years, in 2000, by 2018, a vast majority of 72% of the members were aged 50 or older, resulting in an average age of 56 years. In other words, the member base generation seems not to have changed very much over the observed period. 79% of the members are women. Despite the apparent endurance of TBSG since its foundation, the time bank has failed to rejuvenate its member base. The base's ageing points to the organization's creeping decline, and it reinforces calls for research on the transience of time banks, in particular, and organized forms of alternative economic practices, more generally.

A Longitudinal Network Analysis

We use original relational data on over 6,000 transactions over a period of nine years between 2009 and 2017 to examine the structural characteristics and dynamic changes underlying and shaping the community-building process of TBSG. As members provide a considerable number of services to the time bank itself as organizational assistance, these services would distort the picture of social interaction among members and we have therefore discarded them from the analysis presented here. This leaves 4,477 transactions among a total of 192 participants over a period of more than eight years. We grouped these transactions year by year to construct eight directed networks, which vary in size (number of nodes) as people enter and leave the time bank through the years. As only incomplete data was available for the years 2009 and 2018 and a comparison with the other years is accordingly not possible, we have discarded these years from the dynamic analyses. Although people can of course have more than one transaction in a given time period, we have coded a tie from A to B as being present (1) if there is at least one account of A receiving a service from B and as absent (0) otherwise. Note the encoding of tie directions, which here follows the flow of currency: the tie A ➜ B indicates that A paid an amount of talents to B in return for a service provided by B to A.

In accordance with previous classifications (Collom, 2012), we distinguish 13 classes of goods and services that are traded through the time bank, plus a "miscellaneous" category for non-classifiable transactions. In Table 7.1, we present the distribution of participants and transactions as well as a few network statistics across the 14 types of goods and services. In Fig. 7.1, we display the corresponding visual graphs for each category of traded services. From a network perspective, the sum of

Table 7.1 Type, number, and connectivity of traded services and goods

	N	Transactions/Ties	Suppliers	Consumers	Density	InCentral	OutCentral
Arts and Crafts Production	97	186/158	65	75	.017	.11	.10
Beauty and Spa	107	299/222	78	86	.020	.14	.16
Cleaning, Light Tasks and Errands	116	338/261	82	103	.020	.12	.10
Computer and Technology	121	373/271	79	100	.019	.12	.10
Construction, Installation, Maintenance and Repair	119	312/241	92	92	.017	.12	.08
Entertainment and Social Contact	96	210/162	65	73	.018	.12	.21
Events and Program Support	52	57/54	33	34	.020	.16	.16
Foods	145	881/506	98	128	.024	.28	.12
Health and Wellness	138	601/383	100	119	.020	.09	.06
Office and Administrative Support	70	89/78	45	49	.016	.10	.10
Sales and Rentals of Items	89	143/124	54	67	.016	.08	.06
Transportation and Moving	129	499/358	95	115	.022	.19	.14
Tutoring, Consultation and Personal Services	79	130/106	49	60	.017	.16	.06
Miscellaneous	125	359/239	86	106	.015	.11	.07

Note. Source: Design by authors

                                                    J. Glückler and J. Hoffmann

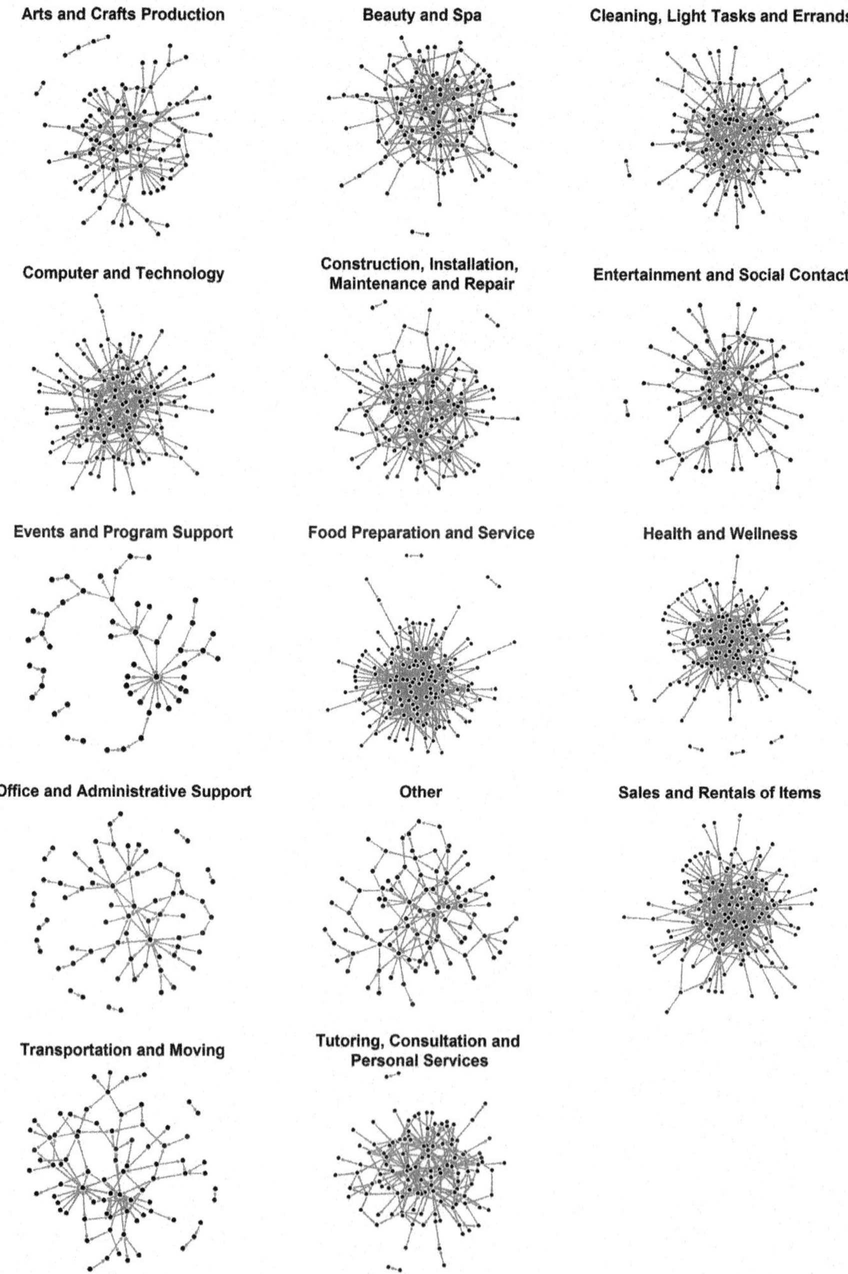

Fig. 7.1 Network graphs of fourteen types of goods and services exchanged in TBSG. Source: Design by authors

these different category networks represents a multiplex network with 14 layers as they represent different types of ties. Considering raw counts of transactions and participating members, we observe considerable variation across the different service categories. Among the most frequent are exchange of food and other item trades and health services, followed by computer-related services. Less prominent are event support, office and administrative support, and transportation.

Network density is used to calculate the proportion of the total number of possible ties that is actually realized in a network. It is thus a measure of overall network connectivity and varies somewhat across the different category networks, with food being the most dense and office support and item sales being the least dense. More interestingly, degree centralization is used to assess to what extent a network's transactions are concentrated on a single actor. Centralization varies between 0 and 1, with 1 representing a star-configuration, where all ties are focused on a single actor. We distinguish here between centralization of indegree and outdegree as proxies for assessing the concentration of supply (indegree centralization) and demand (outdegree centralization), respectively. Here again, trade in food peaks with high indegree centralization, indicating a relatively small number of highly active members who supply food to a larger group of members. Other product categories, such as health and wellness, have much lower centralization in both indegree and outdegree, a sign of a more equally spread exchange structure. Tutoring and personal services are also characterized by a discrepancy in supply and demand concentration. Although the number of suppliers is generally lower than the number of consumers across all goods and services, differences are moderate and no trade category is fully monopolized in that only one or very few people supplied a service exclusively.

Evolution and Demise of the TBSG Network

In the following, we focus on a descriptive analysis of the evolution of TBSG's network structure. Displaying simple aggregate statistics on a year-by-year basis reveals that the number of members, ties, and transactions had initially risen to then revert to a decline of overall activity by 2012/2013. This demise is also reflected in the degree centralization, which started declining equally in 2012 (Fig. 7.2). Gross network indicators such as the number of actors and the number and structure of transactions thus suggest an evolution from initial rise to creeping decline of overall activity, which corresponds with an inverted U-shaped development curve. This trend also corresponds Seyfang and Longhurst's finding (2013) that time banks often lack durability. An analysis of the network dynamics allows us to take a deeper look into the structural changes to explore potential mechanisms and processes that help us to understand such demise.

To further examine the pattern of centralization and decentralization of transactions, we identify different trajectories of individual participation in overall exchange. The goal of such an approach is to provide a micro-level analysis of the

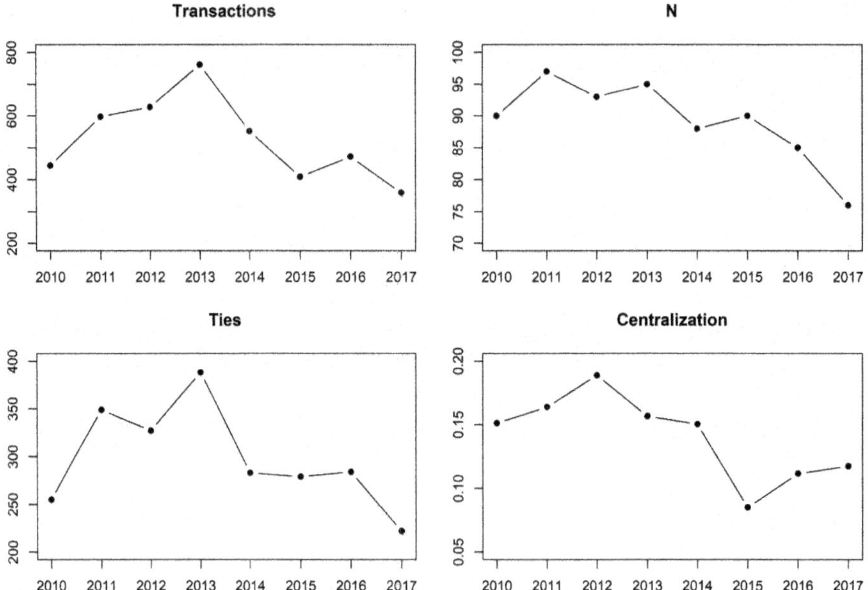

Fig. 7.2 Changes in transactional activity in TBSG, 2010–2017. Source: Design by authors

relational process through which activities decline. Therefore, we consider the activity by network position and time rather than by type of transaction. For this line of analysis, we draw on methods of positional network analysis as well as methods from sequence analysis (Gabadinho, Ritschard, Müller, & Studer, 2011). Positional approaches cluster actors into groups if they are located in equivalent positions within the network (Doreian, Batagelj, & Ferligoj, 2005; Faust, 1988; Glückler & Doreian, 2016). In contrast to conventional clustering approaches, such groups are defined by similarity in relations rather than in characteristics, in other words, by similarity in the way actors are connected to the rest of the network. Among the most discussed positional structures are core-periphery models (Glückler & Panitz, 2016a; Prota, 2016). Such structures are composed of a densely connected core and a periphery, which is loosely connected internally as well as with the core. We here employ stochastic blockmodels (Lazega, Sapulete, & Mounier, 2011; Zhang, Martin, & Newman, 2015) to cluster actors into core and periphery positions for each of the eight annual networks.

Each of the 192 individuals—due to new entries and exits, the number of members exceeds the current number of members in TBSG—can now be assigned to one of three positions for any given point in time: core, periphery, and inactive. As we have eight years of analysis, we have 192 sequences of length eight, using each to summarize a member's positional trajectory of participation in the time bank between 2010 and 2017. We use a hierarchical clustering algorithm and an optimal matching distance measure (Gabadinho et al., 2011) to cluster these sequences into five types of characteristic trajectories (Fig. 7.3).

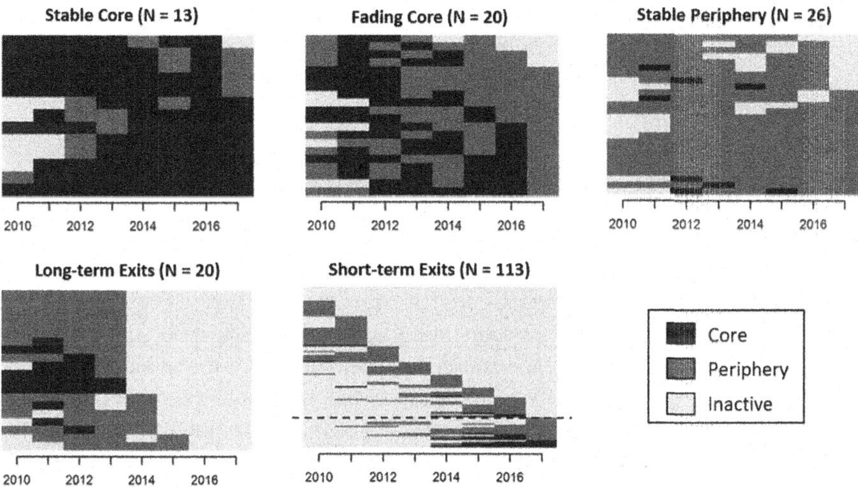

Fig. 7.3 Types of member trajectories through core-periphery positions at TBSG. Source: Design by authors

With each cluster of sequences, we present a distinctive trajectory of involvement in transactions: First, the *stable core* consists of 13 actors who occupy core positions over most of the observation period. Second, in the *fading core*, many members occupy core positions in the beginning of the observed period, yet as time goes on, many members reduce their activity and drift to peripheral positions. Third, the *stable periphery* includes 26 loyal but sporadic members who hold peripheral positions for long periods of time. Together, these three clusters of trajectories make up for the long-term backbone of the time bank but are also a source of declining activity, as can be seen by the fading part of the core. Fourth, *long-term exits* as well as, fifth, *short-term exits* largely consist of drop-outs. Whereas those of the former had maintained longstanding membership before finally becoming inactive, the latter includes people who had entered the time bank and left shortly thereafter. The sheer size of the fifth cluster and the corresponding scale of relational turnover (Lazega, 2017) reflects the remarkable volatility around the smaller core of long-term members. The cluster of short-term drop-outs also holds some newcomers (indicated by the dashed line in Fig. 7.3), which are not enough to fully compensate for the rate of exits, as can be seen by the declining number of participants.

The decomposition of differential histories of involvement presented here reveals several interesting insights into the exchange dynamics of TBSG. First, most exchanges revolve around a relatively small number of core actors who constitute the robust center of the time bank. Second, this core has not been durable throughout the observation period, as can be seen by many members moving to peripheral positions or becoming dropouts. Third, the densely connected core is surrounded by a relatively stable but smaller periphery of casual members as well as by a large and volatile group of short-term and perhaps experimental members. Finally, as researchers have often reported for time banks (Collom, 2005), recruiting new members is hard, as can be seen by the relatively low number of newcomers. As a consequence, the time bank struggles to replenish itself and risks fading out with its long-standing core members.

Conclusion

We have proposed a relational perspective to study time banks as a new type of civic organization to enact alternative economic practices. In seeking to understand the mechanisms of such a civic organization's rise and demise, we applied methods of dynamic social network analysis to analyze the relational processes within a Southern German time bank over a period of eight years. From dynamic social network analysis, one can gain original insight into the ways in which a time bank evolves. Given the repeated observation that time banks and other types of alternative economic practices are often characterized by considerable volatility and potential collapse, relational thinking and network analysis are especially suited for unpacking the underlying relational mechanisms that shape these outcomes of volatility and demise.

We have illustrated the benefits of formal methods of network analysis, but are by no means suggesting that researchers should disregard other ways of studying alternative economic practices. We acknowledge that a relational analysis of an emergent phenomenon, which may be easily misread from a dominant way of "capitalocentric" thinking, will benefit from thick description and interpretative methods to capture new logics of action (Gibson-Graham, 2014). In concluding this, however, we should not sacrifice the value of a detailed micro-relational analysis of the social process and the structural dynamics that these practices create. At their best, researchers conducting studies on civic organization and their practices should consider mixed-method designs that combine the best of both worlds (Small, 2011; Glückler, Panitz, & Hammer, 2020). In any case, it is worthwhile and necessary to explore the empirical nature and dynamics of social practices in civic organizations more deeply, rather than limiting the debate to normative accounts of their potential virtues and liabilities. Relational thinking, quickly advancing methods of social network analysis, and an ever-increasing amount of available relational data are a promising offering to complement the diversity of empirical research approaches to civic life.

References

Batchelor, J. (2003). More than tea and biscuits: The role of time banks and LETS in local economic development. *Local Economy, 18,* 253–270. https://doi.org/10.1080/0269094032000111048a

Bathelt, H., & Glückler, J. (2011). *The relational economy: Geographies of knowing and learning*. Oxford, UK: Oxford University Press. https://doi.org/10.1093/acprof:os obl/9780199587384.001.0001

Bathelt, H., & Glückler, J. (2018). Relational research design in economic geography. In G. L. Clark, M. P. Feldman, M. S. Gertler, & D. Wójcik (Eds.), *The new Oxford handbook of economic geography* (pp. 179–195). Oxford, UK: Oxford University Press. https://doi.org/10.1093/oxfo rdhb/9780198755609.013.46

Borgatti, S. P., Everett, M. G., & Johnson, J. C. (2013). *Analyzing social networks*. Thousand Oaks: Sage.

Borgatti, S. P., & Halgin, D. S. (2011). On network theory. *Organization Science, 22*, 1168–1181. https://doi.org/10.1287/orsc.1100.0641

Boyle, D. (2003). The new mutualism and the meaning of time banks. *Local Economy, 18*, 253–270. https://doi.org/10.1080/0269094032000111048b

Brailly, J. (2016). Dynamics of networks in trade fairs: A multilevel relational approach to the cooperation among competitors. *Journal of Economic Geography, 16*, 1279–1301. https://doi. org/10.1093/jeg/lbw034

Burt, R. S. (1988). The stability of American markets. *American Journal of Sociology, 94*, 356–395. https://doi.org/10.1086/228995

Burt, R. S. (1992). *Structural holes: The social structure of competition*. Cambridge, MA: Harvard University Press.

Cahn, E. S., & Gray, C. (2015). The time bank solution. *Stanford Social Innovation Review, 13*(3), 40–45.

Cahn, E. S., & Rowe, J. (1992). *Time dollars: The new currency that enables Americans to turn their hidden resource time into personal security & community renewal*. Emmaus: Rodale.

Carnero, M. A., Martinez, B., & Sánchez-Mangas, R. (2015). Explaining transactions in time banks in economic crisis. *Applied Economics Letters, 22*, 739–744. https://doi.org/10.108 0/13504851.2014.975323

Clement, N., Holbrook, A., Forster, D., Macneil, J., Smith, M., Lyons, K., & McDonald, E. (2016). Timebanking, co-production and normative principles: Putting normative principles into practice. *International Journal of Community Currency Research, 21*, 36–52. https://doi. org/10.15133/j.ijccr.2017.004

Collom, E. (2005). Community currency in the United States: The social environments in which it emerges and survives. *Environment and Planning A, 37*, 1565–1587. https://doi. org/10.1068/a37172

Collom, E. (2008). Engagement of the elderly in time banking: The potential for social capital generation in an aging society. *Journal of Aging & Social Policy, 20*, 414–436. https://doi. org/10.1080/08959420802186282

Collom, E. (2012). Key indicators of time bank participation: Using transaction data for evaluation. *International Journal of Community Currency Research, 16*, 18–29. https://doi.org/10.15133/j. ijccr.2012.002

Collom, E., Lasker, J. N., & Kyriacou, C. (2012). *Equal time, equal value: Community currencies and time banking in the US*. London: Routledge. https://doi.org/10.4324/9781315580159

del Moral-Espín, L. (2017). Sharing is caring: Mediterranean time banking in a multidimensional crisis scenario. *International Journal of Community Currency Research, 21*, 33–50. Retrieved from https://ijccr.files.wordpress.com/2017/09/5-del-moral-003.pdf

Diprose, G. (2016). Negotiating interdependence and anxiety in community economies. *Environment and Planning A, 48*, 1411–1427. https://doi.org/10.1177/0308518X16638659

Dittmer, K. (2013). Local currencies for purposive degrowth? A quality check of some proposals for changing money-as-usual. *Journal of Cleaner Production, 54*, 3–13. https://doi. org/10.1016/j.jclepro.2013.03.044

Domínguez, S., & Hollstein, B. (Eds.). (2014). *Mixed methods social networks research: Design and applications*. Structural Analysis in the Social Sciences: Vol. 36. New York, NY: Cambridge University Press. https://doi.org/10.1017/CBO9781139227193

Doreian, P., Batagelj, V., & Ferligoj, A. (2005). *Generalized blockmodeling*. Structural Analysis in the Social Sciences: Vol. 25. Cambridge, UK: Cambridge University Press. https://doi. org/10.1017/CBO9780511584176

Faust, K. (1988). Comparison of methods for positional analysis: Structural and general equivalences. *Social Networks, 10,* 313–341. https://doi.org/10.1016/0378-8733(88)90002-0

Gabadinho, A., Ritschard, G., Müller, N. S., & Studer, M. (2011). Analyzing and visualizing state sequences in R with TraMineR. *Journal of Statistical Software, 40*(4). https://doi.org/10.18637/ jss.v040.i04

Gibson-Graham, J. K. (2008). Diverse economies: Performative practices for 'other worlds'. *Progress in Human Geography, 32,* 613–632. https://doi.org/10.1177/0309132508090821

Gibson-Graham, J. K. (2014). Rethinking the economy with thick description and weak theory. *Current Anthropology, 55*(S9), S147–S153. https://doi.org/10.1086/676646

Glückler, J. (2007). Economic geography and the evolution of networks. *Journal of Economic Geography, 7,* 619–634. https://doi.org/10.1093/jeg/lbm023

Glückler, J. (2013). Knowledge, networks and space: Connectivity and the problem of non-interactive learning. *Regional Studies, 47,* 880–894. https://doi.org/10.1080/0034340 4.2013.779659

Glückler, J., & Doreian, P. (2016). Editorial: Social network analysis and economic geography—positional, evolutionary and multi-level approaches. *Journal of Economic Geography, 16,* 1123–1134. https://doi.org/10.1093/jeg/lbw041

Glückler, J., Lazega, E., & Hammer, I. (Eds.). (2017). *Knowledge and networks.* Knowledge and Space: Vol. 11. Cham: Springer. https://doi.org/10.1007/978-3-319-45023-0

Glückler, J., & Panitz, R. (2016a). Relational upgrading in global value networks. *Journal of Economic Geography, 16,* 1161–1185. https://doi.org/10.1093/jeg/lbw033

Glückler, J., & Panitz, R. (2016b). Unpacking social divisions of labor in markets: Generalized blockmodeling and the network boom in stock photography. *Social Networks, 47,* 156–166. https://doi.org/10.1016/j.socnet.2016.07.002

Glückler, J., Panitz, R., & Hammer, I. (2020). SONA: A relational methodology to identify structure in networks. *Zeitschrift für Wirtschaftsgeographie, 64,* 121–133. https://doi.org/10.1515/ zfw-2020-0003

Granovetter, M. S. (1973). The strength of weak ties. *American Journal of Sociology, 78,* 1360–1380. https://doi.org/10.1086/225469

Granovetter, M. S. (1992). Problems of explanation in economic sociology. In N. Nohria & R. G. Eccles (Eds.), *Networks and organisations: Structure, form, and action* (pp. 25–56). Boston, MA: Harvard Business School Press.

Gregory, L. (2009). Spending time locally: The benefit of time banks for local economies. *Local Economy: The Journal of the Local Economy Policy Unit, 24,* 323–333. https://doi. org/10.1080/02690940903026852

Hayashi, M. (2012). Japan's Fureai Kippu time-banking in elderly care: Origins, development, challenges and impact. *International Journal of Community Currency Research, 16,* 30–44. https://doi.org/10.15133/j.ijccr.2012.003

Hoffmann, J., & Glückler, J. (2021). Evolution of a time bank: How navigation practices shape the structure of exchange under uncertainty. (Working Paper).

Lasker, J., Collom, E., Bealer, T., & Niclaus, E., Young Keefe, J., Kratzer, Z., Baldasari, L., Kramer, E., Mandeville, R., Schulman, J., Suchow, D., Letcher, A., Rogers, A., & Perlow, K. (2011). Time banking and health: The role of a community currency organization in enhancing well-being. *Health Promotion Practice, 12,* 102–115. https://doi.org/10.1177/1524839909353022

Lazega, E. (2016). Synchronization costs in the organizational society: Intermediary relational infrastructures in the dynamics of multilevel networks. In E. Lazega & T. A. B. Snijders (Eds.), *Multilevel network analysis for the social sciences: Theory, methods and applications* (pp. 47–77). Methodos Series (Methodological Prospects in the Social Sciences): Vol. 12. Cham: Springer. https://doi.org/10.1007/978-3-319-24520-1_3

Lazega, E. (2017). Organized mobility and relational turnover as context for social mechanisms: A dynamic invariant at the heart of stability from movement. In J. Glückler, E. Lazega, &

I. Hammer (Eds.), *Knowledge and networks* (pp. 119–142). Knowledge and Space: Vol. 11. Cham: Springer. https://doi.org/10.1007/978-3-319-45023-0_7

Lazega, E. (2018). Networks and institutionalization: A neo-structural approach. *Connections, 37,* 7–22. https://doi.org/10.21307/connections-2017-001

Lazega, E., Sapulete, S., & Mounier, L. (2011). Structural stability regardless of membership turnover? The added value of blockmodelling in the analysis of network evolution. *Quality & Quantity, 45,* 129–144. https://doi.org/10.1007/s11135-009-9295-y

Lazega, E., & Snijders, T. A. B. (Eds.). (2016). *Multilevel network analysis for the social sciences: Theory, methods and applications.* Methodos Series (Methodological Prospects in the Social Sciences): Vol. 12. Cham: Springer. https://doi.org/10.1007/978-3-319-24520-1

Meier, D. (2001). *Tauschringe als besondere Bewertungssysteme in der Schattenwirtschaft: Eine theoretische und empirische Analyse* [Time banks as specific evaluation systems in the informal economy: A theoretical and empirical analysis]. Beiträge zur Verhaltensforschung: Vol. 41. Berlin: Duncker & Humblot. https://doi.org/10.3790/978-3-428-50210-3

Mitchell, J. C. (1969). The concept and use of social networks. In J. C. Mitchell (Ed.), *Social networks in urban situations: Analyses of personal relationships in Central African towns* (pp. 1–50). Manchester, UK: Manchester University Press.

Nomaler, Ö., & Verspagen, B. (2016). River deep, mountain high: Of long-run knowledge trajectories within and between innovation clusters. *Journal of Economic Geography, 16,* 1259–1278. https://doi.org/10.1093/jeg/lbw035

Ozanne, L. K. (2010). Learning to exchange time: Benefits and obstacles to time banking. *International Journal of Community Currency Research, 14,* 1–16. https://doi.org/10.15133/j.ijccr.2010.002

Pachucki, M. A., & Breiger, R. L. (2010). Cultural holes: Beyond relationality in social networks and culture. *Annual Review of Sociology, 36,* 205–224. https://doi.org/10.1146/annurev.soc.012809.102615

Perrow, C. (1991). A society of organizations. *Theory and Society, 20,* 725–762. https://doi.org/10.1007/bf00678095

Polanyi, K. (1944). *The great transformation: The political and economic origins of our time.* Boston: Beacon.

Prota, L. (2016). Toward a polanyian network analysis: Market and non-market forms of coordination in the rice economy of Vietnam. *Journal of Economic Geography, 16,* 1135–1160. https://doi.org/10.1093/jeg/lbw039

Sánchez-Hernández, J. L. (2017). *Las prácticas económicas alternativas en perspectiva geográfica* [Alternative economic practices in geographical perspective]. Salamanca, Spain: Universidad de Salamanca.

Sánchez-Hernández, J. L., & Glückler, J. (2019). Alternative economic practices in Spanish cities: From grassroots movements to urban policies? An institutional perspective. *European Planning Studies, 27,* 2450–2469. https://doi.org/10.1080/09654313.2019.1644295

Seyfang, G. (2001). Community currencies: Small change for a green economy. *Environment and Planning A, 33,* 975–996. https://doi.org/10.1068/a33216

Seyfang, G. (2003a). Growing cohesive communities one favour at a time: Social exclusion, active citizenship and time banks. *International Journal of Urban and Regional Research, 27,* 699–706. https://doi.org/10.1111/1468-2427.00475

Seyfang, G. (2003b). 'With a little help from my friends': Evaluating time banks as a tool for community self-help. *Local Economy, 18,* 257–264. https://doi.org/10.1080/0269094032000111048c

Seyfang, G. (2004). Working outside the box: Community currencies, time banks and social inclusion. *Journal of Social Policy, 33,* 49–71. https://doi.org/10.1017/S0047279403007232

Seyfang, G., & Longhurst, N. (2013). Growing green money? Mapping community currencies for sustainable development. *Ecological Economics, 86,* 65–77. https://doi.org/10.1016/j.ecolecon.2012.11.003

Small, M. L. (2011). How to conduct a mixed methods study: Recent trends in a rapidly growing literature. *Annual Review of Sociology, 37,* 57–86. https://doi.org/10.1146/annurev.soc.012809.102657

Stuart, C. (2003). "All you need is love"? Assessing time banks as a tool for sustainable economic development. *Local Economy: The Journal of the Local Economy Policy Unit, 18,* 264–267. https://doi.org/10.1080/0269094032000111048d

ter Wal, A. L. J., & Boschma, R. A. (2009). Applying social network analysis in economic geography: Framing some key analytic issues. *The Annals of Regional Science, 43,* 739–756. https://doi.org/10.1007/s00168-008-0258-3

Thrift, N. (2002). The future of geography. *Geoforum, 33,* 291–298. https://doi.org/10.1016/S0016-7185(02)00019-2

Uzzi, B., & Spiro, J. (2005). Collaboration and creativity: The small world problem. *American Journal of Sociology, 111,* 447–504. https://doi.org/10.1086/432782

Valor, C., & Papaoikonomou, E. (2016). Time banking in Spain: Exploring their structure, management and users' profile. *Revista Internacional de Sociología, 74,* e028. https://doi.org/10.3989/ris.2016.74.1.028

Vedres, B., & Stark, D. (2010). Structural folds: Generative disruption in overlapping groups. *American Journal of Sociology, 115,* 1150–1190. https://doi.org/10.1086/649497

Wasserman, S., & Faust, K. (1994). *Social network analysis: Methods and applications.* Structural Analysis in the Social Sciences: Vol. 8. Cambridge, UK: Cambridge University Press. https://doi.org/10.1017/CBO9780511815478

Whitham, M. M., & Clarke, H. (2016). Getting is giving: Time banking as formalized generalized exchange. *Sociology Compass, 10,* 87–97. https://doi.org/10.1111/soc4.12343

Williams, C. C., Aldridge, T., Lee, R., Leyshon, A., Thrift, N., & Tooke, J. (2001). Bridges into work? An evaluation of local exchange and trading schemes (LETS). *Policy Studies, 22,* 119–132. https://doi.org/10.1080/01442870120096367

Zhang, X., Martin, T., & Newman, M. E. J. (2015). Identification of core-periphery structure in networks. *Physical Review E, 91,* 1–10. https://doi.org/10.1103/PhysRevE.91.03280

Part III
Spaces, Networks and Fields

Chapter 8
Civil Society as Networks of Issues and Associations: The Case of Food

Mario Diani, Henrik Ernstson, and Lorien Jasny

Civil Society: Aggregative Versus Relational Perspectives

In this chapter, we provide an empirical illustration of how to apply a relational approach to the study of civil society. By this we mean an approach with which one can combine attention to the traits of civil society actors *and* to the relations between them, and use network data to explain and understand civil society, its collective processes, and its role in wider society. Such an integrated approach has not proved easy to develop, as we are striving to combine two fundamental dimensions of civil society, its communicative and organizational ones. In contrast, most analysts have either focused on the communicative/ideational elements (e.g., Alexander, 2006; Seligman, 1995) or the organizational/associational ones (e.g., Maloney & van Deth, 2008, 2010; for more discussions on defining civil society, see Calhoun, 2001; Edwards, 2004). Among the former approaches, analysts have portrayed civil society primarily as a discursive space, delineated by the communicative practices through which core societal values are defined, criteria of civility are established, collective goals are formulated, and collective identities are constructed (e.g.,

An earlier version of this paper was presented at the 12th Organizational Studies Workshop on "Food Organizing Matters," Chania, Crete, May 18th–20th, 2017.

M. Diani (✉)
Department of Sociology and Social Research, University of Trento, Trento, Italy
e-mail: mario.diani@unitn.it

H. Ernstson
Centre for Public Policy Research, School of Education, Communication and Society, King's College London, London, UK
e-mail: henrik.ernstson@manchester.ac.uk

L. Jasny
Department of Politics, University of Exeter, Exeter, UK
e-mail: L.Jasny@exeter.ac.uk

J. Glückler et al. (eds.), *Knowledge and Civil Society*, Knowledge and Space 17,
https://doi.org/10.1007/978-3-030-71147-4_8

Alexander, 2006; Habermas, 1989). In the latter group, researchers have largely equated civil society to voluntary organizations' contributions to the development of political capacity, the strengthening of social cohesion and the quality of democratic life, and the definition and production of collective goods (Anheier, 2004, 2007; Deakin, 2001; Maloney & van Deth, 2010).

These standard approaches share a further underlying problem for empirical research, namely, what we have called an "aggregative approach" to collective processes (Diani, 2015, Chap. 1). Researchers have often tended to treat civil society as a set of aggregated *a priori* properties or "traits," frequently adhering to formal definitions of civility, by which different actors and organizations are said to be defined. Following this logic, they then describe the structure of civil society as the distribution of such actors' traits, and gauge the strength of civil society in reference to the number of citizens who, for instance, value tolerance, rational debate, and the pursuit of the common good over private gain, those who express their trust in institutions (e.g., Norris & Inglehart, 2002; Putnam, 2000) or promote collective action on public issues (Maloney & Roßteutscher, 2006; Maloney & van Deth, 2010). Unquestionably, aggregative approaches have generated important insights. Yet, this has often been detrimental to the analysis of how the same actors relate to each other in complex patterns (for exceptions, see: Anheier & Themudo, 2002; Knoke & Wood, 1981; Laumann & Pappi, 1976).

In this chapter, we sketch the contours of a relational approach to civil society with which we attempt to address both difficulties: how to better integrate ideational and associational dimensions of civil society, and how to focus on the relational structures between civil society actors, rather than simply on their traits. Building on our previous work (Diani, 2015; Diani, Ernstson, & Jasny, 2018), we rely on social network analysis (henceforth, SNA) to explore civil society as a set of (a) multiple networks connecting a multiplicity of collective agents and (b) ideational elements that assign a specific meaning to collective action.[1]

SNA provides a number of methodological tools to explore the connections between different elements of a population (Borgatti, Everett, & Johnson, 2013; Kadushin, 2012; Knoke & Yang, 2008). In contrast to standard statistical techniques, it does not require independence of cases; to the contrary, its utilizers focus on such cases' interdependencies. Accordingly, civil-society analysts are able to go beyond the properties of civic agents to instead focus on the relations between them. Not only that: researchers may apply SNA to map the connections between non-agentic ideational elements, including symbols, words, concepts, or other cultural products (e.g., Carley, 1994; Diesner & Carley, 2011). Even network analysts have not commonly linked agents and ideas; most have focused either on networks of exchanges between specific organizations, or on networks of ideational elements (Ferguson, Groenewegen, Moser, Borgatti, & Mohr, 2017), with less genuine

---

[1] See Diani (1995), Ernstson (2011), and Bassoli and Theiss (2014) for additional examples of this logic of analysis, covering specific civic networks in Italy, Sweden, and Poland.

integration of these two levels (for exceptions: Basov & Brennecke, 2017; Oberg, Korff & Powell, 2017; von Atteveldt, Moser, & Welbers, 2017).

In our social network study, agents corresponded to large sets of voluntary organizations in three different cities, which all mobilized around variable combinations of service delivery and political advocacy. We conceived the ideational elements as issue priorities identified by those same agents. Admittedly, "issue priorities" might be regarded as a poor, partial proxy for cultural and ideational elements. However, claims about the issues that organizations regard as of primary relevance for them should not be dismissed as the mere identification of specific problems or the target of fleeting initiatives. Rather, surveying how each actor ranks issues' relevance provides a core indicator of how organizations position themselves in the context of larger collective action fields—in other words, of how they distribute and prioritize scarce internal resources, or represent their activities to members, potential members, and the larger public. Furthermore, we approach issue priorities in relational terms, unpacking how issues never have single, uncontroversial meanings. To the contrary, and following a now consolidated tradition in the study of culture (DiMaggio, 1987; Mohr, 1998; Mohr & Duquenne, 1997), issues may be subject to different interpretations by different agents, depending on the symbolic context in which they are embedded, just like other cultural elements such as attitudes or beliefs. For example, concerns about the issue of urban pollution may take a very different meaning if actors connect it to global environmental problems than to upper-middle class concerns about status and urban lifestyle. By sampling a wider set of actors, researchers can unpack such contrasting interpretations through a relational network approach. Indeed, a strength with our approach is that we can identify how a sub-set of issues are central to a sub-set of civil society agents, with which we can in turn explain how issues are interconnected by those mobilizing on them, how single issues are woven into broader agendas, and how cultural frames for collective action (Snow, 2004; Snow, Rochford, Worden, & Benford, 1986) emerge out of the interaction between actors and issues.

Although civic organizations may be regarded as connectors between issues, issues may likewise be regarded as facilitators or obstacles to the activation of links between organizations. Accordingly, one might be led to believe that issues mapped on to organizing patterns, with organizations sharing some issues being automatically connected in distinctive, dense clusters of relations. However, reality has proven more complicated, with the authors of one study on civic-organization networks in British cities suggesting that although the presence or absence of the traditional traits of protest organizations did characterize specific network positions in some cities, this what not the case in others (Diani, 2015). Thus, whether identification with a set issues (or lack of it) creates boundaries that facilitate or discourage organizational alliances (Tilly, 2005) becomes a matter for empirical investigation. With our relational approach, we respond to this task in how we analyze issue priorities and network patterns. Rather than distinct and neat clusters of collaborative organizations that all share the same issues, what we can uncover is a more nuanced story of how civil society organizations create deeper-lying "modes of coordination" (Diani, 2015) that cut across the boundaries of specific groups or associations and develop complex cooperative networks on themes of common interest.

Our case study in this chapter is food, as it provides a good starting point to explore how civic organizations combine an interest in relatively specific issues with attention to other themes. We then explore if and how an interest in food defines specific clusters of cooperation within broader civil society networks (Levkoe, 2014; Levkoe & Wakefield, 2014; Luxton & Sbicca, 2021; Sumner & Wever, 2015). In doing so, we draw upon data from urban settings as diverse as Cape Town in South Africa and Bristol and Glasgow in the UK. This enables us to conduct a rare comparative analysis of organizational networks,[2] in contexts that differ substantially in terms of urban inequality as well as in the salience of major political cleavages.

Exploring Civil Society in British and South African Cities

Our evidence comes from two projects, "Networks of Civic Organizations in Britain," conducted in Bristol and Glasgow between 2001 and 2003,[3] and "Socioecological Movements and Transformative Collective Action in Urban Ecosystems," conducted in Cape Town between 2012 and 2014.[4] Admittedly, these data are far from recent. As we will point out in the discussion of our findings, the specific local agendas may well have changed substantially since data were collected. Still, we do not regard this as a problem, because this article is not an account of contemporary urban dynamics and should not be taken as such. Rather, we are illustrating an approach—and a method—to integrate the cultural and organizational dimensions of civil society. In such a context, data at different points in time can be useful, if they help analysts to explore network mechanisms in polities that differ on theoretically relevant grounds. In our case, this means looking at networks in settings with different levels of democratic consolidation and cleavage salience. In this regard, an exploration of South African and British cities may be treated as a most dissimilar design comparison (Dogan & Pélassy, 1984), despite their sharing a relatively similar institutional system by virtue of South Africa's colonial past as part of the Commonwealth. On a smaller scale, significant differences in opportunities for civic activism may also be found between British cities, although they may appear quite homogeneous by comparison to urban areas elsewhere in the world (Diani 2015, pp. 46–47, pp. 194–198).

---

[2]Examples of comparative analyses of social networks include Eggert (2014); Entwisle, Faust, Rindfuss, and Kaneda (2007); Fischer (2011).

[3]Funded by UK's Economic and Social Research Council (contract L215 25 2006) with Mario Diani as PI.

[4]Funded by the Swedish Research Council Formas (contract 211–2011–1519) with Henrik Ernstson as PI.

In relation to our particular focus, three dimensions are worth pointing out. First, although inequality has risen consistently across the globe in the last few decades, the depth of social divisions and their embeddedness in race and class have historical and deeper patterns in South Africa (Maharaj, 2020; Seekings, 2000). The country often scores among the most unequal countries in the world according to the Gini index, which has continued to deteriorate under the African National Congress (ANC) government, especially since its neo-liberal policy turn in the late 1990s (Ballard, Habib, Valodia, & Zuern, 2006b, pp. 13–14), and further under Zuma's presidency 2009–2018.[5] As for UK cities, despite a common shift from an industrial to a service economy, inequality and deprivation were still more pronounced in Glasgow than in Bristol at the time of the study (Diani, 2015, p. 30).

Second, the salience of main political cleavages differed as well: in South Africa, proximity to or distance from the dominant ANC party and its partners in the so-called tripartite alliance (Sanco, the federation of anti-apartheid civic organizations, and Cosatu, the unions' confederation) shaped the city's alliance patterns (Diani, Ernstson, & Jasny, 2018; this despite ANC having lost Cape Town to its rivals since 2006). The same applied in a significant way to organizations close to or distant from Glasgow's Labour party (the study was conducted before the growth of the Scottish National Party), although this was not the case in Bristol, where lines of political identification were multiple and not as consolidated (Baldassarri & Diani, 2007, p. 752).

The third important element to consider was the variable weight of contentious repertoires of action in the three cities. The most significant differences lay between the UK and South Africa, with the latter displaying exceptionally high levels of radical contention (Ballard, Habib, & Valodia, 2006a; McFarlane & Silver, 2017; Mottiar & Bond, 2012). This may be at least partially due not only to the stronger salience of cleavages in that country, but also to ANC's electoral domination, akin to a one-party rule, coupled with the legitimacy gained by ANC, given its role in anti-apartheid struggles. This has, especially in the early post apartheid period from 1994 to around 2010, made it recognizably harder to build wider multi-sectoral popular platforms outside the tripartite alliance to link local protests into a broader national opposition of ANC's neoliberal policies (Ballard, Habib, & Valodia, 2006a).[6] Accordingly, the radicalization of repertoires of action may be related to a

---

[5] The Southern African Labour and Development Research Institute reported that between 1993 and 2008, the Gini coefficient increased from 0.66 to 0.70, surpassing Brazil, with the income of the average black person actually falling as a percentage of the average white person from 1995 (13.5%) to 2008 (13%), with even worse poverty figures recorded in urban areas (Bond, 2011, p. 113).

[6] We recognize national one-issue campaigns, such as the successful Treatment Action Campaign from 1998 for free access to treatment for HIV/Aids. We also note how the political party situation is changing in South Africa; although ANC's dominance in 2019's general election was still intact at the national and most regional levels, they had lost Cape Town by 2006 and Western Cape by 2011 to their conservative-liberal rival, the Democratic Alliance, and lost several more metropolitan regions in 2016 and 2019. The emergence of a left-wing opposition in the Economic Freedom Fighters is also interesting, gaining almost 11% in 2019.

lingering lack of political opportunities for challenging groups, and their shortage of political resources, beyond the very local level (on radicalization, see e.g., Alimi, Demetriou, & Bosi, 2015). As for the UK, the continued perception of Glasgow's civil society as more confrontational than Bristol depended to a large measure on the stronger ties between protest organizations in Scotland than in the South-West of England (Diani, 2012, 2015, Chap. 9).

The depth of social divisions, the salience of major cleavages, and the variation in action repertoires may all affect the structure of alliances within civil society (Diani, 1995, 2015). They may similarly influence the way in which issues are shaped and connected to each other. Food represents a notable case to illustrate these mechanisms. Like many large and multi-dimensional issues, it has been associated to quite different agendas and represents a focus of mobilization for highly diverse actors and coalitions. It may be part of classic environmental agendas, linking actions on the environmental impact of food production to the protection of the natural environment mainly based in a (new) middle class and moderate perspectives; but it may also be strongly connected to approaches focusing on inequality and social deprivation within affluent societies, possibly from a "right-to-the-city" perspective, as well as to global justice proponents arguing for a radical change in the relationship between food corporations and the small producers in the global south. Interest in food may drive attempts to transform the behavior of individual consumers and consolidate new markets, but it can also provide the basis for collective actions oriented to the practice of alternative lifestyles, as exemplified by environmental groups supporting food-growing allotment gardens in seeking a greener, more self-sustaining urban lifestyle. Attention to food as a public issue may be found across major political cleavages, involving quite diverse actors, from left-wing radical groups—as was historically the case with Black Panthers in US cities, who developed the Free Breakfast for Children programs as a mode of fighting structural injustice—all the way to liberal, conservative, and religious groups supporting charity "food banks" (Barthel, Parker, & Ernstson, 2013; Battersby & Haysom, 2019; Cherry, 2006; Forno, 2019; Halkier, 2019; Herring, 2014; Jallinoja, Vinnari, & Niva, 2019).

We collected our data among organizations that combined in a variable measure interest in social and ecological issues. In the UK, they focused on three main types of issues: environment, social exclusion and inequality, and minorities and migrants. Given the impossibility of mapping the whole of civil society, those issues were chosen because (a) they provided a sufficiently broad illustration of core urban problems and (b) they were distinct enough to be the target of specific campaigns or even nimby activism, yet could also serve to link into broader, more encompassing agendas. Apart from the major organizations operating on a city-wide scale, groups included in the study came from relatively deprived areas of the two cities: the Southside in Glasgow, characterized by a massive historical presence of working class, including neighborhoods such as Govan, Govanhill, Gorbals, and Pollokshields; and the neighborhoods of Easton, Knowles, Withywood, and Hartcliffe in Bristol, featuring a strong presence of ethnic minorities. Altogether,

124 organizations in Glasgow and 134 in Bristol were included in the study (Diani, 2015, Chap. 2).

The Cape Town study was part of a larger research program on urban ecology and urban political ecology (Ernstson, 2011, 2013; Ernstson & Sörlin 2019; Lawhon, Ernstson, & Silver, 2014), in which researchers conceived the urban environment broadly to include both ecological as well as social issues. The organizations surveyed ranged from classic environmental groups working on conservation issues to action committees addressing fundamental environmental justice themes such as access to energy, sanitation, and health, as well as the quality of food and housing. Barring the limited attention to migrants' rights, the themes addressed by civic organizations in Cape Town are otherwise largely comparable to those addressed by UK civic organizations. Complete data were collected for 129 organizations in Cape Town, once again located in areas with a very diverse socio-economic status, from affluent Constantia to environmentally and socially deprived areas of Cape Flats (Diani, Ernstson, & Jasny, 2018).

In all three cities, respondents were asked to identify their priorities out of a long list of issues (about 50 issues in the UK, 30 in Cape Town), among which those linked to food attracted considerable attention (Table 8.1). In both Bristol and Glasgow, about one organization out of five expressed an interest in generic food issues, and a similar share combined this with a more specific attention to genetically modified food (henceforth, GM). In Cape Town, the wording of the issues was different, and so was the distribution of responses: 30% of organizations claimed an interest in "urban farming and food security," but only three in GM food. Coupled with the fact that two of those groups also claimed an interest in the former, this low figure resulted in the Cape Town analysis only differentiating between organizations interested or uninterested in food issues, without further qualification.

How did interest in food relate to other issues? As a preliminary step, we submitted the list of items in the three cities to a standard data reduction technique, principal component analysis (henceforth, PCA). In Bristol and Glasgow, we thus identified five underlying dimensions, which we labeled *social exclusion, environment, minority citizenship, global justice*, and *housing* (Diani, 2015, pp. 41–42; see also Table 8.11 in the appendix for details); in Cape Town, we identified four dimensions, grouping together issues linked to *global environmental justice, urban conservation, right to the city*, and issues aligned along the alternative between *urban sustainability* (i.e., a managerial approach to urban issues) and *social rights* (Diani,

Table 8.1 Interest in food-related issues

	Bristol	Glasgow	Cape Town
No interest	62%	62%	70%
Interest in generic food issues, but not GM food	20%	16%	
Interest in both generic food issues and GM food	18%	22%	
Interest in urban farming and food security			30%
N	134	124	129

Note. Source: Design by authors

Ernstson, & Jasny, 2018; see also Table 8.12 in the appendix). We then proceeded to build networks of issues. We assumed a connection between two issues if a relatively high number of organizations indicated both among their priorities. We calculated the link's strength through the Jaccard coefficient (Borgatti & Halgin, 2011, p. 421), which takes into account the fact that the strength of the connection between pairs of issues, sharing the same number of organizations interested in them, may actually be quite diverse, depending on the ties such issues may have to other issues. For example, the fact that ten organizations claimed an interest in both GM food and, say, animal rights would imply quite a different tie strength between the two if there were no organizations claiming an interest in GM food and urban pollution or environmental protection (or any other issue) than if many such existed. More specifically, we concentrated on the strongest ties, defined as those at least one standard deviation above the average strength of ties in any specific network. In the figures that follow, color and shape of nodes will correspond to the different sets of issues, identified through principal component analysis. This will offer us a preliminary way to start unpacking the two fundamental dimensions of civil society, its communicative and organizational dimensions, which we can now operationalize through comparing two criteria of group issues together in our data: correlation in the case of PCA, and co-occurrences in the issue networks.

The Structure of Issue Networks: Insights into the Discursive Space Produced by Civil Society

Starting with the Bristol case, the graph of the strongest connections between issues (Fig. 8.1) well matches the sets identified by PCA (Table 8.11 in the appendix): a set of environmental issues, which includes food along with nature conservation, pollution, forestry, energy, and transport among others, can be seen on the bottom right of the graph (white squares), whereas minority and migrants' issues are on the left side (green triangles) and social deprivation (black triangles) and housing issues (white circles) are mostly at the network center. The only set of themes lacking a clear network position were those broadly associated with global justice (black circles); although correlated, they did not display consistently strong ties to each other. Interestingly, organizational representatives perceived GM food issues as connected to global justice themes (probably a reflection of their role in conflicts between strong corporations and producers in the global South) rather than to environmental ones, as was the case with generic food themes. However, even that connection does not appear to be particularly robust, as in terms of strong ties GM food was rather distinctive. This does not imply its marginality in local civil society, as interest in the theme was quite significant (see Table 8.1). Rather, it illustrates the difficulty to locate it within a specific discourse or a specific agenda.

The position of generic food issues was quite different, as we show in Fig. 8.2, reporting their ego-network. On the one hand, Bristolian organizations perceived

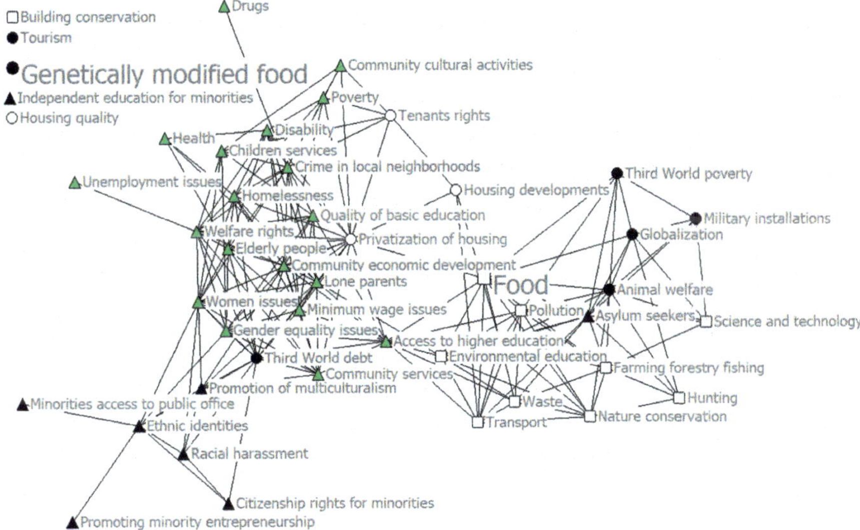

Fig. 8.1 Issue network in Bristol (cut off point 0.41, one s.d. above mean). Green triangles: inequality and deprivation issues; black triangles: minorities and migrants' issues; black circles: global justice issues; white squares: environmental issues; white circles: housing issues. Source: Design by authors

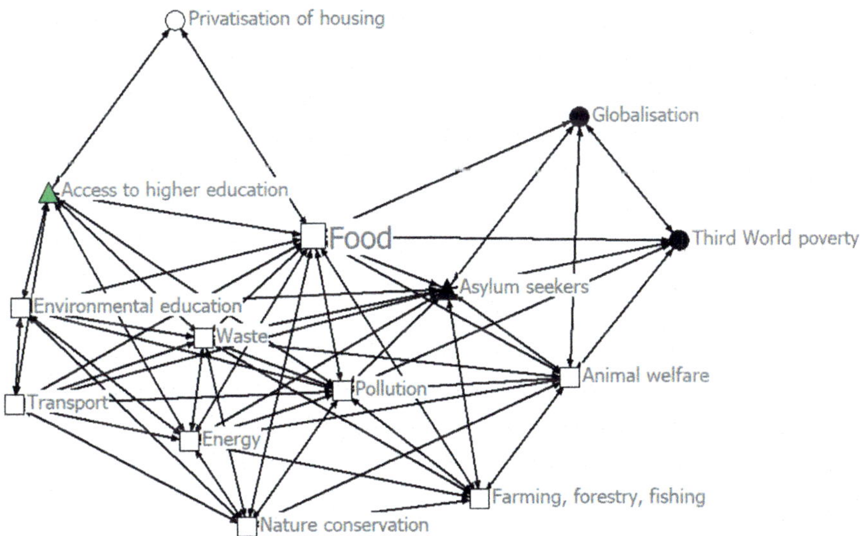

Fig. 8.2 Ego-network of food issues in Bristol (cut off point 0.41, one s.d. above mean). Green triangles: inequality and deprivation issues; black triangles: minorities and migrants' issues; black circles: global justice issues; white squares: environmental issues; white circles: housing issues. Source: Design by authors

food as strongly connected to a broad range of environmental issues; on the other, they also assigned it some significant connections to social issues, such as access to higher education and housing, or globalization and migration dynamics. Apart from being embedded in distinctive sets of issues, food issues were also highly central in the whole issue network. In Table 8.2, we report two standard centrality measures, degree and betweenness.[7] Out of 49 issues, food ranked eighth in terms of degree, with thirteen other issues being strongly connected to it (about one standard deviation above the average of eight); it was even more central in terms of betweenness, part of a very small set of issues with particularly high scores on that particular measure. As we also show in Fig. 8.1, food was often in an intermediate position on the paths connecting other issues in the network. We take this as a signal of how food could play a central role in constructing wider frames for collective action.

Based on the structure of the issue network in Glasgow, we believe that foods occupies a more distinct and far less central position here than in Bristol, despite its overall popularity among civic organizations being very similar (Fig. 8.3). In Glasgow, food was part of a distinct component of the network, detached from the main one, and only consisting of three other heavily correlated issues: animal welfare, hunting, and science and technology. As for GM food, it was as isolated as in Bristol, at least in terms of strong connections, yet in a context in which most themes correlated with ideas of "global justice"—and indeed of environmentalism as well—were peripheral to the network. The other two components, distinct from the main one, again consisted of environmental themes (transport and energy) and those linked to global justice (globalization, Third World poverty, and asylum seekers). Social issues related to deprivation and community development, housing, and minority rights heavily dominated the main component. Similar considerations apply to the analysis of issue centrality. In both cities, most central issues referred to inequality and social exclusion. However, many central issues in Bristol also referred to environmental and global justice problems. This did not happen in Glasgow, where food was not among the most central issues (Table 8.3). In a nutshell, although similarly relevant in terms of appeal, food issues occupied very different positions in the two cities. In Bristol, they were at the intersection of several different agendas, combining different sets of issues; in Glasgow, they were strongly related to a small, distinctive set of themes, which combined in a very specific agenda.

Moving to the issue network in Cape Town provides still a different account of the position of food-related issues. It is not, it has to be said, a fully comparable account, as the list of issues submitted to organization representatives was different, and reflective of the project's focus. In particular, whereas in Britain the reference was to generic "food issues," in Cape Town it was more specific, to "urban farming and food security" (GM food was also represented, as in Britain). As a consequence, the search for macro-issues generates partially different factors from the ones

---

[7] "Degree" consists of the number of direct connections (adjacencies) one node in a network has to other network members; "betweenness" measures the extent to which one node is located in an intermediate position on the shortest paths (geodesics) connecting other nodes (Knoke & Yang, 2008, pp. 62–69).

Table 8.2 Centrality of issues in Bristol (network dichotomized at 0.41 cutoff; issues marked by an asterisk are central in both UK cities)

	Degree	Norm degree	Betweenness
Privatization of housing*	18	0.37	209.96
Third World debt	15	0.31	100.19
Crime in local neighborhoods*	15	0.31	61.48
Community economic development*	15	0.31	22.87
Access to higher education	14	0.29	177.17
Single parents*	14	0.29	72.15
Women's issues*	14	0.29	51.15
Food	13	0.27	172.70
Asylum seekers	13	0.27	50.70
Welfare rights*	13	0.27	49.19
Elderly people*	13	0.27	12.01
Minimum wage*	13	0.27	8.50
Gender equality*	12	0.24	48.08
Animal welfare	12	0.24	27.25
Homelessness*	12	0.24	11.23
Energy	11	0.22	27.25
Pollution	11	0.22	23.09
Community services*	11	0.22	7.46
GM food	0	0.00	0.00

Note. Source: Design by authors

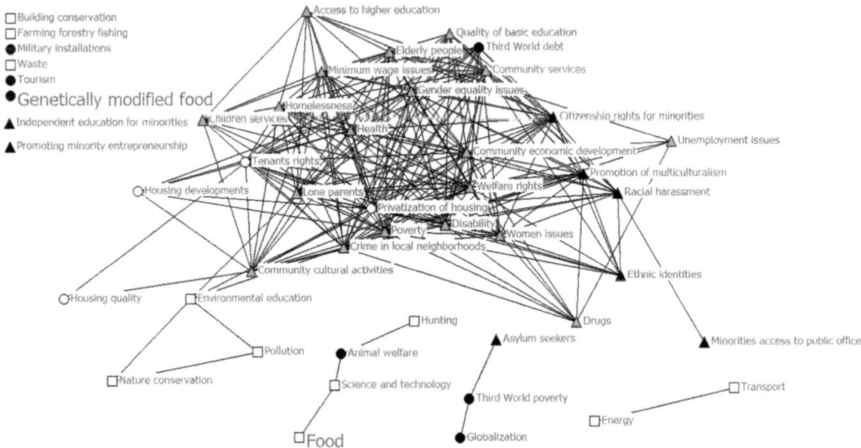

Fig. 8.3 Issue network in Glasgow (cut off point 0.451, one s.d. above mean). Green triangles: inequality and deprivation issues; black triangles: minorities and migrants' issues; black circles: global justice issues; white squares: environmental issues; white circles: housing issues. Source: Design by authors

Table 8.3 Centrality of issues in Glasgow (network dichotomized at 0.51 cutoff; issues marked by an asterisk are central in both UK cities)

	Degree	Norm degree	Betweenness
Privatization of housing*	25	0.51	50.61
Poverty	24	0.49	16.53
Disability	23	0.47	11.66
Crime in local neighborhoods*	22	0.45	36.28
Community economic development*	22	0.45	14.83
Welfare rights*	22	0.45	13.79
Single parents*	20	0.41	22.68
Health	20	0.41	10.30
Elderly people*	20	0.41	8.26
Women's issues*	20	0.41	6.64
Citizenship rights for minorities	19	0.39	4.95
Minimum wage*	19	0.39	2.97
Tenant's rights	18	0.37	19.74
Gender equality*	18	0.37	5.75
Community services*	18	0.37	4.78
Homelessness*	17	0.35	2.79
Food	1	0.02	0.00
GM food	0	0.00	0.00

Note. Source: Design by authors

identified in Britain (see Fig. 8.4): Whereas "urban conservation" and "global environmental justice" broadly correspond to the "environmental" and "global justice" factors in the UK, in Cape Town social inequality and community development issues combined under two different headings: one labeled "social rights," addressing labor, gender, and youth conditions as well as health, and another labeled "right to the city," combining community development issues with claims for the strengthening of urban democracy (Diani, Ernstson, & Jasny, 2018). In Cape Town, the issue network was split into two different components, one consisting of "global justice" issues, which included GM food (similarly to the UK), and another in which "right to the city" seemed to provide a bridge between "urban environmental conservation" and "social rights" themes.

The centrality of the "urban farming and food security" issue closely matched that of generic food issues in Bristol in terms of the overall volume of connections, as the normalized degree scores were very similar (0.27 in Bristol vs. 0.23 in Cape Town: Table 8.4). However, the issue's capacity to connect other types of themes and discourses seemed very limited, as its betweenness score was extremely low. It was, in fact, even lower than that of GM food, despite the latter's peripheral position within a component limited to global justice issues (Fig. 8.4). The explanation for this apparent paradox lies in the structure of the ego-network of food security issues (Fig. 8.5): Although it was of a comparable size to the Bristolian one, it was more homogenous, consisting almost exclusively of other environmental issues, and most importantly, highly dense. This substantially reduced betweenness scores,

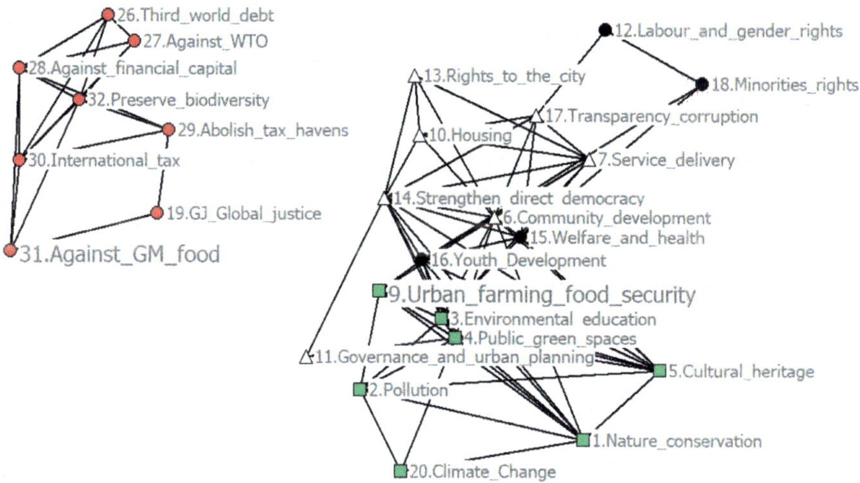

Fig. 8.4 Issue network in Cape Town (cut off point 0.21, one s.d. above mean). Red circles: global environmental justice issues; green squares: urban conservation issues; black circles: social rights issues; white triangles: right to the city issues. Source: Design by authors

Table 8.4 Centrality of issues in Cape Town (network dichotomized at 0.21 cutoff)

	Degree	Normalized degree	Betweenness
Strengthen direct democracy	12	0.39	22.70
Community development	12	0.39	18.12
Public green spaces	10	0.32	13.38
Youth development	10	0.32	13.12
Environmental education	10	0.32	6.12
Nature conservation	9	0.29	7.55
Cultural heritage	9	0.29	3.42
Welfare and health	8	0.26	6.76
Service delivery	8	0.26	4.00
International tax	7	0.23	10.92
Urban farming and food security	7	0.23	0.93
Transparency corruption	6	0.19	11.40
Against financial capital	6	0.19	2.92
Preserve biodiversity	6	0.19	2.92
Pollution	6	0.19	1.28
GM food	4	0.13	6.00

Note. Source: Design by authors

suggesting that food issues be primarily contained within a fairly specific environmental discourse.

A few comparative comments may be in order before shifting the focus to the relationship between food issues and alliance structures. First, the popularity of GM

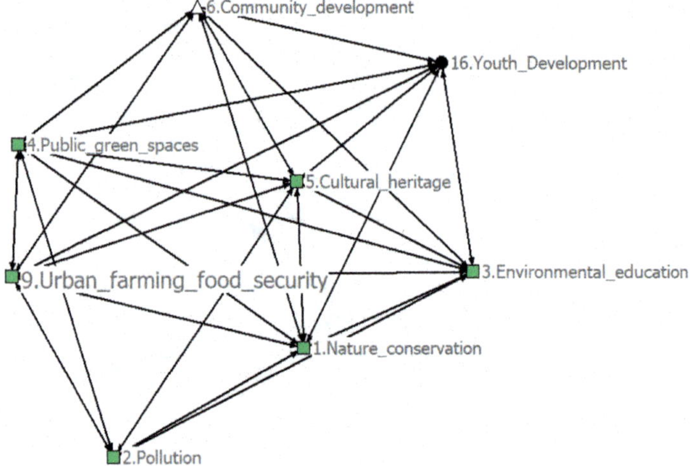

Fig. 8.5 Ego-network of Food security issues in Cape Town (cut off point 0.21, one s.d. above mean) Green squares: urban conservation issues; black circles: socialrights issues; white triangles: Right to the city issues. Source: Design by authors

food issues differed substantially, being high in the two British cities and very low in Cape Town (although the size of that difference may have been partially due to differences in research design). When it comes to embeddedness in broader agendas, however, the only meaningful cluster of issues comprising GM food was actually found in Cape Town, in the context of global environmental justice initiatives. In Bristol and Glasgow, GM food seemed to stand out as an issue with a peculiar profile, that was difficult to connect systematically to one specific agenda. The three cities were more similar in the popularity of other food issues (generically defined in the UK study, linked to urban farming in the case of Cape Town), with 30% to 40% of organizations claiming an interest in them. However, the three cities differed substantially in the centrality of food issues in relation to broader agendas. In Glasgow, these were part of an isolated component. In Cape Town, they had high centrality, but this depended largely on their embeddedness in environmental agendas, and was not matched by strong links to other issues. Only in Bristol did they seem to play a central role in establishing connections between different agendas within civil society. The finding about Cape Town is particularly intriguing: given the city's high levels of deprivation, one might have expected a stronger connection between food and social inequality issues. This would also be consistent with the very high number of groups and organizations that were documented to be active on food issues just after our fieldwork (Battersby et al., 2014), a paradox we will return to in the conclusions.

The Structure of Alliance Networks: Insights into the Associational Space Produced by Civil Society

In the previous section we explored the connections that organizations create between different issues by including them among their priorities. Here we reverse the perspective and ask if and to what extent organizations interested in food-related issues occupied distinctive positions within civil society networks. In the case of the UK, one can differentiate between organizations that did not identify food as a priority, those who were interested in generic food issues, and those who combined such interest with a more specific attention to GM food. Studying the graph showing inter-organizational collaborations in Bristol, of any intensity, one can see that groups with an interest in GM food (triangle-shaped nodes in Figs. 8.6 and 8.8) were more densely interconnected. Groups only interested in generic food issues also displayed some level of connectedness, but with a higher proportion of unlinked organizations and rather engaged in alliances with groups focused on other issues (Figs. 8.7 and 8.8).

A more formal test of the distribution of ties between three types of organizations confirms the visual impression (Table 8.5). Ties between organizations interested in food but not in GMOs were slightly denser than a random distribution would suggest (the ratio between observed and expected ties under conditions of independence was about 1.5), whereas ties between organizations also focused on GM food were more than three times above what one should expect if the issue had no effect whatsoever on alliance patterns. These differences are highly significant, suggesting that attention to food issues actually characterized the local civic network in some meaningful ways. This was not the case, however, if we concentrated on the

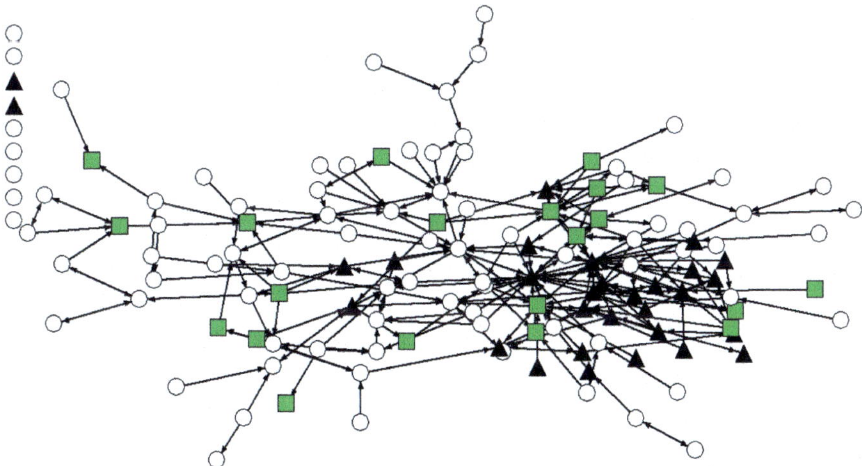

Fig. 8.6 Inter-organizational cooperations in Bristol (white circles: not interested in food; green squares: interested in food issues, but not in GMO; black triangles: interested in both types of issues). Source: Design by authors

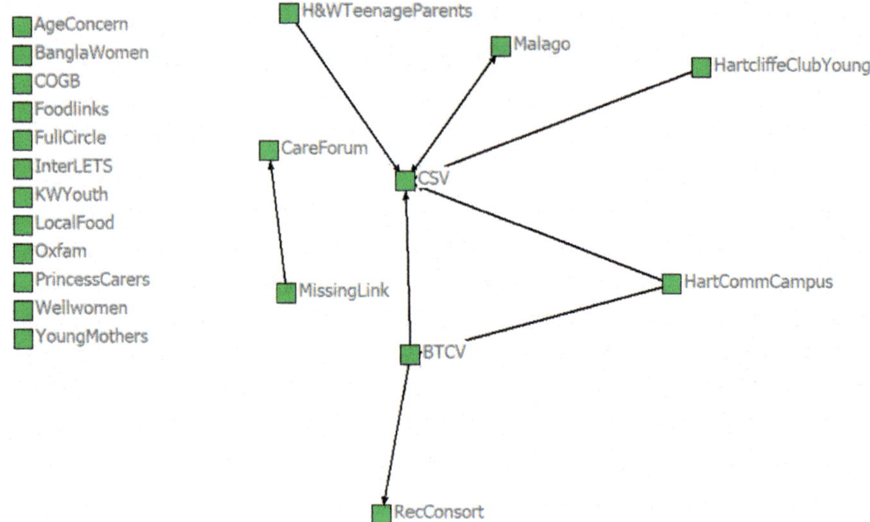

Fig. 8.7 Cooperations in Bristol between organizations interested in food issues but not in GMO. Source: Design by authors

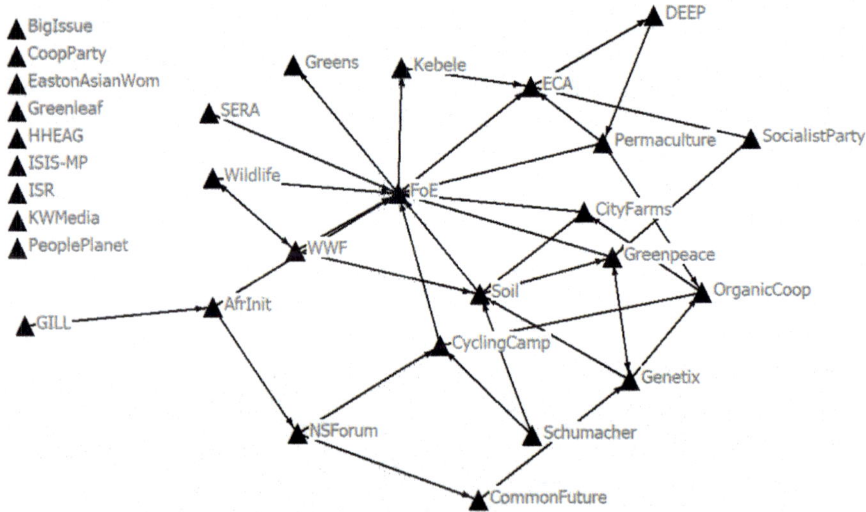

Fig. 8.8 Cooperations in Bristol between organizations interested in both generic food issues and GMO. Source: Design by authors

strongest ties, in other words, those that combined exchanges of resources with the deeper connections created by shared core members or strong interpersonal ties ("social bonds": Baldassarri & Diani, 2007). Here, no significant discernible pattern emerged. If anything, organizations sharing a similar position on food issues seemed less, rather than more, likely to be connected by strong ties (Table 8.6).

Table 8.5 The salience of food issues in the Bristol civic network

	Observed/expected ties		
	1	2	3
1. Not interested in food	0.78	0.94	0.85
2. Interested in food, but not in GM food	0.86	1.46	2.27
3. Interested in both issues	0.49	1.94	3.21
Significance: 0.000			

Note. Source: Design by authors

Table 8.6 The salience of food issues in the Bristol civic network (strong ties only)

	Observed/expected ties		
	1	2	3
1. Not interested in food	0.87	0.93	0.87
2. Interested in food, but not in GM food	1.18	0	1.89
3. Interested in both issues	1.39	1.21	0.62
Significance: 0.25			

Note. Source: Design by authors

A broadly similar pattern can be detected in Glasgow, if slightly less pronounced, and with a more similar structure of ties among the two sets of organizations with interests in food (Figs. 8.9, 8.10, and 8.11). As in Bristol, inter-organizational connections were most likely among groups with an interest in GM food (Table 8.7); in contrast to Bristol, the ratio between observed and expected ties remained higher for groups mobilizing on GM food also in the case of the strongest "social bonds." However, dense connections also linked these organizations to groups with no interest in food whatsoever, which made it difficult to identify a salient role for food issues in the strong ties network (Table 8.8).

It is worth noting that food issues seemed to have the same salience in the two cities despite being located in so different positions within the issue network. As we described, food was fairly central in Bristol, but quite peripheral in Glasgow. Yet, this did not result in differences in the issue's salience in the inter-organizational network. In both cities, this was significant in terms of generic resource exchanges, but not in terms of the strongest "social bonds." As we have shown in our previous work, strongest ties are most likely to connect organizations involved in social movement dynamics, or social movement "modes of coordination" (Diani, 2015). In this case, however, British cities displayed network patterns that suggested food was primarily the object of initiatives taking a coalitional form: in other words, relatively dense exchanges of resources, but much lower levels of solidarity and shared identity between organizations interested in the issue.[8] The low ratio between

---

[8] Diani (2015) actually suggested that tie multiplexity, in other words, the coupling of resource exchanges and deep connections created by joint activists, be the distinguishing feature of the social movement way of coordinating collective action, distinct from coalitional, subcultural/communitarian or organizational modes.

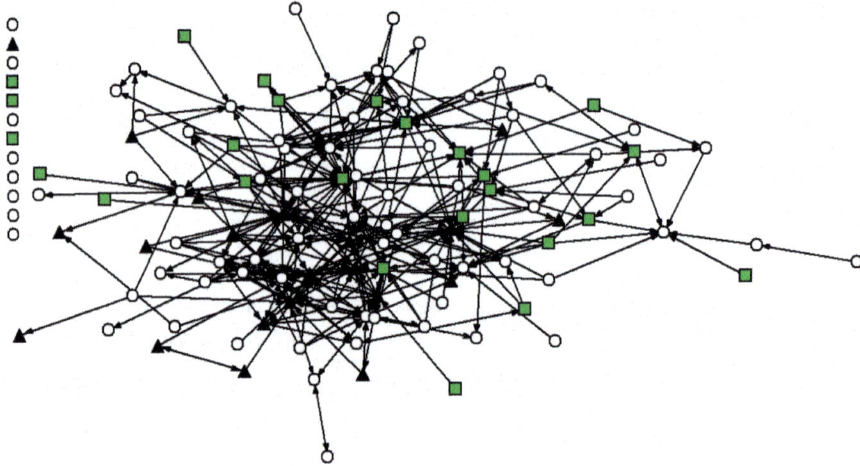

Fig. 8.9 Inter-organizational cooperations in Glasgow (white circles: not interested in food; green squares: interested in food issues but not in GMO; black triangles: interested in both types of issues). Source: Design by authors

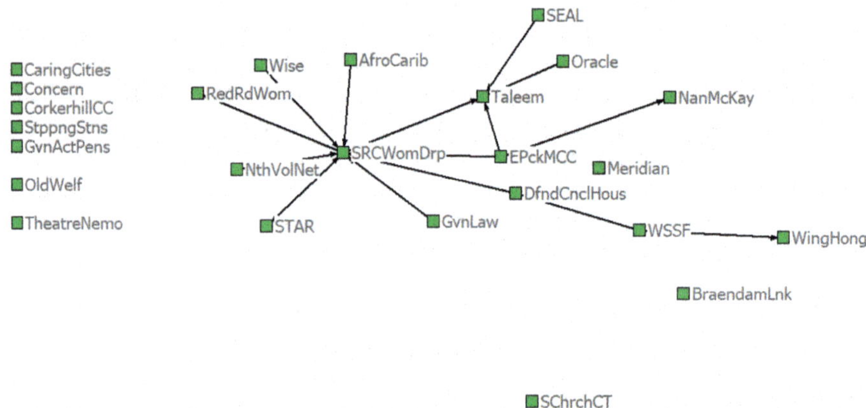

Fig. 8.10 Cooperations in Glasgow between organizations interested in food issues but not in GMO. Source: Design by authors

observed and expected ties among organizations that were uninterested in food also points to the fact that food issues had a modest capacity to stir emotions and to generate strong oppositions. This finding should not be overemphasized: after all, it is fairly normal that ties be denser among actors with a specific interest than among those who only share their disinterest in that particular issue. However, empirical exploration of civic networks suggests that some issues may be more polarizing than others. For example, in our work on Cape Town civic networks (Diani, Ernstson, & Jasny, 2018) we found "urban conservation" and "global environmental justice" issues to be more polarizing than "right-to-the-city" issues.

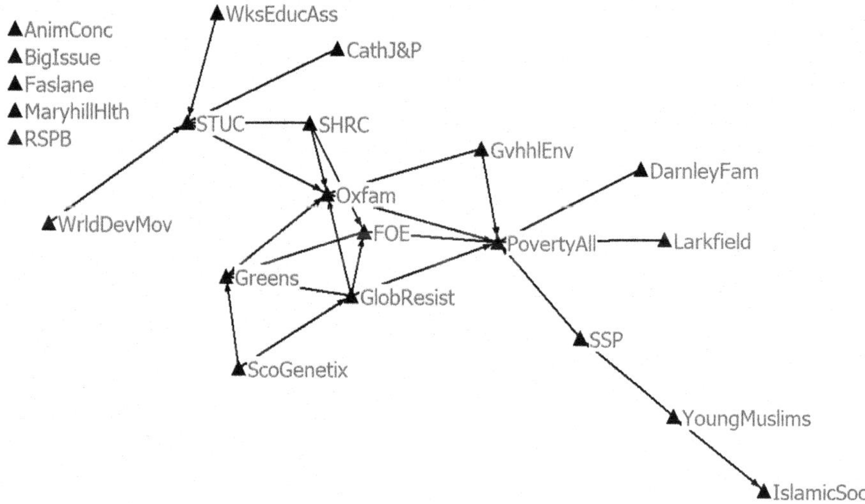

Fig. 8.11 Cooperations in Glasgow between organizations interested in both food issues and in GMO. Source: Design by authors

Table 8.7 The salience of food issues in the Glasgow civic network

	Observed/expected ties		
	1	2	3
1. Not interested in food	0.72	0.95	0.85
2. Interested in food, but not in GM food	0.90	1.23	1.10
3. Interested in both issues	1.13	0.39	2.72
Significance: 0.023			

Note. Source: Design by authors

Table 8.8 The salience of food issues in the Glasgow civic network (strong ties only)

	Observed/expected ties		
	1	2	3
1. Not interested in food	0.98	0.80	1.96
2. Interested in food, but not in GM food	0.57	0.73	0.00
3. Interested in both issues	1.17	0.00	2.39
Significance: 0.11			

Note. Source: Design by authors

Civic networks in Cape Town present a different profile on several grounds. The network consisting of all resource exchanges (Fig. 8.12) suggests quite frequent ties between organizations that differed in their attention to food. Although the majority of organizations interested in food were connected, many others were disconnected in that particular sub-network (Fig. 8.13). As it happens, only four organizations interested in food (indicated by black triangles) were isolated in the full civic network (left-hand side of Fig. 8.12), but 15 were isolated in the network only

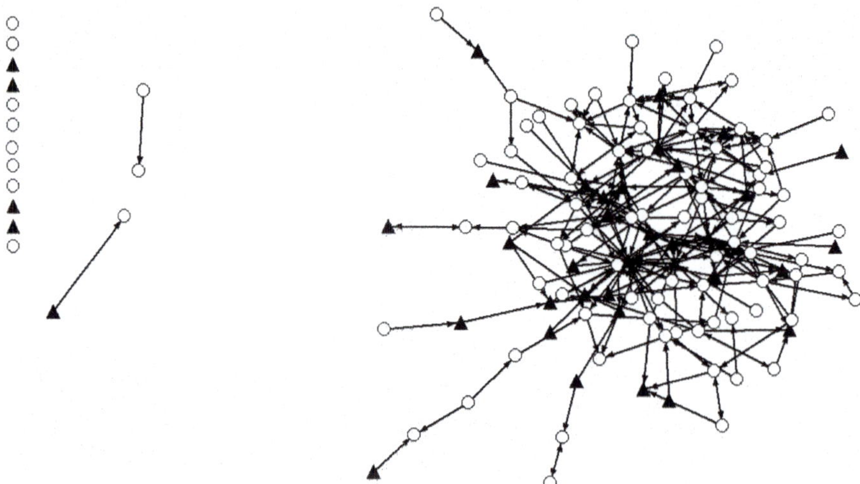

Fig. 8.12 Inter-organizational cooperations in Cape Town (white circles: not interested in food; black triangles: interested in food). Source: Design by authors

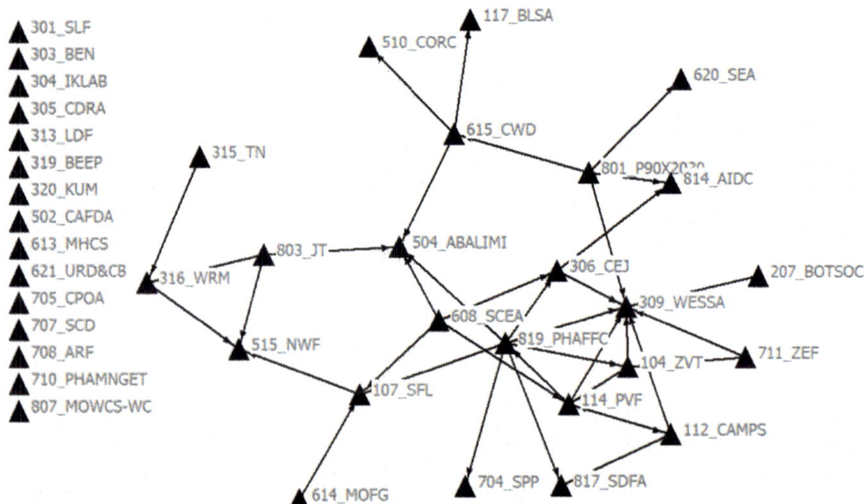

Fig. 8.13 Cooperations in Cape Town between organizations interested in food. Source: Design by authors

consisting of actors mobilizing on food (Fig. 8.13). In Table 8.9, we have confirmed the impression generated by the visual inspection of the graphs: The propensity of groups interested in food to exchange resources or collaborate with each other was only marginally above a random distribution, certainly much lower than in the two British cities (Tables 8.5 and 8.7).

Table 8.9   The salience of food issues in the Cape Town civic network (any tie)

	Observed/expected ties	
	1	2
1. Not interested in food issues	0.90	1.24
2. Interested	0.90	1.62
Significance: 0.14		

Note. Source: Design by authors

Table 8.10   The salience of food issues in the Cape Town civic network (strong ties only)

	Observed/expected ties	
	1	2
1. Not interested in food issues	0.91	0.83
2. Interested	0.87	2.17
Significance: 0.03		

Note. Source: Design by authors

The effect of interest in food on inter-organizational exchanges in Cape Town seems to follow an opposite pattern to what we found in the UK: If we focus only on strong ties, we find significant effects of interest in food on the structure of the network (Table 8.10). The probability of a strong tie between organizations interested in "urban farming and food security" was more than twice what one should expect in case of a random distribution. Again, it was not a polarizing issue (disinterested groups were not strongly connected to each other), yet it seemed to have the capacity of shaping the stronger ties, those that imply some higher level of mutual solidarity, rather than ties that were less demanding and less symbolically charged.

Conclusions

In this chapter, we have proposed an approach to better integrate the ideational and associational dimensions of civil society, which researchers usually treat disjointedly (Edwards, 2004). In doing so, we have attempted to move from an aggregative to a relational view of civil society (Diani, 2015), examining the interactions between its different components rather than focusing exclusively on their traits or properties. More specifically, taking interest in food as our case study, we have explored the relation between ideational elements and associations from two complementary perspectives. On the one hand, we have suggested that by making claims about their priorities and combining them, members of civic organizations define specific systems of meanings, and shape civil society agendas. We have shown that issues do not have an objective meaning, but take different meanings depending on the other themes to which they may be related (DiMaggio, 1987; Mohr, 1998; Mohr & Duquenne, 1997; Pachucki & Breiger, 2010). On the other hand, we have explored the extent to which interest in food issues characterized specific structural positions within civic organizations' networks in different local settings.

It is important to be clear about the limits of the exercise. Admittedly, our treatment of food issues was quite superficial. With the exception of GM food, both studies relied on generic definitions of the issue. In the UK, respondents were only asked about their interest in "food," without further qualification. In Cape Town, the question was more specific, referring to "urban farming and food security," but still broad. A more detailed treatment of the multiple aspects of food (e.g., as part of alternative lifestyles, as dimension of domestic inequality, or as a global issue linked to multinational corporate capitalism) would have certainly sharpened our analysis. Even so, our findings still highlight some of the main differences in the insights that an aggregative and a relational approach to civil society may generate.

In particular, we have found that an issue's popularity (measured by the number of organizations that regard it as a priority) does not necessarily correlate with its location in broader agendas: highly popular issues are not necessarily central to the formation of wider comprehensive frames for collective action. This is an important finding because proponents of an aggregative approach would necessarily take a popular issue to be central for wider collective action. Indeed, utilizing an aggregative approach to the interest in GM food shows that its popularity was much higher (at least at the time of the surveys) in British cities than in Cape Town. Although this is an interesting finding in its own right, suggesting that the topic was more easily addressed by organizations operating in more affluent settings, our relational approach paints a richer picture. Despite its significant appeal to civic organizations, GM food's structural position in the larger issue network was one of isolation in both British cities. Ironically, it was in Cape Town, where its weight was more limited, that GM food was linked into a distinctive cluster of issues. However, that was a set of global themes, isolated from the rest of the issue network—unable, in other words, to connect in a significant way to agendas more closely addressing local issues, whether from a social or an environmental perspective.

A relational approach is similarly rich in insight if one examines generic food issues. Using an aggregative approach, one would conclude that their popularity was pretty constant across the three cities. If, however, one looks at the patterns of relations between issues—or, in other words, at the structures of civic agendas—in different cities, a finer-grained picture emerges. In all three cities, generic food issues were primarily connected to broader environmental concerns *at the time of the surveys*, rather than to social inequality and welfare agendas. But the extent of such connection differed: in Bristol, namely, in the city closest to a post-industrial economy based on high-tech research and an advanced service sector, food issues were at the intersection of environmental and broader social agendas; in Glasgow, they were far more peripheral, as a focus on deprivation still seemed to influence local public discourse in a significant way; [9] in Cape Town, they were firmly located within an environmental conservation agenda.

---

[9] On some basic differences between Bristol and Glasgow see Diani (2015, Chap. 2) and Cento Bull and Jones (2006).

If utilizing a relational approach to issues results in a different story from the one that utilizing an aggregative perspective would, the same applies to alliance patterns between organizations interested in food. We had a similar number of such organizations in the three cities, yet the probability that they worked together was not the same but varied depending on the type of relation. In Bristol and Glasgow, the probability of a collaboration was significantly higher when "collaboration" meant the exchange of resources between two organizations, regardless of the depth of such connection. However, we found no significant difference when we focused on the network consisting of the strongest links, those that also implied sharing core activists and/or strong personal ties between core members of two organizations. In Cape Town, in contrast, organizations interested in food issues represented a distinct cluster within the larger network only when we took the strongest ties into account. Cape Town was the only city in which interest in food issues seemed to characterize clusters of organizations linked by the strong, multiplex ties that are closest to a "social movement mode of coordination" (Diani, 2015).

To further illustrate the power of a network analytic approach, we will close by returning to the paradox of food issues in Cape Town. With our combined findings about the issue and organizational networks, we have generated a profile of the situation in Cape Town that people familiar with the area might find puzzling. Given the amount of deprivation in some communities within the city, the persistent segregation across race and class lines, and the role that urban farming might play in addressing at least partially the link between inequality and poor diet, one might have plausibly expected "urban farming and food security" to be more strongly linked to "social rights" or "right-to-the-city" type of issues, and thus for food to be part of wider-spanning agendas for collective action. As a matter of fact, there is ample evidence that activism on food issues has intensified over the last few years, with major civil society, policy, and scholarly activities around food security being promoted in the city, including in areas that we already widely covered in our study, like the Philippi Horticulture Area (Battersby et al., 2014; Kanosvamhira, 2019). This means that our network survey, if carried out today, might show that food has become a more integrative issue. However, since our goal was to illustrate a logic of analysis, not to provide an up-to-date account of urban politics in specific settings, we can make a more useful final point on how one could expand the relational analysis further.

The fact that food in Cape Town was most strongly linked to conservation issues does not mean that it had no connection to other issues. It simply means that more organizations stressed a link between food and environmental conservation than between food and social inequality issues. This may be due to deep differences in resources within civil society; organizations with a (new) middle-class membership, richer in resources, may find it easier to engage on multiple issues, combining attention to urban farming with conservation issues, whereas grassroots groups representing the most dispossessed communities may be forced to concentrate on specific issues because of their limited resources. To explore this hypothesis within a narrow aggregative approach would be difficult, if not impossible. A relational approach would simply looking separately at the issue networks created by organizations operating in affluent or deprived environments. If many affluent (mostly white) groups indicated food as a priority alongside conservation issues, whereas deprived (black/colored) groups focused mostly on single-issues, that might account for food's more solid link to conservation than to "right to the city" issues. Of course, this is just a working hypothesis. What we have illustrated in this piece, nonetheless, is the power of a network analytic approach to public issues when it comes to identifying non-obvious patterns and new, challenging research questions.

Appendix

Table 8.11 Issues addressed by civic organizations in Bristol and Glasgow, and their popularity

Social Exclusion		Global Justice	
Single parents	39%	Genetically modified food	21%
Children's services	44%	Animal welfare	15%
Drugs	40%	Third World debt	24%
Welfare rights	47%	Third World poverty	27%
Unemployment issues	49%	Globalization	26%
Poverty	57%		
Health	65%	**Environment**	
Disability	50%	Pollution	37%
HIV-related issues	30%	Nature conservation	28%
Crime in neighborhoods	35%	Waste	29%
Homelessness	47%	Energy	33%
Access to higher education	39%	Environmental education	54%
Community Services	61%	Farming, forestry, fishing	20%
Quality of basic education	45%	Science and technology	19%
Minimum wage	24%	Food	35%
Gender equality	47%	Transport	36%
Women's issues	55%		
		Minority Citizenship	
Housing		Racial harassment	42%
Tenants' rights	35%	Minority citizenship rights	35%
Housing quality	38%	Minorities' access to public office	24%
Housing privatization	21%	Multiculturalism	42%
Housing developments	40%	Asylum seekers	44%
		Minority entrepreneurship	23%
N	258	N	258

Note. Reprinted from Diani (2015, pp. 41–42). Copyright 2015 by Cambridge University Press. Reprinted with permission

Table 8.12 Issues addressed by civic organizations in Cape Town, and their popularity

Global Environmental Justice		Right to the City	
Against financial capital	2%	Housing	28%
Against WTO	2%	Service delivery	47%
Third World debt	2%	Community development	57%
Preserve biodiversity	2%	Transparency corruption	21%
International tax	2%	Strengthen direct democracy	42%
Abolish tax havens	2%	Rights to the city	19%
Against GM food	2%		
Global justice	10%	**Urban Sustainability**	
		Renewable energy	9%
Urban Conservation		Curb urban growth	5%
Nature conservation	35%	Public transport	11%
Environmental education	45%	Governance planning	22%
Public green spaces	40%		
Pollution	26%	**Social Rights**	
Cultural heritage	26%	Labor and gender rights	12%
Urban farming food security	29%	Youth development	40%
Climate change	14%	Minorities' rights	14%
		Welfare and health	34%
N	129	N	129

Note. Source: Design by authors

References

Alexander, J. C. (2006). *The civil sphere*. Oxford, UK: Oxford University Press.

Alimi, E. Y., Demetriou, C., & Bosi, L. (2015). *The dynamics of radicalization: A relational and comparative perspective*. New York, NY: Oxford University Press.

Anheier, H. K. (2004). *Civil society: Measurement, evaluation, policy*. London: Earthscan.

Anheier, H. K. (2007). Reflections on the concept and measurement of global civil society. *Voluntas, 18,* 1–15. https://doi.org/10.1007/s11266-007-9031-y

Anheier, H. K., & Themudo, N. (2002). Organizational forms of global civil society: Implications of going global. In M. Glasius, M. Kaldor, & H. K. Anheier (Eds.), *Global civil society 2002* (pp. 191–216). Oxford, UK: Oxford University Press.

Baldassarri, D., & Diani, M. (2007). The integrative power of civic networks. *American Journal of Sociology, 113,* 735–780. https://doi.org/10.1086/521839

Ballard, R., Habib, A., & Valodia, I. (2006a). *Voices of protest: Social movements in post-apartheid South Africa*. Scottsville, South Africa: University of KwaZulu-Natal Press.

Ballard, R., Habib, A., Valodia, I., & Zuern, E. (2006b). Introduction: From anti-apartheid to post-apartheid social movements. In R. Ballard, A. Habib, & I. Valodia (Eds.), *Voices of protest: Social movements in post-apartheid South Africa* (pp. 1–24). Scottsville, South Africa: University of KwaZulu-Natal Press.

Barthel, S., Parker, J., & Ernstson, H. (2013). Food and green space in cities: A resilience lens on gardens and urban environmental movements. *Urban Studies, 52,* 1321–1338. https://doi.org/10.1177/0042098012472744

Basov, N., & Brennecke, J. (2017). Duality beyond dyads: Multiplex patterning of social ties and cultural meanings. *Research in the Sociology of Organizations, 53,* 87–112. https://doi.org/10.31235/osf.io/xpf76

Bassoli, M., & Theiss, M. (2014). Inheriting divisions? The role of catholic and leftist affiliation in local cooperation networks: The case of Italy and Poland. In S. Baglioni & M. Giugni (Eds.), *Civil society organizations, unemployment, and precarity in Europe* (pp. 175–203). London: Palgrave Macmillan. https://doi.org/10.1057/9780230391437

Battersby, J., & Haysom, G. (2019). How food secure are south Africa's cities? In J. Knight & C. M. Rogerson (Eds.), *The geography of South Africa: Contemporary changes and new directions* (pp. 169–178). Cham: Springer. https://doi.org/10.1007/978-3-319-94974-1.

Battersby, J., Haysom, G., Tawodzera, G., McLachlan, M., Marshall, M., Kroll, F., & Crush, J. (2014). Food system and food security study for the City of Cape Town. Retrieved from http://www.afsun.org/wp-content/uploads/2016/08/Final-Food-System-Study-Report_Corrected-_WITH-COUNCIL-REPORT.pdf

Bond, P. (2011). South African splinters: From 'elite transition' to 'small-a alliances'. *Review of African Political Economy, 38,* 113–121. https://doi.org/10.1080/03056244.2011.552690

Borgatti, S. P., Everett, M. G., & Johnson, J. C. (2013). *Analyzing social networks*. London: Sage.

Borgatti, S. P., & Halgin, D. (2011). On network theory. *Organization Science, 22,* 1157–1167. https://doi.org/10.1287/orsc.1100.0641

Calhoun, C. (2001). Civil society/public sphere: History of the concept. In N. J. Smelser & P. B. Baltes (Eds.), *International encyclopedia of the social & behavioral sciences* (pp. 1897–1903). New York: Pergamon. https://doi.org/10.1016/B0-08-043076-7/00115-7

Carley, K. (1994). Extracting culture through textual analysis. *Poetics, 22,* 291–312. https://doi.org/10.1016/0304-422X(94)90011-6

Cento Bull, A., & Jones, B. (2006). Governance and social capital in urban regeneration: A comparison between Bristol and Naples. *Urban Studies, 43,* 767–786. https://doi.org/10.1080/00420980600597558

Cherry, E. (2006). Veganism as a cultural movement: A relational approach. *Social Movement Studies, 5,* 155–170. https://doi.org/10.1080/14742830600807543

Deakin, N. (2001). *In search of civil society*. Basingstoke: Palgrave Macmillan.

Diani, M. (1995). *Green networks: A structural analysis of the Italian environmental movement*. Edinburgh, UK: Edinburgh University Press.

Diani, M. (2012). The 'unusual suspects': Radical repertoires in consensual settings. In S. Seferiades & H. Johnston (Eds.), *Violent protest, contentious politics, and the neoliberal state* (pp. 71–86). Farnham: Ashgate. https://doi.org/10.4324/9781315548104

Diani, M. (2015). *The cement of civil society: Studying networks in localities*. Cambridge, UK: Cambridge University Press. https://doi.org/10.1017/CBO9781316163733

Diani, M., Ernstson, H., & Jasny, L. (2018). "Right to the city" and the structure of civic organizational fields: Evidence from Cape Town. *Voluntas, 29,* 637–652. https://doi.org/10.1007/s11266-018-9958-1

Diesner, J., & Carley, K. M. (2011). Semantic networks. In G. A. Barnett (Ed.), *Encyclopedia of social networks* (pp. 766–769). Thousand Oaks: Sage.

DiMaggio, P. (1987). Classification in art. *American Sociological Review, 52,* 440–455. https://doi.org/10.2307/2095290

Dogan, M., & Pélassy, D. (1984). *How to compare nations: Strategies in comparative politics*. Chatham: Chatham House.

Edwards, M. (2004). *Civil society*. Cambridge: Polity.

Eggert, N. (2014). The impact of political opportunities on interorganizational networks: A comparison of migrants' organizational fields. *Mobilization: An International Quarterly, 19,* 369–386. https://doi.org/10.17813/maiq.19.4.d5p65x6563778xv6

Entwisle, B., Faust, K., Rindfuss, R. R., & Kaneda, T. (2007). Networks and contexts: Variation in the structure of social ties. *American Journal of Sociology, 112,* 1495–1533. https://doi.org/10.1086/511803

Ernstson, H. (2011). Transformative collective action: A network approach to transformative change in ecosystem-based management. In Ö. Bodin & C. Prell (Eds.), *Social network analysis and natural resource management: Uncovering the social fabric of environmental gover-*

nance (pp. 255–287). Cambridge, UK: Cambridge University Press. https://doi.org/10.1017/CBO9780511894985

Ernstson, H. (2013). The social production of ecosystem services: A framework for studying environmental justice and ecological complexity in urbanized landscapes. *Landscape and Urban Planning, 109*, 7–17. https://doi.org/10.1016/j.landurbplan.2012.10.005

Ernstson, H., & Sörlin, S. (2019). *Grounding urban natures: Histories and futures of urban ecologies*. Cambridge, MA: MIT Press.

Ferguson, J. E., Groenewegen, P., Moser, C., Borgatti, S. P., & Mohr, J. W. (2017). Structure, content, and meaning of organizational networks: Extending network thinking, introduction. *Research in the Sociology of Organizations, 53*, 1–15. https://doi.org/10.1108/S0733-558X20170000053013

Fischer, M. (2011). Social network analysis and qualitative comparative analysis: Their mutual benefit for the explanation of policy network structures. *Methodological Innovations Online, 6*(2), 27–51. https://doi.org/10.4256/mio.2010.0034

Forno, F. (2019). Protest, social movements, and spaces for politically oriented consumerist actions—Nationally, transnationally, and locally. In M. Boström, M. Micheletti, & P. Oosterveer (Eds.), *The Oxford handbook of political consumerism* (pp. 69–88). New York, NY: Oxford University Press. https://doi.org/10.1093/oxfordhb/9780190629038.001.0001

Habermas, J. (1989). *The structural transformation of the public sphere: An inquiry into a category of bourgeois society* (T. Burger, Trans.). Cambridge, MA: MIT Press.

Halkier, B. (2019). Political food consumerism between mundane routines and organizational alliance-building. In M. Boström, M. Micheletti, & P. Oosterveer (Eds.), *The Oxford handbook of political consumerism* (pp. 275–292). New York, NY: Oxford University Press. https://doi.org/10.1093/oxfordhb/9780190629038.001.0001

Herring, R. J. (2014). How is food political? Market, state, and knowledge. In R. J. Herring (Ed.), *The Oxford handbook of food, politics, and society* (pp. 3–40). New York, NY: Oxford University Press. https://doi.org/10.1093/oxfordhb/9780195397772.001.0001

Jallinoja, P., Vinnari, M., & Niva, M. (2019). Veganism and plant-based eating: Analysis of interplay between discursive strategies and lifestyle political consumerism. In M. Boström, M. Micheletti, & P. Oosterveer (Eds.), *The Oxford handbook of political consumerism* (pp. 157–180). New York, NY: Oxford University Press. https://doi.org/10.1093/oxfordhb/9780190629038.001.0001

Kadushin, C. (2012). *Understanding social networks: Theories, concepts, and findings*. New York, NY: Oxford University Press.

Kanosvamhira, T. P. (2019). The organisation of urban agriculture in Cape Town, South Africa: A social capital perspective. *Development Southern Africa, 36*, 283–294. https://doi.org/10.1080/0376835X.2018.1456910

Knoke, D., & Wood, J. R. (1981). *Organized for action: Commitment in voluntary associations*. New Brunswick, NJ: Rutgers University Press.

Knoke, D., & Yang, S. (2008). *Social network analysis* (2nd ed.). Thousand Oaks: Sage. https://doi.org/10.4135/9781412985864

Laumann, E. O., & Pappi, F. U. (1976). *Networks of collective action: A perspective on community influence systems*. New York: Academic Press. https://doi.org/10.1016/C2013-0-11049-5

Lawhon, M., Ernstson, H., & Silver, J. (2014). Provincializing urban political ecology: Towards a situated UPE through African urbanism. *Antipode, 46*, 497–516. https://doi.org/10.1111/anti.12051

Levkoe, C. Z. (2014). The food movement in Canada: A social movement network perspective. *The Journal of Peasant Studies, 41*(3), 385–403. https://doi.org/10.1080/03066150.2014.910766

Levkoe, C. Z., & Wakefield, S. (2014). Understanding contemporary networks of environmental and social change: Complex assemblages within Canada's 'food movement'. *Environmental Politics, 23*(2), 302–320. https://doi.org/10.1080/09644016.2013.818302

Luxton, I., & Sbicca, J. (2021). Mapping movements: A call for qualitative social network analysis. *Qualitative Research, 21*, 161–180. https://doi.org/10.1177/1468794120927678.

Maharaj, B. (2020). The apartheid city. In R. Massey & A. Gunter (Eds.), *Urban geography in South Africa: Perspectives and theory* (pp. 39–54). Cham: Springer. https://doi.org/10.1007/978-3-030-25369-1

Maloney, W. A., & Roßteutscher, S. (2006). *Social capital and associations in European democracies: A comparative analysis.* London: Routledge.

Maloney, W. A., & van Deth, J. W. (2008). *Civil society and governance in Europe: From national to international linkages.* Cheltenham: Edward Elgar.

Maloney, W. A., & van Deth, J. W. (2010). *Civil society and activism in Europe: Contextualizing engagement and political orientations.* Abingdon: Routledge.

McFarlane, C., & Silver, J. (2017). The Political City: 'Seeing sanitation' and making the urban political in Cape Town. *Antipode, 49,* 125–148. https://doi.org/10.1111/anti.12264

Mohr, J. W. (1998). Measuring meaning structures. *Annual Review of Sociology, 24,* 345–370. https://doi.org/10.1146/annurev.soc.24.1.345

Mohr, J. W., & Duquenne, V. (1997). The duality of culture and practice: Poverty relief in New York City, 1888–1917. *Theory and Society, 26,* 305–356. https://doi.org/10.1023/A:1006896022092

Mottiar, S., & Bond, P. (2012). The politics of discontent and social protest in Durban. *Politikon, 39,* 309–330. https://doi.org/10.1080/02589346.2012.746183

Norris, P., & Inglehart, R. (2002). Islam & the West: Testing the Clash of Civilizations thesis. SSRN Scholarly Paper 316506. https://doi.org/10.2139/ssrn.316506

Oberg, A., Korff, V. P., & Powell, W. W. (2017). Culture and connectivity intertwined: Visualizing organizational fields as relational structures and meaning systems. *Research in the Sociology of Organizations, 53,* 17–47. https://doi.org/10.1108/S0733-558X20170000053001

Pachucki, M. A., & Breiger, R. L. (2010). Cultural holes: Beyond relationality in social networks and culture. *Annual Review of Sociology, 36,* 205–224. https://doi.org/10.1146/annurev.soc.012809.102615

Putnam, R. D. (2000). *Bowling alone: The collapse and revival of American community.* New York: Simon & Schuster.

Seekings, J. (2000). After apartheid: Civic organizations in the 'New' South Africa. In G. Adler & J. Steinberg (Eds.), *From comrades to citizens: The South African civics movement and the transition to democracy* (pp. 205–224). London: Palgrave Macmillan. https://doi.org/10.1057/9780230596207

Seligman, A. B. (1995). *The idea of civil society.* Princeton, NJ: Princeton University Press.

Snow, D. A. (2004). Framing processes, ideology, and discursive fields. In D. A. Snow, S. A. Soule, & H. Kriesi (Eds.), *The Blackwell companion to social movements* (pp. 380–412). Malden: Blackwell. https://doi.org/10.1002/9780470999103

Snow, D. A., Rochford, E. B., Worden, S. K., & Benford, R. D. (1986). Frame alignment processes, micromobilization, and movement participation. *American Sociological Review, 51,* 464–481. https://doi.org/10.2307/2095581

Sumner, J., & Wever, C. (2015). Cultivating alliances: The local organic food co-ops network. *Canadian Journal of Nonprofit and Social Economy Research, 6*(2), Article 2. https://doi.org/10.22230/cjnser.2015v6n2a204.

Tilly, C. (2005). *Identities, boundaries, and social ties.* Boulder: Paradigm.

von Atteveldt, W., Moser, C., & Welbers, K. (2017). Being apart together: Convergence and divergence in the field of Dutch politics. *Research in the Sociology of Organizations, 53,* 49–64. https://doi.org/10.1108/S0733-558X20170000053004

Chapter 9
The Geography of Giving in the Philanthropic Field

Johannes Glückler and Laura Suarsana

Economic geography is a field of research that takes an interest in the spatial diversity of economic activity as well as the specific trajectories along which regional economies evolve, and how these trajectories differ between places and across space. In this chapter, we look at the geography of philanthropy and explore the role of financial giving in regional development. Citizens and wealthy patrons donate, foundations and associations engage in and finance benevolent activities, and private businesses assume social responsibility for regional, national, and global communities. Mainstream philanthropy research has largely been analyzing charitable activities from the perspective of the third sector, and has often pursued actor-specific divisions of research into types of giving organizations, such as charities and foundations, patrons and wealthy individuals, non-governmental organizations, and civic associations. This practice has enabled researchers to explore these specific types of actors in depth, yet it has somehow inhibited an evolving understanding of the playing field, in which all these activities come together, especially in geographical, regional contexts. Therefore, and to overcome the evident boundaries of sectorial segmentation, we propose the concept of the philanthropic field to capture the interdependency and interrelations between all benevolent giving across sectors and among diverse types of actors. In this chapter, we seek to explore what we can learn about philanthropy when taking a relational and geographical perspective of fields.

The aim of this chapter is to shift our view from actors to agency of philanthropic giving, to identify differences in engagement, and to explore patterns of collaboration and labor division among different actors in joint projects. After

J. Glückler (✉)
Department of Geography, University of Heidelberg, Heidelberg, Germany
e-mail: glueckler@uni-heidelberg.de

L. Suarsana
Institute Labour and Economy, University of Bremen, Bremen, Germany
e-mail: laura.suarsana@uni-bremen.de

J. Glückler et al. (eds.), *Knowledge and Civil Society*, Knowledge and Space 17,
https://doi.org/10.1007/978-3-030-71147-4_9

conceptualizing the notion of the philanthropic field as an analytical framework, we present an in-depth, multi-method case study of the Southern German region of Heilbronn-Franconia. In our analysis, we draw on a detailed multi-year media analysis of published cases of donations and financial giving between regional donors and recipients.[1] We show that apart from third-sector organizations, private businesses also play a central role as promoters in the region by offering financial support to social, educational, and charitable purposes. In addition, different types of actors collaborate across the analytic boundaries of public, private, and civic sectors, a key insight that remains opaque when only focusing on one type of actor. In Heilbronn-Franconia, for instance, foundations and firms joined financial and human resources to make major projects possible in the field of education. In essence, our empirical case study serves as a showcase of how using the perspective of a philanthropic field emphasizes not the actions of one type of organization, but the interaction of all actors involved in the philanthropic field in a specific regional context. Finally, we are inviting a conversation about the role of philanthropic involvement in regional governance and development.

We begin by developing the concept of the philanthropic field as our analytical framework, and then present our case study including data and methods. The presentation of the findings is organized around four dimensions of the philanthropic field: its morphology, the diversity of actors, the connectivity of giving, and the geography of benevolent activity. We conclude by reassessing the philanthropic field's potential to capture benevolence and giving in regional societies and by exploring the interrelation between philanthropy and social and economic development of regions.

The Philanthropic Field

Researchers of philanthropy in the social sciences have adopted a broad variety of definitions. We conceive philanthropy as voluntary, charitable, or welfare-oriented action, which takes place through the use of financial means, material resources, or time and without expectation of direct compensation (Acs & Phillips, 2002; Andreoni, 2001; Glückler & Ries, 2012). With this definition, we imply that philanthropic engagement not only applies to nonprofit actors such as foundations or nonprofit associations, but also to those actors who, apart from pursuing their economic goals, also act benevolently or contribute to the public good (Phillips & Jung, 2016; Wiepking & Handy, 2015). Scholars in the interdisciplinary research field of philanthropy have studied organizational diversity and the various practices, mechanisms, and modes of philanthropic involvement as well as its social antecedents and effects (Bekkers & Wiepking, 2011; Brown & Ferris, 2007; Diani, 2013; Diani &

---

[1] The empirical findings presented in this chapter are based on work conducted between 2011 and 2013 as part of the research project "Regional Philanthropy and Innovation in Heilbronn-Franconia" (Glückler & Suarsana, 2013, 2014; Suarsana & Glückler, 2016).

Pilati, 2011; Galaskiewicz & Wasserman, 1989; Graddy & Wang, 2009; Herzog & Yang, 2018; Maclean & Harvey, 2016; Marquis, Glynn, & Davis, 2007; Ostrander, 2007).

Many researchers have pursued sectoral perspectives or have focused on individual types of actors and organizations (Bekkers & Wiepking, 2007). Whereas researchers focusing on the antecedents of charitable giving and generosity (Andreoni, 2006; Bekkers & Wiepking, 2011; Havens et al., 2007; Havens & Schervish, 2005; Wiepking & Maas, 2009) examine philanthropic commitment and the willingness of the population to donate, those studying elite philanthropy have a particular focus on wealthy individuals and patronage (Faller & Wiegandt, 2010, 2015; Glückler, Ries, & Schmid, 2010; Hay & Muller, 2014; Kischel, 2009; Ostrower, 1995; Saunders-Hastings, 2018). Researchers studying civil society, the third sector, or nonprofit sector (Anheier, 2005; Anheier & Ben-Ner, 1997; Anheier, Priller, Seibel, & Zimmer, 1997; Anheier & Seibel, 1990; Hammack & Smith, 2018; Powell & Steinberg, 2006; Salamon & Anheier, 1992, 1998; Zimmer & Simsa, 2014) compare and assess the characteristics, activities, development, and national conditions of civil society and nonprofit organizations, often focusing on specific types of organizations such as foundations and associations (Adloff, 2010; Anheier, 2003; Birkhölzer, Klein, Priller, & Zimmer, 2005; Hammack & Smith, 2018; Zimmer, 2007), and on these organizations' interactions with state and market organizations (Salamon, 1995; Salamon & Toepler, 2015). Recently, scholars have challenged sectoral perspectives (Salamon & Wojciech Sokolowski, 2016) and suggested extending the view, for instance, through concepts of hybridization (Anheier & Krlev, 2014; Evers, 2020).

In addition, Corporate Social Responsibility (CSR), Corporate Citizenship (CC), and Corporate Philanthropy approaches have been established to examine social and welfare-oriented activities of economic actors, (Beschorner, 2010; Burt, 1983; Carroll, 1999; Crane, Matten, & Moon, 2010; Galaskiewicz & Burt, 1991; Gautier & Pache, 2015; Henderson & Malani, 2009; Hurd, Mason, & Pinch, 1998; Matten & Crane, 2005; Porter & Kramer, 2006; Schwartz & Carroll, 2003; Wolch & Geiger, 1985). Philanthropic activities are often considered part of the overall concept of CSR or CC (Habisch, Wildner, & Wenzel, 2008; Sasse & Trahan, 2007), whereas some authors do not include philanthropic activities in their definition of CSR because of their distance to the company's core business (Schneider, 2012). This view is often linked to demands that entrepreneurial social or regional commitment should be wedded to corporate strategy and the corporation's core (Porter & Kramer, 2002, 2006). Moreover, a number of new approaches have emerged in recent decades, their proponents discussing philanthropy from the angle of efficiency and strategy, economic and market-oriented perspectives, such as venture or creative philanthropy, social entrepreneurship, or philanthrocapitalism (Adloff & Degens, 2017; Anheier & Leat, 2006; Letts, Ryan, & Grossman, 1997; McGoey, 2012, 2014; Moody, 2008; Salamon, 2014).

Although focusing on sectors or organizational types contributes to a differential understanding of groups of actors, it entails the danger of neglecting the entirety of philanthropic engagement and the interaction among the actors in specific social and geographical contexts. Alternatively, network approaches help researchers understand interorganizational relationships and the importance of social capital and the institutional embedding of philanthropic actors (Adloff, 2016; Brown & Ferris, 2007; Burt, 1983; Faulk, Lecy, & McGinnis, 2012; Galaskiewicz & Burt, 1991; Guo & Acar, 2005; Harrow, Jung, & Phillips, 2016; Johnson, Honnold, & Stevens, 2010; Krashinsky, 1997; Letts, 2005; Marquis et al., 2007; see also Chap. 8 by Diani).[2] Moreover, conducting geographical studies sheds light on the regional dimension of fundraising, the "philanthropy market," and the formative effect of the community context on philanthropic donor behavior (Wolch & Geiger, 1985; Wolpert & Reiner, 1984). Scholars have found that local contexts and geographical disparities set important conditions for regional variations in philanthropy and giving (Bekkers, 2016; Card, Hallock, & Moretti, 2010; Clerkin, Paarlberg, Christensen, Nesbit, & Tschirhart, 2013; Lengauer & Tödtling, 2010; Wolpert, 1988, 1995) at various geographical scales (Bekkers, 2016, p. 124; Havens & Schervish, 2005; Heinemann, 2010; von Schnurbein & Bethmann, 2010). Cross-national comparison reveals the impact of the political, economic, and social and cultural context on philanthropic giving as well as on the size and scope of the not-for-profit sector (Salamon & Anheier, 1998; Wiepking & Handy, 2015, p. 597)[3]. Those utilizing network approaches have often focused on interrelations between philanthropic organizations at the expense of the role of geography, whereas those conducting geographical studies have put emphasis on regionalizing the activity of actors typically of just one sector at the expense of grasping the connectivity between them and across a broader set of diverse actors.

To overcome the limitations of these approaches, we propose the concept of the philanthropic field (Glückler & Suarsana, 2014). With it, we capture the totality of philanthropic activities, diverse actors, and the interconnection amongst all kinds of benevolent actors and their recipients in a geographical context. We have based the concept of the philanthropic field on institutional theory, in which an organizational field comprises the totality of all organizations that form a "recognizable area of institutional life" (DiMaggio & Powell, 1983, p. 148; Lawrence & Phillips, 2004). The notion of the field exceeds the narrow boundaries of sectors, markets, and networks. First, it exceeds the logic of sectors, which are constituted by homogenous types of organizations that offer similar products or services, by looking at diverse actors from private, public, and civic sectors. Second, it exceeds markets, which are defined by

---

[2] In his reflection on philanthropy, Adloff (2016, p. 66) argues that philanthropy "takes place within specific social contexts. [...] Interaction on the level of face-to-face contacts must also be taken into account, as well as cultural, social, and institutional frameworks."

[3] Bekkers and Wiepking (2011, pp. 927–943) identified as mechanisms driving charitable giving on the household and individual level: "(1) awareness of need; (2) solicitation; (3) costs and benefits; (4) altruism; (5) reputation; (6) psychological benefits; (7) values; (8) efficacy." Wiepking and Handy (2015, pp. 610–611) identified eight common facilitating factors for philanthropy, including "1. a culture of philanthropy; 2. public trust, issues of transparency, accountability and effectiveness; 3. regulatory and legislative frameworks; 4. fiscal incentives; 5. the state of the nonprofit sector; 6. political and economic stability or growth; 7. population changes; 8. international giving."

competition and trade, to include cooperation, collaboration, cocreation, solidarity, charity, volunteering, and so forth. Third, it exceeds networks, which are defined by connectivity and cohesion, to emphasize the significance of geography, such as the political, institutional, and cultural specificity of place or the proximity in space.

In analogy to physics, a field is the spatial distribution of a social (rather than physical) force that acts on social actors (rather than physical objects). The fundamental idea to be translated into the context of social science is that the force drives or affects social actors in similar ways yet in varying magnitude. In social life, such a force is found in the institutional pressures on individuals and organizations to gain legitimacy by complying with the expectations held in the respective social community or society. Accordingly, one of the axiomatic conjectures in neo-institutional theory is that those organizations belonging to an organizational field will respond to the institutional pressure with isomorphic conversion into similar organizational forms (DiMaggio & Powell, 1983). Similarly, we conceive the philanthropic field as a spatial distribution of benevolent giving that includes actors being exposed to a common set of institutional expectations for legitimacy and who are involved in the structuring of this phenomenon of philanthropy in a specific geographical context. Consequently, the field does not stop at the boundary of the third sector or nonprofit organization; it also encompasses the benevolent giving of private businesses and public organizations, as well as individual citizens, who together co-constitute the field in their roles as employees or mandated representatives in decision making, or as donors, volunteers, or recipients. In essence, a philanthropic field links the geography of giving with the networks of benevolent activities across the domains of private, public, and civic sectors (Fig. 9.1).

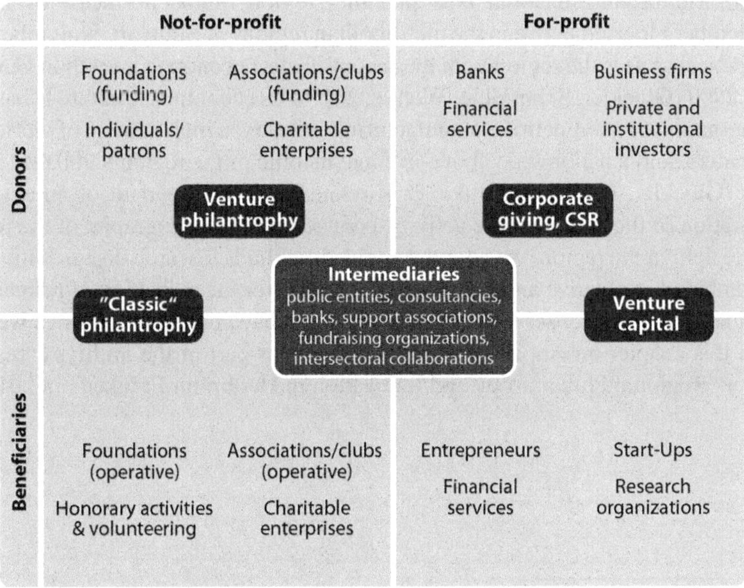

Fig. 9.1 Types of actors in the philanthropic field. Source: Design by authors

To leverage the concept for empirical analysis, we specify any empirical philanthropic field along four dimensions. First, *field composition* comprises the location and constitution of the diverse participants who contribute benevolent activity in the field. Second, *field activity* comprises the sources and magnitude of benevolent giving as well as the diverse uses of philanthropic donations. Third, *field connectivity* encompasses the interactions and interrelations between benevolent actors in the field, including direct collaboration on large joint projects and the division of labor that emerges from specialization and segmentation into often complementary activities. Fourth, *field geography* is the regional specificity, spatial reach, and interregional relations in philanthropic activities and cooperation. Together, these four dimensions make up the philanthropic field. One of our central objectives in this chapter is to deploy this concept as an analytical framework for empirical exploration in a case study of philanthropy in the Southern German region of Heilbronn-Franconia.

Case Study: Data and Methods

Study Region

In our case study, we draw on intensive research in the rural region of Heilbronn-Franconia, located in the federal state of Baden-Württemberg, Germany. With a GDP of over €500b, Baden-Württemberg would be number 22 in a world ranking of global economies, with a magnitude of economic output similar to Sweden and Poland. Heilbronn-Franconia is a planning region in the northeast of Baden-Württemberg located between the metropolitan regions of Stuttgart, Nuremberg and Rhine-Neckar. It is the region with the second-fastest economic growth in Germany since 2000 (Glückler, Schmidt, & Wuttke, 2015). Its economic structure is based on an internationally competitive manufacturing industry, a high density of world market leaders, and a nationwide above-average income of the region's 900,000 inhabitants (Glückler, Punstein, Wuttke, & Kirchner, 2020). In pursuit of an extensive exploration of the composition, activity, connectivity, and geography of the philanthropic field in the region, we adopted a mixed-methods research design with which we combined qualitative and quantitative methods for the collection of primary and secondary empirical observations (Table 9.1). We have based the findings we present in this chapter on empirical work carried out as part of the multiyear research project "Regional Philanthropy and Innovation in Heilbronn-Franken" in 2012.[4]

---

[4] For a more detailed discussion of the study design and methods, see Glückler and Suarsana (2013).

Table 9.1 Methods and sources of empirical data collection

Methods	Actions and observations	Empirical database
Regional analysis	• Analysis of regional income and private wealth as well as of registered foundations, associations, and charitable organizations	• Official statistics on income • Public registers of associations and foundations
Media analysis	• Identification of charitable donations by actors of all sectors in the region that were mentioned in newspapers and magazines, 2004–2011	• 2,297 donations between 920 donors and 1,234 recipients with a total volume of €129m
Social network analysis	• Transformation of the textual data retrieved in the media analysis into a network database, indicating the direction and value of donation relations between actors	• 789 donors and 1,103 recipients, total volume of €93.4m
Survey of foundations	• Survey of all 186 judiciable foundations in the region	• 101 responses (response rate 54.3%), of which 98 were charitable foundations (52.7%)
Qualitative interviews	• Interviews with philanthropists, recipient organizations, and intermediaries from both not-for-profit and for-profit sectors	• 33 semi-structured interviews

Note. Source: Design by authors

Identification of Field Actors

To identify the actors contributing to the philanthropic field of Heilbronn-Franconia, we consulted official registries from the Land of Baden-Württemberg on the number of charitable clubs and associations as well as of judicable foundations and associations[5] with legal capacity. We then decided to take a more detailed look at the foundations located in the region as well as at other regional field actors, drawing on two sources of primary data collection (Table 9.1). First, we conducted a standardized survey of all the identifiable 186 judicable foundations in the region to get information on organizational characteristics and profiles, yet most importantly to learn about interactions and cooperation with other foundations as well as additional partners in benevolent giving. Because our study met high levels of interest and acceptance, a remarkable number of 98 nonprofit foundations (response rate 52.7%) responded to the survey. Secondly, we carried out 33 qualitative interviews with representatives of foundations, nonprofit associations, private businesses, and public entities to explore additional actors in the field, assess their roles, and understand the diversity of philanthropic practices.

---

[5]Registered associations can be retrieved at the local district courts, whereas we collected the number (though not the identity) of charitable associations from the regional tax offices.

Measure of Field Activity: Donations

We aimed at creating a maximally complete database of philanthropic giving in the region to capture the magnitude, structure, and connectivity of philanthropic engagement in the field. In the absence of official statistics and due to the limitations of survey techniques regarding response rates and willingness to declare donations, we conducted a media analysis to capture all "publicized" donations within the region. Of course, not all donations are published—for instance, donors may act discreetly or newspapers may restrict reports as a matter of policy. With our analysis, we have covered all cases of giving between 2004 and 2011 that were published in eight regional daily newspapers, each having partial coverage of selected districts in the region (Fig. 9.2). We used a set of 90 keywords and keyword combinations to

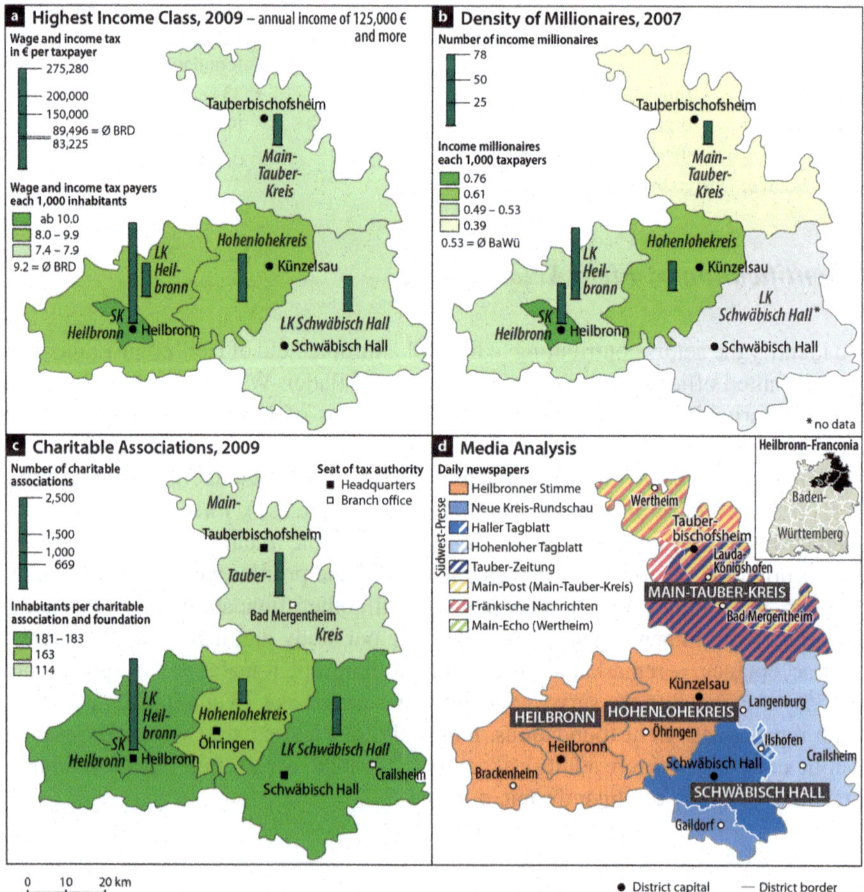

Fig. 9.2 Geographical distribution of newspapers, income, wealth, and civic associations. Source: Design by authors

search the digital archives of these eight newspapers and screened all individual reports manually to verify the transaction and avoid double counting of transactions in cases of multiple reports. After checking each transaction, we created a database on philanthropic relationships between donors and recipients, including the purpose and the amount of each donation.[6] The database contains a total of 2,297 cases of charitable donations and donations between 920 donors and 1,234 beneficiaries, amounting to a sum of 129 million euros. Of course, this database only provides insights into the activities voluntarily published in the press. The results are subject firstly to the selection criteria of the responsible editorial offices of the media involved and secondly to our selection criteria in the course of our research.

Field Composition: Who are the Actors?

The region of Heilbronn-Franconia includes the city of Heilbronn at its core and the four rural districts of *Heilbronn, Hohenlohe, Main-Tauber,* and *Schwäbisch Hall.* As a consequence of our multiple-method approach, we identified the following groups of actors who represent the potential for philanthropy in the region: wealthy individuals, charitable associations and foundations (funding/grant making and operative), and private businesses. In addition, we included cooperative and less institutionalized entities such as events and project in the philanthropic field (Table 9.3). Together, these constitute a diverse group of donors and sources of benevolent activity.

First, identifying private wealth in Germany on the ground of public statistics is not without its difficulties. In the mid-1990s, the German government abandoned wealth taxes and the state consequently lost transparency over the magnitude and distribution of private wealth. Today, researchers only have forward projections or surveys of small population samples with which to estimate the magnitude and distribution of private wealth. Rather than looking at the assets, we therefore focus on the flows of income. In aggregate, the region enjoys an above-average per capita income, with a peak in the city of Heilbronn. More specifically—and this one can learn in great detail from the official statistics—the region also hosts a great number of income millionaires. Although the sheer number of 179 income millionaires reflects the mean in the spatial distribution across Germany, the income millionaires in Heilbronn-Franconia were, in aggregate, exceptionally rich: The regional average was about double as high as the German average. These statistics of prosperity resonate with the observation of quite a number of patrons and wealthy individuals

---

[6] We recorded activities for which a transfer of financial or physical resources took place or for which we could allocate a monetary value to the grant. With this analysis step one can only draw conclusions about actors whose activities were published in the media. However, given the general opacity of the field of charitable activities, this appears to be one of the few possible ways to capture all philanthropic activities in the region. For a detailed discussion of the conception and a critical evaluation of the method, see Glückler, Ries, and Schmid (2010).

who have become known for the civic engagement and benevolent giving in the region.

Second, regarding associational life and organized civil society, we found 5,131 publicly registered clubs and associations, of which 1,200 clubs were registered under the legal status of a charitable club, a status that exempts them from paying corporation tax in return for charitable commitment. Third, apart from the charitable associations, a total of 186 judicable foundations under civil and public law were registered with the Stuttgart Regional Council in 2012. There were also 19,551 legally responsible foundations under civil law alone in Germany and 2,847 in Baden-Württemberg (Bundesverband Deutscher Stiftungen, 2013, pp. 112–114). The responding foundations in Heilbronn-Franconia had relatively larger endowments than the average endowments of all German foundations (Table 9.2). Although one learns little about actual philanthropic activity from the mere number of nonprofit organizations, the structure of household incomes and foundation assets is consistent with a solid financial basis for philanthropic commitment within the region. The majority of the foundations in the survey (71.1%) categorized themselves as funding/grantmaking foundations. A further 20.6% are both operative as well as grant-making, whereas 8.2% pursue only operational activities.

Finally, we observed that the regional population had a remarkable level of involvement with philanthropy and civic engagement. Based on our analyses of the number of organizations and of our foundation survey, we conclude that in addition to 1,200 charitable support clubs and associations with an unspecified number of tens of thousands dedicated members, another approximately 1,400 citizens regularly volunteered on an honorary basis for almost all the regional foundations. Apart from the few hundred people directly involved with a foundation, we counted a total of 252 individuals who acted as members of management or supervisory boards, thus being directly responsible for decisions about their foundation's activities. Finally, two thirds of all foundations reported sustaining advisory boards with a total of 391 board members who typically share their expertise, experience, prestige, and social networks to leverage the work of a foundation.

Table 9.2 Financial equity of charitable foundations in Heilbronn-Franconia (n = 88 foundations)

Equity 2012	Region Heilbronn-Franconia		Germany	
	No. of foundations	Share (%)	No. of foundations	Share (%)
Up to €100,000	21	23.9	2,209	28.4
Up to €1 mil.	44	50.0	3,478	44.7
Up to €10 mil.	20	22.7	1,720	22.1
More than €10 mil.	3	3.4	379	4.9

Note. Values for Germany: Bundesverband Deutscher Stiftungen (2012). Source: Design by authors

Field Activity: What are the Practices of Giving?

Drawing on a detailed analysis of published media reports on donations in the region, we found that the philanthropic commitment in Heilbronn-Franconia had increased significantly between 2004 and 2011. Within this short period of only seven years, the annual number of published transactions more than doubled to over 400. Despite the steady rise of donations, the grant volumes had been volatile over time, with an unprecedented peak in 2010 (€42 million). Despite the relative volatility, there is a trend towards increasingly more donations to beneficiaries. In total, we found donations with an aggregate value of 129 million euros through our media analysis.

The media analysis not only shows that considering only one isolate type of philanthropic donor would be inadequate but also that wealthy individuals and private businesses also play a significant role in philanthropic giving. Charitable foundations accounted for the majority share (61.7%) of all funding volume, with one foundation making up 45.9% of the total sum (€59.37m).[7] Yet the second most important group of donors were private business firms who accounted for 10.5% of the volume and 20.3% of the number of donations. Excluding private businesses from the perspective of the field would thus leave out a substantial share in overall regional benevolent engagement. When ranked by the volume of donations, wealthy individuals come third. Although individual patrons have a minimal share in the number of transactions, their donations amount to the third largest share of 8.4% in the volumes of money donated. Although clubs and associations are largest in terms of the number of transactions, they fall to only fourth place in terms of the amounts of money donated. This diversity of actors is a significant insight to be gained from a field perspective. Public organizations and entities were the largest recipients, with 55% of the total amount given. Whereas foundations and private businesses together accounted for the lion's share of 70% of funding, clubs and associations accounted for the highest number of individual transactions (Table 9.3A). The not-for-profit sector received the largest flow of donations, comprising a total of 94.6 million euros, that is, 73.2% of the total amount of all grants. Cooperation between for-profit and not-for-profit organizations received the second largest share (€34.5 million, 26.7%) (Table 9.3B).

One of the fundamental advantages of building a transaction database by using media reports is that we could carefully read every news article and thus extract more detailed information on the donors, beneficiaries, and donation purpose. Hence, we were able to distinguish a variety of different purposes, ranging from the most popular purposes of "education, academia, and research" and "charity and

---

[7] When including this regional actor, the maximum increases from 3.5 to 20 million euros and the total funding amount of foundations from 17 to 76.3 million euros. The regional field is therefore divided: One organization with very high annual income on the one hand and a larger number of smaller foundations on the other. If the largest foundation is excluded, the mean amount donated by foundations still exceeds that of companies.

Table 9.3 Sources and recipients of donations by sectors and organizational forms

A. Donors	No. of donations	Share of donations	Amounts (EUR)	Share of volumes	Mean volumes
For-profit					
Business firms	462	20.3%	13,025,848	10.5%	28,194
other (events, projects, etc.)	10	0.4%	198,386	0.2%	19,839
Cooperation/across sectors					
Events, projects, groups, etc.	51	2.2%	112,192	0.1%	2,200
Not-for-profit					
Foundations	532	23.4%	76,284,331	61.7%	143,392
Clubs and associations	616	27.0%	9,424,336	7.6%	15,299
Individuals, e.g., patrons	92	4.0%	10,410,470	8.4%	113,157
Public entities	205	9.0%	8,934,932	7.2%	43,585
Other (events, projects, etc.)	299	13.1%	4,839,844	3.9%	16,187
Not-for-profit enterprises	11	0.5%	444,500	0.4%	40,409
B. Recipients					
For-profit					
Business firms	7	0.3%	42,155	0.0%	6,022
Other (events, projects, etc.)	4	0.2%	158,500	0.1%	39,625
Cooperation/across sectors					
Events, projects, groups, etc.	199	8.7%	33,099,841	25.6%	166,331
Public-private partnerships	10	0.4%	1,360,192	1.1%	136,019
Not for-profit					
Foundations	192	8.4%	6,562,983	5.1%	34,182
Clubs and associations	790	34.4%	7,147,524	5.5%	9,047
Individuals	35	1.5%	188,890	0.1%	5,387
Other (events, projects, etc.)	321	14.0%	9,067,648	7.0%	28,248
Public entities	739	32.2%	7,1640,822	55.4%	96,943

Note. We have not included 19 cases (0.8% of all transactions, 4.3% of the total sum), as information on the sector was unavailable. Source: Design by authors

Table 9.4 Number and volume of donations by purpose, 2004–2011

	Volume (EUR)			Transactions	
	Total	Mean	Share	No.	Share
Education, academia, & research	80,894,895	198,272	62.6%	408	17.8%
Charity and humanitarian aid	23,631,219	22,722	18.3%	1,040	45.3%
Culture & arts	8,391,146	55.941	6.5%	150	6.5%
Local heritage & traditions	6,694,029	41,321	5.2%	162	7.1%
Health & medicine	3,069,780	15,197	2.4%	202	8.8%
Religion & worldviews	2,010,044	39,413	1.6%	51	2.2%
Other	1,706,217	32,812	1.3%	52	2.3%
Sports	1,290,726	11,628	1.0%	111	4.8%
Leisure (without sports)	701,765	23,392	.5%	30	1.3%
Environment & animal care	377,706	5,104	.3%	74	3.2%
Economy	149,500	24,917	.1%	6	.3%
Interest groups	3,500	1,750	.0%	2	.1%
Politics and public administration	429	429	.0%	1	.0%
Unknown/not specified	347,600	43,450	.3%	8	.3%
Total	129,268,556	56,277	100.0%	2,297	100.0%

Note. Source: Design by authors

humanitarian aid" to more niche purposes such as "leisure," "environment and animal care," or even "economy" (Table 9.4). The distribution of donations across the many purposes was highly skewed. The greatest number of donations fell in the area of charity and humanitarian aid, which represents the classic destination of philanthropic support. In total, over 1,000 donations, corresponding to almost half of all transactions, were dedicated to his purpose, yet these transactions represent only 18.3% of the volume of donated money. In turn, whereas education, academia, and research received only 17.8% of the number of donations, its cumulative value amounted to almost 81 million euros and made up 62.6% of the volume of donated assets. These figures may reflect a recent trend that education has become an increasingly popular target of philanthropy (Glückler & Ries, 2012), but also reflects the impact of the largest regional foundation, with its focus on education, that was responsible for 59,273,500 euros of the total amount given.

Field connectivity: How Does Giving Create a Network of Cooperation?

The third dimension of connectivity is used to focus on the network of giving as well as the divisions of labor and interactions among donor organizations in terms of collaboration in philanthropic projects as well as across the traditional nonprofit and for-profit sectors.

Regarding field connectivity, we analyzed the topology of the transactional network generated by the aggregate of philanthropic donations. In our media analysis, we retrieved 920 donors who made 2,297 donations to 1,234 recipients worth over

129 million euros. Because some of the donors were nonidentifiable, we were able to include a slightly reduced number of 789 donors and 1,103 recipients in our social network analysis, amounting to a total volume of 93.4 million euros. Bilateral and nonrecurring donor-recipient relationships dominate the network. The main component includes 62% of the actors, 75% of the relations, and 42% of the aggregate grant value (Fig. 9.3). A small patronage elite faces a broad civic commitment. The small number of large donations is offset by a large number of small donations. The median donation is less than 2,500 euros. Using more detailed techniques of network analysis (Glückler & Panitz, 2021), such as a triadic census, we revealed that giving is spread widely across the field and does not tend to cluster very much. Donors mostly supported several beneficiaries, whereas beneficiaries tended to receive grants from the same donors.

Although the endowments, objectives, and strategies of public, private, and civic organizations differ, we expect all these types of actors to shape and influence their philanthropic activities together and to be interrelated in the philanthropic field

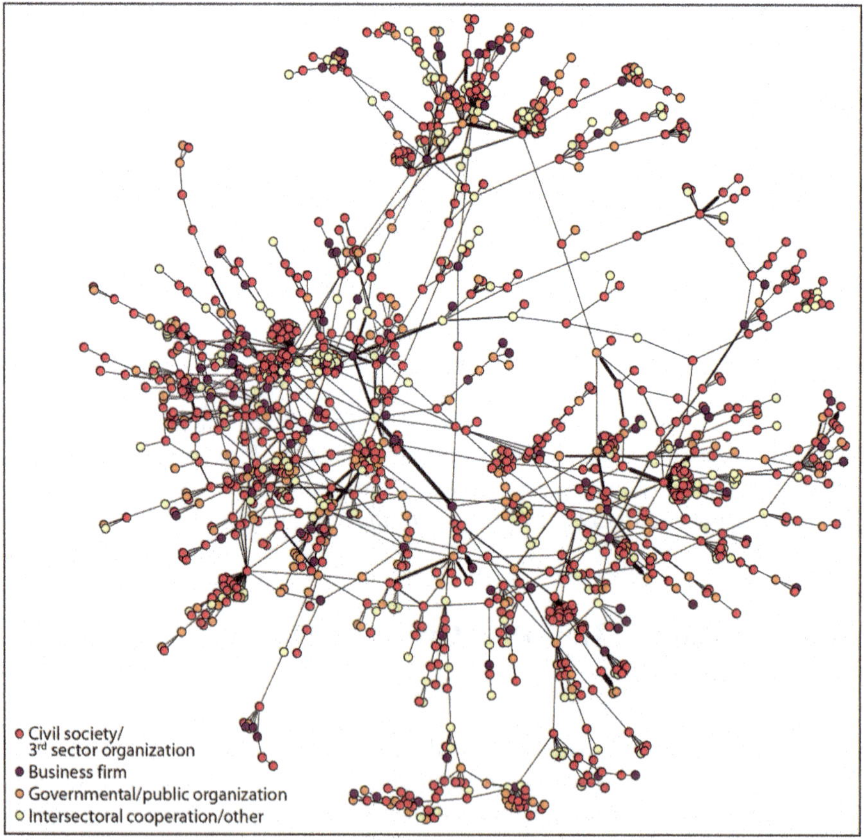

Fig. 9.3 The philanthropic network of Heilbronn-Franconia (main network component). Source: Design by authors

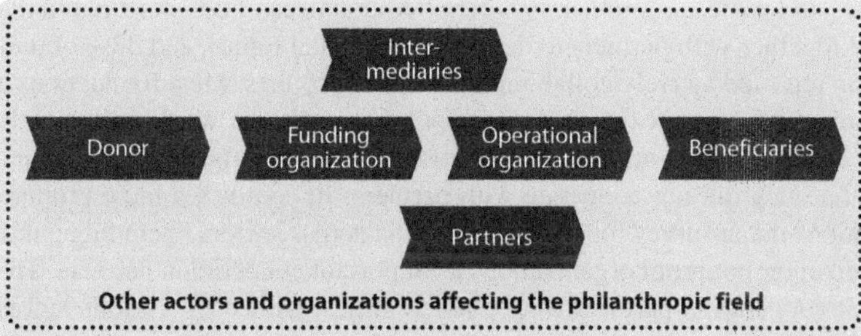

Fig. 9.4 Flows of giving in the philanthropic field in Heilbronn-Franconia. Source: Design by authors

(Glückler & Ries, 2012). From a geographical perspective, therefore, questions arise about their interaction and possible forms of complementarity, specialization, and cooperation between them with a view to achieving benevolent goals in a philanthropic field. We draw on the notion of the value chain to distinguish different stages of involvement in the chain of giving, ranging from original donations and financial support, the collection of assets in funding organizations, and operational activities to the final recipients. The stages of individual giving, organizational fundraising, and operational charity are complemented and interlinked by intermediary actors (e.g., public entities, authorities, organized events, interest groups) and supported by cooperation partners, for example by syndicated donations or operational collaboration among operational foundations (Fig. 9.4).

Although the donation network we drew from the media reports comprises a large number of financial donations, it does not include the specialization and collaboration between the different actors in the division of philanthropic giving. To obtain additional information on these relations, we carried out a survey of all 186 judicable foundations registered with the regional council in Stuttgart. With this survey, we focused on how foundations had specialized on certain stages and collaborated with other partners in the provision of philanthropic giving. With 98 charitable foundations taking part, we achieved a response rate of 52.7% of the entire regional population of foundations. More than half of the questionnaires were completed by a board member; in one third of cases the managing director answered. With this survey, we learned that 71% of the foundations acted exclusively as sponsors—that is, they only donated money for charitable purposes—whereas 20.6% engaged in both funding and their own project operations, and a minor share of 8.2% exclusively pursued operational activities, depending on financial support from other organizational and individual donations.

This pattern of specialization reflects the contours of horizontal and vertical divisions of labor, in which operational foundations seek and receive donations from sponsoring organizations that are concentrated on fundraising, including from individual donors and citizens. In the horizontal dimension of the chain of giving, two types of cooperation emerged from the survey. First, 71% of surveyed foundations stated that cooperation with partners consisted of *co-financing* common charitable purposes and projects. Another 49% reported practices of *co-operation* in that they worked together with partners to develop themes and topics, and 38% of the charities even reported actively collaborating on joint projects. Most foundations agreed that cooperating more extensively with other foundations would increase the efficiency of charitable work. However, more than half of the surveyed foundations stated that they did not cooperate with partners. In contrast, a large proportion of foundations in the survey reported cooperation across sectors, including public, private, and other nonprofit organizations as important cooperation partners. The most frequent cooperation partners were public entities, named by 27 foundations, followed by associations and private businesses. In most cases, the cooperation developed through existing personal contacts. Nevertheless, a quarter of surveyed foundations confirmed that they were also actively seeking new partners.

In the vertical dimension of the chain of giving, we learned from our survey that funding relationships largely exist between not-for-profit actors. The majority of the foundations were tied up in fixed funding relationships with both donors and recipients. This pattern of linkages appeared to be quite stable and rather inert, reflecting long-term established channels of philanthropy. On the one hand, these established channels guaranteed continuous dedication to the same purposes and recipients; on the other, this rigidity incurred problems for those foundations that aimed to access new donors to expand their activities. Overall, the region's foundations desired better access to and more visibility vis-à-vis potential sponsors. Moreover, they reported that they were less visible to potential donors and multipliers than to recipients. From several interviews, we discovered the relevance of connectivity and formal as well as informal relations between regional actors for philanthropic practices, with personal relations bridging gaps between organizational logics of action. A representative of a regional business firm, associated with a charitable foundation, characterized the regional division of labor among the regional foundations and their relations with regional philanthropists:

> We were in conversation with [Philanthropist A] very often and he asked: "What shall we do together?" He is also strongly connected within the region, and we are now working very closely together with our foundations.... We work together locally, where there is no competition. [Philanthropist B], he says he works on the topic "children," and then we stay out of that. Because there is no use if we do that as well. (Representative, business firm C)

The activities of business firms, foundations and other charitable and public actors were intertwined in many different ways: The degree of cooperation among foundations and between foundations and public and private businesses varied widely. The surveyed foundations reported a stronger interest in forms of cooperative regional involvement than business firms. In our set of qualitative interviews with selected business representatives, interviewees conveyed that sufficient local possibilities for funding existed. We learned from the discussions that businesses had their philanthropic strategies well defined and that they counted on sufficient regional and local cooperation opportunities through personal and organizational networks. In turn, foundations were particularly interested in new, creative forms of cooperation, such as opportunities for short-term project collaboration. They also welcomed the idea of cooperation being orchestrated by intermediaries who could provide support in finding partners, initiating cooperation, or forming consortia for joint funding. Furthermore, some foundations emphasized the social benefit of a stronger pooling of funds in order to enable joint funding offers that small or individual foundations could not provide. However, not all foundations were so open to additional cooperation. For example, interviewees feared the resources required to establish new cooperations and the loss of organizational independence.

Despite the independence of most philanthropic actors, several large charitable projects had been realized in the Heilbronn-Franconia region, projects characterized by the cooperative interaction of business firms, foundations, and other actors. One showcase of the complex pattern of intersectorial collaboration among a diverse group of actors is the regional *Pakt Zukunft* [pact for future].

The *Pakt Zukunft Heilbronn-Franken* was founded in 2007 by regional stakeholders as a partnership with the purpose of jointly representing regional interests. A total of 134 municipalities, private businesses, and civic organizations participated in this initiative and met regularly for network meetings, lectures, and working groups. At the same time, the Chamber of Industry and Commerce (IHK) established the nonprofit enterprise *Pakt Zukunft Heilbronn-Franken gGmbH* to raise money from the largest corporations in the region and to fund charitable projects in the region. The purpose was to promote the overall well-being of the Heilbronn-Franconia region, especially in the areas of education and upbringing, youth and elderly care, and science and research. Three years later, in 2010, the pact failed, and members withdrew from the original organizational structure. However, the shareholders of the nonprofit enterprise relied on their growing solidarity and interest in continuing joint activities within the framework of Corporate Social Responsibility. From then on, the participating business firms concentrated on financially supporting nonprofit projects in the region. Since 2011, when a leading automotive manufacturer joined the enterprise as a shareholder, *Pakt Zukunft* supported more than 40 regional projects with an increasing focus on education and science. Interview partners emphasized several factors of the successful establishment and co-operation in the *Pakt Zukunft* enterprise. First, the initiative is built on existing personal relationships and trust, which provided the glue and confidence to engage in joint financial cooperation. Second, the initiative benefited from the opportunity for a number of regional entrepreneurs to become more involved in their region, actors who thus responded gratefully to such an inclusive nonprofit initiative. Third, the shareholders appreciated the serious framework in order to jointly promote more experimental projects in fields requiring action in the longer term. If merely entrepreneurial commitment had been involved, there would have been a risk of attracting negative attention. Fourth, the *Pakt Zukunft* partners acknowledged the Chamber of Commerce's central role as a trustworthy intermediary who offered an impartial, serious, and reliable framework needed for project sponsors and funding recipients to be able to balance competing interests. In addition, using the Chamber of Commerce's existing infrastructure for administration and communication provided additional advantages and prevented the implementation of unnecessary infrastructure:

> "Lernende Region Heilbronn-Franken e.V." [Learning Region, charitable association] and "Pakt Zukunft": These are cooperations that fortunately are set up, controlled, and supervised by the IHK [regional chamber of industry and commerce]. In order to achieve an

effect, the companies in the region really join forces in order to advance such significantly larger projects. That, of course, suits us very well. We don't have so many employees here on site that we can now run such larger projects ourselves and look after them sustainably. This really is an institution. And the associations that are behind it are very valuable to really make this an investment for us that is pursued consistently and does not have a one-time character. (Business firm representative B)

Field Geography: How Does Geography Shape Philanthropy?

Finally, we examine the geographical dimension as the fourth element of the philanthropic field. Specifically, we assess the extent to which geography makes a difference for the way that philanthropy works. Social commitment is often synonymous with local commitment. Most transactions took place locally within a county (61.8%) and were dedicated to the immediate local environment within a district or the city of Heilbronn. All types of donors focused on the local level as the geographic focus of philanthropic grant relationships between donors and recipients. This finding is consistent with earlier studies on the geography of philanthropy (Wolpert, 1988; Wolpert & Reiner, 1984). Business firms, foundations, and other organizations such as associations, federations, service clubs, and the like directed at least 80% of their activities and financial resources to recipients within the region (Table 9.5).

Whereas most donations were made locally, the largest amount of funding, constituting less than a third of transactions, was directed at the regional level. Only 17.7% of all transactions, but 42.7% of the total volume, crossed a district border within the region.

The region is divided into four areas: Heilbronn, Hohenlohe, Main-Tauber, and Schwäbisch Hall. Because these areas maintain only limited social and economic exchange with each other, we found the probability of a philanthropic relationship between two actors from different districts within the region to be no greater than that with actors outside the region. One donor located in the city of Heilbronn district accounted for 92.5% of grants for the city of Heilbronn and 97.3% of grants for other regions in Germany (Fig. 9.5).

Regarding interregional philanthropic relations, we observed a negative balance: 29.5% of the funds, mostly in the form of large donations, but only 14% of all transactions, went to beneficiaries outside the region. Only 6.9% of donations came into the Heilbronn-Franconia region from outside (Table 9.6).

In addition to geographical diversification, there were also differences in the governance of the commitment—from simple donor-recipient relationships and multilateral divisions of labor between business firms and corporate foundations or foundations with associated support associations, to complex interorganizational associations, such as the *Pakt Zukunft Heilbronn Franken gGmbH* (see previous section). Further, the geography of giving varied by the type of donor. Business firms used a significantly higher proportion of their funds than foundations at the

Table 9.5 Geographical distribution of donations

	Funding volume (EUR)			Transactions	
	Total	Mean	Share	No.	Share
Local level	26,259,737	18,811	20.9%	1,396	61.8%
Regional level[a]	53,479,011	133,364	42.7%	401	17.7%
Region, outgoing	37,014,782	121,759	29.5%	304	13.5%
Region, incoming	8,618,259	54,203	6.9%	159	7.0%
Total	125,371,789[b]	55,474	100%	2,260	100%

Note. [a] Includes 110 transfers totaling €1,368,3445 for which donors or recipients were located in the region but we could clearly allocate them to a group, [b] Because we could not precisely locate some donors and recipients, we could classify only €112.9 million of the total of €129 million in grants. Source: Design by authors

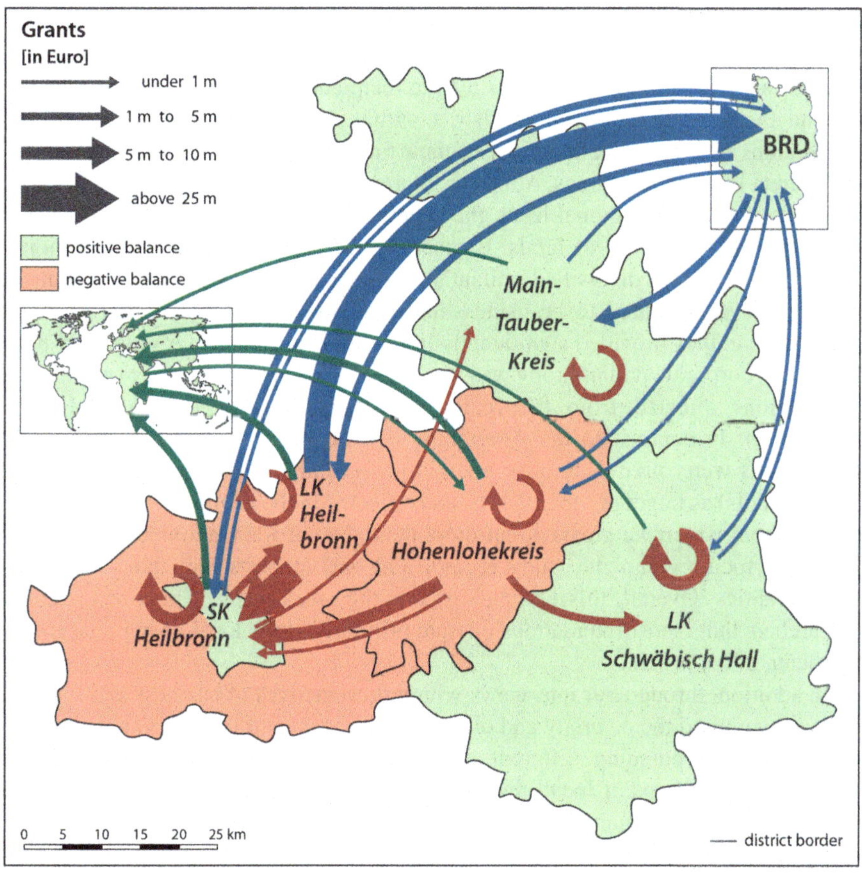

Fig. 9.5 The geography of the philanthropic field of Heilbronn-Franconia. Source: Design by authors

Table 9.6 Geographical distributions of donations by organization

	Share of (%)	Businesses	Foundations[a]	Other	Total
Local level	Transactions	58.5%	63.7%	65.0%	63.4%
	Volume	21.6%	51.3%	47.5%	43.1%
Regional level[a]	Transactions	22.7%	20.5%	12.8%	16.6%
	Volume	47.6%	7.7%	33.9%	29.5%
Extra-regional, outgoing	Transactions	12.0%	3.8%	17.7%	13.4%
	Volume	20.9%	16.0%	10.8%	14.4%
Extra-regional, incoming	Transactions	6.8%	12.0%	4.5%	6.7%
	Volume	10.0%	25.0%	7.8%	13.1%

Note. [a] We excluded the largest donor, a foundation, due to the high distortion of the total values. This donor spent a total of 59.3 million, or 46% of the total amount raised. For the latter, 7% of the activities and 0.4% of the total are at the local level, 79% of the activities and 52% of the total are at the regional level and 14% of the activities and 47% of the total are at the national level. Source: Design by authors

regional level (Glückler & Suarsana, 2014). In spite of the large number of transactions, they committed only 21.6% of their funds to the local level. Instead, they directed almost half of all funds (47.5%) to recipients at the regional level, that is, beyond their own administrative district within the broader region. In contrast, foundations directed more than half of their financial donations to beneficiaries in their direct local surroundings. Although the foundations recorded a similar number of grant cases at the regional level, they supported recipients at the regional level with only just under 8% of funds. Business firms' stronger focus on the regional level reflects a more diversified philanthropic commitment. For example, firms at the local level appeared to be using smaller amounts of money, whereas at the regional level they provided significantly larger financial support. A greater diversification of corporate philanthropy was also reflected in a higher number of activities corporations directed from the region to the national or international level (Table 9.6). In contrast to the geographical diversification of private donations, foundations were often statutorily bound to local purposes or local organizations (e.g., schools) as target groups. This is also reflected in the results of our foundation survey, from which we gleaned that more than 80% of foundations had their geographical focus within the study region, and half alone within their respective municipalities. Overall, this finding supports the assessment of previous studies' researchers that "most foundations operate primarily at the local or regional level" (Anheier, 2003, p. 70).

In addition, through our interviews with representatives of business and foundations we captured the diversity and different significance of the geographical reference levels for pursuing different strategic goals. The interviewed businesses pursued combinations of local, regional, and national activities. They aimed their local commitment at gaining acceptance and improving the quality of the local environment. Business firms were committed to ensuring good relations in the local environment, including a prosperous and attractive labor market. Locally rooted entrepreneurs said they wanted to "give back" to their home region and combine generosity with economic interest:

> And that is really the core belief of [the philanthropist and corporate owner] that it is his job to not only to look after the company, but also to look after this region. And not only out of gratitude and goodwill, to a certain extent you also have to look at it from the perspective of agglomeration, it influences the environment in which he wants to continue to be successful as an entrepreneur in the future. (Business firm representative B)

In contrast, nationwide commitment tended to raise the visibility of CSR activities. This relates to the different logics of the action of market-oriented corporations on the one hand and nonprofit organizations such as charitable foundations on the other—differences that researchers must account[8] for in an integrated analysis of a regional philanthropic field. Differences became apparent in the three dimensions: organizational purpose, finance, and flexibility.

First, regarding the organizational purpose: From their legal form and profit orientation as well as their market and economic-success-oriented logic of action, one can conclude that a business firm's philanthropic activities are linked to direct and indirect benefit expectations, such as positive reputation, employee recruitment, and so forth (Hiß, 2006; Maaß, 2009, pp. 27–28). In contrast, foundations—though these may also seek legitimacy and public awareness—are constituted by formal statutes and the requirements of charitable law for achieving charitable goals. [9]

Second, with respect to finance, business firms cover philanthropic donations with their profits. Due to the earnings expectations of investors and employees, business firms face opportunity costs and are thus pressured to justify activities in the public interest. The philanthropic commitment of firms, therefore, must always be traded off against alternative forms of profit placement. In contrast, foundations are not faced with the question of alternative uses of financial resources for private economic purposes due to their statutory obligation to promote public-interest objectives. However, because foundations are bound to their income from the existing foundation assets, they are dependent either on additional donations or the increase of the foundation assets through endowments or other incoming funds. In this respect, it is to be expected that foundations tend to seek relationships with institutional and individual donors or partners if they wish to expand their funding performance.

Third, business firms are more flexible in their behavior than foundations because they set their goals, strategies, and agendas internally. Although a CSR strategy adopted and communicated in the long term can have a binding effect on future activities, firms can always adapt and change objectives and practices if necessary or if corporate objectives change. On the other hand, foundations have less freedom

---

[8] The following relates to not-for-profit foundations within the meaning of German nonprofit law and to profit-oriented companies.

[9] There are also differences within each sector. Existing research, for example, refers to particular features of the structure of the commitment depending on the size and form of the business firm (Bertelsmann Stiftung, 2007; Fischer, 2007). The differences among foundations must also be pointed out (Hof, 2003), whereas we apply our argument exclusively to nonprofit foundations.

of choice and flexibility with regard to their commitment, the topics dealt with, and the target group of beneficiaries, due to the statutes' binding nature and the requirements of nonprofit law. It can therefore be assumed that business firms can firstly show greater adaptability to new needs of charitable support and secondly promote the diversity of these social needs with greater flexibility.

The philanthropic activities of the firms, foundations, and other local actors we covered in fieldwork were all affected by social and spatial proximity between organization representatives, benevolent individuals, and beneficiaries. In choosing topics and projects, they followed locally perceived needs and opportunities to realize local projects together with local partners, to whom again often long-term relations existed beforehand. Existing personal relations, successful cooperation across sectors in the past, and the integration into local associations and networks were referred to as opportunities for the acquisition of partners and donors and as a place where new projects and ideas were developed. From these interviews, we can underline the specific nature of the regional context and unique conditions for the regional philanthropic field.

Conclusion: Strategizing the Philanthropic Field?

We have proposed the philanthropic field as an analytical framework to conceive and capture the interrelations of benevolent activities across the domains of private, public, and civic sectors in a geographical context. The concept of the philanthropic field offers a comprehensive view of philanthropic engagement beyond the sectoral boundaries of civic, public, and private actors.

Through our exploratory case study of the Southern German region of Heilbronn Franconia, we have illustrated that its philanthropic field was territorially constrained, loosely connected, and fragmented, as well as highly diversified in terms of its actors, and with a certain division of labor between them. Through interviews we uncovered close associations between local key actors in the field of philanthropy and the influence of their networks on the selection of recipients, flows of donations, and their willingness to cooperate on the local or regional level.

Moreover, through the field perspective and the use of methods of network analysis we have conveyed that different actors collaborate on big projects that none of the individual actors could have pursued or realized separately. In this way, regional philanthropy has had a considerable impact on education and knowledge creation in Heilbronn-Franconia. The largest share of all donations we covered in our analysis was directed towards science and education and led to the establishment of an entirely new university campus in the region. The vast majority of foundations reported that they had contributed to the creation of new ideas and concepts in other areas of societal development, such as cultural heritage, education, sports, religious practices, and so forth.

Overall, we have used our analysis of the geography of giving in the Heilbronn-Franconia region through the lens of the philanthropic field to show that not only the isolated work of diverse sets of actors, but also the collaborative engagement and interaction of partners from the first (state), second (business), and third sector (civil society) can produce successful contributions to solving social challenges at the regional level. We found both complementary as well as collaborative practices of giving. Coordinated cooperation enables positive economies of scale through the pooling of resources or the combination of complementary competencies. One possible implication for regional development is to include a region's philanthropic field in processes of regional governance (Glückler et al., 2020), on the one hand in order to promote charitable commitment, but also to orchestrate this commitment more strongly towards public goals and regional development. However, the integration of philanthropy into network governance requires further reflection (Glückler, Herrigel, & Handke, 2020; Jung & Harrow, 2015). Although interviewees named personal contacts and integration into regional networks as positive opportunities for the collaboration between for-profit and not-for-profit activities, we must highlight that individual involvement in local networks may also constrain some agency within the philanthropic field. Conflict- or problem-laden personal relations may quickly constrain the prospect for joint efforts in collaborative philanthropy.

When attempting to use regional commitment as a strategic resource for regional development politicians and planners should respect the individuality of the actors and take into account the diversity of their goals and strategies, as well as their unique combination of field activity and connectivity: In all efforts, it must be acknowledged that social commitment depends on the actors' regional involvement, self-determination, and initiative (Klein, 2015). Individual organizational or personal goals range from spontaneous or random motives to long-term strategic goals and therefore require broad approaches to governance. Commitment often develops over very long periods of time and within specific contexts. Personal relationships, private initiative, and sympathies and antipathies often determine whether business firms, foundations, municipalities, and other organizations in the various sectors are willing and able to successfully cooperate. External willingness to control and the goal of linking it with strategic regional development may stand in contrast with the philanthropic practices of business firms, foundations, associations, patrons, and volunteers. Recognition of this is a central prerequisite for any regional initiative aiming at the integration of philanthropic involvement in regional development strategies. To use the concept of the philanthropic field is to emphasize the interrelations between the diverse actors and may thus help regional stakeholders to discover new linkages and to initiate new forms of cooperation in pursuit of realizing large projects.

References

Acs, Z. J., & Phillips, R. J. (2002). Entrepreneurship and philanthropy in American capitalism. *Small Business Economics, 19,* 189–204. https://doi.org/10.1023/A:1019635015318

Adloff, F. (2010). *Philanthropisches Handeln: Eine historische Soziologie des Stiftens in Deutschland und den USA* [Philanthropy: A historical sociology of donating in Germany and the USA]. New York/Frankfurt: Campus.

Adloff, F. (2016). Approaching philanthropy from a social theory perspective. In T. Jung, S. D. Phillips, & J. Harrow (Eds.), *The Routledge companion to philanthropy* (pp. 56–70). London: Routledge. https://doi.org/10.4324/9781315740324

Adloff, F., & Degens, P. (2017). „Muss nur noch kurz die Welt retten.": Philanthrokapitalismus: Chance oder Risiko? [Just quickly have to save the world: Philanthrocapitalism: Opportunity or risk?]. *Forschungsjournal Soziale Bewegungen, 30,* 43–55. https://doi.org/10.1515/fjsb-2017-0085

Andreoni, J. (2001). Philanthropy, Economics of. In N. J. Smelser, & P. B. Baltes (Eds.), *International encyclopedia of the social & behavioral sciences* (pp. 11369–11376). Oxford: Elsevier. https://doi.org/10.1016/B0-08-043076-7/02298-1

Andreoni, J. (2006). Philanthropy. In S.-C. Kolm, & J. M. Ythier (Eds.), *Handbook of the economics of giving, altruism and reciprocity* (Vol. 2, pp. 1201–1269). Handbooks in Economics: Vol. 23. Amsterdam: North-Holland. https://doi.org/10.1016/S1574-0714(06)02018-5

Anheier, H. K. (2003). Das Stiftungswesen in Deutschland: Eine Bestandsaufnahme in Zahlen [The foundation system in Germany: An inventory in numbers]. In Bertelsmann Stiftung (Ed.), *Handbuch Stiftungen: Ziele—Projekte—Management—Rechtliche Gestaltung* (2nd ed., pp. 43–85). Wiesbaden: Gabler. https://doi.org/10.1007/978-3-322-90317-4_3

Anheier, H. K. (2005). *Nonprofit organizations: Theory, management, policy.* London: Routledge. https://doi.org/10.4324/9780203500927

Anheier, H. K., & Ben-Ner, A. (1997). Economic theories of non-profit organisations: A Voluntas symposium. *VOLUNTAS: International Journal of Voluntary and Nonprofit Organizations, 8,* 93–96. https://doi.org/10.1007/BF02354188

Anheier, H. K., & Krlev, G. (2014). Welfare regimes, policy reforms, and hybridity. *American Behavioral Scientist, 58,* 1395–1411. https://doi.org/10.1177/0002764214534669

Anheier, H. K., & Leat, D. (2006). *Creative philanthropy: Toward a new philanthropy for the twenty-first century.* London: Routledge. https://doi.org/10.4324/9780203030752

Anheier, H. K., Priller, E., Seibel, W., & Zimmer, A. (Eds.). (1997). *Der Dritte Sektor in Deutschland: Organisationen zwischen Staat und Markt im gesellschaftlichen Wandel* [The third sector in Germany: Organizations between the state and the market in societal change]. Berlin: edition sigma.

Anheier, H. K., & Seibel, W. (1990). *The third sector: Comparative studies of nonprofit organizations.* De Gruyter Studies in Organization: Vol. 21. Berlin: De Gruyter. https://doi.org/10.1515/9783110868401

Bekkers, R. (2016). Regional differences in philanthropy. In T. Jung, S. D. Phillips, & J. Harrow (Eds.), *The Routledge companion to philanthropy* (pp. 124–138). London: Routledge. https://doi.org/10.4324/9781315740324

Bekkers, R., & Wiepking, P. (2007). Understanding philanthropy: A review of 50 years of theories and research. Retrieved from https://core.ac.uk/download/pdf/148194198.pdf

Bekkers, R., & Wiepking, P. (2011). A literature review of empirical studies of philanthropy: Eight mechanisms that drive charitable giving. *Nonprofit and Voluntary Sector Quarterly, 40,* 924–973. https://doi.org/10.1177/0899764010380927

Bertelsmann Stiftung. (2007). Das gesellschaftliche Engagement von Familienunternehmen: Dokumentation der Ergebnisse einer Unternehmensbefragung [The social commitment of family businesses: Report of the results of a business survey]. Retrieved from https://www.familienunternehmen.de/media/public/pdf/publikationen-studien/studien/Studie_Stiftung_Familienunternehmen_Das-Gesellschaftliche-Engagement-von-Familienunternehmen.pdf

Beschorner, T. (2010). Corporate Social Responsibility und Corporate Citizenship: Theoretische Perspektiven für eine aktive Rolle von Unternehmen [Corporate social responsibility and corporate citizenship: Theoretical perspectives for an active role of companies]. In H. Backhaus-Maul, C. Biedermann, S. Nährlich, & J. Polterauer (Eds.), *Corporate Citizenship in Deutschland: Gesellschaftliches Engagement von Unternehmen. Bilanz und Perspektiven* (2nd ed., pp. 111–130). Bürgergesellschaft und Demokratie: Vol. 27. Wiesbaden: VS Verlag für Sozialwissenschaften. https://doi.org/10.1007/978-3-531-91930-0_5

Birkhölzer, K., Klein, A., Priller, E., & Zimmer, A. (Eds.). (2005). *Dritter Sektor/drittes System : Theorie, Funktionswandel und zivilgesellschaftliche Perspektiven* [Third sector/third system: Theory, functional change and civil society perspectives]. Bürgergesellschaft und Demokratie: Vol. 20. Wiesbaden: VS Verlag für Sozialwissenschaften. https://doi.org/10.1007/978-3-663-05985-1

Brown, E., & Ferris, J. M. (2007). Social capital and philanthropy: An analysis of the impact of social capital on individual giving and volunteering. *Nonprofit and Voluntary Sector Quarterly, 36,* 85–99. https://doi.org/10.1177/0899764006293178

Bundesverband Deutscher Stiftungen. (2012). Stiftungen und Vermögen in Klassen: Stand 31.12.2012. [Classification of foundations and private wealth: As of 31.12.2012.]. Retrieved April 1, 2013, from http://www.stiftungen.org/fileadmin/bvds/de/Presse/Grafiken_Zahlen_Daten/Stiftungsvermoegen_Klassen_2012.pdf

Bundesverband Deutscher Stiftungen (Ed.). (2013). *Stiftungsreport 2013/14: Auftrag Nachhaltigkeit: Wie Stiftungen Wirtschaft und Gemeinwohl verbinden* [Foundation report 2013/14: Mission sustainability: How foundations combine business and the common good]. Berlin: Bundesverband Deutscher Stiftungen.

Burt, R. S. (1983). Corporate philanthropy as a cooptive relation. *Social Forces, 62,* 419–449. https://doi.org/10.1093/sf/62.2.419

Card, D., Hallock, K. F., & Moretti, E. (2010). The geography of giving: The effect of corporate headquarters on local charities. *Journal of Public Economics, 94,* 222–234. https://doi.org/10.1016/j.jpubeco.2009.11.010

Carroll, A. B. (1999). Corporate social responsibility: Evolution of a definitional construct. *Business & Society, 38,* 268–295. https://doi.org/10.1177/000765039903800303

Clerkin, R. M., Paarlberg, L. E., Christensen, R. K., Nesbit, R. A., & Tschirhart, M. (2013). Place, time, and philanthropy: Exploring geographic mobility and philanthropic engagement. *Public Administration Review, 73,* 97–106. https://doi.org/10.1111/j.1540-6210.2012.02616.x

Crane, A., Matten, D., & Moon, J. (2010). The emergence of corporate citizenship: Historical development and alternative perspectives. In H. Backhaus-Maul, C. Biedermann, S. Nährlich, & J. Polterauer (Eds.), *Corporate Citizenship in Deutschland: Gesellschaftliches Engagement von Unternehmen. Bilanz und Perspektiven* (2nd ed., pp. 64–91). Bürgergesellschaft und Demokratie: Vol. 27. Wiesbaden: VS Verlag für Sozialwissenschaften. https://doi.org/10.1007/978-3-531-91930-0_3

Diani, M. (2013). Organizational fields and social movement dynamics. In J. van Stekelenburg, C. Roggeband, & B. Klandermans (Eds.), *The future of social movement research: Dynamics, mechanisms, and processes* (pp. 145–168). Minneapolis, MN: University of Minnesota Press. https://doi.org/10.5749/minnesota/9780816686513.003.0009

Diani, M. (2022). Civil society as networks of issues and associations: The case of food. In L. Suarsana, H. D. Meyer, & J. Glückler (Eds.), *Knowledge and civil society* (pp. 149–177). Knowledge and Space: Vol. 17. Cham: Springer. https://doi.org/10.1007/978-3-030-71147-4_8

Diani, M., & Pilati, K. (2011). Interests, identities, and relations: Drawing boundaries in civic organizational fields. *Mobilization: An International Quarterly, 16,* 265–282. https://doi.org/10.17813/MAIQ.16.3.K301J7N67P472M17

DiMaggio, P. J., & Powell, W. W. (1983). The iron cage revisited: Institutional isomorphism and collective rationality in organizational fields. *American Sociological Review, 48,* 147–160. https://doi.org/10.2307/2095101

Evers, A. (2020). Third sector hybrid organisations: Two different approaches. In D. Billis & C. Rochester (Eds.), *Handbook on hybrid organisations* (pp. 294–310). Cheltenham: Edward Elgar. https://doi.org/10.4337/9781785366116.00027

Faller, B., & Wiegandt, C.-C. (2010). Die geschenkte Stadt: Mäzenatentum in der deutschen Stadtentwicklung [The donated city: Patronage in urban development in Germany]. *vhw FWS, 6,* 329–336. Retrieved from https://www.vhw.de/fileadmin/user_upload/08_publikationen/verbandszeitschrift/2000_2014/PDF_Dokumente/2010/FWS_6_2010/FWS_6_2010_Faller_Wiegandt.pdf

Faller, B., & Wiegandt, C.-C. (2015). Mäzenatentum in Deutschland: Eine Chance für die Stadtentwicklung [Patronage in Germany: A chance for urban development]? *Geographica Helvetica, 70,* 315–326. https://doi.org/10.5194/gh-70-315-2015

Faulk, L., Lecy, J. D., & McGinnis, J. (2012). Nonprofit competitive advantage in grant markets: Implications of network embeddedness (Andrew Young School of Policy Studies Research Paper Series No. 13-07). https://doi.org/10.2139/ssrn.2247783

Fischer, R. (2007). *Regionales corporate citizenship: Gesellschaftlich engagierte Unternehmen in der Metropolregion Frankfurt-Rhein-Main* [Regional corporate citizenship: Socially committed business firms in the Frankfurt-Rhine-Main metropolitan region]. Rhein-Mainische Forschungen: Vol. 127. Frankfurt: Rhein-Mainische Forschung des Instituts für Humangeographie der Johann-Wolfgang-Goethe-Universität.

Galaskiewicz, J., & Burt, R. S. (1991). Interorganization contagion in corporate philanthropy. *Administrative Science Quarterly, 36,* 88–105. https://doi.org/10.2307/2393431

Galaskiewicz, J., & Wasserman, S. (1989). Mimetic processes within an interorganizational field: An empirical test. *Administrative Science Quarterly, 34,* 454–479. https://doi.org/10.2307/2393153

Gautier, A., & Pache, A.-C. (2015). Research on corporate philanthropy: A review and assessment. *Journal of Business Ethics, 126,* 343–369. https://doi.org/10.1007/s10551-013-1969-7

Glückler, J., Herrigel, G., & Handke, M. (2020). *Knowledge for governance.* Knowledge and Space: Vol. 15. Cham: Springer.

Glückler, J., & Panitz, R. (2021). Unleashing the potential of relational research: A meta-analysis of network studies in human geography. *Progress in Human Geography,* 1–27. https://doi.org/10.1177/03091325211002916

Glückler, J., Punstein, A. M., Wuttke, C., & Kirchner, P. (2020). The 'hourglass' model: An institutional morphology of rural industrialism in Baden-Württemberg. *European Planning Studies, 28,* 1554–1574. https://doi.org/10.1080/09654313.2019.1693981

Glückler, J., & Ries, M. (2012). Why being there is not enough: Organized proximity in place-based philanthropy. *The Service Industries Journal, 32,* 515–529. https://doi.org/10.1080/02642069.2011.596534

Glückler, J., Ries, M., & Schmid, H. (2010). *Kreative Ökonomie: Perspektiven schöpferischer Arbeit in der Stadt Heidelberg.* [Creative economy: Perspectives of creative work in the city of Heidelberg]. Heidelberger Geographische Arbeiten: Vol. 131. Heidelberg: Geographisches Institut der Universität Heidelberg.

Glückler, J., Schmidt, A. M., & Wuttke, C. (2015). Zwei Erzählungen regionaler Entwicklung in Süddeutschland: Vom Sektorenmodell zum Produktionssystem [Two tales of regional development in Southern Germany: From a sectoral model to the production system]. *Zeitschrift für Wirtschaftsgeographie, 59,* 171–187. https://doi.org/10.1515/zfw-2015-0303

Glückler, J., & Suarsana, L. (2013). *Regionale Philanthropie und Innovation in Heilbronn-Franken: Studie in Kooperation mit der Industrie- und Handelskammer Heilbronn-Franken* [Regional philanthropy and innovation in Heilbronn-Franconia: Study in cooperation with the Heilbronn-Franconia Chamber of Commerce and Industry]. Heidelberg: Professur für Wirtschafts- und Sozialgeographie.

Glückler, J., & Suarsana, L. (2014). Unternehmerisches Engagement im philanthropischen Feld: Das Beispiel Heilbronn-Franken [Civic engagement of business firms in the philanthropic field: The example of Heilbronn-Franconia]. *Berichte Geographie und Landeskunde, 88*(2), 203–221.

Graddy, E., & Wang, L. (2009). Community foundation development and social capital. *Nonprofit and Voluntary Sector Quarterly, 38,* 392–412. https://doi.org/10.1177/0899764008318609

Guo, C., & Acar, M. (2005). Understanding collaboration among nonprofit organizations: Combining resource dependency, institutional, and network perspectives. *Nonprofit and Voluntary Sector Quarterly, 34,* 340–361. https://doi.org/10.1177/0899764005275411

Habisch, A., Wildner, M., & Wenzel, F. (2008). Corporate Citizenship (CC) als Bestandteil der Unternehmensstrategie [Corporate citizenship as part of business strategy]. In A. Habisch, R. Schmidpeter, & M. Neureiter (Eds.), *Handbuch Corporate Citizenship: Corporate Social Responsibility für Manager* (pp. 3–43). Berlin: Springer. https://doi.org/10.1007/978-3-540-36358-3_1

Hammack, D. C., & Smith, S. R. (Eds.). (2018). *American philanthropic foundations: Regional difference and change.* Bloomington, IN: Indiana University Press.

Harrow, J., Jung, T., & Phillips, S. D. (2016). Community foundations: Agility in the duality of foundation and community. In T. Jung, S. D. Phillips, & J. Harrow (Eds.), *The Routledge companion to philanthropy* (pp. 308–321). London: Routledge. https://doi.org/10.4324/9781315740324

Havens, J. J., Hindley, B., McQueen, A., Meisner, M. J., Schervish, P. G., & Trueblood, D. (2007). *Geography and giving: The culture of philanthropy in New England and the nation.* Boston: Boston Foundation. Retrieved from https://folio.iupui.edu/bitstream/handle/10244/699/GeoGivingReport2007.pdf

Havens, J. J., & Schervish, P. G. (2005). *Geography and generosity: Boston and beyond.* Boston: Boston Foundation. Retrieved from https://folio.iupui.edu/bitstream/handle/10244/714/Geography%20and%20Generosity%20report.pdf?sequence=2

Hay, I., & Muller, S. (2014). Questioning generosity in the golden age of philanthropy: Towards critical geographies of super-philanthropy. *Progress in Human Geography, 38,* 635–653. https://doi.org/10.1177/0309132513500893

Heinemann, F. (2010). Voluntary giving and economic growth: Time series evidence for the US (ZEW Discussion Paper No. 10-075). https://doi.org/10.2139/ssrn.1695417

Henderson, M. T., & Malani, A. (2009). Corporate philanthropy and the market for altruism. *Columbia Law Review, 109,* 571–627. https://doi.org/10.2139/ssrn.1116797

Herzog, P. S., & Yang, S. (2018). Social networks and charitable giving: Trusting, doing, asking, and alter primacy. *Nonprofit and Voluntary Sector Quarterly, 47,* 376–394. https://doi.org/10.1177/0899764017746021

Hiß, S. (2006). *Warum übernehmen Unternehmen gesellschaftliche Verantwortung? Ein soziologischer Erklärungsversuch* [Why do companies take on social responsibility? A sociological attempt at explanation]. Campus Forschung: Vol. 907. New York/Frankfurt. Campus.

Hof, H. (2003). Zur Typologie der Stiftung [On the typology of the foundation]. In Bertelsmann Stiftung (Ed.), *Handbuch Stiftungen: Ziele—Projekte—Management—Rechtliche Gestaltung* (2nd ed., pp. 765–796). Wiesbaden: Gabler. https://doi.org/10.1007/978-3-322-90317-4_27

Hurd, H., Mason, C., & Pinch, S. (1998). The geography of corporate philanthropy in the United Kingdom. *Environment and Planning C, 16,* 3–24. https://doi.org/10.1068/c160003

Johnson, J. A., Honnold, J. A., & Stevens, F. P. (2010). Using social network analysis to enhance nonprofit organizational research capacity: A case study. *Journal of Community Practice, 18,* 493–512. https://doi.org/10.1080/10705422.2010.519683

Jung, T., & Harrow, J. (2015). New development: Philanthropy in networked governance: Treading with care. *Public Money & Management, 35,* 47–52. https://doi.org/10.1080/09540962.2015.986880

Kischel, M. (2009). Das gesellschaftliche Engagement von vermögenden Personen [The social engagement of wealthy people]. In T. Druyen, W. Lauterbach, & M. Grundmann (Eds.), *Reichtum und Vermögen: Zur gesellschaftlichen Bedeutung der Reichtums- und Vermögensforschung* (pp. 184–199). Wiesbaden: VS Verlag für Sozialwissenschaften. https://doi.org/10.1007/978-3-531-91752-8_14

Klein, A. (2015). Der Eigensinn des Engagements als Voraussetzung guter Engagementpolitik [The self-will of engagement as a prerequisite for good engagement policy]. *Forschungsjournal Soziale Bewegungen, 28,* 144–149. https://doi.org/10.1515/fjsb-2015-0119

Krashinsky, M. (1997). Stakeholder theories of the non-profit sector: One cut at the economic literature. *VOLUNTAS: International Journal of Voluntary and Nonprofit Organizations, 8,* 149–161. https://doi.org/10.1007/BF02354192

Lawrence, T. B., & Phillips, N. (2004). From Moby Dick to Free Willy: Macro-cultural discourse and institutional entrepreneurship in emerging institutional fields. *Organization, 11,* 689–711. https://doi.org/10.1177/1350508404046457

Lengauer, L., & Tödtling, F. (2010, September 14–17). *Regional embeddedness and corporate regional engagement: Evidence from three industries in the Austrian region of Styria.* Paper presented at the eighth European Urban & Regional Studies Conference, Vienna, Austria. Retrieved from http://www.dur.ac.uk/resources/geography/conferences/eursc/16-09-10/LengauerandTodtling.pdf

Letts, C. W. (2005). Effective foundation boards: The importance of roles (KSG Working Paper No. RWP05-054). https://doi.org/10.2139/ssrn.642562

Letts, C. W., Ryan, W. P., & Grossman, A. S. (1997). Virtuous capital: What foundations can learn from venture capitalists. *Harvard Business Review, 75*(2), 36–44.

Maaß, F. (2009). *Kooperative Ansätze im Corporate Citizenship: Erfolgsfaktoren gemeinschaftlichen Bürgerengagements von Unternehmen im deutschen Mittelstand* [Cooperative approaches in corporate citizenship: Success factors for joint civic engagement of medium-sized German companies]. Munich: Rainer Hampp.

Maclean, M., & Harvey, C. (2016). "Give it back, George": Network dynamics in the philanthropic field. *Organization Studies, 37,* 399–423. https://doi.org/10.1177/0170840615613368

Marquis, C., Glynn, M. A., & Davis, G. F. (2007). Community isomorphism and corporate social action. *Academy of Management Review, 32,* 925–945. https://doi.org/10.5465/amr.2007.25275683

Matten, D., & Crane, A. (2005). Corporate citizenship: Toward an extended theoretical conceptualization. *The Academy of Management Review, 30,* 166–179. https://doi.org/10.5465/amr.2005.15281448

McGoey, L. (2012). Philanthrocapitalism and its critics. *Poetics, 40,* 185–199. https://doi.org/10.1016/j.poetic.2012.02.006

McGoey, L. (2014). The philanthropic state: Market-state hybrids in the philanthrocapitalist turn. *Third World Quarterly, 35,* 109–125. https://doi.org/10.1080/01436597.2014.868989

Moody, M. (2008). "Building a culture": The construction and evolution of venture philanthropy as a new organizational field. *Nonprofit and Voluntary Sector Quarterly, 37,* 324–352. https://doi.org/10.1177/0899764007310419

Ostrander, S. A. (2007). The growth of donor control: Revisiting the social relations of philanthropy. *Nonprofit and Voluntary Sector Quarterly, 36,* 356–372. https://doi.org/10.1177/0899764007300386

Ostrower, F. (1995). *Why the wealthy give: The culture of elite philanthropy.* Princeton, NJ: Princeton University Press. https://doi.org/10.1515/9781400821853

Phillips, S. D., & Jung, T. (2016). Introduction: A new 'new' philanthropy: From impetus to impact. In T. Jung, S. D. Phillips, & J. Harrow (Eds.), *The Routledge companion to philanthropy* (pp. 5–34). London: Routledge. https://doi.org/10.4324/9781315740324

Porter, M. E., & Kramer, M. R. (2002). The competitive advantage of corporate philanthropy. *Harvard Business Review, 80*(12), 56–68.

Porter, M. E., & Kramer, M. R. (2006). Strategy and society: The link between competitive advantage and corporate social responsibility. *Harvard Business Review, 84*(12), 78–92.

Powell, W. W., & Steinberg, R. (Eds.). (2006). *The nonprofit sector: A research handbook* (2nd ed.). New Haven, CT: Yale University Press.

Salamon, L. M. (1995). *Partners in public service: Government-nonprofit relations in the modern welfare state.* Baltimore, MD: Johns Hopkins University Press.

Salamon, L. M. (2014). *New frontiers of philanthropy: A guide to the new tools and actors reshaping global philanthropy and social investing.* Oxford, UK: Oxford University Press. https://doi.org/10.1093/acprof:oso/9780199357543.001.0001

Salamon, L. M., & Anheier, H. K. (1992). In search of the non-profit sector. I: The question of definitions. *VOLUNTAS: International Journal of Voluntary and Nonprofit Organizations, 3,* 125–151. https://doi.org/10.1007/BF01397770

Salamon, L. M., & Anheier, H. K. (1998). Social origins of civil society: Explaining the nonprofit sector cross-nationally. *VOLUNTAS: International Journal of Voluntary and Nonprofit Organizations, 9,* 213–248. https://doi.org/10.1023/A:1022058200985

Salamon, L. M., & Toepler, S. (2015). Government-nonprofit cooperation: Anomaly or necessity? *VOLUNTAS: International Journal of Voluntary and Nonprofit Organizations, 26,* 2155–2177. https://doi.org/10.1007/s11266-015-9651-6

Salamon, L. M., & Wojciech Sokolowski, S. (2016). Beyond nonprofits: Re-conceptualizing the third sector. *VOLUNTAS: International Journal of Voluntary and Nonprofit Organizations, 27,* 1515–1545. https://doi.org/10.1007/s11266-016-9726-z

Sasse, C. M., & Trahan, R. T. (2007). Rethinking the new corporate philanthropy. *Business Horizons, 50,* 29–38. https://doi.org/10.1016/j.bushor.2006.05.002

Saunders-Hastings, E. (2018). Plutocratic philanthropy. *The Journal of Politics, 80,* 149–161. https://doi.org/10.1086/694103

Schneider, A. (2012). Reifegradmodell CSR: Eine Begriffsklärung und -abgrenzung [Maturity model CSR: A definition and demarcation]. In A. Schneider & R. Schmidpeter (Eds.), *Corporate Social Responsibility: Verantwortungsvolle Unternehmensführung in Theorie und Praxis* (pp. 17–38). Berlin: Springer. https://doi.org/10.1007/978-3-642-25399-7_2

Schwartz, M. S., & Carroll, A. B. (2003). Corporate social responsibility: A three-domain approach. *Business Ethics Quarterly, 13,* 503–530. https://doi.org/10.5840/beq200313435

Suarsana, L., & Glückler, J. (2016). Vernetztes regionales Engagement: Das Beispiel Heilbronn-Franken [Interconnected regional engagement: The example of Heilbronn-Franconia]. *Standort, 40,* 25–32. https://doi.org/10.1007/s00548-016-0407-3

von Schnurbein, G., & Bethmann, S. (2010). *Philanthropie in der Schweiz* [Philanthropy in Switzerland]. CEPS Forschung und Praxis: Vol. 1. Basel, Switzerland: Centre for Philanthropy Studies (CEPS), University of Basel. https://doi.org/10.5451/unibas-ep28292

Wiepking, P., & Handy, F. (2015). *The Palgrave handbook of global philanthropy.* London: Palgrave Macmillan. https://doi.org/10.1057/9781137341532

Wiepking, P., & Maas, I. (2009). Resources that make you generous: Effects of social and human resources on charitable giving. *Social Forces, 87,* 1973–1995. https://doi.org/10.1353/sof.0.0191

Wolch, J. R., & Geiger, R. K. (1985). Corporate philanthropy: Implications for urban research and public policy. *Environment and Planning C: Government and Policy, 3,* 349–370. https://doi.org/10.1068/c030349

Wolpert, J. (1988). The geography of generosity: Metropolitan disparities in donations and support for amenities. *Annals of the Association of American Geographers, 78,* 665–679. https://doi.org/10.1111/j.1467-8306.1988.tb00237.x

Wolpert, J. (1995). Giving and region: Generous and stingy communities. *New Directions for Philanthropic Fundraising, 1995*(7), 11–30. https://doi.org/10.1002/pf.41219950703

Wolpert, J., & Reiner, T. (1984). The philanthropy marketplace. *Economic Geography, 60,* 197–209. https://doi.org/10.2307/143809

Zimmer, A. E. (2007). *Vereine: Zivilgesellschaft konkret* [Civic associations: Civil society in the real] (2nd ed.). Grundwissen Politik: Vol. 16. Wiesbaden: VS Verlag für Sozialwissenschaften. https://doi.org/10.1007/978-3-531-90626-3

Zimmer, A. E., & Simsa, R. (Eds.). (2014). *Forschung zu Zivilgesellschaft, NPOS und Engagement: Quo vadis?* [Research on civil society, NGOS, and engagement: quo vadis?]. Bürgergesellschaft und Demokratie: Vol. 46. Wiesbaden: Springer VS. https://doi.org/10.1007/978-3-658-06177-7

Chapter 10
Global Authenticity, Local Authority: Epistemic Power, Discursive Geographies, and the Creation of Civil Society Knowledge Networks

E. Fouksman

Introduction

Knowledge is both the fuel and the product of international development practice. Development interventions are premised on knowledge and ideas—both on understandings of the needs of the majority world (the nature of the problem), and on ideas of how to engage with and ultimately resolve such needs (how to solve it). At the same time, this process inevitably creates new knowledge in its wake, both among those who work in the development sector, and those whom the sector attempts to help. This is an iterative, interconnected process that is embedded in wider epistemic currents and world views (Verkoren, 2010). Out of it arise the paradigms and ideas that have come and gone in development practice—from microcredit to cash transfers, from women in development to gender mainstreaming, from resilience to adaptation. This chapter is concerned with the question of knowledge sources in development practice—how do ideas and knowledge currents (and the people that represent them) find ascendency within development practice, both among global epistemic currents and their field-applications? How do development actors, particularly development-focused civil society organizations, prioritize and legitimize certain ideas? Why do such organizations select, accept, and choose to apply certain ideas over others?

To answer these questions, it is crucial to look at the way development practitioners *themselves* understand, categorize, and utilize ideas and knowledge sources. This chapter will use two multi-sited studies of *aidland* (Fechter & Hindman, 2011; Marcus, 1995; Mosse, 2011) to demonstrate the ways in which development professionals repeatedly create, enact, utilize, and privilege two categories or typologies of knowledge: "expert" or global knowledge and participatory or "local"

E. Fouksman (✉)
Centre for Public Policy Research, School of Education, Communication and Society, King's College London, London, UK
e-mail: liz.fouksman@kcl.ac.uk

J. Glückler et al. (eds.), *Knowledge and Civil Society*, Knowledge and Space 17,
https://doi.org/10.1007/978-3-030-71147-4_10

knowledge. Of course, such a binary distinction between expert and local is not normative but descriptive. While it has been contested in the academic literature,[1] this chapter will demonstrate that it continues to be used in development practice; hence the logic behind its use must be described and understood. I argue that both categories are used in international development to give practitioners legitimacy to act, and yet that each also plays a separate role in development projects: referencing expert knowledge gives development interventions authority, while laying claim to local knowledge grants authenticity. Thus, both categories carry power. Yet I will argue that this power is more than simply a form of cultural imperialism founded on ideas about the professional, the expert, and expertise (Kothari, 2005, p. 427). This power is used to produce, co-opt, and justify development work rather than only repress or control its subjects—in the words of Lewis and Mosse (2006), it is power "that comes from below as well as above, that is heterogeneous, diffuse, immanent and unstable" (p. 3).

The category of expert knowledge has a long history in development interventions,[2] as well as in the colonial administrations that were international development's predecessors.[3] It is global in scope and typically Western-based in origin. It is technical in its extent and focus, often concentrating on formalized methodological approaches to problem-solving, be they log frames[4] or survey instruments. It is rooted in a common language (not only English, but also the particular discourse of international development) and its practitioners bear the insignia of authority, such as Western degrees and international experience (Fechter & Hindman, 2011; Mosse, 2011). The individuals and organizations that are the source of this knowledge are part of what Adler, Haas and others have called *epistemic communities* (Adler & Haas, 1992; Haas, 1990)—"a network of professionals with recognized expertise and competence in a particular domain and an authoritative claim to policy-relevant knowledge" (Haas, 1992, p. 3). These are consultants (and consultancies), foundations, academics, monitoring and evaluation specialists, expats, and *development nomads* (Chambers, 2005) working in the higher rungs of the country offices of transnational development institutions. All share "the will to improve" (Li, 2007, p. 1) under-developed societies as a core aim.

In short, the sources of expert knowledge are the individuals and organizations that act as what John Meyer (1999, 2010) has termed *advisors* in dispensing their expertise to development projects. As will be argued below, expert knowledge is used to give legitimacy and authority to already existing development practice as much as to develop new knowledge and new ideas. It reproduces the epistemic and discursive consensus of transnational movements, and often incorporates academic knowledge or credentials. Expert knowledge has its own spaces of consensus

---

[1] See Aronsson, 2007; Cooke and Kothari, 2001; McKinnon, 2006; Mitchell, 2002.

[2] Evans and Stephens, 1988; Ingham, 1993; Mitchell, 2002; Scott, 1998.

[3] Adas, 1989; Cohn, 1996; Said, 1978/1994.

[4] Log frames, or the Logical Framework Approach (LFA), is used in international development projects as a formalized way of organizing project design and monitoring. It largely consists of drawing and filling in tables with the details of various project objectives and goals.

building, such as conferences, workshops, and trainings—indeed, both knowledge building and knowledge transfer are important goals of such "experts." In the words of Uma Kothari (2005), "knowledge of development professionals and the Western notions of 'progress' embodied within them continue to be reinforced through the power embedded in the relationship between donor and beneficiary" (p. 428).

Yet expert knowledge is not the only source of legitimacy for development practice. Over the course of the last few decades, another form of knowledge in development has become equally vital: local (also known as "citizen," "grassroots," "indigenous," or "traditional"[5]) knowledge (Briggs, 2005). This pushback is intertwined with postmodern perspectives and post-development theory, whose proponents reject development's universalist aims at global betterment (Escobar, 1995). They privilege and emphasize specificity and context-dependence, and promote "the validity and salience of local knowledge" (Beinart, 2000, p. 277)—for example, emphasizing the value of indigenous conservation systems (Berkes, 1999; Berkes, Colding, & Folke, 2000), or culturally specific ways of interpreting gender relations, such as Islamic feminism (Mahmood, 2005). In development practice, such knowledge emerges out of local leaders, participatory rural appraisals, and partnerships with grassroots organizations and activists. The development actors that prize such knowledge understand it to be locally tied and spatially bound (Fernando, 2003), and "time, place and culture specific" (Speranza, Kiteme, Ambenje, Wiesmann, & Makali, 2010, p. 296). The people and institutions that provide such knowledge are as much advisors and harbingers of legitimacy to development practice as the experts, but rather than being part of global epistemic communities and movements, they represent the authentic needs and perspectives of the individuals and communities with whom development civil society hopes to engage. Such "knowledge from below" has come to be increasingly privileged with the rise of participatory approaches to development—indeed, discovering and implementing local knowledge plays an essential role in such approaches (Chambers, 2005; Cooke & Kothari, 2001). Beyond granting a different kind of legitimacy to development practice, local knowledge also grants authenticity to global development-focused civil society by seeming to move it out of Western-centred, transnational movements and approaches to the perspectives and desires of the subjects of development.

Development practitioners use both typologies to justify their attempts to represent the "universal" needs and rights of the world's peoples, and to operate off a widely accepted (but not uncontested) assumption of the moral universality of their values (Anderson & Rieff, 2005). In this work, I not only examine the ways that development-focused civil society uses these two typologies of knowledge to signify legitimacy and authenticity, but also the relationship between the two. Global civil society organizations can invoke both categories simultaneously and at times in contradiction, and this chapter examines the way such organizations navigate

---

[5] I would echo Sillitoe (2010) in dismissing the semantic debates between these various terms as peripheral to an examination of the subject itself and the role it plays in the valuing and categorizing of knowledge.

such tensions and contradictions. Expert and local knowledge typologies are also used by the very individuals and organizations to whom they are applied, often in savvy, knowing ways in order to access both global funds and opportunities and local trust and cooperation. Yet the distinction between expert and local knowledge is itself blurry and contested, and the individuals and collectives to which such categories are applied often move between the two. Indeed, this chapter subverts these categories by pointing out the difficulties and contradictions in the way development-focused civil society attempts to categorize and demarcate different types of knowledge.

To do so, I draw on data from two multi-sited qualitative case studies of global development organizations and their in-country partners. Fieldwork for these case studies was conducted between 2011 and 2014, and utilised in-depth semistructured interviews (with over 200 interviews conducted in total), many more informal conversations and discussions, textual analysis of the written materials produced by the networks, and participant observation inspired by ethnographic methodology. I spent weeks with each of the organizations, attending meetings, shadowing workers, conducting interviews with as many people in each organization as possible, going out for informal social events, and in many cases actually staying as a guest in the homes of members of these organizations, often for multiple weeks at a time. Often it was the informal interactions that generated far more insight and sparked new questions rather than formal interviews. The interviews themselves consciously incorporated a variety of voices and vantage points across staff positions in the civil society organizations, where I interviewed nearly everyone I could access, allowing for a broad and nuanced picture of the organizations, their cultures, and the ways they created, took up, privileged, and transmitted ideas. When possible, I have conducted multiple rounds of individual interviews with the same key actors.

As this project examines connections and flows via discourse and practice, I have designed its methodological approach to utilize conversations as a window into attitudes, actions, and values. The methodology is thus centred around what Heyl (2001) describes as ethnographic interviewing: emphasizing time, openness, and repeated interactions with participants in order to build rapport and engage the participants in the research process itself. Rather than seeking only specific pieces of information and approaching the interview "as a pipeline for transmitting knowledge" (Holstein & Gubrium, 1995, p. 3), I approached interviews as a two-sided social encounter, and the knowledge produced by them as emerging out of the interaction between myself as interviewer, the person being interviewed, and any third party such as a translator. Thus, I approached these interviews as moments of mutual meaning making from both interviewer and respondent. In practice, this often meant entering the interview with a preconceived range of topics and questions, and making use of an interview guide for interviews at each tier of the process outlining the thematic areas I wished to cover, but at the same time actively engaging with the content of the interview, challenging answers, asking for depth, allowing the improvisation of new questions, adumbrating new interpretations, or privileging the development of certain topics over others. Such flexibility allows for a depth and richness of data that is particularly suited to the complexity of mapping such knowledge networks (Beinart, 1991; Wengraf, 2001).

The first of the two case studies encompasses the Christensen Fund (TCF), a US-based foundation working internationally with a mandate of supporting and promoting biocultural diversity (the intersection of biological and cultural diversity, such as the protection of sacred sites or traditional agroecological practices (Loh & Harmon, 2005)). The case study includes their partners in Kenya—Kivulini Trust, a small nonprofit based in Nairobi, and Waso Trustland, and even smaller NGO based in the north Kenyan town of Isiolo. Both organizations were supporting projects connected to biocultural diversity in the pastoral communities of the northern part of the country, and are examined in the context of a forest conservation project that they support in a small village in Isiolo district of Kenya. The second case study is of the Aga Khan Foundation (AKF), a large implementing foundation[6] that runs development projects around education, health, natural resource management, and economic development in a number of regions around the globe. The case study looks closely at AKF's work in Kyrgyzstan, drawing data from immersive qualitative fieldwork with its Kyrgyzstan branch (AKF Kg) and local implementing partner NGO (called the Mountain Society Development Support Programme Kyrgyzstan, or MSDSP Kg) in the context of their climate-change adaptation programme.

These two case studies provide insights into two very different organizations and development networks, with different scopes, approaches, and goals, and two different cultural and political contexts for their work. The USA-Kenya network encompasses far smaller organizations, concerned less with mainstream development and more with indigenous and ecological problems, and with much of the connections in the network built on personal relationships and a strong emphasis on empowering local leaders. The Swiss-Kyrgyz network involves larger organizations, which are deeply embedded in the aidland of international development. While these organizations are interested in ecological issues, they are deeply rooted in more mainstream development concerns around livelihood, education, and health. Despite the contrast, both networks create and utilize the two typologies or categories of knowledge discussed above. In this chapter, I draw on aspects and examples from each to examine ways of knowing and of privileging knowledge in development-focused civil society. I argue that civil society organizations create this morphology of knowledge in order to signal authority and authenticity both to others and themselves, thus enacting power. Yet these categories are also fluid and porous, and can at different times be used by the same individuals and organizations. This chapter demonstrates the way these two typologies are simultaneously used, contested, and undermined by both the agents and "beneficiaries" of development. The power their use confers is dynamic and complex, and lies beyond simple hierarchies and top-down interventions—and can thus be captured by multiple agents, in multiple positions of power and resistance, within the development project.

---

[6] That is, AKF draws on its own internal funding and runs its own projects—though in fact AKF also applies for and uses external funding for its programs.

Creating Authority out of Expert Knowledge

Expert Expats in Bishkek

The Kyrgyzstan office of the Aga Khan Foundation (AKF Kg) demonstrates the ways in which development-focused civil society seeks and utilizes expertise and expert knowledge. This expertise is largely Western, though, as described below, its producers prefer to think of themselves as global.[7] When I visited the organization in 2013, expats held the three top positions in the organization: Karl,[8] a German, was the CEO; Jack,[9] a Canadian, was in charge of fundraising and grant-writing; and Nicolle, an American, was the head of the research, monitoring, and evaluation unit. All three are development veterans, having worked for many years in Africa or Asia before coming to AKF Kg. The organization's culture was thus dominated by expat authority, and by the distinction between the expats and locals working in the organization. When I asked Karl how most of decisions, particularly those related to creating programs when applying for new grants, were made, he said that this was done by Jack in conversation with himself and Nicolle. Karl was not the only one to say so: during my interviews, most of the Kyrgyz staff members at AKF Kg stated that Jack created ideas around programming, and there was a strong sense in both AKF Kg and its implementing partner NGO MSDSP that expats and their networks made decisions in Bishkek. This deferral to foreign expertise was also reflected in AKF Kg's climate-change adaptation programming, then a new area for AKF and MSDSP. Another expat (Laurie, an American) was specifically hired as a consultant to refine, evolve, and shape the program's implementation.

These positions are all crucial to the way broad trends and global movements are transformed into AKF programming, and the way the programming is implemented, evaluated, altered, and tailored. The climate-change adaptation program is a case in point: both Karl, then the CEO of AKF Kg, and David, at the time the head of the environmental fund of the Aga Khan Foundation, called the Prince Sadruddin Aga Khan Fund for the Environment (PSAKFE), described the climate-change adaptation program in Kyrgyzstan as pragmatic, and valuable for being able to tap into broader interest (and thus funding) within the global development community. Both credited Laurie with the main idea and impetus behind the program—despite the fact that Talant, the Kyrgyz head of MSDSP, told me that he was one of the program's original instigators. Thus, it is Western experts like Laurie or Jack who are given the task of interpreting the interests and trends of the broader development community into programming in particular countries. This is not to say that their

---

[7] Indeed, the very term *global civil society* carries this conceit (Anderson & Rieff, 2005; Kaldor, 2003; Keane, 2003).

[8] Participants in the case studies were given the option to change their name to preserve anonymity, or to use their real given/first name. Most preferred to use their real given or first name; some chose to have their full name used, and some names has been changed upon request.

[9] Named changed on request.

motives are purely pragmatic—Laurie is genuinely and deeply concerned with the effects of climate change on communities in the developing world. But such genuine concern does not negate the more pragmatic advantages of creating connections into global movements and consensus that has funding behind it. Wielders of expert knowledge then both adopt norms and create them. Experts become what the sociologist John Meyer refers to as the *consultants* or *others* (i.e., not actors or nation states) who create and enforce a world polity—collectives that take part in and mutually create a world culture, that produce norms and advice by speaking in terms of higher truths and moral laws, such as climate change and its moral imperatives for development (Meyer, 1999).

These experts are able to exercise power and find legitimacy in part by relying on the claim that their knowledge emerges from working in the development sector all over the globe and with a variety of different programs. They are part of a development epistemic community, in the sense of "networks of knowledge-based experts" with "authoritative claim to policy-relevant knowledge" (Haas, 1992, p. 2–3). Their claims to policy-relevance and professionalism lend them authority, and the internationalization of their knowledge, and their connection to wider development currents—often through conferences, workshops, and international meetings—grants legitimacy by giving a transnational scope to their ideas.

Indeed, this is the corner stone of the epistemic community idea—an international consensus in the applicability and the verity of certain forms of knowledge. Epistemic communities have a shared way of knowing, which includes shared values, causal beliefs, and, importantly, shared discursive practices. In AKF's in-country branches, connections to epistemic communities in this sense were created and fostered through trainings (discussed below), the hiring of experts, and attendance at conferences. This use of expert knowledge is coordinated by the head office of the Aga Khan Foundation in Geneva, which is the key player in integrating AKF into a global community, advising country branches, creating connections, and following up on funding opportunities. Mark, the head of AKF's natural resource management (NRM) program in AKF's head office, told me that the Geneva office's main function is to "stay in touch with global best practices" and to "engage with international programs"—and to spread these practices through trainings for country office staff and by bringing a handful of staff members from each country to a few international conferences or events every year.

This alignment with broader, transnational ideas and ways of knowledge gives expats in the development arena not only legitimacy but also power. Local staff at both AKF Kg and MSDSP would refer and defer to expat expertise, in particular to Laurie's role in the climate-change adaptation program. Pirjan, who ran the climate-change adaptation program, Aizada, who was the program coordinator, and Talant, the director of MSDSP—all Kyrgyz staff members at MSDSP—repeatedly mentioned "the international consultant" or "reports prepared by an international consultant" or some fact "according to the international consultant"—although it was clear that I knew Laurie and her role in the program. Mentioning the *international consultant* gave legitimacy and gravitas to whatever fact, argument, or piece of work they were discussing, in a way that mentioning the specific person (Laurie) who did the work did not. The fact that this power was granted to a consultant, specifically in a knowledge- and advice-giving role, echoes Meyer's (2010) arguments about the role of consultants, advisers, and others (that is, non-actors) in creating consensus and agreement transnationally. At the same time the use of the very word "international" by Kyrgyz staff members denotes a level of authority to the knowledge produced by this figure (and Laurie's role was largely producing knowledge—reports, training manuals, syntheses of village assessments).

Thus, the power to decide on what global movements, organizations, and programs to engage with, as well the power to transform this (initially knowledge-based) engagement into action, lies with the international, and in fact Western, expats in AKF Kg. When I asked local staff members, both at MSDSP and at AKF, whether they had any decision-making power in the selection and design of new programs, they largely agreed that they had ceded it to Mark (together with Nicolle, Karl, and, in the case of the climate-change adaptation program, Laurie). However, they did insist that the programs had to conform to the organization's current strategic plan, and that they had a role in deciding what that plan contained at the two organizations' annual meeting and retreat. Yet even here it is significant that these meetings were attended by Western staff from AKF Geneva, and that the AFK Geneva office had to approve the new strategic plan. In short, even when key decision-making was nominally given to local staff, it was still controlled, and indeed even controlled directly, by the global node of the Kyrgyz network.

Creating Local Experts: Language, Education, and Training Trips in Kyrgyzstan

The weight and authority given to experts is echoed in the background and educations of the local staff members who are allowed to take on powerful roles in AKF Kg and MSDSP. Almost all the staff members of AKF Kg and at MSDSP's head office in Osh are fluent in English, not a common thing even amongst Kyrgyzstan's highly educated. Nicolle once expressed concern that staff hired in Bishkek and Osh are selected on their language abilities rather than their knowledge or skills in development. Many had English Language as their university degree, and AKF Kg tended to prize their ability to connect with expat authorities as well as global partners. Many staff members are sent abroad for trainings, which are inevitably held in English.

Pirjan is one of the few staff members who did not speak English, whose experience and abilities overrode this requirement when he was being hired. On several occasions, Pirjan mentioned to me that he felt disadvantaged by this fact: He found it difficult to communicate with Laurie and to attend joint AKF-MSDSP meetings, and in fact the job advertisement both for his job and for the coordinator of the third iteration of the climate-change adaptation (a job he applied for and did not get) contained an explicit requirement of English fluency.

By contrast, Rahat, the new coordinator for the third iteration of the climate-change adaptation program, has a master's degree from Manchester. Leila, the reporting manager for MSDSP—which is the one position at MSDSP besides that of Talant, the director, that involved communicating with donor organizations outside of Kyrgyzstan—did her master's in Washington, D.C., and worked there for several years. Molvoda, the communications manager at AKF, lived for several years in New York. All three of these staff members are key in the way the intermediaries' actions and ideas are presented to outsiders (Molvoda and Leila), including those outside of Kyrgyzstan, or in the way programming is transformed into action (Rahat). Again, language is the key denotation of expert knowledge here—both English, but also the discourse necessary to communicate to donors and international development organizations.

There are occasional exceptions to the power held by expert knowledge in the organizations. Over a dozen staff members attended the kick-off meeting for the third iteration of the climate-change adaptation program, including several who could not speak English and several expats that could not speak Russian. Though the meeting started in English, Laurie insisted that it switch to Russian so that all the local staff could understand and participate in the discussions, and the discussion itself was a lively one, with proposals from MSDSP staff that actually changed some of the details in the way the program was implemented. However, multiple staff members later informed me that this was the exception rather than the norm, and that such meetings were usually dull and achieved little. Also, even in this open meeting, the local staff's suggestions went through a filtering process when they were translated by Talant to Laurie (who then actually chose which ones to implement). Talant privileged some suggestions over others in his translation and funnelled them into his own vision of how the program should look. So, despite (or even within) such exceptions, knowledge of English or experience in the West ultimately grants development expertise, as well as the power to transform ideas into practice.

Those Kyrgyz staff members without a background or experience in the West are sent to trainings and workshops held by AKF global staff from Geneva or other transnational organizations (such as the climate-change training held by GIZ that Pirjan attended), or even go all the way to Geneva for trainings in the AKF head office. For instance, Leonora, the human resources manager at MSDSP, went to Geneva during my time there for training. This begs the question: what can be taught or transmitted about human resources in Switzerland that cannot be explained or understood in Kyrgyzstan? I would argue that the trainings abroad are another kind of epistemic glue, creating consensus around expert knowledge and the privileging of the West as the central source of knowledge within development practice—even (or perhaps particularly) with the managerial aspects of such practice, such as managing human resources. Thus, examining the network in Kyrgyzstan reveals the creation and privileging of a category of knowledge with the weight of authority and claims to a global geography: a knowledge privileged for its expertise, and on this basis accorded weight in the creation of development practice.

Bottom-Up Expertise: Experts Designated by the Local in Kenya

It is not only globally connected institutions that privilege and see the pragmatic need for expert knowledge. This privileging of expert knowledge also happens at the grassroots. Local people, too, see the advantages that leveraging experts who have access to certain tools, ideas, and language can have in the world of development projects and funding. This is demonstrated clearly in the second case study of this chapter: a forest conservation project in a north Kenyan village called Beliqo. The project is funded by the Christensen Fund (TCF), a biocultural diversity-focused foundation based in San Francisco, USA, but was instigated and run with the help of a small regional NGO called Waso Trustland (WTL), based in the town of Isiolo in Kenya's north. Waso Trustland itself is connected to the Christensen Fund through another non-profit, the Kivulini Trust, run out of Nairobi by Dr. Hussein, himself a former Program Officer for the Christensen Fund. The development organizations in this network are far more independent and loosely connected than those of AKF, AKF Kg, and MSDSP Kg. With its biocultural diversity focus, the Christensen Fund privileges local knowledge and shies away from designating expertise as explicitly as the Aga Khan Foundation. All members of the Christensen Fund's partner organizations in Kenya are actually Kenyans, though Dr. Hussein is Western educated (another example of the roots and insignia of expert knowledge). And yet, even in a local NGO far closer to the grassroots than MSDSP, expert knowledge is privileged and acknowledged.

This can be seen in Waso Trustland's charismatic founder, head and director, Hassan Shano.[10] Although Dr. Hussein described Shano to me as a local or indigenous elder, Hassan Shano both sees himself and is seen by village communities in Northern Kenya as bringing information, knowledge, and skills from the global development communities. Indeed, one of Waso Trustland's main activities is running "sensitization" workshops in the region's villages, which educate local people about legal and political issues connected to land and natural resource use. This includes pragmatic knowledge of the Kenyan state and its legal instruments. Hassan Shano brought knowledge of the 2005 Kenyan Forest Act that granted power to community groups over local forests to concerned locals at the start of the TCF-funded forest conservation project in Beliqo. Shano also provided connections with civil society organizations with access to resources (including the Christensen Fund) who could help the village with its concerns. Indeed, most people I spoke to in Beliqo would tell me the community forest association and its forest conservation project was funded and supported by Waso Trustland—they very rarely acknowledged the Christensen Fund, despite the fact that Christensen staff members had visited the previous year, and that most people in the village were aware that WTL's funding came from foreigners.

---

[10] Indeed, Waso Trustland is almost a one-man show: Besides Hassan Shano, there is only an administrative assistant and jack-of-all-trades (Liban), and sometimes a legal intern sponsored by a partnering NGO.

Shano also brought the model of a Community Forest Association to the village, mimicking those started earlier all around Kenya. These ideas and connections might not have originated with Shano, but for people in the village, he was the expert with national and global links who brought such knowledge. Finally, Shano had the specific knowledge necessary for forging access to international support: Not only did he speak English, which is essential for access to development programs and aid, but he also had experience with global civil society, knew how to write grant applications, and had access to information technology and a sense of international funders and non-profits. As Beliqo did not have electricity or a mobile phone signal, its residents also saw Shano's ability to use the internet as a skill and an advantage, a kind of development expertise. As I will discuss below, other development actors and organizations Shano interacted with did not see him as an expert. Nevertheless, to the people of Beliqo and many other locals in the region, he was as much the expert, and the harbinger of expert knowledge, as Laurie was to Pirjan or Talant at MSDSP.

Rhetorics of Local Knowledge and the Claim to Authenticity

Aspirations towards Local Knowledge at the Aga Khan Foundation

While the knowledge, legitimacy, and authority of experts and expertise is privileged in development practice, the rhetoric of international foundations and development charities simultaneously privileges the very opposite: the knowledge of the grassroots. This can be seen in the rhetoric—if not the practice—at the Geneva headquarters of the Aga Khan Foundation. Although AKF's Kyrgyz office and implementing partner NGO seek expertise and expert knowledge, staff members at the Geneva headquarters were fully and unequivocally committed to the global norms and ideas around participatory development. Participation, local knowledge, and local needs repeatedly came up unprompted during my interviews with staff at AKF's Geneva office, and were referenced many times in the Foundation's public discourse. Mark, then the head of Natural Resource Management at AKF, repeatedly referred to AKF's work as "community based" and insisted that AKF focuses on what the communities want, that it respects community perspectives, and thus that its priorities shift with community priorities. Indeed, Mark characterized AKF's mission as "working with communities to address their needs"—echoing the discourse of community-needs-based approaches.[11] He said the same of the natural resource management program he oversees—its priority is to respond to people's (economic) needs, and in the case of the climate-change adaptation program, "community is central—climate change is second." The words "community" and "needs"

---

[11] See, for instance, Chambers, 1983, 1986, 2004; Hickey and Mohan, 2004.

came up frequently in our conversation, and Mark attributed this emphasis to the Aga Khan himself, who told the staff at AKF to build on community interests and local knowledge and to trust the local people.

Mark applied this participation rhetoric specifically to AKF's climate-change adaptation program. In his words, community participation in program management and planning is "done all along," and AKF does not push fads onto communities or distort community needs. Mark argued that pushing fads is how one loses community support and that this is the danger with climate-change adaptation. For this reason, it had to be integrated and "mainstreamed" into "real concerns" such as pasture and water management (Conveniently, AKF Kg and MSDSP are already well-versed in and have the expert knowledge for these programs). Indeed, Mark showed acute awareness of the weaknesses of development organizations when working with local communities—he spoke of the danger that development projects could distort people's interests and create local groups that fell apart the minute a project ended. Mark reiterated that the climate-change adaptation project should engage already existing groups and build on people's interests by mainstreaming a climate-change perspective into key resource management. The ideal of using pre-existing CBOs (community-based organizations) as a way of ensuring both participation and success (indeed, the two seem to be synonymous for AFK Geneva) was also echoed by David, at the time the head of AFK's environmental fund,[12] when he stressed that the climate-change adaptation program "empowered village organizations," and that this is the AKF "mode"—along with bottom-up planning, which is a hope if not always a reality.

This vision of participation differs quite strongly from the way the climate-change adaption program ran on the ground—though the ideals and the rhetoric of participation exist throughout the network. The program's reality was largely centred around top-down knowledge, teaching about climate change and adaptation through workshops run by MSDSP, followed by an adaptation project which was selected and run by the community, but in practice was based on examples given during the workshops. The workshops themselves echo MSDSP's previous programs and areas of expertise. However, AKF headquarters is ideologically committed to the idea of participation and participatory development, despite also being committed to finding technical solutions to problems it deems largely economic. Its promotional material stresses that the foundation gives money to "local organizations interested in testing new solutions, in learning from experience and in being agents of lasting change" (Aga Khan Foundation, 2006, p. 3). This is repeated in the Foundation's annual report, which states that AKF focuses on "inclusive, community-based development approaches, in which local organizations identify, prioritize and implement projects with the Foundation's assistance" (Aga Khan Foundation, 2007, p. 7).

Such an emphasis on local knowledge directly echoes the language of participatory development, which stresses the importance of local participation and idea

---

[12] The Prince Sadruddin Fund for the Environment (PSAKFE).

creation—in other words, local knowledge—as an antidote to the many problems and inefficiencies of top-down development (Hickey & Mohan, 2004; Mansuri & Rao, 2013). Community involvement and input is itself part of a transnational consensus or an epistemic community on development practice. However, I would argue that the Aga Khan Foundation is not searching for greater effectiveness in their programming, or even for the ideals of democratic civil involvement. The most central theme in the above quotes is the search for authenticity for the foundation itself. AKF's claims center around the organizational actors' awareness of real concerns and their response to real interests and existing problems. The emphasis on local reality gives the Aga Khan Foundation claim to authentic knowledge and experience—in other words, "street cred." This is not to say that the organization's emphasis on utilizing local knowledge is cynical. Their belief in its importance for development is likely entirely genuine, but it is notable that the higher up the organizational ladder I went, the more likely staff were to bring up participatory approaches and the importance of local knowledge. This points to a philosophical or ideological, rather than a practical or applied, concern with grassroots participation and input—a search for organizational authenticity.

Authenticity and Indigenous Knowledge: Funding Choices at the Christensen Fund

Much like the Aga Khan Foundation, the Christensen Fund uses the language of participation and locally led development. Indeed, because the Christensen Fund's mission is to promote biocultural diversity, privileging and prizing indigenous or traditional knowledge is core to the organization's mandate and aspirational rhetoric. Wolde Tadesse, the Program Officer for the East Africa region until 2014, told me that decisions must be made from the bottom, with community involvement and ownership of projects and project resources, and that the emphasis of TCF's work must be on inclusion rather than marginalization. Ken Wilson, the director of the Christensen Fund until 2015, reiterated the point and linked it to the decentralized nature of the Fund, telling me that the program officer for every region has their own unique strategy for funding distribution that is "shaped by context, by what is important to people, and what they'd like to change."

TCF went so far in emphasizing local needs and participation that it effaced and minimized its own role. In Ken's words, "institutions are essential for mobilizing resources, but can make complications and difficulties for movements: movements, individuals and issues should be core [to our work], not funding institutions." This is tied to the radical self-vision that TCF cultivates of itself, particularly in comparison to other international foundations. Ken stated that in trying to be "responsive to the goals and objectives of the leaders of [local] movements," TCF is "fairly extreme" in its decentralized approach: not only are its program officers located "on the ground"—that is, they reside in regions where they oversee funding[13]—but TCF's programs "involve multiple initiatives and grantees evolving in context," as opposed to the much larger initiatives of other foundations that are centralized. Tadesse echoed this when he flatly told me that "we're not telling [the grantees] what to do"—that TCF's goal is to work with the approaches in indigenous cultures to biodiversity, and that TCF thus purposefully does not implement or operate any projects to this end, so that, in Tadesse's words, these are "not our projects."

Indeed, TCF is not primarily an operating or implementing foundation (unlike the Aga Khan Foundation). This seemed a point of pride with Ken Wilson, even on pragmatic grounds. He stated that operating foundations such as AKF operate in a "closed circle"—they themselves "decide what's important, how to solve it, try to solve it themselves, and then evaluate." Ken argued that this is inefficient, costs a lot more, and lacks critical feedback. He depicted TCF as the opposite of a closed loop—by focusing on building capacity, it outsources the task of both finding and fixing problems. Fundamentally, TCF sees itself as promoting grassroots inputs into the biocultural diversity movements—picking up ideas and giving them voice and support. Unlike the Aga Khan Foundation, TCF views the input of local or indigenous knowledge as going beyond specific, localized projects. Its staff members believe that this knowledge must be fed into global movements and knowledge commons—for instance to create and bolster the global indigenous rights movements. The foundation's role thus becomes not simply to apply local knowledge, but to link it to the global or the expert. However, I would argue that the search for organizational authenticity and legitimacy is central in the Christensen Fund's repeated insistence on their use of indigenous knowledge. Indeed, it is even more fundamental to their organizational mandate, since it is a fundamental part of biocultural diversity. TCF can only be authentic in its claims to promote and support biocultural diversity if it promotes and supports indigenous or traditional knowledge.

Transcending the Categories: Blurring the Lines between Global Authority and Local Authenticity

Hassan Shano at Conferences: Crossing the Lines

In this chapter, I have thus far suggested two categories of knowledge both created and prized by development organizations: expert and local. However, although development professionals maintain these two categories for difference purposes and uses, the distinctions and separations between them are not firm. Not only do they sometimes blur into each other—as in the case of TCF and MSDSP staff discussed below—but they are permeable, and the same individuals can cross between

---

[13]Although Tadesse is the exception, residing in Oxford, his replacement in 2014 resides in Nairobi, Kenya.

being the source of expert and the source of indigenous knowledge based on context. This allows for shifting uses of power, and the occasional decentering of "the legitimacy and authority of Western modernity" (Kothari, 2005, p. 443) in development.

Hassan Shano, the head of Waso Trustland, is a particularly compelling example of this transcendence. As argued above, in the setting of his own organization and the communities it serves in the north of Kenya, Shano fulfils the role of the expert, bringing the knowledge and skills that can connect these communities both to international development organizations and trends and to legal knowledge of the Kenyan state. However, for TCF or even its Kenyan partner Kivulini, Shano is an *indigenous elder*. Dr. Hussein brought Shano to speak at both the 2005 World Conference on Ecological Restoration in Zaragoza, Spain, specifically as an indigenous elder on the role of indigenous knowledge in environmental restoration, as well as to a number of events around the UN Conference on Indigenous Peoples in Geneva. In both of these settings, Shano switched from his expert role in northern Kenya to being a representative of authentic indigenous knowledge.

In our conversation about these conferences, Shano seemed to be uncomfortable with the switch, preferring his role of expert in Isiolo to representing an indigenous elder in Geneva or Spain. However, Shano credits these conferences with making him realize the importance of culture and traditional knowledge and their value within global development and environmental organizations. Hassan Shano described the first time he attended the conference in Geneva, where during a day of cultural sharing, Maasai representatives, from Kenya came with "marvellous" traditional dress and performances. Hassan Shano described how he felt embarrassed that he did not have the same cultural artefacts to share, asking himself, "What about our Borana culture?"[14] Shano credited this moment of shame, brought about by the exposure afforded by an international conference, with awakening his awareness of the significance of culture in the global realm, strengthened in turn by the Christensen Fund's emphasis on biocultural diversity. Particularly startling in this story is the fact that Shano had to travel all the way to Switzerland in order to be exposed to the cultural assertion and strategies of another Kenyan ethnic group and to realize the value ascribed to such cultural expressions, and to local or indigenous knowledge more broadly, in global forums.

International conferences are not only an avenue for exposure to (both local and expert) knowledge—such as seeing Maasai culture presented—but also to the value and uses the international community ascribes to such knowledge. Thus, expert and local categories fuse and mix, just as Shano himself crossed the boundaries between the two depending on context and audience. As Smith and Jenkins (2012) have pointed out, "middling NGO activists" such as Shano "can play roles that challenge 'either/or' characterizations of development action, such as in being professionalized as opposed to political, elite as opposed to grassroots, and are at the centre of

---

[14] Borana is both Hassan Shano's ethnic group and also the ethnic background of the majority of village communities he works with. For a classic ethnography of the Borana, see Dahl (1979); for more on the political and social place of the Borana within Kenya, see Arero (2007).

the way such meanings are negotiated and played out through the machineries of development" (pp. 646–647). Shano thus complicates the local-expert binary. He is able to "exploit the artificial distinction between professional and local knowledges to claim authority and exert power" (Nightingale, 2005, p. 600)—both in Beliqo and in the global, expert setting of international conferences.

TCF and MSDSP Staff: Local or Expert?

The staff members of both the Christensen Fund and the Aga Khan Foundation, particularly at their implementing NGO MSDSP Kg, also illustrate the fluid boundaries between expert and local. As described above, MSDSP and AKF Kg prized local staff members who spoke fluent English, had experience in international organizations, and often had Western degrees. However, the promotional material described above, AKF made much of using local organizations and local staff members. Thus, AKF and MSDSP could benefit from having staff that simultaneously had the authority of experts and the authenticity of locals. This is even more obvious with the staff of the Christensen Fund. When I asked Ken Wilson about the gap between the foundation and actors on the ground, he went out of his way to depict how TCF attempts to forge closer links with the grassroots by employing staff that themselves could be considered part of the movements and peoples TCF attempts to help. He made the case that program staff members are "tangled up in the movements they fund" and thus are ultimately insiders and participants. Thus, Ken Wilson seemed to be presenting TCF staff almost in an intermediary role, a position they are able to take up because they claim to belong to the grassroots.

These claims are somewhat tenuous: the majority of TCF staff have a Western education and now live in the West. For instance, though Yeshi, then a grant associate at TCF, is from Ethiopia, she has a master's degree from the Institute of Social Science (ISS) in the Netherlands. Yet what these assertions emphasize is TCF's need to demonstrate its close connection to the grassroots, a connection that would legitimize the foundation's discourse privileging the local as the authentic repository of indigenous knowledge and as the crux of the foundation's work. In an interview two years later Ken reiterated the point, emphasizing the wide diversity of world views and perspectives and the "depth of knowledge" held by TCF staff, for instance of local languages and contexts, songs, and plants. In Ken's words, being a "staff-rich foundation" meant that TCF is able to "work on complex issues." Staff diversity is thus linked with insider knowledge, and enabled what Ken termed the "human relationships between staff and communities," the closeness and authentic knowledge of the grassroots. Just as "indigenous knowledge is becoming professionalized" (Laurie, Andolina, & Radcliffe, 2005, p. 476), so too can professional or expert knowledge become indigenized by way of claims to local authenticity and identity. But I would argue that this is more than simply "adverse incorporation" (Kothari, 2005, p. 429)—it shows the conceptual power that notions of grassroots, indigenous or local knowledge hold within the development project, even at its most globalized spatial levels.

Holding Typologies of Knowledge in Tension: AKF's View of Climate-Change Adaptation and TCF's Involvement in Programming

How do foundations like the Aga Khan Foundation and the Christensen Fund reconcile their simultaneous privileging of the authority of expert knowledge and the authenticity of local knowledge? These two typologies of knowledge seem to be distinct paradigms for the two organizations. It was only in response to direct questioning that staff members spoke of the fact that the two must interact, and even then, they tended to stress the importance of either one form of knowledge or the other. For instance, when asked whether TCF itself brought new knowledge to the communities whose indigenous knowledge it prizes, Ken Wilson stressed that TCF barely introduces imperatives to the grassroots, but rather presents knowledge and offers "new horizons of what can be achieved and ways to achieve this." Indeed, in its mission statement explication TCF depicts the organization as a "buttress":

> The Fund is choosing to 'buttress' these [grassroots] efforts, not just fund them—that is, we will back them, bolster them, support them and, in a gentle solid way, engaged in co-creation at times, but not ourselves seeking to direct the process, just as the 'buttress' on the wall of an ancient tower or rampart serves to secure and yet not dominate the crucial wall. (The Christensen Fund, 2010)

By utilizing this metaphor, TCF is engaging with the tension between local autonomy and TCF's involvement, between bottom-up indigenous knowledge and the globalized, expert knowledge of the organization itself. Thus, TCF rejects "direct[ing] the process" but acknowledges that its influence and involvement go beyond funding. When asked directly if TCF changes its grantees, Ken Wilson's answer was "Yes, definitely." He termed TCF's involvement as "thick grant making," that "the program officer influences projects and organizations through dialogue, [he or she] probes, asks questions, pushes, brings information." Yet such involvement remains in fine balance with TCF's protests that the Fund does not impinge on local autonomy or ideas. Yeshi TekleMichael, the grant associate at TCF who works under Tadesse, told me that Tadesse might push or encourage communities, but tries not to impose—in her words, he "just gives voice to what they want to do." In short, the Fund attempts to resolve the tension between valuing both its own influence and local ideas by insisting that although influence and knowledge might come from TCF, autonomy and ownership remains with the local.

The Aga Khan Foundation's headquarters are also caught between two visions of its epistemic approach. Thus, Mark admitted that although His Highness the Aga Khan wants AKF to build on local knowledge, this could also be too narrow a perspective for its work. He asserted that the foundation is not "slavish" to community knowledge, that it seeks to bring to communities outside expertise and "independent channels of information," and to develop knowledge and reduce ignorance. Both Mark and David highlighted the process of spreading knowledge while implementing the ideals of bottom-up development as a challenge that AKF is actively struggling with. In David's words, using bottom-up planning is a hope for AKF, but the foundation relies heavily on Western knowledge. Mark told me that AKF is "looking for new ways that knowledge and ideas are shared", and that this is a continuing struggle for AKF. He argued that filling broad knowledge gaps is a rocky and slow process with "high costs of information transfers." Mark argued that the Foundation is doing this by involving local institutions (linking back to its participatory rhetoric), as well as by providing overhead for "information transfer processes" that the foundation co-ordinates and facilitates.

This tension is particularly obvious in the case of the climate-change adaptation program. The climate-change adaptation literature has criticized bottom-up programming for ignoring the multiscale nature of climate change: local communities cannot easily engage with national or global priorities for adaptation (Thornton & Manasfi, 2010). Despite his repeated emphasis on the importance of local needs and local ideas, when pressed Mark admitted that the foundation sometimes had to "educate" local communities, and that they could not be expected to know about issues such as climate change. Indeed, Mark framed knowledge transfers as an issue of responsibility in a climate-change adaptation program—he told me that AKF does recognize "the responsibility to raise the [climate change] issue with the community." Thus, when pushed Mark admitted that both knowledge from above and below was vital. How AKF resolves tensions and contradictions between the two—for instance, if local communities were not interested in or did not believe in climate change—was never explicitly explained or addressed.

Conclusion

The case studies above have demonstrated the propensity of development organizations to both create and make use of two categories of knowledge: the expert and the local. The first brings development organizations not only legitimacy, but also authority, and despite its pretensions of global roots it often in fact represents Western training, ideas, or consensus. The second connects the development project to the (now global) idea of participatory or community-based development, and gives global civil society a claim to authenticity through its connections to citizen or indigenous knowledge. However, the two are deeply integrated, despite the propensity of global foundations such as AKF and TCF to treat them as distinctly separate categories. Not only are the lines between the two nebulous and at times crossed by the same actors, but expert knowledge both gains legitimacy from local knowledge and local knowledge itself can be constituted by global movements, such as those which privilege traditional culture or indigenous rights.

Civil society knowledge networks (Fouksman, 2017) such as the two described in this chapter act as vectors for ideas that emerge from a variety of geographies and integrate this knowledge into development interventions. Actors in the networks who can claim to be indigenous or local can wield power by granting authenticity to global organizations, the way Hassan Shano does with TCF, in the process getting local concerns heard or funded—but also shaping these concerns to global interests. And sometimes, the very same actors can claim authority by drawing on expert knowledge—the way Hassan Shano does in the village communities he works with, for instance by his ability to write successful grant applications. Indeed, this need not be a cynical transformation or manipulation: not only are the categories fluid, but they can in fact be open and accessible, dependant on context, object, and subject. Thus, civil society knowledge networks allow different ideas, needs, and visions of development to interact and shape each other, not in a simple hierarchy of global over local, but rather in a complex interaction, often leading to the emergence of something hybrid—be it the integration of infrastructural needs into climate-change adaptation or a community forest association that allows pastoralists to control the usage rights of local land.

In theory, a locally-bound, participatory, and context-specific approach has challenged the Western-based and expert-led modernization approach that characterized development practice in the 1950s and 60s. But how deep has this challenge been? Alongside the rhetoric of context specificity, local knowledge, and community participation, development as both a universal aim and practice has continued to be "the central organizing concept of our time" (Cowen & Shenton, 1995, p. 27). For instance, although participatory approaches became ever more prominent in development practice in the early 2000s, so too did the widespread acceptance of the UN's Millennium Development Goals and now the Sustainable Development Goals, which set the overall, universal aims of development. The privileging and lauding of local ideas, itself a universalizing discourse rooted in Western interest in Romantic Orientalism (Washbrook, 1999) and continued in postmodernist cultural relativism and participatory approaches to development, coexists alongside a continued search for knowledge of universal development aims and solutions, rooted in the Enlightenment and then colonial views of progress and shared humanity. As I have demonstrated in this chapter, the development project has become the key place of negotiation and enactment of these two visions, often held simultaneously by the same development actors.

Unpicking this negotiation is vital to understanding the way certain ideas and projects are justified and supported over others. The Christensen Fund embodies the power of these categories when Ken Wilson speaks about bringing local activists and local leaders to international conferences and UN meetings. In so doing, TCF sees itself as using its expert status within these international circles to promote local knowledge on the global stage. In selecting which local activists and which local ideas are brought to and promoted at these global (and largely Western) gatherings, TCF utilizes the category of local knowledge to promote the agenda and ideas it holds dear, while demonstrating that these ideas are in fact authentically local. Authenticity and authority are tightly interwoven in such an interplay of local and expert knowledge categories.

In examining this interplay, I have demonstrated that although the development project creates, relies on and privileges both categories, power and knowledge is still enacted in the Foucauldian sense—the West is able to exercise power over the local in the South. In part, this is simply a distribution of resources and historical power, but the West continues to justify and explain this very distribution by laying claim to global or universalizing discourse. Thus, expert knowledge becomes global knowledge and this global claim is bolstered by the rhetoric of local participation and citizen knowledge. This chapter has shown the way development practitioners try to lay claim to both knowledge typologies: they see themselves as in touch with the local, but as possessing instruments of expert knowledge such as log frames and impact assessments to demonstrate that their interventions are objectively correct. This brings the argument back to the Enlightenment paradigm of universal, scientific knowledge—now represented as expert knowledge, which continues to play a key role in the development project, despite the apologetics of the particularism and relativism of the local. And yet the discourse of the local and the participatory holds power too, by conferring authenticity as well as legitimacy to the development project. Thus, power becomes not a top-down imposition, but rather "individuals… and communities absorb, assume, resist, claim and interface with power and they too are implicated in [its] character, form and techniques" (Meade, 2012, p. 891).

Of course, as Beinart, Brown, and Gilfoyle (2009) point out, there is real utility for both what is categorized as scientific and as local knowledge, and to try to divorce and separate the two is simplistic. Perhaps one of the staff members at MSDSP Kg highlights the point—the organization has its own in-house civil engineer to plan and help build its infrastructure projects. This is a Kyrgyz man who has never left the country, was educated locally, and speaks no English. He has nothing to do with international organizations (other than ultimately drawing his salary from one) and does not have to speak the language of grant-writing. His does not fit the typology of expert knowledge, yet his knowledge of civil engineering is in a sense truly global: there is largely global consensus on how to build an irrigation canal or lay a pipe. Thus, the categories and their uses in international development lie in tension and often in contradiction; yet they play a crucial role in development institutions' epistemic search for authority and authenticity.

To critically evaluate the development project now, one must be conscious of the way power is deployed; these typologies of knowledge could be the present's version of the orientalism and scientific Enlightenment universalism of colonialism. Built implicitly into colonial power structures were troubling assumptions about race, geography and culture, be they stereotypes of noble savages or scientifically backward primitives. Today's parallel assumptions might be that there are global experts and authentic locals, and that these can be sharply separated. Indeed, both academia and society more broadly are struggling to bring together the apparent universality of science—and from it, technocratic, evidence-based interventions— with the insights of poststructuralism, cultural specificity, and indigenous knowledge. But rarely does it matter so much to people's lives as in the case of justifying the course of development interventions. This is a key battleground of power, and the structure within which both the actors and the subjects of development must operate.

Acknowledgements Research for this chapter was supported by the Rhodes Trust, the Oxford Department of International Development and the Gilchrist Educational Trust. This research would have been impossible without the generosity and hospitality of the people I met in Kenya and Kyrgyzstan, in particular Hassan Shano, Habiba Ibrahim, Nicolle Neson, Pirjan Manasov, and Eliza and Nurmat Tolumbaiulo, who all welcomed me as a guest into their homes, and without the perseverance and dedication of my translators, Salad Choki and Maksat Kazubekova. My thanks also to the organizers and participants of the Knowledge and Civil Society Symposium held at the University of Heidelberg for the opportunity to workshop the ideas and arguments that form the basis of this work.

References

Adas, M. (1989). *Machines as the measure of men: Science, technology, and ideologies of Western dominance*. Ithaca, NY: Cornell University Press.

Adler, E., & Haas, P. M. (1992). Conclusion: Epistemic communities, world order, and the creation of a reflective research program. *International Organization, 46,* 367–390. https://doi.org/10.1017/S0020818300001533

Aga Khan Foundation. (2006). Environment and development. Retrieved from https://d1zah1n-kiby91r.cloudfront.net/s3fs-public/Publications/2006_akf_environment.pdf

Aga Khan Foundation. (2007). *Aga Khan Foundation Annual Report 2006*. Retrieved from https://www.yumpu.com/en/document/read/34893361/akf-annual-report-aga-khan-development-network

Anderson, K., & Rieff, D. (2005). Global civil society: A sceptical view. In M. Glasius, M. Kaldor, & H. Anheier (Eds.), *Global civil society 2004/5* (pp. 26–39). London: Sage. https://doi.org/10.4135/9781446211908.n2

Arero, H. W. (2007). Coming to Kenya: Imagining and perceiving a nation among the Borana of Kenya. *Journal of Eastern African Studies, 1,* 292–304. https://doi.org/10.1080/17531050701452598

Aronsson, I.-L. (2007, October). On knowledge production and local participation. Paper presented at the NOHA-ECHO Presidency Seminar on Changing Scope of Humanitarian Action, Lisbon, Portugal. Retrieved from http://uu.diva-portal.org/smash/get/diva2:173934/FULLTEXT01.pdf

Beinart, W. (1991). Speaking for themselves. *African Studies, 50,* 11–38. https://doi.org/10.1080/00020189108707733

Beinart, W. (2000). African history and environmental history. *African Affairs, 99,* 269–302. https://doi.org/10.1093/afraf/99.395.269

Beinart, W., Brown, K., & Gilfoyle, D. (2009). Experts and expertise in colonial Africa reconsidered: Science and the interpenetration of knowledge. *African Affairs, 108,* 413–433. https://doi.org/10.1093/afraf/adp037

Berkes, F. (1999). *Sacred ecology: Traditional ecological knowledge and resource managment*. Philadelphia: Taylor & Francis.

Berkes, F., Colding, J., & Folke, C. (2000). Rediscovery of traditional ecological knowledge as adaptive management. *Ecological Applications, 10,* 1251–1262. https://doi.org/10.1890/1051-0761(2000)010[1251:ROTEKA]2.0.CO;2

Briggs, J. (2005). The use of indigenous knowledge in development: Problems and challenges. *Progress in Development Studies, 5,* 99–114. https://doi.org/10.1191/1464993405ps105oa

Chambers, R. (1983). *Rural development: Putting the last first*. London: Routledge.

Chambers, R. (1986). Putting the last first. In P. Ekins (Ed.), *The living economy: A new economics in the making* (pp. 306–323). London: Routledge. https://doi.org/10.4324/9780203169063

Chambers, R. (2004, November). Ideas for development: Reflecting forwards (IDS Working Paper No. 238). Brighton, England: Institute of Development Studies. Retrieved from https://citeseerx.ist.psu.edu/viewdoc/download?doi=10.1.1.487.8068&rep=rep1&type=pdf

Chambers, R. (2005). Critical reflections of a development nomad. In U. Kothari (Ed.), *A radical history of development Studies: Individuals, institutions and ideologies* (pp. 67–87). London: Zed.

Cohn, B. S. (1996). *Colonialism and its forms of knowledge: The British in India*. Princeton, NJ: Princeton University Press.

Cooke, B., & Kothari, U. (2001). The case for participation as tyranny. In B. Cooke & U. Kothari (Eds.), *Participation: The new tyranny?* (pp. 1–15). London: Zed.

Cowen, M., & Shenton, R. (1995). The invention of development. In J. Crush (Ed.), *Power of development* (pp. 25–42). London: Routledge. https://doi.org/10.4324/9780203975985

Dahl, G. (1979). *Suffering grass: Subsistence and society of Waso Borana* (Doctoral thesis). Department of Social Anthropology, Stockholm University, Stockholm, Sweden. Retrieved from http://su.diva-portal.org/smash/get/diva2:687864/FULLTEXT01.pdf

Escobar, A. (1995). *Encountering development: The making and unmaking of the Third World*. Princeton, NJ: Princeton University Press.

Evans, P., & Stephens, J. D. (1988). Studying development since the sixties: The emergence of a new comparative political economy. *Theory and Society, 17*, 713–745. https://doi.org/10.1007/BF00162617

Fechter, A.-M., & Hindman, H. (Eds.). (2011). *Inside the everyday lives of development workers: The challenges and futures of aidland*. Sterling: Kumarian.

Fernando, J. L. (2003). NGOs and production of indigenous knowledge under the condition of postmodernity. *The Annals of the American Academy of Political and Social Science, 590*, 54–72. https://doi.org/10.1177/0002716203258374

Fouksman, E. (2017). Civil society knowledge networks: How international development institutions reshape the geography of knowledge. *Third World Quarterly, 38*, 1847–1872. https://doi.org/10.1080/01436597.2016.1233490

Haas, P. M. (1990). Obtaining international environmental protection through epistemic consensus. *Millennium: Journal of International Studies, 19*, 347–363. https://doi.org/10.1177/03058298900190030401

Haas, P. M. (1992). Introduction: Epistemic communities and international policy coordination. *International Organization, 46*, 1–35. https://doi.org/10.1017/S0020818300001442

Heyl, B. S. (2001). Ethonographic interviewing. In P. Atkinson, A. Coffey, S. Delamont, J. Lofland, & L. Lofland (Eds.), *Handbook of Ethnography* (pp. 369–383). Los Angeles: Sage.

Hickey, S., & Mohan, G. (2004). Towards participation as transformation: Critical themes and challenges. In S. Hickey & G. Mohan (Eds.), *Participation: From tyranny to transformation? Exploring new approaches to participation in development* (pp. 3–24). London: Zed.

Holstein, J. A., & Gubrium, J. F. (1995). *The active interview*. Qualitative Research Methods Series: Vol. 37. Thousand Oaks: Sage. https://doi.org/10.4135/9781412986120

Ingham, B. (1993). The meaning of development: Interactions between 'new' and 'old' ideas. *World Development, 21*, 1803–1821. https://doi.org/10.1016/0305-750X(93)90084-M

Kaldor, M. (2003). *Global civil society: An answer to war*. Cambridge: Polity.

Keane, J. (2003). *Global civil society?* Cambridge, UK: Cambridge University Press. https://doi.org/10.1017/CBO9780511615023

Kothari, U. (2005). Authority and expertise: The professionalisation of international development and the ordering of dissent. *Antipode, 37*, 425–446. https://doi.org/10.1111/j.0066-4812.2005.00505.x

Laurie, N., Andolina, R., & Radcliffe, S. (2005). Ethnodevelopment: Social movements, creating experts and professionalising indigenous knowledge in Ecuador. *Antipode, 37*, 470–496. https://doi.org/10.1111/j.0066-4812.2005.00507.x

Lewis, D., & Mosse, D. (2006). Encountering order and disjuncture: Contemporary anthropological perspectives on the organization of development. *Oxford Development Studies, 34,* 1–13. https://doi.org/10.1080/13600810500495907

Li, T. M. (2007). *The will to improve: Governmentality, development, and the practice of politics.* Durham, NC: Duke University Press.

Loh, J., & Harmon, D. (2005). A global index of biocultural diversity. *Ecological Indicators, 5,* 231–241. https://doi.org/10.1016/j.ecolind.2005.02.005

Mahmood, S. (2005). *Politics of piety: The Islamic revival and the Feminist subject.* Princeton, NJ: Princeton University Press.

Mansuri, G., & Rao, V. (2013). *Localizing development: Does participation work?* A World Bank Policy Research Report. Washington, D.C.: World Bank. https://doi.org/10.1596/978-0-8213-8256-1

Marcus, G. E. (1995). Ethnography in/of the world system: The emergence of multi-sited ethnography. *Annual Review of Anthropology, 24,* 95–117. https://doi.org/10.1146/annurev.an.24.100195.000523

McKinnon, K. I. (2006). An orthodoxy of 'the local': Post-colonialism, participation and professionalism in northern Thailand. *The Geographical Journal, 172,* 22–34. https://doi.org/10.1111/j.1475-4959.2006.00182.x

Meade, R. R. (2012). Government and community development in Ireland: The contested subjects of professionalism and expertise. *Antipode, 44,* 889–910. https://doi.org/10.1111/j.1467-8330.2011.00924.x

Meyer, J. W. (1999). The changing cultural content of the Nation-State: A world society perspective. In G. Steinmetz (Ed.), *State/culture: State-formation after the cultural turn* (pp. 123–144). Ithaca, NY: Cornell University Press.

Meyer, J. W. (2010). World society, institutional theories, and the actor. *Annual Review of Sociology, 36,* 1–20. https://doi.org/10.1146/annurev.soc.012809.102506

Mitchell, T. (2002). *Rule of experts: Egypt, techno-politics, modernity.* Berkeley, CA: University of California Press.

Mosse, D. (2011). Introduction: The anthropology of expertise and professionals in international development. In D. Mosse (Ed.), *Adventures in aidland: The anthropology of professionals in international development* (pp. 1–31). Studies in Public and Applied Anthropology: Vol. 6. New York: Berghahn.

Nightingale, A. J. (2005). 'The experts taught us all we know': Professionalisation and knowledge in Nepalese community forestry. *Antipode, 37,* 581–604. https://doi.org/10.1111/j.0066-4812.2005.00512.x

Said, E. W. (1994). *Orientalism.* New York: Vintage. (Original work published 1978)

Scott, J. C. (1998). *Seeing like a state: How certain schemes to improve the human condition have failed.* New Haven, CT: Yale University Press.

Sillitoe, P. (2010). Trust in development: Some implications of knowing in indigenous knowledge. *Journal of the Royal Anthropological Institute, 16,* 12–30. https://doi.org/10.1111/j.1467-9655.2009.01594.x

Smith, M. B., & Jenkins, K. (2012). Existing at the interface: Indian NGO activists as strategic cosmopolitans. *Antipode, 44,* 640–662. https://doi.org/10.1111/j.1467-8330.2011.00888.x

Speranza, C. I., Kiteme, B., Ambenje, P., Wiesmann, U., & Makali, S. (2010). Indigenous knowledge related to climate variability and change: Insights from droughts in semi-arid areas of former Makueni District, Kenya. *Climatic Change, 100,* 295–315. https://doi.org/10.1007/s10584-009-9713-0

The Christensen Fund. (2010). *Understanding Christensen's Mission.* Retrieved from http://www.christensenfund.org/wp-content/uploads/2010/12/Christensen_Mission_Explication.pdf

Thornton, T. F., & Manasfi, N. (2010). Adaptation—Genuine and spurious: Demystifying adaptation processes in relation to climate change. *Environment and Society: Advances in Research, 1,* 132–155. https://doi.org/10.3167/ares.2010.010107

Verkoren, W. (2010). Learning by southern peace NGOs. *The Journal of Development Studies, 46,* 790–810. https://doi.org/10.1080/00220380903012706
Washbrook, D. A. (1999). Orients and occidents: Colonial discourse theory and the historiography of the British Empire. In R. W. Winks (Ed.), *Historiography* (pp. 596–611). The Oxford History of the British Empire: Vol. 5. Oxford, UK: Oxford University Press.
Wengraf, T. (2001). *Qualitative research interviewing: Biographic narrative and semi-structured methods.* London: Sage.

Part IV
Doing Civil Society

Chapter 11
Democracy Movement and Alternative Knowledge in Hong Kong

Kin-man Chan

Introduction: Trial and Alternative Knowledge

I was supposed to write this book chapter in the fall of 2018 after attending the Heidelberg Seminar. The writing plan was disrupted by a trial in which I stood as the second defendant together with eight activists identified by the prosecutor as the leaders of the Umbrella Movement in Hong Kong in 2014. We were accused of committing crimes related to conspiracy and incitement to cause public nuisance. After several rounds of pretrial hearings, the formal trial took place in December 2018 and lasted for three weeks. The "event" attracted enormous attentions from local and international media. Hundreds of citizens went to the court to hear the trial and chant slogans of support outside the courthouse. The trial's highlights were my testimony, the submission by the first defendant who was a law professor, and the mitigation speech by the third defendant who was a retired pastor. There were tears and laughter among the audience. At the end, the first defendant and I were sentenced to 16 months of imprisonment and the other two sentenced to eight months. I was unable to write this book chapter until I was released in the spring of 2020.

During the trial, I found that the courtroom became a public space to contest for different interpretations of history. The prosecutor believed that the prolonged blockage of some major avenues during the 79-day occupation was caused by the defendants' provocative speeches, whereas the defendants argued that it was Beijing's denial of *universal suffrage* that triggered the whole saga. The defense lawyers also summoned a respectable professor to prove that the unnecessary use of tear gas against peaceful demonstrators was a more prominent factor in bringing hundreds of thousands of citizens to the protest, according to the polls his team conducted. A documentary film was also shown in the court for the first time, revealing how young protesters made their own decisions to occupy while refusing to

K.-m. Chan (✉)
Center for Social Innovation Studies, The Chinese University of Hong Kong,
Shatin, New Territories, Hong Kong

© The Author(s) 2022
J. Glückler et al. (eds.), *Knowledge and Civil Society*, Knowledge and Space 17,
https://doi.org/10.1007/978-3-030-71147-4_11

identify some of the senior defendants as their leaders. The court debates, broadcast through news and social media, aroused unprecedented reflections on the movement. People accused the government of scapegoating the defendants and reiterated their free will in joining the protest. Compared to the extremely depressing mood in the movement's aftermath, the trial uplifted the movement's spirits by once again making the issues of democracy and civil disobedience the focus of public agenda. Alternative knowledge, that is, facts and interpretations of social reality beyond official prescriptions, such as polls conducted by independent scholars and documentaries made by independent directors, was disseminated through the court as a contested space. This is why the judicial process is deemed a part of the struggle in civil disobedience, as it provides a stage for the participants to explain their causes to the public. In the historical trials of Gandhi and Mandela, the court provided a most dramatized context that critiques the status quo and in which alternative visions of society are effectively communicated to the people when their emotions are provoked.

My aim in this chapter is then to discuss the production and dissemination of alternative knowledge by social actions, using the mobilization of the Umbrella Movement from March 2013 to September 2014 as an example. I focus my discussion on the *deliberation days* and the civil referendum conducted by the organizing team of the Occupy Central with Love and Peace (OCLP) movement led by the Occupy Trio, two professors and one retired pastor who later became the first three defendants in the Umbrella Movement Trial. Readers need to be forewarned that the author of this chapter is also a key player in this case. Although the involvement provided insider information and sympathetic understanding of the movement actors, constant reflections and cross references of alternative interpretations are needed to maintain scientific integrity.

Production and Dissemination of Knowledge in Social Movement

Civil society as a structure of self-organization plays a critical role in holding the state accountable to the will of the people. In order to do so, civil society members need to control state policies from the viewpoint of their consistency with the "socially constitutive value systems" (Frentzel-Zagorska, 1990, p. 760). They must also exercise self-defense in cases when this consistency is violated. But how does a society develop its socially constitutive values systems? Frentzel-Zagorska argued that it is initially through the elaboration of these normative structures that group identities and interest are defined. For example, workers could develop a sense of belonging to a certain industry and understand the importance of labor rights through joining a trade union. Upon this social base, an encompassing collective identity will develop to provide definition of its traditions, its hierarchy, and norms of social behavior.

Adopting this analytical schema assumes a certain degree of free communication within and across social groups. Unofficial or alternative information and perspectives are also available for civil society to check state policies' consistency with the socially constitutive value systems. In a more mature and responsible civil society, social groups will also propose alternative policies. In view of this, production and dissemination of alternative knowledge through civil society is an issue deserving scholarly attentions. Authors of the scanty studies in this area have found that unlike Frentzel-Zagorska's schematic development, the relationship between knowledge formation and self-defense is more complex. Very often, people only pay attention to social issues when their emotions are duly aroused. Intuition or elusive moral sense plays a significant role in making initial response to an emergent controversy in society. Acquisition of information and reflections on personal values will become more intense only after people are drawn into the social movement.

In his classic study of learning in informal education, Griff Foley (1999) found that "some of the most powerful learning occurs as people struggle against oppression, as they struggle to make sense of what is happening to them and to work out ways of doing something about it"(pp. 1–2). From a Gramscian perspective, Foley maintained that the unlearning of "dominant discourses" and the learning of "resistant discourses" is central to this learning. For Foucault, discourses are about "what can be said and thought, but also about who can speak, when, and with what authority" (Ball, 1990, p. 2 as cited in Foley, 1999, p. 15). In view of this, Foley's task of "unlearning" comprises the debunking of ideology justifying the existing arrangements of the distributions of power and resources. The "learning" thus refers to the acquisition of alternative or *counter-knowledge* (against the status quo) produced and disseminated through social actions.

With his case study (1999), Foley revealed that these unlearning and learning processes could be very painful. Those experiencing them were often disillusioned about expertise when professionals could offer no technical solutions (see also Heifetz, 1994). They also found that state officials did not always act to protect public interest. When they were finally fed up with the bureaucracy's idiosyncratic mode of tackling public issues, they decided to take things in their own hands. This awakening enabled people "to make sense of, and act on, their environment, and to come to understand themselves as knowledge-creating, acting beings" (Foley, 1999, p. 64). But this is only the beginning of another painful journey of working with fellow citizens without standard procedures and absolute authority. In response, social movement organizations and leadership attempt to give a more durable and predictable order to the definition of the situation and formulation of actions (Melucci, 1988).

Following this vein of argument, Donatella della Porta and Elena Pavan (2017) suggested that social movement provides "repertoires of knowledge practices" (p. 300), meaning the set of organizational practices that foster the coordination of disconnected, local, and highly personal experiences and rationalities within a *shared cognitive system* from which movements and their supporters can draw a common orientation for making claims and acting collectively to produce political and cultural change. Della Porta and Pavan named this cognitive system an "alternative epistemology" that produces "counter-knowledge" (p. 298). Citing Gramsci (1971), they called this "good sense" (p. 298), in other words, knowledge derived from "the popular practice" (p. 298) in everyday life, in contrast to "common sense" (p. 298) that crystallized the hegemonic system of social relationship.

In past studies of social movement, scholars either paid too much attention to resources and organization (old social movements such as labor movements) or value and identity (new social movements such as environmental and feminine movements) while neglecting that it is also a process of knowledge creation, through which "alternative political imaginaries and theories about how to actualize these imagined possibilities" (Chesters, 2012, p. 147) are collectively identified. But in their study about framing, David Snow and Robert Benford (1988) already pointed out the importance of the alignment between the frame and social reality. They define framing as assigning meaning to and interpreting relevant events and conditions in ways that are intended to mobilize potential adherents and constituents, to garner bystander support, and to demobilize antagonists. One of the core framing tasks is diagnostic faming, in other words, the identification of a problem and the attribution of blame or causality. In order to effectively perform this framing, movement organizers must take into account its empirical credibility, meaning the fit between the framing and events in the world, such as giving evidence when claiming that we are in the midst of the global wave of democracy. Snow and Benford also discussed the idea of experiential commensurability, that is, whether the solutions the movement suggests really harmonize with the ways those affected have experienced the situations. For example, it would be foolish to treat democracy as a panacea to economic crisis when many Western democracies have been struggling with austerity since the 2008 financial crisis. Those engaging in these discussions demonstrated that social movement organizations need to produce a set of creditable knowledge with which one could identify the problematic situation, the cause of injustice, and the possibility of change. This set of knowledge will be challenged by experts and authorities from the establishment as well as critics in public sphere.

Due to the lack of resources, the alternative knowledge produced by social movement is often represented in the forms of testimony and storytelling rather than with systematized data (Esteves, 2008 cited by della Porta & Pavan, 2017). Their strength is to provide a thick description of counter examples to challenge the domination discourses or common sense. This knowledge is spatially and temporally grounded and is also an expression of actors' reflexivity and accountable to the places they aim to affect (Eyerman & Jamison, 1991, p. 52). In some cases, however, movement activists would engage with existing scientific knowledge with different degrees of criticism, addressing controversies in different academic fields or creating professional counter-expertise that becomes a resource for academic and political debates. In the latter situation, academic and professionals play a significant role in altering the power imbalance in the production of knowledge by bridging the gap between activists and experts in the field (della Porta & Pavan, 2017).

One of the most outstanding cases of the production of counter-expertise is the campaign against global warming. Political elites such as Al Gore and experts in academia and industry are also involved. They need to debate with experts from the traditional energy sector as well as with political figures and parties supporting the firms and workers in this sector. Actors have conducted research to uncover the hidden injuries of nature and people due to flood and drought originated from global warming. They have held international forums and signed treaties to raise consciousness and reach agreement on reducing carbon emission. Although some activists criticize that the campaign actors have aimed at the development of green business while neglecting fundamental changes in economic development and lifestyle, these actors have demonstrated the possibility of social movement to produce alternative knowledge on a global scale and make climate change knowledge a field of contention (Jamison, 2010).

In this chapter, I will discuss the mobilization process of the Umbrella Movement in Hong Kong as a case to show how social movement produces and disseminates alternative knowledge. In particular, I will analyze how the movement impacted public agenda setting, contested the interpretation of constitution and initiated an alternative reform proposal. Klandermans (1992) argues that an issue can spark protest only if interested actors gain access to public discourse. Although public attention is a scared resource, how to mobilize public attention to the concerned issue is the first task a social movement needs to consider. The Umbrella Movement was successful in changing the public agenda through numerous creative actions, including organizing a series of deliberation days. The movement used social media to compete with mainstream news media to disseminate alternative interpretations of the Basic Law, the mini constitution of Hong Kong, particularly regarding the meaning of universal suffrage. It also used deliberation days and the civil referendum to mobilize a popular initiative in submitting constitutional reform proposals. Besides massive mobilization, scholars and professionals were involved in debating with progovernment experts and facilitating online and offline platforms to develop alternative knowledge and policy proposals. Though movement organizers struggled to handle tensions coming from both external and internal divisions, they appreciated the liberating experience of subjectivity through producing alternatives in the face of hegemonic discourse.

Agenda Setting and Alternative Interpretations of the Constitution

The Umbrella Movement was a prodemocracy protest in a form of occupying some main streets in the central business district (CBD) of Hong Kong. It lasted from September 28 to December 15, 2014, following a student strike in late September 2014 due to Beijing's decision to impose severe restrictions on the election of the Chief Executive (CE) of Hong Kong. However, preparations for the demonstration had been in the works since March 2013 by OCLP, a movement led by law professor Benny Tai, retired pastor Yiu-ming Chu, and myself, the author of this chapter, who the media collectively dubbed the Occupy Trio. Under the Occupy Trio, an

organizing committee was established with representatives from different oppositional parties and civil society organizations. Various functional groups for matters
related to media and communication, fund-raising, social actions, deliberation days,
and the civil referendum were formed. Hundreds of volunteers were involved,
including scholars, IT experts, mediators, media experts, and film makers,
among others.

The movement's aim was to fight for universal suffrage for the election of the CE
of Hong Kong. Beijing had already promised to implement universal suffrage
according to Article 45 of the Basic Law, the mini constitution of Hong Kong, in
2017. Any constitutional reform proposal, however, must be initiated by the CE and
approved by Beijing before it can be submitted to the Legislative Council of Hong
Kong for approval by two thirds of the council members. The approved bill will be
then vetted by the CE and Beijing before becoming law. As the reform will fundamentally change the political system of Hong Kong and involve complex legislative
processes, OCLP suggested that the government should conduct a public consultation as soon as possible so that a reform proposal could be submitted to Beijing for
vetting in 2014 and for further approval by different authorities in 2015.

As Peter Bachrach and Morton S. Baratz (1962) have argued, agenda setting is a
hidden face of power that the dominant groups exercise to preempt policy suggestions with potential threat to the status quo. In other words, the regime reduces the
visibility of certain policy issues by avoidance and inaction. On the contrary, public
attentions will be stirred up when issues are placed on the public agenda, such as
being mentioned in presidential policy addresses, discussed in government cabinet
or parliamentary committees, or debated in public hearings, and so forth. In view of
this, a regime's responsiveness is always selective and biased. Unless civil society
is able to contest with the dominant groups in terms of agenda setting, the regime
tends to set policy priority according to the preferences of its keen supporters, if not
its own organizational interests. Social movement, however, could impact on public
agenda setting by creating "repertoires of knowledge practices" (della Porta &
Pavan, 2017, p. 300) to mobilize public attentions. OCLP was the set of organizational practices whose utilizers foster the coordination of disconnected views within
a shared cognitive framework. Its use also provided a common orientation for making claims and acting collectively to produce political change.

The OCLP held its first press conference in a small but elegant church on March
27, 2013. The set was deliberately chosen, as the serene atmosphere helped send the
message of "love and peace." The Occupy Trio's professional backgrounds as
scholar and clergyman, widely respected in the community, also helped build the
integrity of the movement as nonpartisan and public serving. Against this backdrop,
the trio made a polemic claim that any election method of the CE election should be
open and fair and that the word universal suffrage stipulated in the Basic Law must
be interpreted according to *international standards*. If the government refused to
abide by these standards, the movement would resort to civil disobedience, that is,
occupying the CBD.

C.Y. Leung, then CE of the Hong Kong government, rejected OCLP's suggestion
of holding public consultation on constitutional reform, as he believed that

livelihood issues such as housing should be given top priority in the public agenda. This avoidance strategy did not work, as a retired senior Chinese official responsible for Hong Kong and Macau affairs decided to respond. He maintained that only "patriotic" persons should be allowed to run the CE election and also named two major opposition leaders as examples of unqualified candidates. He then argued that the meaning of universal suffrage should be understood in the context of the Basic Law instead of any international standards. Ironically, these exchanges of words immediately sparked public debates on the urgency of constitutional reforms and the meanings of universal suffrage. The media extensively covered the controversial idea of civil obedience, that is, peaceful but unlawful protest, proposed by these seemingly moderate figures including a law professor. Vowing that they were prepared to shoulder the legal consequences including imprisonment, the Trio successfully mobilized public attentions by dramatizing the urgency of constitutional reforms. They were also able to attract incessant media coverage by holding varying types of innovative events.

Regardless of the government's refusal to hold public consultation, OCLP immediately organized a series of deliberation days (D-Day) to gather people's views on the coming constitutional reform. Deeply influenced by Jürgen Habermas's theory of the public sphere and deliberative democracy, as well as the idea of deliberation day advocated by Bruce Ackerman and James S. Fishkin (2004), OCLP's D-Day encouraged citizens to discuss matters related to constitutional reform in a fair and rational manner. The subjects discussed included the importance of democracy to Hong Kong, movement strategies, and a specific reform proposal.

The first deliberation day (D-Day 1) was held in Hong Kong University on June 9, 2013 with around 700 participants coming from different opposition parties and civil society organizations. Before attending D-Day, they were advised to visit a website to view articles expressing contending views concerning OCLP's demand for an election method that met the international standards of universal suffrage. According to OCLP's understanding of these standards, not only should the election be as inclusive as possible in terms of one-person-one-vote, it should also be sufficiently competitive. No unreasonable restrictions should be imposed to block people from different political backgrounds from standing for election. This discussion of what constitutes genuine universal suffrage was pertinent because the Basic Law stipulates the establishment of a *nominating committee* to screen candidates for CE elections. OCLP argued that unless the constitution of the nominating committee was truly broadly representative as stipulated in the Basic Law or the threshold for nomination was sufficiently low, the committee would become an obstacle to free elections. Pro-Beijing people, however, opinioned that the nominating committee is a gatekeeper to safeguard national security by screening out disloyal candidates.

D-Day 1 began with an open session, allowing participants to express their views. It was followed by a breakout session in which randomly formed groups of a dozen or more participants met, led by a moderator responsible for maintaining fair discussion procedures. All group members, regardless of position, were given equal time to express their views. The breakout session's results were then reported during a closing session. Given my sociological training, I was assigned to summarize the views expressed in different breakout sessions. I observed that participants were very excited to join this form of *town meeting*. They particularly appreciated the equal opportunity for expressing views and the sense of solidarity created by meeting democracy supporters face-to-face. The D-Day's smooth rundown and the involvement of a large number of well-trained volunteers also boosted people's confidence towards the movement. The event was widely covered by both mainstream and social media.

Despite the positive responses, many participants reminded the organizers to bridge the idea of democracy with the concerns of different sectors in the community. Social worker participants expressed that their clients with working class backgrounds found the academic setting of the university too intimidating and the rundown of the discussion too rigid. A more casual chat in a familiar setting would be crucial if the organizers wanted people to fully express their views and emotions. In view of this, OCLP decided to change D-Day 2 into a series of discussions held in different communities, such as cafes for investment bankers, churches for Christians, community centers for women and laborers, public space under footbridges for homeless people, and so forth. D-Day 2 lasted for four months until January 2014, resulting in the number of participants growing to 3000.

At the same time, the Occupy Trio was frequently invited to give speeches in different communities and debate with progovernment antagonists. The public was then exposed to alternative views regarding the constitutional reform. Unlike other social movements, OCLP was not supposed to produce counter-expertise because they were experts themselves. Among the trio, Benny Tai is a constitutional law professor. Kin-man Chan is a political sociologist studying civil society and democracy and was also a leader of a scholars' group encompassing many prodemocracy political scientists. In order to counteract the movement, a group of progovernment scholars and businessmen then established Silent Majority to mobilize support for the regime. Whereas OCLP advocated the idea of genuine universal suffrage as crucial to good governance in a modern society like Hong Kong, Silent Majority emphasized the importance of stability in maintaining prosperity. Instead of adopting Beijing's xenophobic discourse, such as accusing Western democracy of posing a threat to national security, the group mainly targeted the Hong Kong middle class, who found the idea of civil disobedience too radical and occupying CBD detrimental to the economy. One of the economists in Silent Majority warned that the stock market would lose billions of Hong Kong dollars in a few days of occupation. They also released a consultancy report predicting that traffic across the city would be crippled should one area of the CBD get blocked.

Although none of this ultimately happened, these warnings were effective in creating fears not just among well-off people but working class people who were constantly worried about losing their jobs. Notwithstanding these worries, Radio Hong Kong Television conducted a survey and found that people in the lower-middle class and with a higher education level were most supportive of radical actions. Age was also significant in determining one's attitude towards these debates. The Chinese University of Hong Kong conducted a survey and found that although the community held divided views of the movement (38% in support and 36%

opposed), among respondents aged 15–24, some 62% were in support, 30% were neutral, and only 7.7% opposed (Chan & Vitrierat, 2017).

The intervening factor for these relationships can be attributed to the medium of information. Working class and elderly people relied heavily on television and newspapers to receive information about matters related to the constitutional reform. These mainstream media, except Apply Daily, had already been criticized for practicing self-censorship due to their business connections with China. In view of this, OCLP relied mainly on social media such as Facebook and other internet news platforms such as House News (renamed as Stand News later) to deliver its messages. Young and more educated people were more receptive to these media than many of their counterparts. The information gap then led to political diversion. The controversies over the implementation of a free election and the means to strive for it brought Hong Kong into unprecedented splits in different domains of life. In churches, people debated whether democracy is central to their faith and whether committing an unlawful act is against Christian teaching. In families, husbands and wives quarreled over their political stances, and parents pressured their children not to participate in the demonstration.

Formation of a Policy Proposal and Internal Split of the Movement

By April 2014, the deliberation days had already lasted for 10 months. The movement then employed D-Day 3 and the civil referendum to draw up a reform proposal to be submitted to the government. D-Day 3 was held in five different locations simultaneously on May 6, 2014. Before it was held, the School of Law of Hong Kong University invited a group of international experts on constitutional laws to vet all the proposals made by the political parties and groups from different backgrounds during that period of time. The criteria these experts adopted to scrutinize whether the proposals could guarantee fairness and sufficient competition in the election indirectly proved the existence of international standards of universal suffrage. Ultimately, 15 proposals, including one from a member of Silent Majority, were tabled for selection by 2500 participants of D-Day 3. They were asked to select three proposals to be considered by the public in the upcoming civil referendum.

The selection process was controversial, with some of the more radical opposition parties such as People's Power mobilizing participants to select only those proposals with a provision for "public nomination," in other words, those specifying that a certain number of registered voters could nominate candidates. Moderate democrats criticized this provision as a violation of the Basic Law and a measure that would be difficult for Beijing to accept. They also complained that the OCLP movement had been hijacked by radicals and that the selection process on D-Day 3 was exactly the kind of political screening that people opposed. At the end, three proposals with a public nomination provision were selected but the democracy movement was split.

The moderates, particularly Hongkong 2020 led by former senior government official Mrs. Anson Chan, were dissatisfied with the results. Mrs. Chan doubted whether the upcoming civil referendum could offer people a genuine choice if proposals without a provision for public nomination were excluded. Students and radicals counterattacked, accusing her of being out of touch with the masses who had no trust at all in the nominating committee specified in the Basic Law. When the movement was on the verge of collapse, Cardinal Joseph Zen played a critical role in rebuilding solidarity. He urged both sides to stop attacking the other. In order to encourage moderate supporters to vote in the referendum, OCLP added an additional motion to represent the baseline of the movement's goal: "The Legislative Council should veto any proposed election method violating international standards of universal suffrage that fails to provide voters genuine choice" (SCMP, 2014).

To urge people to take the referendum seriously, the Occupy Trio pledged to step down from the movement's leadership if they failed to draw 100,000 votes. Led by Cardinal Zen, a Democracy March was organized to promote the referendum for seven consecutive days and nights across Hong Kong. The march was successful in conveying a strong image of solidarity, with opposition leaders from different wings urging people to vote while marching through various communities. Right before the referendum, however, Beijing issued a white paper on the implementation of *One Country, Two Systems*, proclaiming China's "overall jurisdiction" over Hong Kong (SCMP, n.d.). In Chinese, the term was written as "overall administrative power," and was understood as a move undermining Hong Kong's high degree of autonomy. Furthermore, because the white paper's authors also referred to judges in Hong Kong as "administrators," a number of lawyers joined a *silent march* to express their worries over the judiciary's continued independence.

The referendum is described as "civil" because it was purely a civil society initiative without official status. OCLP commissioned the Public Opinion Program at Hong Kong University to operate the referendum. All Hong Kong citizens aged 18 or above were eligible to vote via an electronic platform or at one of the polling stations set up in churches, schools, or temporary shelters in various communities. In order to avoid duplicate voting, besides checking ID numbers, a unique code would be sent to the voter's mobile phone. Despite the public enthusiasm, the Hong Kong government accused the referendum of "having no legal basis," (Kahon, 2014) even though OCLP had never made such a claim.

Before the civil referendum was held from June 20th to 22nd, 2014, the electronic voting system suffered unprecedented attacks by hackers. The scale of these attacks was so large that local network security maintenance companies decided to withdraw from the project, claiming that they lacked the capacity to handle such large-scale attacks. At the same time, however, the attacks sparked overwhelming reactions from the community, because it was widely believed that the hackers had been hired by Beijing to deprive the Hong Kong people of their right to free expression. Fortunately, US-based CloudFlare was determined to defend the voting system. Working day and night, the CloudFlare team finally managed to fix the system.

In the first few minutes after the referendum started, thousands of citizens scrambled to vote. Hearing this exciting news, many people burst into tears while they were finishing the last leg of the Democracy March. On June 22nd, citizens who did not use the internet lined up in front of the polling stations, creating an impressive scene of citizen participation (Chan, 2015).

In the end, around 800,000 voters turned up to the referendum. The proposal of a *three-track system* (nomination from the public, political parties, and the nominating committee), made by the Alliance for True Democracy, received the most votes. Some 88% of voters also agreed that the legislature should veto any government proposal that did not meet international standards of universal suffrage. The massive turnout for the referendum brought the movement to a satisfying climax, as people felt that they had overcome tremendous obstacles to make their voices heard. On July 1, around 500,000 people joined the annual rally organized by the Civil Human Rights Front to demand genuine universal suffrage. More than 500 college students and other citizens stayed behind after the rally to "trial-run" the occupation by sitting down peacefully on a main road in the Central district of Hong Kong and were arrested.

To stop the movement's momentum from accelerating further, the government first denied the referendum's representativeness by releasing a report on the public consultation of constitutional reform, depicting the demand for public nomination as a view held by "some people" and progovernment views as "mainstream" (Hong Kong Government of the Special Administrative Region, 2014). The then Chief Secretary Carrie Lam, senior official leading the government's constitutional reform task force, met the Occupy Trio a month after the referendum. She was extremely arrogant during the meeting and showed no intention whatever to continue the dialogue with the movement. On August 31, 2014, the Standing Committee of the National People's Congress in Beijing made a decision (known as the "831 decision") with which it basically ruled out the implementation of free elections in Hong Kong. With this decision, it laid down three significant hurdles to democracy: The nominating committee's constitution would be modeled on the existing election committee, in other words, comprise 1200 representatives from four sectors of society; support from 50% of nominating committee members would be required for a candidate to qualify for election; and the number of candidates would be restricted to two to three persons. As Beijing has been able to control the results of past CE elections, its stipulation that the CE nomination system be modeled on the existing election committee naturally led to the conclusion that the proposed election would be a restricted one that could not meet the international standards of universal suffrage.

Because the 831 decision was more conservative than any proposals made by pro-China political groups in Hong Kong, people were completely shocked and enraged. More protests flared up. Secondary and college students joined forces to launch class boycotts. By the end of the boycotts, some students decided to storm the government headquarters and occupy the civic square in front of it. Police responded with pepper spray and arrests. Tens of thousands of citizens besieged the spot to support the students and shielded themselves from pepper spray by using umbrellas (why the media later dubbed the movement the Umbrella Movement). The confrontation triggered the Occupy Trio to kick-start the occupation on the spot, although it was neither the time nor the venue they had planned. Police attempted to disperse the crowd with tear gas, but this drew even more people to join. The rest is history.

Discussion

I have documented the above to show that social movements can produce and disseminate alternative knowledge, as in the case of the Umbrella Movement in Hong Kong. The controversy's crux in Hong Kong's 2013–2014 constitutional reform was to define the problematic situation, to reach consensus on whether democratic reform is a solution, and to determine the form of universal suffrage that could meet both the constitutional prescriptions and the people's expectations.

The definition of a problematic situation is related to public agenda setting. CY Leung, then CE of Hong Kong, believed that the housing and inequality issues were caused by the insufficient supply of land resulting from previous administrations' lack of vision and determination. Although the movement did not disagree with this argument, it looked for a more systemic solution to ensure a more responsive government. The movement attacked CE's existing election method, identifying the 1200-strong Election Committee as the root cause of insufficient accountability, as its voting members are mainly from business and pro-Beijing sectors. Apparently, OCLP was able to affect the agenda setting by mobilizing public attentions to focus on constitutional reform. This was made possible by creating a sense of urgency through introducing the idea of civil disobedience and the trio's determination to pay their personal price, including risking imprisonment.

The selection of a reform proposal meeting both the Basic Law and international standards was a more painstaking issue. The regime interpreted the provision of the nominating committee in Article 45 of the Basic Law as a way to protect China's national security by screening out "unpatriotic" candidates in the CE election. In the regime's eyes, there is no such thing as international standards of universal suffrage. The word universal suffrage is subjected to Beijing's interpretation. The business community also believed that screening of candidates is a way to protect Hong Kong's sound economic system from any fundamental changes. In contrast, the most active participants in the deliberation days were more concerned with removing unnecessary obstacles to a free and open election regardless of the provision of the nominating committee prescribed in the Basic Law. They believed that the governance problem's crux lay in the government's lack of accountability to the people. They subscribed to the idea of public nomination, a system practiced in Taiwan and some other democracies, and could not care less about the issue of national security. They did not trust Beijing and were annoyed by the business community's pragmatic and pro-Beijing stances.

This antiestablishment tendency also led to internal strife in the movement, as the moderate factions had attempted to seek solutions to resolve the conflicting expectations of Beijing and the Hong Kong people. For example, a scholars' group suggested that the public nomination could be incorporated into the initial stage of the nominating processes as "public submission" to be vetted by the nominating committee in the second stage. These innovative options, however, were ruled out in D-Day 3 when the more radical groups successfully mobilized attendants to select only proposals with public nomination. Building consensus within the movement was more difficult than the Occupy Trio first expected. In the beginning, they envisioned that participants would become more accommodating if they consulted divergent viewpoints before joining the deliberation. Instead, people's stances became more rigid. One of the reasons is that the participants were the most active members of the opposition parties and civil society organizations, who did not represent the whole spectrum of political stances in the society-at-large. As a result, the venue became an echo chamber for the activists to consolidate their more idealistic thinking. Only in the referendum, which involved a huge number of people, did participants select a comparatively more accommodating proposal.

This chapter is not a venue to decide on the validity of different claims and the merits of different proposals. The above discussion is to demonstrate that definition of situation and interpretation of law could be contested, and alternative knowledge could be produced by a social movement in the process. In this particular case, the original intent of certain provisions in the drafting of the Basic Law was debated. The words uttered by some former senior Chinese leaders were cited to support respective interpretations. Choudry (2010) argues that texts are sites of real struggles. The regime will organize knowledge in particular directions and from particular standpoints, which often include the containment of social movement (Choudry, 2010; Kinsman, 1997). Sometimes, the containment is so overwhelming that creating a vision beyond the official frame is already a difficult task to be recognized as a movement's achievement (Kelley, 2002). Kinsman (1997) suggests that how the media, different publics, governments, NGOs, and social movements read and use those texts in particular contexts and moments is critical to the development of counterhegemonic politics.

Though laymen could also produce powerful counter-expertise knowledge by testimony and storytelling grounded in their everyday lives, involvement of professionals in the movement could directly challenge the evidence base of the dominant discourses. In the present case, both sides of the struggle involved experts in the field. Though OCLP produced counter-knowledge, it was not in a form of counter-expertise, as the movement claimed that they were expert themselves. These experts, including scholars, pollsters, IT professionals, and so forth, played a significant role in altering the power imbalance in the production of knowledge by bridging the gap between activists and experts in the field as well as challenging the scientific base of the dominant discourses. The downside of expert involvement is to gear public debates into technical if not idiosyncratic arguments discouraging popular involvements. OCLP attempted to bridge this gap by cocreating alternative knowledge through deliberation days and the civil referendum. They also extensively employed social media to disseminate alternative views to the public, although with limited success among workers and less educated people. Some housewives expressed that they joined the occupation because of the police's unreasonable use of tear gas and pepper spray. They believed that it was unjust to harm peaceful protesters, particularly students, and their "mother's instinct" urged them to protect these young protesters. They were not aware of the previous discussions about international standards but would support democracy just to make the government accountable to the people (Wong, 2016). It seems that testimonies and storytelling of this kind are equally as powerful as theories and statistics provided by a movement's experts.

This case supports Foley's (1999) argument that some of the most powerful learning occurs when people struggle against oppression, to make sense of what is happening to them and to work out ways of doing something about it (pp. 1–2). OCLP's role during the Umbrella Movement's mobilization period (March 2013– September 2014) was to provide "repertoires of knowledge practices" (della Porta & Pavan, 2017, p. 300), in other words, the set of organizational practices with which one can foster the coordination of disconnected experiences and rationalities within a shared cognitive system that can be used to provide a common orientation for making claims and acting collectively to produce change. The cognitive system here comprises the understandings of the international standards of universal suffrage and the honorable tradition of civil disobedience as a strategy for fighting for justice. It is a shared system because the understandings were cocreated through deliberation days and the civil referendum. Even though the movement was unable to change the political system as people wished, the movement itself demonstrated the capacity of human beings to produce alternative worldviews, interpretations of reality, and policy proposals. The experience of this "subjectivity" is both psychologically and politically liberating. Thus, the most prominent slogan printed on the backdrop of the stage in the Umbrella Movement was "self-determination," a sign of moral autonomy.

Prologue

As I am writing this chapter in the summer of 2019, Hong Kong is under a reign of terror after China imposed the National Security Law to crack down on subversion, secession, terrorism, and collusion with foreign forces regardless of whether violence is involved. Provoking hatred towards the Chinese or Hong Kong government in relation to collusion with foreign forces (under a very broad definition) could be a crime. A special court has been established with judges appointed by the Chief Executive. No jury will be set up in the trial and media attendance could be denied. Serious cases could be extradited to China for interrogation and trial. The penalty is up to life imprisonment. The community was once again shocked by this blatant violation of the One Country, Two Systems policy, in particular the damage caused to the common law system.

Using COVID-19 as an excuse, the authorities have permitted no rallies to express people's objections to the law. They have arrested activists for alleged subversion or secession just for expressing views condemning the regime or supporting Hong Kong independence. Hundreds of policemen raided the office of Apple Daily, the only prodemocracy newspaper in town, and arrested its founder Jimmy Lai and senior management staff for alleged collusion with foreign forces and other financial crimes. Prof. Benny Tai, the cofounder of OCLP, was sacked by Hong Kong University regardless of his tenure appointment. The university gave no explanation to the community except that Arthur Li, the Chair of the University Council, told the media that a "criminal" should not be allowed to teach in the university (Chan, 2020). Later on, Benny Tai was arrested and detained by the authority for his alleged violation of the National Security Law by organizing a primary election among prodemocracy candidates. Back in May 2020, the government lashed out at Hong Kong's examination authorities for "seriously hurting the feelings" of Chinese people who had suffered under Japanese occupation by asking history paper candidates if they agreed that Japan did more good than harm to China in the first half of the last century. In fact, the question covered the period from 1900 to 1945, a time when Sino-Japanese relations was more complicated than just the war. Although more than 5000 students had answered this question in the concerned public examination, the examination authorities were forced to cancel the question just to demonstrate their "political correctness."

These recent crackdowns on independent newspapers and liberal scholars, and tightening control over schools and curricula, are moves to block the production and dissemination of alternative knowledge in Hong Kong. Social movements as repertoires of knowledge practices are also barred under the national security law or the emergency laws due to the pandemic. The regime is determined to back up the hegemonic discourse with white terror. How people unlearn dominant discourses and produce counter-knowledge under such a repressive regime will be an interesting topic to study, but more importantly a vital task to preserve people's sense of moral autonomy and will to change.

References

Ackerman, B., & Fishkin, J. S. (2004). *Deliberation day*. New Haven, CT: Yale University Press.

Bachrach, P., & Baratz, M. S. (1962). Two faces of power. *The American Political Science Review, 56*, 947–952. https://doi.org/10.2307/1952796

Ball, S. J. (Ed.). (1990). *Foucault and education: Disciplines and knowledge*. Routledge Library Editions: Michel Foucault: Vol. 1. London: Routledge.

Chan, H. (2020, July 31). University of Hong Kong governing council chief defends Benny Tai sacking, rejects allegations of outside interference in the decision. *South China Morning Post* (Hong Kong). Retrieved from https://www.scmp.com/news/hong-kong/politics/article/3095411/university-hong-kong-governing-council-chief-defends-benny

Chan, K. (2015). Occupying Hong Kong: How deliberation, referendum and civil disobedience played out in the Umbrella Movement. *SUR: International Journal on Human Rights, 12*(21), 1–7.

Chan, K., & Vitrierat, N. G. (2017). 本土、勇武與犬儒:傘後香港的社會趨勢 [Localism, radicalism and cynicism in post-Umbrella Movement Hong Kong]. *Mainland China Studies, 60*(1), 19–36. https://doi.org/10.30389/MCS.201703_60(1).0002

Chesters, G. (2012). Social movements and the ethics of knowledge production. *Social Movement Studies, 11,* 145–160. https://doi.org/10.1080/14742837.2012.664894

Choudry, A. (2010). Global justice? Contesting NGOization: Knowledge politics and containment in antiglobalization networks. In A. Choudry & D. Kapoor (Eds.), *Learning from the ground up: Global perspectives on social movements and knowledge production* (pp. 17–34). New York: Palgrave Macmillan. https://doi.org/10.1057/9780230112650

della Porta, D., & Pavan, E. (2017). Repertoires of knowledge practices: Social movements in times of crisis. *Qualitative Research in Organizations and Management, 12,* 297–314. https://doi.org/10.1108/QROM-01-2017-1483

Esteves, A. M. (2008). Processes of knowledge production in social movements as multi-level power dynamics. *Sociology Compass, 2,* 1934–1953. https://doi.org/10.1111/j.1751-9020.2008.00146.x

Eyerman, R., & Jamison, A. (1991). *Social movements: A cognitive approach.* Cambridge: Polity.

Foley, G. (1999). *Learning in social action: A contribution to understanding informal education.* London: Zed.

Frentzel-Zagorska, J. (1990). Civil society in Poland and Hungary. *Soviet Studies, 42,* 759–777. https://doi.org/10.1080/09668139008411900

Gramsci, A. (1971). *Selections from the prison notebooks of Antonio Gramsci* (Q. Hoare & G. Nowell Smith, Eds. and Trans.). New York: International.

Heifetz, R. A. (1994). *Leadership without easy answers.* Cambridge, MA: Harvard University Press.

Hong Kong Government of the Special Administrative Region. (2014). *Report on the public consultation on the methods for selecting the Chief Executive in 2017 and for forming the Legislative Council in 2016.*

Jamison, A. (2010). Climate change knowledge and social movement theory. *WIREs Climate Change, 1,* 811–823. https://doi.org/10.1002/wcc.88

Kahon, C. (2014, June 23). Referendum has no legal basis, says justice chief. *China Daily* (Hong Kong). Retrieved from https://www.chinadailyasia.com/hknews/2014-06/23/content_15143362.html

Kelley, R. D. G. (2002) *Freedom dreams: The Black radical imagination.* Boston: Beacon.

Kinsman, G. (1997). Managing AIDS organizing: 'Consultation,' 'partnership' and 'responsibility' as strategies of regulation. In W. K. Carroll (Ed.), *Organizing dissent: Contemporary social movements in theory and practice* (2nd ed., pp. 215–231). Toronto: Garamond.

Klandermans, B. (1992). The social construction of protest and multiorganizational fields. In A. D. Morris & C. McClurg Mueller (Eds.), *Frontiers in social movement theory* (pp. 77–103). New Haven, CT: Yale University Press.

Melucci, A. (1988). Getting involved: Identity and mobilization in social movements. In B. Klandermans, H. Kriesi, & S. G. Tarrow (Eds.), *From structure to action: Comparing social movement research across cultures* (pp. 329–348). International Social Movement Research: Vol. 1. Greenwich: JAI.

South China Morning Post (SCMP). (2014, June 22). What the Occupy Central Rreferendum asks voters. *South China Morning Post* (Hong Kong). Retrieved from https://www.scmp.com/news/hong-kong/article/1538285/what-occupy-central-referendum-asks-voters

South China Morning Post (SCMP). (n.d.). Full text: Chinese State Council white paper on 'One Country, Two Systems' policy in Hong Kong. *South China Morning Post* (Hong Kong). Retrieved from https://www.scmp.com/news/hong-kong/article/1529167/full-text-practice-one-country-two-systems-policy-hong-kong-special

Snow, D. A., & Benford, R. D. (1988). Ideology, frame resonance, and participant mobilization. In B. Klandermans, H. Kriesi, & S. G. Tarrow (Eds.), *From structure to action: Comparing social movement research across cultures* (pp. 197–218). International Social Movement Research: Vol. 1. Greenwich: JAI.

Wong, M. Y. (2016). *Female activists in Hong Kong Umbrella Movement: Body as a site of structure and agency* (Master's thesis). Retrieved from https://repository.lib.cuhk.edu.hk/en/item/cuhk-1292472

Chapter 12
Epistemic Activism in the United States: Examining Meetings Across the Silos of Civil Society

Jen Sandler

The Challenge of Conceptualizing Civil Society's Radical Multiplicity

Researchers of civil society face an ontological problem, well described in the ambiguous introductions to almost all of their major journals and canonical texts: What exactly *is* civil society? What boundaries on the field of civic action ought to be delineated so that some modes of organization can be analyzed as distinctly *civic* phenomena?

Howell and Pearce (2001) in "Civil Society and Development" offer a compelling distinction between two "genealogies" of civil society. In order to account for the ethical and epistemological ambiguity of concepts of civic action in the development world, Howell and Pearce argue that one must distinguish between a "mainstream genealogy" and an "alternative genealogy." The mainstream genealogy is the hegemonic intellectual history of a sphere of civic activity that is separate from the state and the market, in which citizen participation is the driving force. A healthy civil society is said to be functional for democracy, according to the mainstream genealogy, and the question becomes how civil society can be made to thrive, provide the grist for democratic life, and balance out the ethical indifference of the market.

But what of social protest *against* dominant political and economic structures? What of civic *critique* with which one attempts not to complement but to *reveal and shape* the landscape of power in a particular context? The civil society that operates from this mode of critique, Howell and Pearce offer, has a different genealogy. Those adopting this alternative genealogy seek a critical counter-hegemony, in Gramscian terms. It is an epistemic apparatus for making sense of an ever-expanding

J. Sandler (✉)
Department of Anthropology, University of Massachusetts Amherst, Amherst, MA, USA
e-mail: jsandler@anthro.umass.edu

J. Glückler et al. (eds.), *Knowledge and Civil Society*, Knowledge and Space 17,
https://doi.org/10.1007/978-3-030-71147-4_12

range of collective projects, not simply a vantage point for engaging the center from the margins in perpetuity. The dreams of many scholar-actors working within this genealogy today are of variations on an anti-unified field that morphs perpetually on an ever-shifting bedrock of radical multiplicity (e.g., de la Cadena & Blaser, 2018; Escobar, 2020; de Sousa Santos, 2018; Visvanathan, 2006).

In this paper, I lay out and demonstrate the utility of a radically pluralist "big-tent" approach to the study of civil society. Such a project will require appropriating the critical epistemic lens Howell and Pearce have suggested with their alternative genealogy, and which scholars of other fields have elaborated in the intervening decades, to engage with equanimity the entire field of civic action. Once researchers have broadened the field conceptually, the methodological intervention I suggest is to focus on relational and epistemic practices that center around *meetings* to illuminate diverse civil society projects in a new way.

Bringing Civil Society into Epistemic and Relational Focus

My interest in the "big tent" of civic action stems from my lived experience across a broad landscape of overlapping civil society projects that permeates the United States, in each major metropolitan area and at state and federal levels as well. I see a wide swath of this landscape in my various roles as researcher, engaged teacher, and civic actor. My work takes me into the worlds of applied social scientists, grass-roots organizations, social movements, civic engagement projects, national and transnational networks, community care/healing groups, economic cooperatives, traditional labor unions, new labor projects, interfaith base-organizing groups, and policy advocacy organizations. The groups I work with are distinct in ideology, political stance, social identities, structural positionality, organizational structure, resources, and vision.

Most of the robust civic action I find interesting and important appears as highly fragmented and often obscure to the majority of the educated public. The illegibility of the field of civic action as a whole is largely due to the tendency of both main-stream corporate-run media and critical/leftist media to center a narrow range of questions about civic life, which are almost exclusively focus on ideologies and interests. These questions include: What do people believe? What do they want? What determines whether they get what they want? Such essentialist, positivist, and ideological questions are distinctly unhelpful for broad inquiry into the richness of civic life and are particularly unhelpful when considering diverse local contexts. Researchers must find ways to cut the field differently, to think *across* realms of action. The reasons for doing so are as much empirical as theoretical.

The current field of civil society is not a single field of inquiry or practice, but many. Civic action is organized, both conceptually and administratively, in *silos* along several lines: type of organization (social movement, foundation, non-profit); topical focus of organization (public health, housing, food, violence, education); politics (radical, reformist, technical/managerial, neoliberal, reactionary, etc.); and scale (local, statewide, national, transnational/international). That these silos organize how researchers engage with and conceptualize civic action is a problem for several reasons. First, actors—both human and non-human—easily move across all of the currently constituted practice fields, institutional silos, and even political ideologies. Social movement leaders become nongovernmental executives and then policy advocates or even policy makers. Analytically and ideologically distinct projects are interwoven through people's relationships. Within disciplinary silos, the situation even more absurd. Life is lived—and civic action is constituted—in the complex interplay of experiences of health, education, poverty, immigration, and so forth, and analytical or disciplinary convenience is no justification for ignoring people's lived experiences. Long critiqued, the boundaries of civic silos are not only simplistic; they are epistemically dishonest, obscuring the ways that people engage and become with and through intermingled projects, and vice versa.

Upending the silos brings up all sorts of new challenges. Researchers need methodologies with which to interrogate diverse civic projects in an honest way. Without specific ethnographic methods for engaging the field, one cannot see, for example, how development processes are met, in real time and in diverse places, through conferences to legal proceedings, local governance processes and NGO boardrooms, encounters around kitchen tables and in the streets, as part of the same broad civic dialogue about food, or state violence, or climate crisis. Researchers need methods to *see*, not simply theorize, "multiplicity" in civil society. Once one does away with the conceptual apparatus of silos and honestly faces the field of civil society in its multiplicity, questions of ideology recede and epistemic concerns about sense-making come to the fore.

An integrated approach to civic projects requires different questions. Returning to Howell and Pearce, those developing questions from the mainstream genealogy of civil society hold that civil society's main role is to balance competing interests, agendas, and beliefs. My questions, coming out of almost twenty years of engagement with different sorts of civic projects, are primarily epistemic and hail from the alternative genealogy: How do people come together to push upon the major structures of society—state structures, capital structures—to reframe how human thriving is understood? How do groups of people teach power to see and understand their grievances and designs the way they understand them? How do people make structures conform to their visions, or contest their legitimacy and posit alternatives? How does alternative world-making engage with particular existing worlds?

I find that efforts to shift the states', institutions', and various publics' *knowledge practices* (Casas-Cortés, Osterweil, & Powell, 2008; Osterweil, 2013)—which I think of as both ways of making truth(s)/knowledge and making it matter—lie at the core of many of today's most interesting civil society projects. I call such efforts "epistemic activism."

From Participation to Epistemics

In an important way, this approach stems from the limitations of the frame and critique of "participation" in scholarship of civil society and development. For the past 80 years, since the initiation of the global power system delineated following the Second World War, one of the primary tasks of civil society advocates has been to show the virtues of independent citizen participation for democracy. This project was reconfigured with the breakdown of the USSR and the rise of neoliberal global development plans, and notwithstanding debates about its relevance, it continues to animate funders and international bodies. During and following the decolonization period of the mid-20th century, scholars began to call attention to the epistemic violence of the colonial project of citizenship that underlies traditional notions of civil society (Fanon, 1963; Spivak, 2003). Finally, from the 1970s through the "participatory turn," one of the key projects of critical scholars in both the Global South and North has been to object to the failure of the development industry to produce real or meaningful participation-based projects (e.g., Cooke & Kothari, 2001).

Civil society researchers have recently been fixated with the participatory turn that has unfolded since the early 1990s. The participatory turn comprises the fact that global governance, the development industry, and many large private foundations have taken up participation as a primary objective, mandate, and/or metric (see, e.g., the special issue edited by Bherer, Dufour, & Montambeault, 2016). Many critical scholars have engaged in nuanced assessment of the participatory turn, revealing how it serves to shape civic life in such a way that citizens are often used to accomplish essentially Western global economic and political agendas, and also revealing its promise and potential (Williams, 2004). How do we depart from civic participation as a frame for civil society?

The conductors of the major civic action projects of our time are not focused on participation per se, but on advancing other values and ways of thinking: particular philanthropic orientations, "evidence-based" policy advocacy, education and health frameworks, and many of the ecological movements, spiritual movements, and radical social movements. Such diverse re-framing projects would appear obviously analytically incommensurable, and I argue that this is due to their conductors' distinct relationships to civil society's core participation concern. They stand in a different relationship to participation, to be sure: structuring it, demanding it, embodying it, eschewing it, strategizing to get it, innovating it, advocating for it. But they also do other things; they are not just detailing various modes of participation; they are advocating for ways of *knowing* rather than ways of participating or doing. How can we hone the conceptual and analytical resources to see such projects in a more helpful way than the participatory frame allows?

In this paper, I delineate a particular slice of the landscape of social change work in the United States cut along the epistemic dimension. Such projects are interventions into how power constructs the relationship between knowledge and the public good. I think about such efforts as organized "epistemic activist" projects and use this concept as a way of viewing the field of civil society from a different angle.

Civil society around the globe involves a great deal of epistemic activism. It is well understood that the legacy of the post-structuralist, post-colonial, post-modernist movements is not a strong political framework or program, for that failed under the weight of myriad critiques (of irresponsible moral relativism, insufficient materialism, insufficient capacity to engage with rights-based demands, among others). But there is a strong legacy that pervades based on a stubbornly useful descriptive set of insights—Foucault's core insights: that power is inextricable from particular knowledge regimes, that governance entails at its center a relationship between knowledge and power, and that the particular cultural-historical structure of this relationship is a persistently useful field of inquiry. But although the allure of postmodern (and adjacent) theories may have faded, actual *projects* whose conductors offer alternatives to modernist logics have proliferated. I argue here that this insight is actually incorporated into so many political projects, across silos, that it has been difficult to trace. It is articulated and demonstrated by the multitude of civic projects coming from every possible margin (indigenous, queer, feminist, neo-colonial, scientific, religious fundamentalist, spiritual, ecological). My project stands on this critical epistemological foundation. Following scholars like Shiv Visvanathan (2006), Linda Tuhiwai Smith (2012), Arturo Escobar (2008, 2020), and Boaventura de Sousa Santos and his colleagues (2007, 2018), the concept of epistemic activism is a notion of civic world-making as a contested, historically contingent project that is multiple to its core.

Knowledge Practices Within Social Theory

In this paper, I examine civil society (and the cross-field subcategory of epistemic activist projects) as a set of practices, not as a structural object or concept. The civil society of Tahrir Square and Occupy are easy to characterize as things located in space and time: *There* is civil society! But to say so only further mystifies what researchers are trying to understand. Many of the field's researchers examine the role of civil society in relation to the state, examining what civil society "means" or "wants" in particular places and times. This, too, is mystifying: Civil society is not an agenda that, once discovered, can be measured and evaluated. Any robust understanding of such a broad concept must enable the parsing of differences, the unfolding of time, the interactions among actors/actants. In a more grounded approach, researchers can examine any particular mass civic event as a particular consequence of civil society *practices*. The questions become not essentialist but empirical: What practices make this particular sort of civic project?

Practice theory comes out of a 20th-century argument, mostly within the discipline of anthropology, about the relationship between human action and the codification or analytic sense-making thereof. This project is perhaps most clearly delineated in Bourdieu's *The Logic of Practice* (1990). Practice theory became a powerful theoretical and, ultimately, methodological response to structuralist approaches to mapping systems of power and human organization. This approach was later elaborated by a wide variety of anthropologists who asserted that a particular sort of human action, resistance to domination, can: 1) best be understood through their everyday practices (e.g. Willis, 1978; Scott, 2008), and 2) teach the field a great deal about the systems and dynamics of power and domination to which they respond (Ferguson, 1990). In this way, the complex worlds of everyday practices become a key to understanding power, not the other way around.

A robust concept of civil society arguably requires a meaningful way of engaging human intent, action, and the ways that structures are shaped by practices (not simply vice versa). For Sherry Ortner, one of the most attractive aspects of practice theory is its robust engagement with the relationship between structure and agency. Ortner insists that a viable practice theory, which is attentive to power, history, and culture, is the most powerful theoretical lens—and methodological guide—to studying contemporary human conditions across contexts. The virtue of practice theory is that it takes as its starting point the notion that the world is contingent, with structures in constant negotiation through human actions, "the idea that the world is 'made'—in a very extended and complex sense, of course—through the actions of ordinary people also meant that it could be unmade and remade" (Ortner, 2006, pp. 16–17).

Beyond its conceptual foundation, the methods of practice theorists are those with which they best interrogate everyday as well as intentionally collective practices of resistance. Elizabeth Povinelli (2011) takes the relationship between worlds and makers, infused by critical theories of power and culture, quite a bit further than her predecessors by examining the particular violence at work on the margins and in the creases of late liberalism. In *Economies of Abandonment*, Povinelli attempts "to address the question of the endurance, let alone the survival, of alternative forms of life in the gale force of curtailing social winds" (p. 10). There are many such ways to make practice theory accountable to the forces of power and history, to account for not only the dominant and easily-legible modes of civic action but those outside the moral—and, I would argue, epistemic—norms of dominant state and market structures.

For me, the roots as well as the reach of practice theory enable a methodological focus on the organization of people's intentional encounters to make things happen in the civic sphere. I study epistemic activist projects through and around meetings, because it is there that I find it possible to access the real-time "knowledge practices" that produce epistemic projects.

Meetings as Site and Lens

In a concrete sense, the practices of civil society can be described largely in terms of who meets, in what setting, and how. The collective relationality of the meeting, which I define as an intentional encounter of people for a purpose,[1] is the primary container for the production of collective knowledge and power outside the state and markets.

In some sense, this is so obvious as not to be worth stating. But in another sense, scholars often ask questions that circle around the importance of relationality without attending to its actual *practices*. They make much of the networked character of social movements and civic organizations alike, to mapping and measuring who knows and influences whom. Major public events or civic campaigns are described in painstaking detail, often through the work of journalists who interview some combination of assigned spokespeople and whoever happens to be on the scene of a main event (protest, press conference, riot, court appearance, etc.). But the micropolitics of interaction in meetings—the events that form the architecture for every civic event—usually remain uninterrogated. Often, neither reporters nor scholars even bother to let on *whether* planning meetings or post-event meetings occurred, let alone the who, when, where, and how of such meetings. And almost never do scholars of social movements or civic projects reveal the meaning-making processes of smaller factions within the projects: the side-meetings, the conspiratorial decision-making, the grumbling, the meetings to strategize otherwise. Indeed, the collective processes of sense-making and identity-making often seem of far less concern than the sense-making of the researcher or reporter who is there to tell the story.

To be sure, ethnographers of civil society organizations and movements often describe project meetings and micro-politics. But by the time they engage in sector-wide analysis (spanning, e.g., the relationship between donors and NGOs and movements), researchers usually lose this focus on everyday practices, or reduce it to the mapping of nodes of connection and largely speculative interpretation into what these connections signify or produce. Such network analysis is necessary and useful to map knowledge diffusion, and to answer questions about the scale and structure of a particular civil society project. Yet network analysis does not enable scholars to see the relationship between different project iterations across both structure-based and field-based silos of civil society.

Below are brief sketches of two extremely distinct civil society projects. These are projects that would not ordinarily be combined in a single social scientific or theoretical project. Their actors do not encounter one another in competition for

---

[1] The definition of *meeting* is controversial: Many meeting scholars and practitioners believe three people are necessary to constitute a meeting, and some believe that meetings require particular rules related to decision-making and dialogue. For a discussion amongst diverse anthropologists and sociologists about this topic, please see the introduction to "Meeting Ethnography" (Sandler & Thedvall, 2017).

resources or in collaborative endeavors; they do not network with one another or attend the same meetings. They inhabit distinct silos. In many ways, the boundaries of these silos make sense: They correspond to many concrete differences. Yet despite the differences that have justified the development of academic, funding, and popular consciousness silos, these silos elide vital similarities that I aim to address with this project.

I argue that the most salient similarities among these three projects are their knowledge practices, the specific ways that their actors make truths and make truths matter. It is impossible to see knowledge practices by looking at a project's function, attempting to measure its effectiveness, mapping its internal structure, or deconstructing and interpreting its aims or discourses. Knowledge practices are in essence *politics*, ways of mobilizing epistemic agendas, and as Richard Freeman, Steven Griggs, and Annette Boaz note (2011), politics must be examined in terms of practices. The only methods that serve are thus ethnographic—one must "read" epistemic activist projects from the inside.

Meeting ethnography is a method for doing so. Once one has looked through meetings as a way of tracing the epistemic dimension of civic action, I suggest one might see, across the broad field of civil society, a great diversity of projects whose actors are engaged in a struggle not over *what* power thinks, but *how*.

Case 1: Demonstrating Epistemic Unity in a U.S. Reform Coalition

CLI: A Civic Reform Coalition

Civic coalitions are a form of civil society particular to municipalities in the United States. Their specific politics vary, depending on the ideologies and positions of the individuals involved, but they typically consist of local business, civic, professional, and volunteer interests coming together to improve life for people in a particular geographic area. Coalitions are sometimes issue-based, particularly if they were developed out of a particular philanthropic or government funding stream (e.g., in response to drug abuse or violence). But many are standing civic coalitions whose members address a wide range of issues that people in the local area face. The epistemics of civic coalitions are distinctly *localist*: that solutions to local problems must emerge from local experiences and knowledge. Civic coalitions produce "local knowledge" through particular data-gathering practices. These may occur through official settings like town halls or issue forums, where community members voluntarily provide input. But most coalition leaders are committed to broader "participation" and recognize that this requires more active or direct methods.

The Coalition for Local Initiatives (CLI, a pseudonym) is one such organization. CLI was started in the early 1990s by business executives from the large and diverse city of Crossroads (a pseudonym) who attended a "public-private partnerships"-inspired seminar with state government officials. They became upset that millions in tax dollars were allocated for their community without any significant participation or consultation of local people. Over the course of several years, they developed a coalition consisting of renegade bureaucrats, high-profile business executives, and civic and community leaders. To ensure broad participation of community members, the coalition staff engaged community organizers to train neighborhood site coordinators to engage low-income neighborhood people. As the board president (an international corporate executive) put it, site coordinators were trained to become "case managers for the neighborhoods: an extraordinary model!"

CLI had become a large and powerful organization by the time I encountered it in my 2006–2007 fieldwork. But a large and diverse local coalition organization is inherently unstable. In order for coalitions to act as collective bodies, their members must constitute themselves continually through projects, through the *doing*. They become and remain real only through their collective constitution. This is where meetings come in. Meetings, I argue, are the key technologies for bringing the coalition into this being-through-doing.

A wide variety of meetings are designed to provide the "architecture" (Sandler & Thedvall, 2017) of CLI (Sandler, 2017), including:

- 1–1 meetings to build relationships and leadership
- internal meetings to build and influence collective agendas
- internal meetings to develop and influence coalition strategy
- meetings with outsiders to spread localist and "bottom-up" methodology
- meetings to hold public officials accountable
- a perpetual stream of meeting-planning meetings and meeting-debrief meetings
- demonstration meetings

In the next section, I will describe in detail a relatively rare but quite important type of coalition meeting: a demonstration of a successful project, in this case the funding of a school-based health clinic. With this meeting, I illustrate the epistemic project of the Coalition for Local Initiatives.

The most interesting aspect of CLI is the diversity of actors brought together through its projects. Notably, CLI's diversity includes social identities, access to power, structural interests, and also ideologies. CLI's actors espouse a very wide range of politics and ideologies, including ardent beliefs in both weak and strong government, more and less corporate power, public and private solutions, empowerment and sanction of the marginalized. Through interviews conducted with the actors who attended the demonstration meeting, described below, I discovered a particularly wide range of motivations and ideologies for supporting the school-based health clinic, including: Addressing the specter of urban violence (the board member quoted "the rough beast" of Yeats' poem); empowering the Black community; building the kingdom of God on Earth; redistributing government resources in a more effective way; building a community self-help culture so that people would not rely on the government; increasing civic engagement; aiding gentrification and economic development; redressing corporate greed, addressing health disparities, and promoting women's leadership. In CLI, as we shall see, everyone is left to their own ideology; what is shared is an epistemic commitment to local knowledge. Periodically, this shared commitment must be demonstrated.

The Meeting

It was 6pm in a low-slung one-story wing of a large Protestant church in an urban neighborhood of a major metropolitan area. Twelve years earlier, an eight-lane highway had cut this neighborhood off from the rest of the city. In 2006, when this meeting occurred, it was difficult to get in or out of this neighborhood. Most public and private services had located on the other side of the highway, where gentrification was uneven but possible and customers were more assured. On the night of the meeting, people began to arrive at the church to discuss the development of a public school-based health clinic that would bring medical, dental, and mental health screening services to the neighborhood for the first time since the highway, and that would make them affordable for neighborhood residents and free for school children and their families. This meeting was the culmination of hundreds of smaller meetings over the course of two years of organizing. The sense of anticipation and build-up was palpable in the intentionality of the meeting design.

Three coalition staff members—business casual in pressed khaki and button-down shirts—stood near the door. There were rectangular folding tables set up at the back of the room with food: boxes of pizza, a bowl of fruit salad, a plate of carrots, bags of Chips Ahoy cookies, cups and juice, Styrofoam plates and napkins. Neighborhood families with children who filed in were given programs by a coalition staffer who they knew. They were directed to nudge their children to the back to pile food on plates, after which the children were hushed and shuffled away to a separate childcare room. A white man and woman in what I could only discern as old-money-nice clothing—both uber-wealthy Coalition board members—came in and were immediately greeted by coalition professional staff, then handed programs and gently guided the other way from the food tables, to seats at the front of the room facing the podium. The coalition's deputy director, a middle-aged Black woman, placed her coat next to them, effectively assuring they would not have unknown seat-neighbors. Meanwhile, two executives of a private hospital, both wearing drab business suits, had walked in, found the one coalition staffer one of them knew, shaken hands stiffly, and sat down as near the door as possible. A woman in a gray skirt and cotton sweater, with a bulging briefcase, rushed in as the program was about to start and smiled apologetically at one of the coalition staffers, collapsed in a heap in the nearest folding chair, and took out her laptop. She was the state program officer overseeing the large government grant for the health clinic, and the only person who seemed to know no one.

The school-based site coordinator, a white male community organizer with the coalition who had been working with the parent leaders on this project for three years, beckoned two parent leaders (both Black women) once they emerged from dropping off their children. He quietly huddled with them as they expressed anxieties, went over prepared talks, and calmed one another's nerves with words of encouragement. Other parents made their way from the food in the back to the back rows of chairs and took seats, smoothing their dresses or pants and fiddling with the one-page programs. The neighborhood church pastor and the school principal, both of them Black men, came in separately and each seemed to make a show of greeting as many people as possible individually. They each walked through aisles to formally shake hands with all the people in suits, said hello to a parent or two in each aisle, backslapped the male coalition professionals and hugged the female deputy director. They were constantly in motion, each separately leaning in to talk conspiratorially with coalition staff, walking to the back to grab food, walking around and crouching down to speak with different neighborhood folks who were seated, and getting back up again to get more food. When they and the khaki'd coalition door staff were the only people standing, all but one staffer took seats and the pastor strode to the podium, welcomed guests to this special event, and offered a short Christian prayer for the food.

Before I describe anything about what went on during the meeting, it should be clear that the substantive assertion of any sort of collective *identity* was impossible in this context. Any attempt to assert collective interest, to tell a collective story, to create a sense of forced solidarity, would have exposed fractures that were not under the surface but were apparent to all through the aesthetic presentation and bodily comportment of the diverse actors. From the outset, it was clear to all that each of these actors was there for his or her own self-interest, and there was an uneasy sense that the project might not be able to hold the diversity of these interests. The "work" each contingency had done had varied so greatly. The local parents had been organizing one another and pressuring their city council representative to help get zoning changed. The elite board members have made their direct phone calls to encourage the passage of an unprecedented package of state grants. The hospital executives had been half-blackmailed with lawsuits and half-bribed with sweetened contracts to join the deal. CLI staff had been managing each of these pieces, and many more. And most of these people had never encountered one another directly. They had different stakes, leveraged different forms of power, held different visions. In this room, for a moment there, it seemed that there might be no center to hold.

The program itself was short. There were many brief, carefully-crafted acknowledgements that without each contingency's work, this clinic would not be built. The core of the meeting, for everyone, was the three neighborhood women leaders' speeches. They were extraordinarily well prepared, both in their language and delivery. The first presented a sort of testimonial-style account of what it is like to live in a part of the city that has been geographically and structurally cut off from all health services. She attested to her own children's school absences for lack of dental services, her four-bus-ride experiences traveling to the hospital emergency room with her toddler for complex ear infections, how her own mother died of cervical cancer because no one in their neighborhood knew where to get affordable gynecological exams. The next speaker talked about the group of parents that came together to study different models of health clinics. She did not talk about the study, only the group; how much they learned, how capable they felt. The third talked about what her life was going to be like once the clinic went in; that she might be able to keep a job for longer than from the end of one child's flu to the beginning of the next; that she wouldn't have to choose between going to work and taking her kids to the dentist; that her asthmatic ten-year old wouldn't ever again nearly die because she couldn't keep an appointment across town with a doctor who would give them a renewed inhaler prescription.

These were carefully crafted statements. There was no discussion of personal obligation, of deservedness, of the role of the government, of rights or responsibilities. There was no blame or demand—and no thanks, either. Just moving stories of what had been the reality without the clinic, and what would now be possible with it. After the women spoke, one of the coalition's most elite board members got up, shook each of their hands, and said a few words about how the Coalition was about bringing people together around amazing stories like these. He thanked them for sharing and said he was glad to hear their words and be a part of this project with everyone in this room. This elite board member—a billionaire, in fact—did not take credit, appropriate, condescend, or provide any framework for the women's statements, beyond the importance of all coming together around local needs. The lack of specificity was quite deliberate; what was not said created space for everyone to feel more at home in their folding chairs, to imagine the project as their own.

After the meeting concluded, the health clinic project development was done. Each of these so-different bodies could move back out into their own worlds and worldviews; building the clinic would commence immediately, and the coalition would go on to work on its many other projects.

What the Meeting Made

CLI demonstration meetings such as this one are where the local knowledge that has been produced (through a tapestry of other meetings) is assembled in public. It is a demonstration that the project resulting from this local knowledge assemblage—the health clinic—does not become an ideological cudgel. No one owns the meaning, and the project can thus remain sutured to each actor's diverse ideologies and interests. The demonstration meeting enables CLI's core *epistemic* project to serve as the glue that holds the coalition together.

Furthermore, when one looks at this meeting as an ethnographer, it is clear that CLI's core practices are not any of the things proponents of the mainstream civil society approach would have them be. Their core practices are not "rational deliberation," nor anything resembling the communicative action central to a Habermasian public sphere. They are not decision-making occasions, either nominally or substantively. Nor are CLI's meetings anthropological ritual performances of the legitimacy of hierarchies or solidarity. Instead, CLI's core meeting practices are epistemic *events*. Large meetings such as these, at the end of a project, are vital occasions for CLI to constitute—to "make"—the coalition as a whole, by demonstrating the epistemologically unified, performatively singularized "local" subject to the multiple wildly diverse actors who comprise it.

Hegemony, as Gramsci noted a century ago, is never total; it requires constant sense-making work through "intellectual and moral leadership" of both individuals and institutions (Gramsci, 1971, p. 57). I would characterize CLI as a counter-hegemonic project of a particular sort. Its particularly vigilant knowledge practices are necessary for the coalition to survive the constant pull of the hegemonic notion that the world is divided based on ideological interest, material interest, or neoliberal measures of efficiency and outcome. Through diverse meeting forms, CLI shifts how people produce knowledge about the conditions of urban social suffering. Coalition participants *know,* all together, that the health clinic is necessary based on the experiences of those who will use its services. Each is free to *believe* the clinic advances their own interest-laden ideologies of the state, the private sector, philanthropy, and cultural politics. This contingent, ever-becoming coalition is thus constituted in and through practices of believing differently *and* knowing together.

Case 2: Place-Based Movements and the Epistemic Politics of Listening

I now turn to a more ideologically cohesive, social movement form of epistemic activism. Many social movements aim, as Raúl Zibechi (2010) says, to "disperse" power directly to people struggling for lives of dignity, rather than to consolidate power in intermediary institutions or representative bodies. These movements' form of participatory democracy involves an insistence on mass-impact and yet human-scale social and political relations. Although ubiquitous and largely legible to the general populous in many parts of the world, in the U.S. place-based social movements have taken hold in a particularly hybrid-American form. These are movements that coalesce not around an abstract idea or funding silo (health, education, housing, immigration, etc.), but around the particular experiences of a specific group of people in a struggle to stay, return to, or protect their homes, communities, and/or land and natural resources. There are many such movements and organizations in the United States. However, they are generally outside the public eye. To date, there have been virtually no serious mainstream media reports of Black-led farms and land trusts,[2] prison abolition movements, indigenous sovereignty projects, or local municipal movements to occupy or collectivize control over space.

In U.S. cities, these local movements coalesce around the notion of *anti-displacement,* the right to stay in one's home and neighborhood despite

---

[2] Two notable examples of Black-led land projects include the Black- and Indigenous-led farming project Soul Fire Farm (Penniman, 2018) and Jackson Rising, a comprehensive, anti-neoliberal, alternative economic project in Jackson, Mississippi, to build the collective ownership and power of the city's majority Black poor residents (Akuno, Nangwaya, & Cooperation Jackson, 2017).

capitalist and imperialist threats. Anti-displacement movements[3] are generally either ignored or wildly mischaracterized within the dominant media of the United States. There is extremely little coverage of collective resistance to eviction, foreclosure, lack or erosion of local ordinances protecting renters, and the predatory banking and real estate development industry that controls these mechanisms of displacement. Even when they cover large public protests, the U.S. media do not do the work of communicating to the public that the people involved—not their leaders or advocates but their *members*—conceptualize themselves as part of a broad and interconnected social movement, intimately connected to other anti-displacement movements around the world. When seen at all, mainstream institutions generally dismiss such movements as uncompromising, radical, and distinctly *illiberal,* or as naively romantic.

In this section, I describe one such group: Movement for Justice in El Barrio, an anti-displacement movement comprised mostly of low-income immigrant women in East Harlem, New York. For place-based movements like Movement for Justice in El Barrio, the vision is one of both autonomy and solidarity, "a world in which many worlds fit," as the Zapatistas say, a logic of multiple forms of collective thriving whose adopters eschew capitalist, imperial, and colonial "global designs" (Mignolo, 2000). This vision can be seen in practice through the particular dynamics of diverse movement meetings. Through meetings, movements mobilize their epistemic agenda: that what is true, and what to do about it, can only be understood through deep listening. *Listening* is the core epistemological practice that Movement for Justice in El Barrio mobilizes through its particular meeting landscape and leads to all other—more visible—movement practices.

Meetings to Mobilize Listening

Movement for Justice in El Barrio engages in at least four types of meetings.[4]

First, they have a range of internal meetings. I have not been to any of these meetings, because I am not a member and am not conducting research inside the organization. I know only that they happen, because they discuss the ways these meetings structure their work in their pedagogical meetings (see below). Internal meetings take place with people who are "in the struggle," that is, who are directly

---

[3] See the Right To The City movement, which consists of many organizations made up of people fighting foreclosure, gentrification, development policies, predatory landlords, and so forth. See Brenner, Marcuse, and Mayer (2012), and https://righttothecity.org/.

[4] My relationship with Movement for Justice in El Barrio has been to facilitate their members' and organizers' access to universities to teach about their work and introducing students and colleagues to their work through both invitations and visits. My reflections in this section stem from what I have learned as a colleague and friend of the organization. Movement for Justice members and organizers have read and approved each draft of this section and have contributed information to ensure the accuracy of this description of their work. For more information on this movement, please see https://www.movementforjusticeinelbarrio.org/.

affected by gentrification and the threat of displacement. In Movement for Justice's situation, the problem of displacement involves bad landlords, bad government, bad zoning policy, and other threats to the rights of people in El Barrio to live with dignity in their community. Movement organizes building by building (in East Harlem, apartment buildings are large). First, a person with a problem related to their housing approaches Movement for Justice to meet, and the organizers ask if they are willing to organize people in their building. If so, the organizing looks like going door to door through the building to have brief 1–1 meetings, where they listen to tenants' problems and inquire as to whether they want to work with their neighbors toward solutions. The majority of a building's residents must then attend a meeting in the lobby of the building and vote (twice) to become members of Movement. Movement's buildings then hold regular meetings to listen to their neighbors and make decisions about how to struggle together, what fights to take on, and so forth. In addition to building-level strategy meetings, Movement for Justice holds large monthly member meetings to share experiences and make organization-level decisions.

Like many movement organizations, Movement for Justice operates on the principle of self-representation—"each person has voice and vote," as they say—and there is a focus on speaking and listening in order to arrive at collective, consensus-based solutions. David Graeber chronicles some of the issues that arise when radical consensus-based meetings are held by mostly white, relatively nomadic global justice direct action groups (Graeber, 2009). But such meetings look rather different among people like the women of El Barrio, who face a shared set of threats to their homes and shared community.

When home, community, or land is at stake, meetings tend to look less like a protracted debate over ideas, identities, strategies, and logistics, and more like a layered set of *testimonies* to personal experiences and concerns. Arguments are interwoven with testimony, over time, to form a sort of tapestry comprised of many intimately positioned political opinions. In this way, sense making more so than linear decision-making characterizes these collective meeting spaces. The methodology of sense-making requires a meeting form crafted to give absolute priority to unmediated testimonial and collective listening. I have experienced such general-assembly style meetings as a guest and occasional participant in various North American movement settings and have also seen video footage of many movements that seem to be striving toward this general-assembly form.

Movements based on shared struggle for place also have to consider how to invite in outsiders to that place, what the outsiders' roles should be, and how to seek and accept support. What do such *solidarity meetings* look like for place-based movements? Movement for Justice in El Barrio invites people in similar struggles across different contexts to share stories of their struggles through mass meetings called Encuentros, inspired directly by the methods of the Zapatistas in Chiapas. The only goal of Encuentro-style meetings is the development and demonstration of solidarity, a form of relationality based on listening in order to develop and demonstrate empathy with one another's struggle. Unlike other epistemic movement demonstration meetings, those holding Encuentros make no space for collective sense-making or persuasion. *Mutual recognition* is the task, and this happens through sharing stories of struggle. In addition to Encuentros, Movement for Justice members also takes their testimony directly to others by sharing documentary films and answering questions with what they call "people of good heart" in various cities, organizations, and universities. Their goal in these visits is both recognition in the struggle, and also to raise funds in support of their work.

Third, Movement for Justice in El Barrio holds pedagogical meetings for outsiders. These take the form of free workshops in their neighborhood each summer, and locally sponsored workshops when they travel. Movement's workshops are explicit teaching-style meetings, using popular education methods to provoke reflection on various elements of their actors' organizing approach. The most interesting of these to students, from my observation in several rounds of offered workshops, is "the politics of listening," a participatory workshop that involves sharing the Zapatista's 2006 listening campaign and applying its lessons to participants' own work. Placing listening front and center introduces a radically different epistemology. Students must speak only from their own perspectives, not from above or outside. The structure all but requires a humble *curiosity* about displacement, rather than argument or critique, in order to open up space to continue listening. In my experience of Movement's workshops at my university, a wholly distinct interactive atmosphere is created when the skills of listening are prioritized.

Finally, for Movement for Justice in El Barrio the struggle itself often involves meeting-based encounters with structures of power. In these encounters, Movement for Justice members (not outside allies) occupy public spaces and meetings, making visible their demands for recognition and structural capitulation or accommodation. In each action, members demand not simply a particular policy change, but a different *logic* than that of those in power. This logic is that of constantly and systematically listening to the people most affected, or what the Zapatistas call "governing by obeying" (*mandar obrediciendo*). The Zapatistas, as Mariana Mora shows in her ethnographic work with them, organize *manndar obrediciendo* in a very systematic way; it is a challenging logic of governance (Mora, 2017). When Movement for Justice in El Barrio members confront power directly, they expose the broad gap between local rule and *mandar obrediciendo;* they do not request to be heard, but demand that government obey their communities.

Movement for Justice's protest politics to expose this gap and counteract the displacement forces that affect them often include disrupting "normal" liberal democratic meetings, where the logic of collaboration between capital and elected representatives is on display. For example, Movement for Justice members decided to strategically disrupt a local Community Board meeting. "Community Boards" in New York City are appointed by elected officials and tasked with discussing and giving input on proposed city policies. Community Boards have no legislative power; their positions are symbolic. Furthermore, participation on a Community Board is often seen as a stepping-stone to elected office. Because members are appointed, do not necessarily live in the neighborhood, and serve at the will of elected officials, there is a strong incentive for CBs to approve—and thus provide a neighborhood-level stamp of legitimacy for—whatever city policies are proposed.

Thus, it was unusual when in 2017 Community Boards began taking positions against the liberal Mayor's re-zoning plan. The media began paying attention to these incidences of "community" pushback. In El Barrio, Community Board 11 was not expected to take a strong stand against the Mayor's re-zoning plan, which would likely result in the displacement of many of the low-income immigrant families who lived there. Movement for Justice members wanted it known that the interests of people who lived in the community were not being represented, so they decided to strategically attend this meeting. Captured on video, a large group of women with their children showed up to the meeting, held in a small room. They did not participate in the mode of liberal governance on display, but instead began stating their experiences as an interruption, making it clear that their collective demands were being ignored. When the board was forced to make clear that "compromise" with capital and placation of local residents was in fact the agenda, Movement members chanted (in Spanish) "we demand a firm 'no'" over and over, eventually marching out.

Movement members have also highlighted the gentrification designs of both greedy landlords and a progressive mayor in the streets and to the press. They have traveled to Europe, with the support of international allies, to proclaim the cruelty and greed of a British developer who sought to purchase vast amounts of property in their Harlem neighborhood and displace them. Their listening campaign in the UK ultimately prevented the sale. And they have driven out several other predatory landlords by similar means of public declaration that is in effect a shaming: Those who govern must *listen* to the people or be shamed for their failure to do so. The community's experiences must not be ignored in the development of their neighborhood. As Movement's members put it in their vision statement (which they often share in videos and at events): "[T]he houses belong to the people who live in and care for them…no one should own more houses than they can live in."

Listening Leads and Mobilizes New Agendas

Listening, not a static mission statement, has led Movement to choose which struggles that affect members of their community to take on. Members have conducted many *consultas del barrio* or neighborhood consultations in several formats to learn what issues the community faces and for the community to decide what should be at the center. Through community surveys, they organized testimonial-style town hall meetings with members of the community, which led the movement to new agendas. Movement has also decided *not* to take on campaigns, such as a city policy that threatened the income of local street vendors, based on listening to those who were directly affected.

Movement for Justice has also taken on new activities in recent years based on its internal listening practices in combination with emerging political events. For example, in 2018 and 2019, Movement members turned their attention to the Cayuga Centers, a local nonprofit organization that they discovered through an investigative journalist's report had been contracted by Homeland Security and

Immigration and Customs Enforcement (ICE) to receive and hold migrant children who had been separated from their families. Detention, deportation, and the specter of family separation threatens many Movement for Justice in El Barrio's families; when the members discovered that children were being sent to be detained in their own neighborhood, they felt compelled to center solidarity with the children and their parents and held several actions to ask that their solidarity be heard.

In March of 2020, COVID–19 began to hit Movement's members very hard. Most Movement members support their families with low-paid, contingent work. Many work as home aids, in restaurants and food trucks, and as house cleaners and custodians. When the pandemic hit, some were deemed "essential" and were also among the least protected workers. Many have lost jobs, with no access to unemployment assistance or federal stimulus aid due to their undocumented immigration status. Many others have fallen quite ill, with little access to medical care aside from hospital emergency rooms. Tragically, several members died from the virus during the first half of 2020. Movement members immediately pivoted their work to address this crisis, for the first time coordinating basic services such as food, health information, support for sick and grieving families, and other necessary aid. In addition, during COVID–19, Movement for Justice in El Barrio has continued to call for the freedom of all immigrants detained in New York.

Movement for Justice has quickly made this major—if temporary—shift in its orientation from anti-displacement policy and protest campaigns to work focused largely on direct aid to families; indeed, I know of no other non-profit organizations that enacted such a dramatic pivot during the early months of the COVID–19 crisis. Movement's actors did so because it was impossible to sideline their members' urgent needs when *listening* was at the center of their approach to the work. Their work during this time has remained true to a politics of listening. They have listened internally to members' stories and needs in order to learn what their work should consist of during the pandemic. They have held both private and public pedagogical meetings to provide allies with opportunities to listen to members' lived experiences, support them, and help them engage more people. For allies such as myself and my students, listening to Movement members' lived experience and analysis has exposed the current iteration of the gap produced by a government that fails to "govern by obeying" the people. Movement for Justice in El Barrio aims its epistemic politics of listening at keeping in sharp relief the gap—and exploitative dependence—between middle-class U.S. citizens, whose experiences of the pandemic have been mediated by government aid, food and service delivery, and ample opportunities to work and learn from home, and families with mixed immigration status, "essential" low-income work status, and no access to capital, whose experiences of the pandemic have been far more brutal.

Conclusion

I have outlined two quite different sorts of epistemic activist projects operating within a broadly conceived field of civil society in the United States. By attending to how each produces its truths and makes them matter, I hope to suggest the utility of using the epistemic activism concept as a lens through which to see civil society in a different way. I have suggested that "meeting ethnography," in particular, is a methodology for looking through that lens, for making inquiries across a diverse field of civic projects.

With this relational approach to epistemic activism, I focus on the way projects' proponents communicate what their projects are, not as static narratives but as relational *practices* in time and space (whether physical or virtual). The ethnographic mapping of narrative practices through meeting ethnography catapults scholars out of obfuscating silos without allowing researchers to fall into an abyss of abstraction. I hope that this project increases the field's capacity to look *across* civil society's ever-shifting silos (albeit awkwardly, much as actors move across them), ultimately to begin to make inquiries across the field of civil society as a whole. By using relational events—meetings—as a methodology for mapping epistemic activism, I suggest that one may be able both to examine extraordinarily diverse projects in the vernacular of their particular practices and also to consider them within the same theoretical frame. Taking epistemic activism as the object of study has enabled me to engage civic projects that range from the two described in this paper—a large municipal coalition and a grassroots place-based movement organization—to the scientistic movement for evidence-based social policy, emerging movements for epistemological pluralism, and movements against state violence. I expect that this approach should also enable scholars to engage alternative economic movements as well as what are now called "alt-right" movements.

Elizabeth Povinelli (2011, p. 10), whose examination of alternative social projects in "Economies of Abandonment" is a selective guide to civic projects that grow in the neglected folds of late/predatory/disaster capitalism, asks:

> If the possibilities of new forms of life dwell and are sheltered within the variation between the force of existing and the power of acting within these intensified zones of being and not being, then what does immanent critique demand of those who live in these zones?

I argue, ultimately, that it is the role of civil society scholars to describe and contend with the various "forms of life," or social projects, that emerge from the variegated pressures and structures of our time. Contending with the epistemic critiques that animate such projects requires drilling down to their relational practices. Civil society scholars are thrust into the intensified zones of the projects we engage through "meeting ethnography," ethnography of and through meetings, through which the ethnographer focuses on mapping civic projects that enact diverse models and modes of being (and not being, and becoming, and answering the question "for whom?"). It is in these intensified zones that one witnesses the proliferation of zealous resistance against hegemonic ways of knowing, as well as the emergence of alternative narratives whose proponents may engage and even produce new forms of life, if given the chance.

References

Akuno, K., Nangwaya, A., & Cooperation Jackson. (Eds.). (2017). *Jackson rising: The struggle for economic democracy and Black self-determination in Jackson, Mississippi*. Ottawa: Daraja.

Bherer, L., Dufour, P. &, Montambeault, F. (2016). The participatory democracy turn: An introduction. *Journal of Civil Society, 12*, 225–230. https://doi.org/10.1080/17448689.2016.1216383

Bourdieu, P. (1990). *The logic of practice* (R. Nice, Trans.). Stanford, CA: Stanford University Press. (Original work published 1980)

Brenner, N., Marcuse, P., & Mayer, M. (Eds.). (2012). *Cities for people, not for profit: Critical urban theory and the right to the city*. London: Routledge. https://doi.org/10.4324/9780203802182

Casas-Cortés, M. I., Osterweil, M., & Powell, D. E. (2008). Blurring boundaries: Recognizing knowledge-practices in the study of social movements. *Anthropological Quarterly, 81*, 17–58. https://doi.org/10.1353/anq.2008.0006

Cooke, B., & Kothari, U. (Eds.). (2001). *Participation: The new tyranny?* London: Zed.

de la Cadena, M., & Blaser, M. (Eds.). (2018). *A world of many worlds*. Durham, NC: Duke University Press.

de Sousa Santos, B. (2007). Beyond abyssal thinking: From global lines to ecologies of knowledges. *Binghamton University Review, 30*(1), 45–89.

de Sousa Santos, B. (2018). *The end of the cognitive empire: The coming of age of epistemologies of the South*. Durham, NC: Duke University Press.

Escobar, A. (2008). *Territories of difference: Place, movements, life, redes*. Durham, NC: Duke University Press.

Escobar, A. (2020). *Pluriversal politics: The real and the possible* (D. Frye, Trans.). Durham, NC: Duke University Press.

Fanon, F. (1963). *The wretched of the earth* (C. Farrington, Trans.). New York: Grove Weidenfeld.

Ferguson, J. (1990). *The anti-politics machine: 'Development', depoliticization and bureaucratic power in Lesotho*. Cambridge, UK: Cambridge University Press.

Freeman, R., Griggs, S., & Boaz, A. (2011). The practice of policy making. *Evidence & Policy, 7*, 127–136. https://doi.org/10.1332/174426411X579180

Graeber, D. (2009). *Direct action: An ethnography*. Oakland: AK.

Gramsci, A. (1971). *Selections from the prison notebooks of Antonio Gramsci* (Q. Hoare & G. Nowell, Ed. and Trans.). London: Lawrence and Wishart.

Howell, J., & Pearce, J. (2001). *Civil society and development: A critical exploration*. Boulder: Lynne Rienner.

Mignolo, W. D. (2000). *Local histories/global designs: Coloniality, subaltern knowledges, and border thinking*. Princeton, NJ: Princeton University Press.

Mora, M. (2017). *Kuxlejal politics: Indigenous autonomy, race, and decolonizing research in Zapatista communities*. Austin, TX: University of Texas Press.

Ortner, S. B. (2006). *Anthropology and social theory: Culture, power, and the acting subject*. Durham, NC: Duke University Press.

Osterweil, M. (2013). Rethinking public anthropology through epistemic politics and theoretical practice. *Cultural Anthropology, 28*, 598–620. https://doi.org/10.1111/cuan.12029

Penniman, L. (2018). *Farming while Black: Soul fire farm's practical guide to liberation on the land*. White River Junction: Chelsea Green.

Povinelli, E. A. (2011). *Economies of abandonment: Social belonging and endurance in late liberalism*. Durham, NC: Duke University Press.

Sandler, J. (2017). Meetings all the way through. In J. Sandler & R. Thedvall (Eds.), *Meeting ethnography: Meetings as key technologies of contemporary governance, development, and resistance* (pp. 106–125). New York: Routledge.

Sandler, J., & Thedvall, R. (Eds.). (2017). *Meeting ethnography: Meetings as key technologies of contemporary governance, development, and resistance.* New York: Routledge. https://doi.org/10.4324/9781315559407

Scott, J. C. (2008). *Weapons of the weak: Everyday forms of peasant resistance.* New Haven, CT: Yale University Press.

Smith, L. T. (2012). *Decolonizing methodologies: Research and indigenous peoples.* London: Zed.

Spivak, G. C. (2003). *Three women's texts and a critique of imperialism.* In R. Lewis & S. Mills (Eds.), Feminist postcolonial theory: A reader (pp. 306–323). New York: Routledge.

Visvanathan, S. (2006). Alternative science. *Theory, Culture & Society, 23,* 164–169. https://doi.org/10.1177/026327640602300226

Williams, G. (2004). Evaluating participatory development: Tyranny, power and (re)politicisation. *Third World Quarterly, 25,* 557–578. https://doi.org/10.1080/0143659042000191438

Willis, P. (1978). *Learning to labour: How working class kids get working jobs.* London: Routledge. https://doi.org/10.4324/9781351218788

Zibechi, R. (2010). *Dispersing power: Social movements as anti-state force* (R. Ryan, Trans.). Oakland: AK.

Chapter 13
Seeding a New World: Lessons from the FeesMustFall Movement for the Advancement of Social Justice

Adam Habib

The "#RhodesMustFall" and "#FeesMustFall" protests of 2015 and 2016 became the largest student social movement since the dawn of South Africa's democracy in 1994. The protests emanated from two major challenges facing higher education: alienation and access. The #RhodesMustFall movement, in which students at the University of Cape Town (UCT) demanded the removal of a statue of Cecil John Rhodes, captured the alienation of the largely black student population at UCT and reflected valid concerns about institutional racism and/or the slow pace of transformation at all of the country's universities. The #FeesMustFall movement, whose principle concern was access for poor, black students to affordable, quality education, began at the University of the Witwatersrand and spread across the country, culminating in a march on the Union Buildings where former President Jacob Zuma conceded to a 0% fee increase for 2016. However, what began as a social justice movement with widespread support from across society soon turned into violent protests that undermined the university as a safe and free space for ideas. The students lost support and the university activated security protocols, which ultimately led to demobilisation of the movement. The question to be asked then is what lessons can be learnt from the strategies and tactics of social movements such as #FeesMustFall.

In this article, I address this question as part of the broader thematic investigation into knowledge and civil society. Extrapolating lessons from the empirical experience of #FeesMustFall—which I have extensively detailed in the book *Rebels & Rage*, from which this article flows—builds the global knowledge base on social movements, which can in turn enhance the effectiveness of social justice struggles in the future if activists sufficiently internalize them. I discuss the value of social mobilization in effecting change, but demonstrate that this is only sustainable if the protest is structured within certain strategic and ethical parameters. I then proceed

A. Habib (✉)
University of Witwatersrand, Johannesburg, South Africa
e-mail: Adam.Habib@wits.ac.za

J. Glückler et al. (eds.), *Knowledge and Civil Society*, Knowledge and Space 17,
https://doi.org/10.1007/978-3-030-71147-4_13

to interrogate the issues of violence, the framing of the struggle and outcomes, the decision-making processes associated with the protest, and the importance of ethical conduct by leaders and activists. I conclude by underscoring the legitimacy of the social justice struggles, but insist that these must be more effectively conducted if they are to culminate in the establishment of a more humane social order.

I am of course not an impartial observer or assessor of this movement and its challenges and successes. Instead, as vice-chancellor of the University of Witwatersrand and the chairperson of University South Africa during the crucial years of 2015 and 2016, I was a central actor in the struggle of #FeesMustFall. This positionality must be understood for both its strengths and weaknesses. I observed the struggle and the conduct of its leaders and activists from the vantage point of the university's executive, which skews my interpretation and analysis in significant ways. Yet this same vantage point allows for a unique insight into how institutional and system decision-makers operate, the influences on their internal deliberations on when to permit and how to contain social struggles, and how to effectively use them for the reform of the system itself.

#RhodesMustFall and #FeesMustFall were, as I suggested earlier, the largest student social struggles in South Africa's democratic era. Its causal pathways lie very much in the policy choices and behavior of the post-apartheid government in the massification of higher education and the resultant decline in per-capita subsidy to universities; in university executives' lack of responsiveness to students' acclimatization to their environment; and frankly in the political opportunism of post-apartheid political elites who spoke with forked tongues, articulating social justice concerns on party platforms while simultaneously promulgating conservative policy prescriptions in government. Their focus on enabling access for poor and middle-class students, and addressing these students' alienation from the universities' institutional cultures and architectures generated enormous sympathy across society and throughout the world. The social struggles as such shook the very foundations of the political and postsecondary education system, and led to significant reforms in the financing of higher education. They also have prompted significant reflections on the movement, its legitimacy, and strategy and tactics from a variety of political perspectives and actors, including among others university executives, student leaders, academics, and journalists (Booysen, 2016; Chantiluke, Kwoba, & Nkopo, 2018; Chikane, 2018; Habib, 2019; Heffernan & Nieftagodien, 2016; Jansen, 2017).

Social justice has to be advanced in the world that exists, not the one activists wish existed. This obvious statement is perhaps the single most important lesson that advocates of social justice need not only to realize, but also internalize. Radical activists of a variety of ideological persuasions, including of the Marxist traditions—Lenin, Trotsky, Luxembourg, and Gramsci—devoted more than a century of study to strategies and tactics for challenging the political and economic order and advancing social justice. Many in the social justice community, including theorists, now recognize that the overthrow and/or transcendence of the political and socio-economic order will not be a single event, but a drawn-out process of advances and retreats. Thus, for social activists who are committed to change, strategies and tactics are paramount. They should develop strategies and tactics not from what they think is fair in an abstract worldview, but rather from what will work in the realities of the current context. This does not mean forgetting their ultimate goal, but rather understanding the possibilities of achieving their goals not from a rule book or formula from a time that is past, but from the contextual realities of the present. Too often, too many demand reforms that are compatible with an alternative social order, rather than those that are viable in the present, and yet push the boundaries of what is acceptable to enable a political dynamic of continuous social change—what Hardt and Negri (2017) describe as a strategy of antagonistic reformism.

Perhaps this has to do with the fact that most activists are often so emotionally invested in their cause that they cannot imagine that there are others who are not the enemy, but may not share the same strategies, or even passion, for the social justice issue at hand. It is often said that anger and rage are essential in mobilizing against injustice, but what is often forgotten is that it also blunts actors' ability to dissect the forces arraigned against them critically and determine how to neutralize or demobilize these to register social gains. All of this was evident in the #FeesMustFall movement. It may be valuable to extricate the movement's lessons, not only for the advancement of the struggle for free education, but also for those associated with other social justice causes.

Social Mobilization

Perhaps it is best to begin this reflection with a recognition that mass action and social mobilisation is an essential component of the strategic arsenal required for changing the world. This is the most obvious lesson to emerge from the #FeesMustFall movement. As I have explicitly and publicly stated on a number of occasions, the students achieved in ten days what vice-chancellors had been debating for ten years. The difference between these two interventions was that the students' engagement took the form of social mobilization. In the process, they redefined the systemic parameters of what was possible and opened up policy options and financial concessions that had not been seriously considered in normal daily engagements. Some of these outcomes exceeded those expected by the student leadership themselves. For example, the Wits Student Representative Council (SRC) president's original proposal to the University Council was not for no fee increase, but rather for a more measured one in the region of 9%. When the protests kicked off, this demand shifted to no increase; when this was achieved, it shifted again to free university education. This was not the first time that these demands had been made. Indeed, they had been made regularly across the country for some time, but government and, more particularly, Treasury and the Presidency had not been responsive to them. But when the 2015 protests erupted and took on the scale that they did, generating widespread support from stakeholder groups across society, not only was a significant financial concession made, but a policy process was also initiated to change the financing of universities fundamentally.

Similarly, the insourcing of vulnerable workers was never on the agenda until the 2015 protests fundamentally changed the environment. The Wits executive had recognized for years that outsourcing practices were exploitative and incompatible with the institution's human rights obligations. Addressing outsourcing would require trade-offs that internal stakeholders were not collectively willing to agree to at that stage. The student protests changed this, again by opening up the systemic parameters and allowing options to emerge that had not previously been considered. The collective willingness to incur these costs was not always present; it only emerged in the wake of the #FeesMustFall protests.

In both these cases, then, social mobilization was essential for putting policy and financial options that had not previously been available on the systemic agenda. But its value cannot be unqualified. Social mobilization is incredibly important for opening up systemic parameters, but some forms of mobilization can also undermine the possibility of social justice being realized. This was evident in the #FeesMustFall movement. As social mobilization became more violent and increasingly started to violate the rights of the institutional community, it also became more factionalized and lost the broader support of the public. As importantly, it forced authorities, both institutional executives and national government, to begin to activate security protocols in an effort to protect universities and the broader public. The net effect was that, in a number of institutions—including Wits—stringent security measures contained the violent social mobilization. This created huge controversy, not only between institutional executives and student protesters, but also within the broader progressive community itself.

Social mobilization on its own does not translate into progressive social outcomes. For such outcomes to be realized, social mobilization needs to be institutionalized through processes of deliberation and policy formulation. It also requires the presence of intra-institutional actors who are willing to use the opportunities that it enables to craft new social policy. Again, this was evident in the #FeesMustFall movement. The fact that it occurred within a democratic society, and in a context where the governing party was deeply polarized, ensured responsiveness from some institutional actors. South African society's democratic character and the civil society's vibrancy meant that options such as all-out repression were not on the agenda, as would be the case in more repressive societies. It is also worth bearing in mind that the student protests emerged soon after the Marikana massacre, where police killed 34 workers in a mining labor dispute. This event traumatised South Africans, deeply delegitimized the police and parts of the government, and paralyzed the police in their management of the student protests. South African society's democratic character, the divisions within the governing party, the widespread support of the social movement, and the paralysis of policing in the aftermath of the Marikana massacre all created a resonance for the demands of #FeesMustFall within the institutional apparatus of the state itself.

None of what I am suggesting here would be unfamiliar to those well versed in the literature on social movements. Scholars writing in the traditions of political process theory and political opportunity structure, such as Charles Tilly (1978, 2003), Doug McAdam (1983), Sidney Tarrow (1994), and Donatella della Porta

(1995, 2013, della Porta & Diani, 2006), have for some time explored the dynamics of how political systems and institutional actors significantly influence, and are in turn conditioned by, the evolution of social movements and their outcomes. But social movement actors and their leaders have never understood this sufficiently well. Even their academic supporters, some of whom are familiar with the literature on social movements, have neither sufficiently internalized this nor allowed it to inform their practice. This is urgently required if movements are to become more effective in achieving social justice outcomes.

Violence as Strategy

Effective social struggle depends on more than a simple reflection of the dynamics of the struggle and the complex interplay between social and institutional actors. It also requires deep consideration of the strategies deployed by social movements themselves. Perhaps the most important of these for consideration is the use of violence to achieve desired outcomes. It must be said that, at least at the rhetorical level, most of the leaders of #FeesMustFall professed a commitment to peaceful action. Peaceful mobilization also seemed to be the substantive intent of the vast majority of its supporters. But it is also indisputable that the movement, or at least elements of it, became substantively violent in the course of the struggle itself.

Activists and even their supporters have suggested that this violence was inspired by the actions of the police and security. Although the behavior and actions of police and security personnel may well have caused individual incidents, the general picture is one of police and security being deployed only when some protesters had begun to perpetrate violence and/or when the widespread abuse of rights was becoming evident. In 2015, for instance, police were only deployed on campus when the bookshop and a vehicle were burnt on the evening of October 27th. In January 2016, private security was only brought in when protesters repeatedly refused to allow registration and continued to assert that if there was "no free education, there shall be no education at all." Similarly, the university only embarked on a comprehensive security response in October 2016 after the failure of repeated attempts to negotiate with the protesters, through the mediation of previous leaders of the SRC and the Black Students Society.

Some academics, particularly within the university, were highly critical of the security response but were unable to provide coherent or unified responses as to what the university should have done instead. Jane Duncan, for example, argued that instead of calling private security, we should have used "the least restrictive means [which] would be to prevent the perpetrators from registering, punish them through the disciplinary process and lay charges against those guilty of criminal conduct, to dissuade others from following suit" (Duncan, 2016). But herein lies the problem with her suggestion. The essential issue with what she recommends is that, when Wits acted along these lines, this same collective of academic supporters accused the university of authoritarian behaviour and violating the right to protest action. Indeed, when student activists became violent in August 2015 and the management suspended them, this same group of academics essentially criticised the response as too heavy handed. Others, when asked what they would have recommended as an alternative to deploying private security, answered not for the suspension and rigorous deployment of disciplinary processes against perpetrators, but the closure of the campus and the suspension of activities—in effect, capitulation to the protesters' demands, even if the vast majority of the community was against this and it impacted negatively on the poor.

It should be noted that at no time in January 2016 or even later in the year were protests or meetings not allowed at Wits, as was the case at some other universities. Indeed, Wits continued to allow for protest and its coverage by journalists; during the events of January 2016, private security was simply mandated to secure the two buildings where registration occurred and to regulate access to them. Private security was deployed, and not police, not only because the latter could not commit for a long period of time, but also because, in the case of private security, the Wits management could specify that no serious weapons would be carried. Was this, then, not acting in the least restrictive of ways as required by the Constitution? Yet this same collective group of anarchist-oriented scholars opposed our measures and tried to disrupt them.

But the problem is not simply one of coming to terms with the need for security in selected circumstances. It is also some leaders' actual advocacy of violence. There is no doubt that resorting to violence was, in part, facilitated by strands of the movement that deliberately adopted it as a strategy. In fact, violence and arson were particularly romanticized by some of the movement's activists and leaders. This was cogently and evocatively expressed by student leaders at a Ruth First lecture at Wits University in August 2016. Unsurprisingly, the speakers' central message was that black people are confronted with structural violence daily, as they have to experience the consequences of inequality, poverty, and corruption. In their view, it is therefore legitimate to respond with black violence to protest this structural violence. In one of the student leader's evocative words, violence is the "aesthetics of rage" (Fikeni, 2016). Although his original reference was throwing feces at the Rhodes statue at UCT and the "fuck white people" graffiti at Wits, in the course of the engagement he spoke approvingly of the burning of university infrastructure, seeing all of these acts as "a common aesthetics" to the movement, "an insistence on moving beyond the boundaries of 'civil' discourse towards attacking the symbols of white supremacy through disruptive acts of rage" (Fikeni, 2016).

In discussing rage and violence, another student leader highlighted "a generational fault line" (Naidoo, 2016), in which she held that:

> the spectre of revolution, of radical change, is in young peoples' minds and politics, and it is almost nowhere in the politics of the anti-apartheid generation . . . Many in the anti-apartheid generation have become anesthetized to the possibility of another kind of society, another kind of future . . . And they can no longer be trusted with the responsibility of the future. When they dismiss the student movement's claim on the future, its experiment with time, when they belittle it, shoot it down, well, then pain becomes anger, anger becomes rage, even fire. (Naidoo, 2016)

Ignoring the fact that the claim of revolutionary consciousness being present among young people and absent among the anti-apartheid generation has no empirical basis, what is notable in this student leader's argument is her highlighting of the generational challenge. There is indeed a restlessness among young people across the world—in the Americas, Asia, Europe and Africa—that is reflected in contradictory phenomena like #BlackLivesMatter, the Bernie Sanders movement, the rise of the far right, and the migration crisis in the Mediterranean. Some of this restlessness does have structural dimensions, in particular the rise of insecurity among young people as a result of the technological shifts of the global economy and the unemployment it portends for those with no or limited skills. A generational conflict that has not been seen in fifty years is, indeed, possible—and may even be necessary. But it does not have to be violent, and yet this is exactly where some want it to go. Student leaders are fond of quoting Frantz Fanon's celebrated remarks that "each generation must out of relative obscurity discover its mission" (Fanon, 2007, p. 145). However, as Mangcu (2017) reminds us, Fanon follows this statement with another:

> We must rid ourselves of the habit, now that we are in the thick of the fight, of minimizing the action of our fathers or of feigning incomprehension when considering their silence and passivity . . . if the echoes of their struggle have not resounded in the international arena, we must realize that the reason for this silence lies less in their lack of heroism than in the fundamentally different international situation of our time. (Fanon, 2004, pp. 145–146)

A humbler and more measured response may be required if student leaders want to honor Fanon's words.

It needs to be noted that the rationality of these arguments for violence breaks down when it is subjected to even a little scrutiny. First, Fanon (2004) and Biko (2002) wrote about revolutionary violence in the crucible of the colonial struggle. Is it legitimate to transpose these ideas onto a democratic era which, however flawed, provides the space not only for protest, but also the right to vote out the political elite? And even if one did believe in the legitimacy of violence given Fanon's criticisms of the compromising and profiteering character of the newly emergent nationalist elite, what of Arendt's (1969) searing critique of both Fanon and Sartre's views on violence when she suggested that violence inevitably contaminates and destroys the end for which it was originally deployed? Essentially, comparing democratic South Africa to colonial societies is not only intellectually unsustainable, but also suggests that student leaders are incapable of distinguishing between different types of political systems and the forms of protest that can be legitimately deployed against them.

Second, how is the struggle against structural violence advanced by attacking other students and destroying university property that is intended for housing and teaching the students themselves? If anything, such actions are likely to consolidate the very effects of the structural violence against the poor and marginalized. Indeed, if the presence of structural violence can legitimate individual acts of violence in a democratic society, the consequences are too horrendous to contemplate: It could justify not only violent attacks on any public authority or their representatives, but also rape and murder against any individual simply on the basis that a perpetrator belongs to a community that is historically disadvantaged, and the act is committed against someone who belongs, by accident of birth, to a community that is historically advantaged. It would, in essence, violate the very social pact on which democratic society derives its philosophical legitimacy. Finally, as a result of this very social pact on which democratic society is founded, violent actions compel the state to respond with force to protect public property and the rights of other citizens, thereby creating a securitized atmosphere that works against the immediate interests of the protesters and the legitimacy of the protests themselves.

Part of the problem with much of the writings and reflections used to advocate for or condone violence is that their authors confuse violence with rage. It is important to distinguish between the two. Feelings of rage can be important and useful if they inspire collective action against injustice and drive progressive social change. Canham (2017) argued in an essay in the *Du Bois Review*: "Black rage [can be] . . . seen as an expression of black self-love in that it is the ultimate cry for freedom" (p. 442). Yet he also cautions against romanticizing black rage because it has the potential to harm the poor and vulnerable, and not only the system. As importantly, one must never confuse explaining and understanding black rage with condoning it, especially when it works against the agenda of freedom. My own view is that black rage need not be violent in our present circumstances to achieve positive outcomes, as the national student protest in 2015 demonstrated. Moreover, rage must not cause leaders to act emotionally and impulsively. It must not blunt them from critically assessing the forces arraigned against the social justice cause, and determining how to overcome these without compromising the end goal itself. Rage is necessary, violence is not; when the two get confused, the cause of social justice itself maybe delegitimized or defeated.

The same can be said of contentious politics and social struggles. Activists and radical scholars often refer to the importance of disruption in enabling change. This is entirely valid. Yet, as Martin Luther King Jr.'s ideas and practices reflect, social activism must impose systemic costs to create the political will among decision-makers to enable social change. But he also states that this must not be violent, for it then becomes immoral and self-defeating (Luther King Jr., 1968/2010). This understanding poses an important question for the leaders and supporters of #FeesMustFall. Would resorting to a permanent shutdown of the university not have entailed a cost that exceeds what is socially acceptable, given the fact that its immediate victims were the poorest among the student community and it did not automatically create the impetus for change among the institutional decision-makers? Moreover, was resorting to violence not unacceptable in these circumstances? Did violence as a strategy not become self-defeating?

It is worth noting that the issue of violence is not only about social movements' deploying it strategically, but also about how the social justice community approaches policing in a democracy. During the protests, Mbembe (2016) questioned whether all security arrangements are inimical to freedom. The automatic opposition to policing by so many in the social justice community suggests that too many would respond affirmatively to this question. But as Mbembe (2016) suggests, this is untenable—freedom does not automatically lead to security, so there is a need for decision-makers to act pragmatically, to contextually analyze each moment and incident. A de facto, automatic response is neither legitimate nor appropriate for a democracy, for it would violate the very essence of the social pact on which a democratic society itself is founded.

Perhaps the dilemma and how it was addressed can be better understood through a reflection of the scholarly work of della Porta and Diani (2006), who suggest that social movements become violent under two conditions: when police are deployed and engage in a repressive response, and when movements are factionalized and compete with each other to claim victories. Scholars used their work and its conclusions to suggest that police should not have been deployed at the universities, even if violence was being committed. But again, this conclusion was flawed; it was morally problematic and did not logically flow from a nuanced understanding of the empirical facts. As indicated earlier, the violence at Wits preceded the deployment of police, largely as a result of the second factor that della Porta and Diani identify. But their first causal factor was also evident, because the violence did indeed escalate immediately after the police deployment and subsided only a few days later, after those who had committed it had been arrested and restrictive security protocols had been activated, at least temporarily, to stabilize the situation.

The question that emerges is this: What is the responsibility of institutional and societal decision-makers in a context where protests turn violent as a result of the second factor, the factionalizing of the movement? Can responsible leadership refuse to deploy the police because of the fear of the first causal factor, the escalation of the violence as a result of the deployment? Our answer as institutional executives at Wits to this question was not to concede to the framing of this debate. To refuse to deploy police would have enabled the violation of the rights of the vast majority within the university, and would have made public institutions and society vulnerable to any group that was willing to commit violence to realize its ends, an untenable situation in a democratic society. Even in the context of a lack of adequate police training, the answer was not to deny their legitimacy to manage security challenges. Rather, the appropriate strategic response in the medium term is to urge their training and organization so that they can fulfil their constitutional responsibility in a democratic society. In the interim, the mitigation measure was to urge them to act with restraint through an engagement with police leadership and the political authorities to whom they reported. The mitigation was also in the recognition, publicly expressed in my review of the 2016 protests (Habib, 2016), that a security solution was not sustainable in the long term, which influenced our interventions to find a political solution through both institutional initiatives negotiated with the SRC and student leaders, and systemic ones such as the National Education Crisis Forum (NECF) and the Heher Commission.

Finally, it is worth noting that the broader progressive community has never developed a coherent approach to the matter of security in a democracy. But this agnosticism is no longer tenable, especially given the violent character of South African society and the rising populist threats to it. Bringing violence under control in this society, which is essential for the sustainability and vibrancy of democracy, will require concerted action on the part of both social movements and societal stakeholders, and the police themselves. All stakeholders need to become the collective agents of the future they desire and claim to want to build.

Framing Social Justice Outcomes

The struggle for social justice must contain within itself the imagery of the outcome it desires. This means that it should be framed in a language, and its activities should be organized in a way, that is compatible with the intended social justice outcome. This strategic principle has a particular resonance for #FeesMustFall: It is here where the movement floundered, which influenced its trajectory dramatically towards factionalism and violence. In 2015, the movement was largely framed and organised in antiracist and nonracial terms. The protests' goal was lowering the cost of higher education, thereby enabling the poor and the middle classes to access universities more easily. Its marches comprised students from across class and racial lines, and drew support from stakeholders across the political spectrum. As political parties tried to intervene to gain control of the movement, it became more factionalized and racialized. Some students started to wear t-shirts bearing racialised statements, whereas others began to frame the movement in explicitly racial terms. As this happened, and other parts of the movement refused to condemn and marginalize these elements, broader groups of students withdrew. The net effect was that the 2016 protests had neither the nonracial flavor nor the broad support that the movement had experienced a year earlier.

This is why it is so important for those interested in social justice to frame their movement in explicit antiracial or nonracial terms. There are two reasons for this. The first is an instrumentalist rationale. If a social movement is to be successful, it must draw on the support of the vast majority of society. In the language of the UDF of the 1980s, one needs to maximize support for the movement and minimize that for the advocates of the status quo. Framing the movement in more racial terms with explicit racist and/or prejudicial statements and activities weakens support for the movement and allows adversaries to caricature it as an agent of division and hatred.

The second rationale is perhaps even more fundamental, for it speaks to the desired social justice outcome. A central political tension that confronts all oppressed communities in their struggle is whether the movement should be framed as a retreat into nativism, where the previously oppressed become the master, or as progress towards the construction of a nonracial, cosmopolitan society in which all have a future. This political divide was perhaps most dramatically evident in the struggle for the allegiance of the African-American community by Martin Luther King Jr.'s Southern Christian Leadership Conference and Stokely Carmichael's (Kwame Ture's) Black Power movement. Too often, however, the divide is caricatured as one between mainstream integration and co-option on one side and radical exclusionary politics on the other. Yet, as he demonstrates in his "Where Do We Go from Here: Chaos or Community?", Luther King Jr.'s (1968/2010) ideas were much more complex and defied this simple caricature. In this book, Luther King Jr. criticises the segregationist and militaristic impulses of the Black Power movement and advances a vision of radical change that is more cosmopolitan and inclusionary. Yet the radicalism of his ideas speaks not only to racial integration, but also to socioeconomic inclusion, calling for a guaranteed income for all citizens in an effort to banish poverty in the United States. Moreover, as indicated earlier, Luther King Jr.'s mobilizational and organizational strategy was not one of appeasement, as is often suggested. Indeed, with his brand of contentious politics he recognized the importance of disorder and disruption for there to be systemic social costs to create the impetus for change. But he also drew an explicit boundary at violence, which the Black Power movement too often ignored. This book, Luther King Jr.'s last, is worth going back to in these fractured times, when social inclusion and fundamental change are back on the global agenda.

Scholars in other settings have also reflected on this central political tension in the struggles of oppressed communities. In "When Victims Become Killers: Colonialism, Nativism, and the Genocide in Rwanda," Mamdani (2001) tries to develop an understanding of the Rwandan genocide by exploring how colonial authorities manipulated tribal divisions in Rwandan society, framing the Hutus as subjects and the Tutsis as citizens. The Tutsis were thus constructed as settlers by colonial authorities and by the Hutu administration in the postcolonial era. Once this defining and labeling happened, the genocide was a logical consequence. It was, Mamdani maintains, not an ethnic but a racial cleansing in which newly established citizens were ridding themselves of the settler presence. This work is a timely warning of the long-term societal consequences that can emerge from present-day political choices and behavior.

These cases essentially underscore the fact that the path a society takes—towards nativism or towards a nonracial common humanity—is not crafted at the point of victory when one ascends to political power. Rather, it originates from the character of the movement that led to that point, and the strategies and tactics its members employed. Hardt and Negri (2017) remind us about the following:

> Rather than asking only how to take power, we must also ask what kind of owner we want and, perhaps more important, who we want to become . . . We must train our eyes to recognise how the movements have the potential to redefine fundamental social relations so that they strive not to take power as it is but to take power differently, to achieve a fundamentally new democratic society and, crucially, to produce new subjectivities. (pp. xiii–xiv)

Essentially, the new society's imagination is seeded in the struggle itself. Acts of racial prejudice, or silence in the face thereof, are not simple theatrics of social struggle—they are the building blocks of consciousness that will ultimately define the very character of the society that is to be born. Ultimately, the trajectory of the #FeesMustFall movement reveals that antiracist framing and organization is essential if social justice struggles are to contain within them the nonracial, inclusive community that social justice activists desire.

Mass Organization and Structural Considerations

The final strategic consideration that the trajectory of the #FeesMustFall movement warrants is the argument of some in its leadership that representative institutions and vertically organized structures of leadership are no longer compatible with social justice struggles and outcomes. This was reflected in the demands of some elements of the #FeesMustFall movement to locate decision making solely in the mass meeting and disband or reform all governance structures, including the Council, Senate, and SRC. Part of the motivation for this lay in some of the activists' deep fear that individual leaders are too easily co-opted by business, government, and institutional elites. But the insistence on making decisions in mass meetings was also driven by a political logic in which small, fringe political groups could easily dominate proceedings through a "politics of spectacle"—one that silenced ordinary, pragmatic voices. Lacking political acumen and experience, the leadership of other student groups were incapable of challenging these voices and repeatedly found themselves on a strategic path more compatible with the agenda of competitor political parties. And so, whether by design or default, an anarchist tradition of decision making, captured in the language of participatory governance, took root in the #FeesMustFall movement.

This tradition is not as democratic as it professes to be. Many students who supported the #FeesMustFall campaign but wanted to return to class were harangued and intimidated in mass meetings by a group of self-appointed political commissars. Individuals who proposed measured and pragmatic solutions were labeled as sellouts, betrayers of a generational cause. Extreme choices were deemed as radical and were enabled in the meetings through demagogic speeches and rhetorical fervour, where sloganeering dominated and complex issues were trivialized. Essentially, the mass meeting was as much a mechanism of silencing ordinary, pragmatic voices as it was of mobilizing others.

The lesson to be learnt for the social justice community is that greater thought needs to be given to how to structure decision making so that it can be more socially accountable. Hardt and Negri (2017) use their concept of "assembly" to make a number of proposals in this regard. Although I am sceptical of their recommendation to locate strategic decision making in the multitude and confine leadership to tactical considerations, they do nevertheless enable thoughtful deliberation about the matter. We need further considered engagement along these lines, especially between multiple stakeholders, so that the reform of governance structures within the university does, ultimately, manage the tensions between different forms of decision making and organization. Only then will we be able to develop universities and public institutions that are socially accountable, yet progressively pragmatic and practical, focused on being responsive to both the short-term needs of different internal constituencies and the long-term institutional mandates defined by the broader society.

Maintaining the Ethics of the Movement

A final set of deliberations that the evolution of #FeesMustFall poses for the advancement of social justice is whether there should be an ethics in the conduct of social justice struggles. Perhaps the most important ethical value to underscore is the importance of movement leaders being consistent in their public and private engagements. Far too many of the leaders of the movement acted duplicitously. Many claimed publicly that executive management was not willing to meet them when they had personally met me and other executives, and pleaded with us not to reveal these engagements. Many who interacted with me on a face-to-face basis were utterly charming and respectful, but their personas seemed to change fundamentally on Twitter. There, they engaged in the most virulent, extreme manner, which was frankly reminiscent of far right behavior. One student leader repeatedly made the most scurrilous remarks about me and my family, but then sent me an SMS to say that he respected me and that his actions were not personal. In interactions outside the university, other student leaders also suggested that their actions were not personal, apologized for any discomfort that they may have created, and then promptly behaved even more obnoxiously in the months that followed. Some repeatedly criticized the presence of private security and police, but then indicated in personal discussions that they understood why we needed it and felt safer as a result. A few who had called for a boycott of lectures and examinations privately approached individual executive managers and asked whether they could write their examinations in secret, so that other students would not see them. This kind of behavior was not exclusive to Wits University. Vice-chancellors and executives across the system had similar experiences and interactions with student leaders of all political persuasions.

The problem with much of this behavior is not simply the individual duplicities, but that it seems to emanate from a belief that astute politics involves saying one thing in public and doing another in private. Student leaders across the spectrum seem to have become captured by a politics of spectacle, believing that they are obliged to be extreme, rude, and obnoxious in public, and pragmatic and polite in their engagements outside the public eye. There is also the belief that the overriding goal is to win through any means. This kind of duplicity should be of particular concern to all of us. It suggests that, despite their criticisms of the existing political elite, some of the prominent leaders among this new generation of activists are displaying behavioral traits that are typical of the most venal of South Africa's current politicians.

The leaders and activists of the #FeesMustFall movement have also displayed an astonishing level of intolerance. On many occasions, student leaders have tried to implicate one another and get the university to invoke its disciplinary processes against others in an effort to rid themselves of potential political and electoral rivals. Students outside the movement were treated with far more disdain, and those who dared to organize formally outside the #FeesMustFall fold were harassed, threatened, and often pilloried as stooges of white interests or executive management.

This intolerance was also reflected in the disruption of meetings—numerous university executives' meetings were disrupted across the system, as were national meetings convened by government and even the NECF. Essentially, some #FeesMustFall leaders and activists shared a widespread belief that anyone who did not fully share their views was a legitimate target for silencing.

These incidents were not exclusive to Wits University. Academic, professional, and administrative staff, students, and executives across the system have increasingly reported similar intolerance. But the challenge also extends to external stakeholders. Some academics outside South Africa undertook lazy solidarity action in which they pronounced on a course of action by the university, at the prompting of an academic colleague, without any independent investigation of the issues on the ground. When confronted, very few even bothered to engage further. Similarly, progressive public lawyers refused to think through the political implications of their legal representation, pleading that their profession required a political agnosticism of them. Finally, civil society activists, even notable ones who had demonstrated incredible bravery in the struggle against apartheid, remained silent in the face of student leaders' intolerance, while at the same time privately communicating with me about how unacceptable their behavior was. Most of this was inspired by a mistaken belief that they could earn student leaders' trust and then slowly encourage them to behave in more acceptable and principled ways. These activists had forgotten that, if left unchecked, these behavioral patterns could generalise themselves across society, consolidate a new generation of venal politicians and, in the process, compromise the very social justice outcome that the protest desired.

The challenge of these ethical violations among leaders, activists, and supporters of #FeesMustFall is not only that they delegitimize the social movement, but also that they consolidate a cynical view of politics within broader society. People come to see all politics, politicians, and political activists as duplicitous and unprincipled, saying one thing and doing another. As I suggested earlier, a movement seeds an imagining of the alternative society that it envisions. This requires not only that its strategies are compatible with the outcome, but also that its participants practise a politics that is distinctive, and more ethical than that which prevails in the current political system—one that can incubate an alternative behavior that is compatible with the social outcome that the movement desires.

Lessons for Advancing Social Justice

If there is one lesson that the trajectory of #FeesMustFall can impart, it is that the dynamics, strategies and practise of politics in a social justice movement must be very different from what the political system normally practises. This is a lesson not only for South African social movements, but also for social struggles across the globe. It is worth noting that, in many ways, South Africa is two worlds in one: an advanced, competitive, and successful world, surrounded by another that reflects underdevelopment's most tragic features. Its contradictions, then, are as global as they are local. It is fair to say, perhaps, that social struggles are more accentuated in South Africa and that, as a result, political fault lines are more dramatically exposed. This makes South Africa a centre of political protest, but also an incredible social laboratory from which to investigate global challenges and potential solutions.

The struggles of #FeesMustFall—the high costs of education, minimum wages and inhumane working conditions for vulnerable workers, and socially inclusive communities—are not unique to South Africa. Indeed, they are the global struggles of this era. As a result, movements similar to #FeesMustFall have emerged across the world, including in North America and Western Europe. The social struggles that these movements organize, and their success, are essential to heal our world, address its inequalities and political polarization, and build more inclusive cosmopolitan communities and societies. To do this, there is a need to learn from past struggles in both the local and global setting. If reflections on #FeesMustFall can help at least a little in this regard, then the protests, and the difficulties that accompanied them, would have been worth it—for South Africa and the rest of the world.

References

Arendt, H. (1969). *On violence*. Orlando: Harcourt.

Biko, S. (2002). *I write what I like*. Chicago, IL: University of Chicago Press.

Booysen, S. (2016). *Fees must fall: Student revolt, decolonisation, and governance in South Africa*. Johannesburg, South Africa: Wits University Press. https://doi.org/10.18772/22016109858

Canham, H. (2017). Embodied black rage. *Du Bois Review: Social Science Research on Race, 14*, 427–445. https://doi.org/10.1017/S1742058X17000066

Chantiluke, R., Kwoba, B., & Nkopo, A. (Eds.). (2018). *Rhodes must fall: The struggle to decolonise the racist heart of empire*. London: Zed.

Chikane, R. (2018). *Breaking a rainbow, building a nation: The politics behind #mustfall movements*. Johannesburg: Picador Africa.

della Porta, D. (1995). *Social movements, political violence and the state: A comparative analysis of Italy and Germany*. New York, NY: Cambridge University Press. https://doi.org/10.1017/CBO9780511527555

della Porta, D. (2013). *Clandestine political violence*. New York, NY: Cambridge University Press. https://doi.org/10.1017/CBO9781139043144

della Porta, D., & Diani, M. (2006). *Social movements: An introduction* (2nd ed.). Malden: Blackwell.

Duncan, J. (2016, December 8). Playing into the Hands of the Securocrats: A Response to Adam Habib. *Daily Maverick* (Johannesburg). Retrieved from https://www.dailymaverick.co.za/article/2016-12-08-playing-into-the-hands-of-the-securocrats-a-response-to-adam-habib/

Fanon, F. (2004). *The wretched of the earth*. New York: Grove.

Fanon, F. (2007). *The wretched of the earth*. New York: Grove.

Fikeni, L. (2016). *Protest, art and the aesthetics of rage: Social solidarity and the shaping of a post-rainbow South Africa*. Paper presented at the 15th annual Ruth First Memorial Lecture, Johannesburg, South Africa. Retrieved from http://witsvuvuzela.com/wp-content/uploads/2016/08/Final-1-Lwandile-2016.pdf

Habib, A. (2016, December 5). Op-ed: The politics of spectacle—Reflections on the 2016 student protest, *Daily Maverick* (Johannesburg). Retrieved from https://www.dailymaverick.co.za/article/2016-12-05-op-ed-the-politics-of-spectacle-reflections-on-the-2016-student-protests/

Habib, A. (2019). *Rebels and rage: Reflecting on #FeesMustFall*. Johannesburg: Jonathan Ball.

Hardt, M., & Negri, A. (2017). *Assembly*. New York, NY: Oxford University Press.

Heffernan, A., & Nieftagodien, N. (Eds.). (2016). *Students must rise: Youth struggle in South Africa before and beyond Soweto '76*. Johannesburg, South Africa: Wits University Press.

Jansen, J. D. (2017). *As by fire: The end of the South African university*. Pretoria: Tafelberg.

Luther King Jr., M. (2010). *Where do we go from here: Chaos or community?* Boston: Beacon. (Original work published 1968)

Mamdani, M. (2001). *When victims become killers: Colonialism, nativism and the genocide in Rwanda*. Princeton, NJ: Princeton University Press.

Mangcu, X. (2017). Imagining our institutions as they should be. Retrieved from https://projectrise.news24.com/xolela-mangcu-time-re-imagine-way-lead/

Mbembe, A. J. (2016, January 19). Theodor Adorno vs Herbert Marcuse on student protests, violence and democracy. *Daily Maverick* (Johannesburg). Retrieved from https://www.dailymaverick.co.za/article/2016-01-19-theodor-adorno-vs-herbert-marcuse-on-student-protests-violence-and-democracy/

McAdam, D. (1983). Tactical innovation and the pace of insurgency. *American Sociological Review, 48*, 735–754. https://doi.org/10.2307/2095322

Naidoo, L.-A. (2016). *Hallucinations*. Paper presented at the 15th annual Ruth First Memorial Lecture, Johannesburg, South Africa. Retrieved from http://witsvuvuzela.com/wp-content/uploads/2016/08/Hallucinations_RUTHFIRST_August2016_FINAL.pdf

Tarrow, S. G. (1994). *Power in movement: Social movements, collective action and politics*. New York, NY: Cambridge University Press.

Tilly, C. (1978). *From mobilization to revolution*. Reading: Addison-Wesley.

Tilly, C. (2003). *The politics of collective violence*. Cambridge, UK: Cambridge University Press. https://doi.org/10.1017/CBO9780511819131

Chapter 14
Civility, Education, and the Embodied Mind—Three Approaches

Heinz-Dieter Meyer

> *[H]ow can we make our teaching so potent in the emotional life*
> *of man, that its influence should withstand the pressure of the*
> *elemental psychic forces in the individual?*
>
> (Albert Einstein, 1938)
>
> *The sage gives free rein to his desires and fulfills all of his*
> *emotions, but having been regulated they accord with*
> *civilized norms.*
>
> (Xunzi)

In 1998, reflecting on the atrocities in Srebenica, Bosnia, the philosopher Richard Rorty published an essay entitled "Human Rights, Rationality, and Sentimentality," in which he considered the ease with which heretofore peaceful people were mobilized to participate in genocidal violence. In the essay, Rorty pointed out that an education focused on reason alone does not get us past the kind of "person whose treatment of a rather narrow range of featherless bipeds is morally impeccable, but who remains indifferent to the suffering of those outside this range, the ones he or she thinks of as pseudo-humans" (p. 124). He suggested that such "primitive parochialism" cannot be overcome "by using that paradigmatic human faculty, reason" (p. 124). Rather, an answer, Rorty argued, must inevitably have recourse to the shaping of the *sentiments*—that complex of feelings, perceptions, preferences, tastes, sensibilities, and inclinations—which includes the capacity to feel empathy and compassion in the face of suffering—our own and others'—and respond accordingly. The sentiments are crucially involved in shaping how we experience the world, but play little to no role in contemporary education that is focused with increasing exclusivity on cognitive skill and competence alone. A similar idea was expressed by Albert Einstein in 1938. Five years after many in Germany applauded the National Socialists' ascent to their rein of terror, Einstein wondered how we could make our education powerful enough so it would "withstand the pressure of

H.-D. Meyer (✉)
Professor of Education Governance and Policy, Department of Educational Policy and
Leadership, University at Albany, State University of New York, Albany, NY, USA
e-mail: hmeyer@albany.edu

© The Author(s) 2022

J. Glückler et al. (eds.), *Knowledge and Civil Society*, Knowledge and Space 17,
https://doi.org/10.1007/978-3-030-71147-4_14

the elemental psychic forces in the individual," including such "primary impulses" as "pride, hate, and need for power." "If men as individuals surrender to the call of their elementary instincts, avoiding pain and seeking satisfaction only for their own selves, the result for them all taken together must be a state of insecurity, of fear, and of promiscuous misery." These observations prompted Einstein to ask: "how can we make our teaching so potent in the emotional life of man, that its influence should withstand the pressure of the elemental psychic forces in the individual?" (Einstein, 1938).

The reflections of these eminent scholars are à propos at a time when the readiness for violence in the public sphere—by means of speech and conduct—is again dramatically on the rise. For just one example, according to one US study, the number of Americans who feel "justified to use violence to advance political goals" has risen sharply and alarmingly during the past three years from under ten percent to 33%.[1] In light of these reflections, we are entitled to wonder how much hope there is for a stable civil society unless nonviolence and self-government in our *external* affairs is coupled with and buttressed by nonviolence and self-government *internally*—in our ability to regulate, govern, and harness our *affective selves*. In fact, this seems to me the challenge of education par excellence: How to train our sentimental and cognitive faculties, our heart and minds, so that we are able to listen to our better angels especially in times of stress and conflict.

In this respect we should derive great encouragement from the currently emerging confluence of philosophical and cultural traditions which point to a profound agreement on key points that our dominant educational model does not now recognize. One of them is that reason alone does not guarantee right conduct and that in order to educate men and women who are able to reason, reflect and reconcile well, they must learn to also properly develop their *affect*. In other words: Education must reach the heart. It must be minimally embodied. It must go beyond the cognition--centered learning that now dominates our competition- and economic-growth oriented educational practices (Meyer & Benavot, 2013).

The Embodied Mind: A Confluence of Traditions

Given how deeply our Western (and increasingly global) model of education is focused on training the rational faculties, it is exciting to see how the long held assumptions about the individual's ability to rationally self-govern are now being challenged from a number of directions representing lines of thought that were, heretofore, noncommunicating. According to many researchers now at work, it is becoming increasingly clear that there is, in fact, a relationship between the rationalist-centered approach to education and the ease with which we observe well-educated people slipping into conduct espousing hatred, greed, and violence. One of them is the psychologist Robert Sternberg, who coined the term "smart fool"

---

[1] Roper, W. (2020, October 7). Feelings of political violence rise. Retrieved from https://www.statista.com/chart/23124/political-violence/https://www.statista.com/chart/23124/political-violence/

and points that people fail in career and life more because of a lack of wisdom than a lack of IQ-type intelligence (Sternberg, 1990, 2001; Sternberg, Reznitskaya, & Jarvin, 2007). The thus educated person is clever, "smart," or "rational" but not "wise." Other leading psychologists are similarly working on understanding the relationship between moral character, intellectual learning, and subjective experience of happiness (Duckworth, 2016; Haidt, 2006; Seligman, Ernst, Gillham, Reivich, & Linkins, 2009).[2]

Of the growing number of writers working on redressing this imbalance, many do so by returning to Aristotelian and Socratic philosophy more broadly (e.g., Dunne, 1993/1997; Jacobs, 2001; Snow, 2015; Steel, 2014). Their efforts have yielded a robust body of work on the intersection of virtue ethics and education (Carr, 2018; Dunne & Hogan, 2004; Kristjánsson, 2015), showing how far our contemporary utilitarian educational ethic has strayed from the moral development and character-oriented educational ethic of those forebears. Much of this work—especially the groundbreaking "Back to Rough Ground: Practical Judgment and the Lure of Technique" (Dunne, 1993/1997) and Steel's (2014) "The Pursuit of Wisdom and Happiness in Education"—have yet to find their proper reception in education scholarship.

There is, however, a more recent development that I shall highlight in this paper—one that is prompted by and important for the possibility of a global civil society. This concerns an emerging confluence of Western and Eastern moral traditions, which, perhaps for the first time, offer the possibility of what Einstein (1938) called "a universal moral attitude"—a moral and civil stance that might unite people across different traditions and world views and that would be of great significance for our ability to live in harmony in a global world. If we can identify areas of obvious agreement among these traditions, this would greatly assist an "embodied" reorientation of education. By engaging that confluence, we can not only attain a sense of the degree to which our modern rationalist education is aberrant; but also some pointers as to the direction in which we might find a reorientation.

In what follows I'll explore these areas of intersection regarding the integration of head and heart, affect and reason, and sentiment and cognition as pursued in three distinct traditions:

- the Confucian and Daoist debate on the relationship between "hot and cold" cognition in the process of self-cultivation or "inner cultivation" as recently reconstructed in the pioneering work of Edward Slingerland (2014);
- the idea of *sophrosyne* or self-regulation in accord with wisdom that was for many centuries the chief educational ideal of the Greek cultural cosmos (North, 1966/2019).

---

[2] Scholars in the field of "positive psychology" like Seligman and Duckworth tend to use "happiness" in the sense of "life satisfaction." This is different from happiness as advancing on a path of moral development. The latter involves a reordering of tastes and preferences leading to a transformational change of character that will change our preferences and our readiness to forego a limited (e.g., sense) pleasure for the sake of a higher pleasure of inner peace. For a discussion of these differences, see Edelglass (2017).

- and the Buddhist-inspired idea of "mindfulness" which is now finding wide-spread use in education.

All three, I will suggest, agree on a for our contemporary debates crucial point: That the reliably "civil" person is one whose moral development has matured to a point where their intellectual and moral capacities, their heart and mind achieve a degree of balanced integration. As the commonalities of these traditions are coming into view to a global community of education, we have a perhaps a historically unique opportunity to recover a deeper sense of education that goes beyond the mere technical and instrumental competence that now preoccupies educational thought, especially in globally influential reform projects like PISA. Pursuing this path, we may eventually develop a sense of education as the kind of moral universal that Einstein (1938) sought, sufficiently "potent in the emotional life of man" that it can withstand and transform the more destructive "elemental forces" in the individual.

The Embodied Mind (I): Inner Cultivation. Integrating Hot and Cold Cognition

One of the most compelling demonstrations of the need for a principled shift in our thinking about moral and educational formation comes from Edward Slingerland's (2015) pioneering reinvestigating of key debates in Chinese philosophy, issuing in the conclusion that "abstract thought is not a strong enough foundation to support morality" (p. 115).

Drawing on both Confucian and Daoist classics, Slingerland usefully distinguishes between two systems of cognition—hot and cold—and suggests that much modern (Western) conceptions of moral formation rest on the faulty assumption that "cold can go it alone" (p. 63). This is flawed because rational control is, as he summarizes, "physiologically expensive, fundamentally limited in nature, and easily disrupted" (p. 65). The dysfunctions of "cold only" can be seen, for example, in research on "verbal overshadowing" where an emphasis on rational analysis (for example, by asking subjects to verbalize and reason about an experience) weakens their judgment. Similarly, a task like the Stroop Task (where subjects are asked to read words like *LOWER* and *upper*, but say the case, not the word) prove to be difficult and effortful because it pits the cold cognitive system against the hot one, rather than making them work in tandem (p. 33).

Over against this effortful repression of hot by cold, Slingerland seeks to recover the Daoist ideal of *wu-wei* (variously translated as nonaction or effortless action), in which hot and cold are balanced and integrated. Unless individuals achieve such an integration, their conduct is likely to be at the mercy of untamed hot cognition. Compared to the "relatively puny" parts of brain that control executive functions "the rest of the brain *is* very much like a team of wild horses or a surging river of water" (p. 64). The problem is that in the disembodied mind the hot system overpowers the cold one any old day.

Jonathan Haidt (2006) takes a similar approach to distinguishing the two volitional systems in human decision making: one visceral and powerful, the other rational but weak. He uses the elephant and rider metaphor to compare the two, the elephant representing our hot or visceral impulses, the rider the rational ones: "when the elephant really wants to do something, I'm no match for him" (p. 4). Similarly: "Reason and emotion must both work together to create intelligent behavior. . ." (p. 13). We pay too much attention to "conscious verbal thinking" and leave the education of sentiments out of the picture. This is, in Haidt's memorable simile like taking "the rider off the elephant and train him to solve problems on his own . . . The class ends, the rider gets back on the elephant, and nothing changes at recess" (p. 165). Haidt concludes: "Modern theories about rational choice and information processing don't adequately explain weakness of will" (p. 4).

By contrast, the proper aim of education is a state where "the mind is embodied and the body is mindful; the two systems—hot and cold, fast and slow—are completely integrated" (Slingerland, 2014, p. 29). "As with large wild animals and rivers, the answer lies in domestication: channeling the flood waters, or taming the wild animals" (2014, p. 65).

The studies of both Slingerland (2014, 2015) and Haidt (2006) issue in a strong indictment of those forms of education that are almost exclusively focused on "cold only." These ideas go significantly beyond traditional notions of "bounded rationality" (Simon, 1957, p. 198). In bounded rationality the emphasis is on the limitations of cognitive and information-processing capacity. The view of rationality as bounded (limited in its ability for information processing) orients us to seek compensatory organizational and computational capacities and intelligence to compensate for rationality's natural shortcomings by means of organization and technology and, for the rest, be content to "satisfice" (rather than maximize) or "muddle through." What Simon and colleagues ignored was that our rational mind is not merely limited in its information-processing and decision-making capacity, it is easily flooded and hijacked by our hot cognition. This capacity to be overwhelmed by our hot cognition is not addressed by expanded computational power or more modest "satisficing" aspirations. The ideas of embodiment, by contrast, point to the need to work on integrating hot and cold cognition by learning to tame the elephant and make room to use the capacities of rational cognition to its full potential.[3]

There is some debate as to how "effortful" the process of heart-mind integration could or should be according to the Chinese classics. While Slingerland presents the idea of "wu-wei" (effortless action) as a Daoist critique of over-effortful Confucian practice focused on regulating external conduct in accord with filial propriety, Kirkland (2004) cites more recently discovered Daoist texts like the *Nei-Yeh*

---

[3] A forthcoming study by Christopher Gowans on "Self-Cultivation Philosophies" extends the scope of this argument to further non-Western philosophies. The introduction to that book is available at "christophergowans.com/what-are-self-cultivation-philosophieshttps://christophergowans.com/what-are-self-cultivation-philosophies".

("Inward Training"), that exhort the practitioner to daily diligence in the pursuit of "biospiritual" practices like meditation (Kirkland 2004, p. 43).

The Embodied Mind (II): Self-Regulation in Accord with Wisdom: Sophrosyne

In the West, a major source for the rejection of mere cleverness as a sufficient outcome of education is Aristotle (trans. 1999). For him "smartness" is a tool that can be used for good and ill: "Now if the mark be noble, the cleverness is laudable, but if the mark be bad, the cleverness is mere smartness…" (Nicomachean Ethics 1144a 23). The merely clever person lacks wisdom. They cannot distinguish reliably between good and bad. For Aristotle, moral and intellectual excellence was inseparable. He would likely have been bewildered by our modern practice of educating the rational faculties of cognition and leaving the affective, embodied side to the student's private endeavors. As MacIntyre (1984) puts it: "For Aristotle excellence of character and intelligence cannot be separated. Here Aristotle expresses a view characteristically at odds with that dominant in the modern world" (p. 154).

For Aristotle, the rational person is defective in two ways: a) being merely clever or "smart," they cannot distinguish reliably between good and bad. But the lack of practical wisdom (*phronesis*) in the thus educated person is not their only deficit. Another hallmark of this mere technical rationality is *akrasia* or weak-willedness. Even where the akratic knows right, they often do wrong (Ovid: "I see and approve of the better, but I follow the worse"). To counter-act the limitations and fragile nature of mere rational self-control or "continence," Aristotle lays out a path of moral development in the course of which people become "properly affected" (Burnyeat, 1980) issuing in a state of uncoerced self-regulation and self-restraint or "sophrosyne" (North, 1966/2019).

For Aristotle, moral development was not complete until it issued in a degree of self-mastery or temperance whereby the person experienced a transformation of their affects that would lead them to a harmonious balance of reason and appetites, head and heart. The goal is a balance of character where reason and appetites, logos and passions, are both transformed and joined harmoniously. This is notably different from mere rational self-management that uses rational stratagems (epitomized by Ulysses tying himself to the mast to better cope with the allure of the Sirens) to keep untamed appetites in check. At the point of sophrosyne, a person becomes properly affected and reliably chooses the right thing for the right reasons (Kosman, 1980). Aristotle was very clear that cleverness or instrumental reason alone does not guarantee right conduct. He called for a process of moral cultivation that would move us beyond the stage of akrasia by transforming a person's affect (Oksenberg Rorty, 1980).

The Aristotelian alternative to the education of mere rationality or smartness was always a package deal involving virtue, wisdom, and contemplation (*theoria*). Characteristically and consequentially, the life of *theoria* (contemplation),

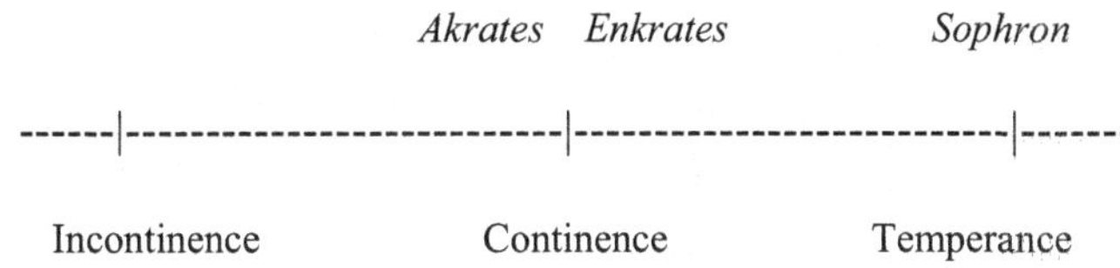

Fig. 14.1 Stages of self-regulation. Source: Design by author.

designated by Aristotle as the highest life, has frequently been mistranslated as "life of study" or even "theoretical life," thereby negating Aristotle's essential dimension of spiritual cultivation. To me, this idea of self-regulation in accord with wisdom and self-knowledge promoted by theoria-contemplation is the most important educational idea suggested by Aristotle and one of the most under-utilized discoveries of our forebears (for the theoria as contemplation concept see Hadot, 1995; Jacobs, 2001, 2012; Pieper, 1952/1998; Smith, 2001; Steel, 2014).

To appreciate Aristotle's thought, it's important to see that his continuum of moral development does not stop at mere continence or rational control of the appetites (see Fig. 14.1). Aristotle distinguishes between incontinence (wantonness, license, lack of control) and continence (control), but also between continence and temperance (Sanderse, 2015). The latter distinction refers to the person who no longer needs to engage in self-coercion to control their appetites. Thus, there is an important distinction between the *akratic* and *enkratic* person on the one hand and between the *enkrates* and the *sophron* on the other. The akrates and enkrates both do battle with the untamed appetites. While the akrates fights and loses, the enkrates fights and wins the battle. But the enkrates still needs to fight and use various means of self-coercion. The point is that the enkrates is not free of inner self-coercion where they need to employ their cold cognition to force the hot system into compliance. They must, in other words, rely on forms of more or less strong *internal violence* that, given certain situational stresses, may burst to the surface.

Reason Does Not Guarantee Right Conduct

A key implication of Aristotle's idea of moral development is that exclusive reliance on reason or rationality do not guarantee right conduct. Where the educational ideal of rationality implies that freedom is the result of the effective suppression of the appetites by means of reason, Aristotle teaches that such a state is still unstable and vulnerable to internal and external violence. It leads at best to oligarchic man's ability to restrain his passions for the sake of another passion: avarice, so as to prevent our passions from getting in the way of our greed. As Albert Hirschman (1977) has shown in his essay on "The Passions and the Interests," this reinterpretation of avarice as the benign passion of self-interest that could be relied upon to keep the more destructive passions in check is, indeed, what the founders of modern political philosophy deemed to be the high-water mark of modern man's moral psychology (see Fig. 14.2).

CONDUCT AND COERCION	With Self-Coercion	Without Self-Coercion
Inappropriate Choice / Conduct	*Akrates* (continent & weak-willed)	*Incontinent*
Appropriate Choice / Conduct	*Enkrates* (continent & self-controlled)	*Sophron* ("temperate," "properly affected")

Fig. 14.2 Conduct and coercion. Source: Design by author.

While enkratic man remains at war with his inclinations, the sophron has succeeded to transform their affect so that they only want what they ought to want.

Notice, that sophrosyne is not "self-restraint above all," but self-restraint in accord with self-knowledge. The rule of virtue is unstable and liable to extremes unless virtue is balanced by self-knowledge and wisdom. History is littered with instances of violence perpetrated in the name of virtue ("let justice be done if the heavens may fall"). So sophrosyne is neither a timid moderation, fuelled by fear of what one may find on the other side of passionate excess or by the boy scout's need for praise. Nor is it the terror of virtue that mercilessly doles out punishment to transgressors from an (often) hypocritical sense of purity. As North's (1966/2019) meticulous reconstruction shows, sophrosyne is far more than what Werner Jaeger called a "humdrum doctrine of peace and contentment," (as cited in North, 1966/2019, p. xii). It is self-restraint in accord with wisdom, supported and guided by insight-knowledge. It is based on the idea that ultimately only the self-restraint that results from self-knowledge and self-insight is free and noncoercive. Insight into the push and pull of the inclinations is the precondition for a kind of self-restraint that is not (self-) coercive (although the process may, initially, require will-power to get going), but which is the free accession to the realization of the kinds of actions which lead to lasting peace and well-being.

While it is often thought that the key step past the akratic's impasse is the firmly self-controlled person, this is not what Aristotle teaches. The enkratic is still doing battle with their appetites and inclinations. They still depend on successfully using various means of self-coercion to avoid transgressive conduct. To get past this point, there is a need for training, guarding, and reordering our tastes and impulses so to become properly affected and want only what we ought to want. The temperate mind is, finally, capable of opening to reason. As North (1966/2019) puts it: "The special importance of sophrosyne in the process of education becomes clear with the assertion that unruly passion is the chief obstacle to learning—because it deafens us to the appeal of reason" (p. 244).

The Embodied Mind (III): Mindfulness

The recent explosion of mindfulness across Western and, indeed, global popular and academic discourse is increasingly noticed by social and political scientists (see, e.g., Mariotti, 2020). It has begun to reshape professional practice in many domains, including health and medicine, business, social work, and, alas, education. Some writers go as far as arguing that mindfulness has the potential to take the place of the Protestant Ethic—now that the latter seems to have shed all ascetic self-restraint and collapsed into unrestrained money making.

My interest here is limited to exploring the parallels between mindfulness and the above two practices of integrating head and heart, or hot and cold cognition, and how this might form the basis for a dialogue that can bring forth the shared educational concerns in these major traditions of moral development.

Although it has entered widespread, even inflationary, usage in the West, the original Pali term *sati* (Sanskrit *smrt*) is actually not easily rendered in one English term. In fact, as Gethin (2011) points out, the term mindfulness was somewhat of an awkward placeholder, arising from the fact that more straightforward translations of *sati* as "calling to mind / bearing in mind / remembering / constant presence of mind / turning one's attention to" are awkward and unwieldy. Often thought of as a moment-to-moment awareness of feelings, thoughts, and mental states ("direct observation of mind and body in the present moment," p. 267), the contemporary uses of mindfulness are often connected to practices aiming at stress reduction, anxiety and other health benefits. These uses shape, in part, the current understanding of the term as a readily available method of lessening one's reactivity and developing a greater sense of calm and ease. This understanding, however, does not capture the full range of the term, incorporating, as it does, several qualities that are not usually combined in a single term in the Western vernacular. There are, in fact, a number of qualities or functions that the term mindfulness combines:

- a quality of awareness and vigilant self-monitoring;
- a quality of guarding and regulating the mind;
- a quality of developing and deepening the mind.

Olendzki (2009) describes the monitoring quality as a "presence of mind that remembers to attend with persistent clarity to the objects of present experience" and "a mode of awareness that is paradoxically both intimately close and objectively removed" (p. 42). The scholar Bhikkhu Bodhi (2011) describes it as "reflexive contemplation of one's own experience" of body, feelings, states of mind, and phenomena, a continuous observation of the object of experience and a "lucid awareness" that is connected to and facilitative of "clear comprehension" (p. 21). Likewise, Bhikkhu Anālayo (2003) ascribes to *sati* the aforementioned functions of monitoring and observing (p. 58), restraining and regulating (p. 56), recollecting and keeping in mind (p. 46) as well as investigating and probing (p. 64) and steering and supervising (p. 55).

An image frequently used in Buddhist scholarship is that of taming and training the mind through mindfulness as a post or anchor to which the mind-in-training is hitched. There is, for example, the simile of the taming of the elephant by way of a post that restrains him. He is then further trained by the tamer's calming words who also provides him with the food that nourishes him. The training includes teaching him to follow commands and standing his ground against attacks (Discourse on the Tamed Stage, MN III 128).

Importantly, this mindfully trained mind is not limited to perfecting one's cognitive powers or to merely calming the mind, although that is an important first step. Rather it includes developing, deepening and transforming the mind towards embodied qualities of "attention that is at once confident, benevolent, generous, and equanimous" (Olendzki, 2009, p. 42). Bhikkhu Bodhi (2011), likewise, holds that "mindfulness and clear comprehension serve as a bridge between the observational function of mindfulness and the development of insight" (p. 34).

A common thread here is the idea of a *self-generating (auto-poeitic) mind*, capable of self-regulating and self-shaping in the process of self-monitoring based on its own innate capacities and powers. This is not an empty vessel mind to be filled with content from the outside; nor is it simply the romanticists' mind that "follows the heart" wherever it may pull. It is a well-trained, well-tamed mind—one that accomplishes this training ultimately by relying on its own, ever deepening powers. This self-generating and self-shaping quality of the mindful mind is expressed nicely in this passage of the Visuddhimagga:

> Sati is that by means of which [the qualities that constitute the mind] remember, or it itself is what remembers, or it is simply remembering. Its characteristic is not-floating [non-distraction, hdm], its property absence of forgetting, its manifestation guarding or being face to face with an object of awareness; its basis is steady perception or the establishing of mindfulness of the body, and so on. Because of its being firmly set in the object of awareness, it should be seen as like a post and, because it guards the gates of the eye and other senses, as like a gatekeeper. (Vism XIV, 141 as cited in Gethin, 2011, p. 272)

A person's mindful development progresses as the practitioner becomes aware of and gradually overcomes obstacles including, in the Buddhist conception, the *five hindrances* of restlessness, sloth, greed, aversion, and skeptical doubt. One result of this development is "clear comprehension" which means, among other things, that practitioners are increasingly unable to deceive themselves. As Gethin (2011) puts it:

> . . . if you consistently 'remember' what it is you are doing in any given moment, you will truly see what it is you are doing; and in truly seeing what it is you are doing, those of your deeds, words and thoughts that are motivated by greed, hatred and delusion will become impossible for you. (p. 265)

Self-deception as an impairment to reason and rationality has been discussed in the literature on rationality (see, especially, Elster, 1986). In our context, it can be seen as a hindrance to moral development. As it deepens, mindfulness makes self-deception about one's intentions and motivations increasingly difficult.

What becomes apparent in this brief consideration of the range of the term mindfulness is that it describes a complex, layered understanding of mind and mental development that brings into view the mind's self-generating capacity for self-regulation and insight. While the "present-moment awareness" as which it is often described captures an important part of the term, much of the deeper underpinnings that come into view as the self-generating mind develops include the transformative deepening of the mind whereby moral conduct and wisdom arise as emergent by-products.

Mindful contemplation thus plays a critical role in moral choice and moral development in at least two ways. First, it assists in practically wise (*phronetic*) action in the here and now, by facilitating the agent's awareness of mental or emotional obstructions to clear seeing and acting. Secondly, mindfulness facilitates a receptive opening and sensitizing the mind for the limitations of self-view, thereby aiding in inclining the mind toward a natural and genuine interest in the well-being of others.

In all this, mindfulness develops qualities that require the integration of hot and cold cognition and run parallel to the idea of sophrosyne. In fact, in this perspective it makes little sense to uphold the strict distinction of heart and mind, emotions and cognition that so strongly characterizes Western thought. Buddhist thought talks instead of the *heart-mind* (*citta*). Both operate together and need to be developed together.

Summary: Educating the Heart-Mind

The three traditions surveyed above share several key concerns regarding education as a process of moral development focused on the formation of the heart-mind—a "faculty" that is distinctly different from the modern Western conception of education as focused on the intellect only. The heart-mind is known to all the traditions considered here as the seat of our experience and action. It is the ensemble of affective and intellectual, moral and cognitive faculties that undergoes transformative change as people learn about their external and internal world.

There are several assumptions that distinguish a heart-mind focused education from that which targets the cold cognition or intellect only:

- reason (or cold cognition) does not guarantee right conduct;
- there are stages of moral and intellectual development. Continence—that stage in which a person is able to refrain from harmful external conduct—is an unstable half-way house on this continuum;
- effective education involves both intellectual and moral development and must reach the affective sentiments;
- a key mechanism of moral development is the cultivation of self-knowledge through mindful self-awareness and self-monitoring.

In practice, this means that a good education must include a nontrivial element of contemplative self-awareness and somatic, embodied practice. Education that wants to reach the heart must include a somatic and contemplative dimension. It must be embodied.

A Note on Heart-Mind as that which Needs Education
Major non-Western (and early) Western traditions share and employ a core concept by which they designate the faculty that requires education as the *heart-mind*—which is distinctly different from the modern Western emphasis on rationality and the "rational" faculties. I will merely adduce some examples without elaboration to give a sense of how these traditions coincide on an understanding of the heart-mind as the core faculty to be trained by education.

Confucianism. Roger T. Ames (2016), in his translation of the classical Confucian commentary "The Great Learning," uses the term "heartmind" (one word in the original) to connote the faculty at which education is aimed (p. 24). Confucius famous passage about the stages of learning also has the heart-mind as that which learns: "From fifteen, my heart-and-mind was set upon learning; . . . from seventy I could give my heart-and-mind free reign without overstepping the mark" (see Lai, 2016, p. 79).

Goldin (2018) argues that the heart-mind is the key concept in the work of the influential Confucian philosopher Xunzi: "In many respects, the heart-mind is the keystone of Xunzi's philosophy, the one piece that links together all the others. The Chinese word xin means 'heart', but Xunzi attributes such strong and varied mental processes to this organ that one has to construe it as not only the heart but also the mind. (The mind was not located in the brain in premodern Chinese philosophy.)," ". . . the heart-mind is the organ that we use to discover the Way" and it is "the only organ that can command the others" (https://plato.stanford.edu/entries/xunzi).

Buddhism. In Pali, the language of the early Buddhist teachings, the heart-mind is *citta*—the seat of experience and of volition. Bhikkhu Bodhi (2000) explains "[c]itta signifies mind as the centre of personal experience, as the subject of thought, volition, and emotion. It is citta that needs to be understood, trained, and liberated" (pp. 769–770).

In Tibetan the term for heart-mind is *kun long*—which is, according to the Dalai Lama (1999), the place "from which all our actions spring" (p. 81).

A classical passage from an early Buddhist Sutta illustrates the importance of *citta* as heart-mind. To the question "[b]y what is the world led around? By what is it dragged here and there? What is the one thing that has all under its control?" the Buddha replies "The world is led around by citta; by mind it's dragged here and there. Mind is the one thing that has All under its control." (Saṃyutta Nikāya.I.62-2).

Greek Philosophical Tradition. The corresponding concept for heart-mind in classical Greek thought is *soul* which, in Plato requires training to achieve the union of *logos* (reason / intellect) and *eros* (affective desire). As discussed above, the development of *sophrosyne* through education aims at both the rational and irrational elements in the soul. (North, 1966/2019, p. 208).

Heeding the lessons about the inherent fragility of the civil society and the essential role of countervailing moral and spiritual forces (see Chap. 2 by Meyer) requires that we dramatically expand our conception of education from a dominant focus on learning about the external world to an equally important focus on learning about our mind. To develop this kind of knowledge, education cannot be limited to conventional learning from texts and lectures. It needs to involve experience through somatic practices that bring the student face-to-face, as it were, with their heart-mind. Only as we advance in "knowing our minds," are we likely to realize the benefits of building and developing it towards not only epistemic knowledge but wisdom. The distinction between book-knowledge and wisdom (and their corresponding types of learning) is famously brought home by Montaigne who points out that we can become knowledgeable with other people's knowledge, but we cannot be wise with other people's wisdom. Wisdom is something we have to develop bit by bit on our own.

Long-standing traditions and recent research on mindfulness, wisdom and self-cultivation in education (Ergas, 2017; Peters 2020; Steel, 2014; Sternberg, 2001; Zajonc, 2009) converge on this point. The right kind of education and schooling that leave room and guidance for mindful self-awareness can initiate students into habits of self-awareness and insight that can lastingly shape their ability of self-reflection and self-regulation.

Can Kindness be Taught?—Education as a Wisdom Culture

Back to Rorty's (1998) "featherless bipeds" who wouldn't dream of harming a member of their flock, but thoughtlessly visit violence on people who look or behave different. Can a different kind of education make a difference? Can kindness be taught?

To staff off a possible misapplication of the above: What is *not* needed is for "Kindness" to become part of national curriculum, where it is "taught" alongside algebra and French grammar. Armies of finger-wagging teachers instructing students in "universal kindness" may undermine any actual transformative education—an education that reaches the heart. It is an axiom of political philosophy that civility-virtue cannot be legislated without lapsing into mental tyranny. Nor, once achieved, can it be taken to be self-perpetuating or self-sustaining. Virtue is a plant that withers under the whip of political coercion as much as under the true believer's totalizing ambition. In short: it cannot be generated by means of actions that directly aim at it. It can only arise as a by-product of types of action and forms of institutions that do not directly aim at generating it.

What *is* needed and is possible, by contrast, is that education develop a wisdom culture, an institutional prioritizing of beliefs and norms that make the development of kindness, compassion and a host of other moral excellences more likely. Sean Steel (2014, p. 293), one of the few to give thought to this idea, enumerates friendship, play, and contemplation as three key factors of such a culture. We need friends to help us see ourselves fully. In Jacobs' (2001)

(continued)

memorable phrase: "the excellent agent is a living norm" (p. 77). This is why "associating with the wise" is a precept in all moral traditions.

A wisdom culture that cultivates friendship, play, and leisure can be developed based on many wisdom traditions, including those surveyed in this paper—or on a pluralist openness to all of them. In fact, a deep pluralism that honors one's own tradition all the while acknowledging and demonstrating the deep interconnections with other traditions (Vélez de Cea, 2013) would seem to be a key requirement of a global educational community. By thus encouraging ourselves and our students to honestly cultivate our minds in an awareness of the shared fund of moral aims we may have as good a chance as human effort can procure for the seeds of human benevolence that we will find in our own minds to grow, so that, when "the other" crosses our path and perchance needs a helping hand, we know what to do.

Widening Circles of Empathy. As an example, consider the idea of teaching universal empathetic kindness in three different traditions. There is the story of Mencius who, encountering a brutal tyrant, teaches him kindness by reminding him how he, the tyrant, felt pity when he saw an ox in distress as he was led to slaughter. Mencius asks the tyrant to similarly notice that his own subjects live in fear and distress and to relax his demands on them just as he decided to spare the ox.

Similarly, there is the story of King David, who, desiring Bathsheba, sends her husband Uriah into battle where he will be killed. When the prophet Nathan tells him the story of the rich man who, upon meeting a hungry traveler, takes not one of his own sheep to feed the traveler, but a poor man's only sheep, David is enraged by the injustice, but comes to see his own unjust deed in the rich man's conduct. Finally, in the Buddhist Metta Sutta, this theme of cultivating a "boundless heart," of developing goodwill for oneself, one's friends and neighbors, and ultimately for all sentient beings, is similarly made the subject of continuous reflection and meditation.[4] In all these stories—and more could be cited from other traditions—moral instruction starts where the "students" are and expands their empathetic and compassionate horizons *in ever widening circles*. Can this principle of "growing the seeds" of universal empathy and compassion become a building block of education today?

---

[4] Metta Sutta: "Wishing: In gladness and in safety, May all beings be at ease. Whatever living beings there may be; Whether they are weak or strong, omitting none, The great or the mighty, medium, short or small, The seen and the unseen, Those living near and far away, Those born and to-be-born—May all beings be at ease! Let none deceive another, Or despise any being in any state. Let none through anger or ill-will Wish harm upon another. Even as a mother protects with her life Her child, her only child, So with a boundless heart Should one cherish all living beings; Radiating kindness over the entire world…" (Snp 1.8. Retrieved from https://www.accesstoinsight.org/tipitaka/kn/snp/snp.1.08.amar.htmlhttps://www.accesstoinsight.org/tipitaka/kn/snp/snp.1.08.amar.html)

Educating the Heart-Mind Mind for Embodied Civility—A Basis for a New Global Dialogue?

The questions raised by Rorty (1998) and Einstein (1938) above show that the experience that our education does not reach deep enough, that it does not reliably put even our best and brightest on a path to an embodied, affective self-regulation in accord with wisdom, are not new to our current condition. But we may today be on the cusp of an encouraging difference: we enjoy today access to ideas from a variety of global traditions that share a common concern for education as the development of the heart-mind. This common fund can help us transcend two sizable obstacles that have, to date, hindered progress along this path. Firstly, it can help us overcome the overt or latent Eurocentrism that can be found in many contemporary discussions, where the problems discussed here are considered only within the tight limitations of European thought and traditions.[5] Secondly, it can also help us realize that questions of moral development are not synonymous with religious framing. They need neither be couched in religious or theistic terms; nor need they be hostile to such a framing.

What emerges here is the possibility of a global coalition for education as a project of moral development, fuelled by the coinciding insights of a family of philosophical and wisdom traditions all of which emphasize the need to develop the heart as much as the head, the sentiments as much as cognition, the affect as well as the intellect. While they differ in important ways that are not to be dismissed, this area of overlapping consensus could prove an important resource of global peace and prosperity—especially in the decades ahead in which global peace may hinge in no small part on our ability to develop cooperative relations between East and West. What is emerging, in fact, is the possibility of a global community of educators, each starting from their own tradition, but with a sincere desire to cultivate cooperation with the members of other traditions. This global community could work towards the building of a global coalition which can include all traditions facilitating the development of the heart-mind. Where education has thus far been couched in terms of nationalist priority or of a merely economic cosmopolitanism in projects like PISA, it can instead be couched in terms of the kind of moral universalism that Einstein invoked many decades ago. Civility can deepen from mere politeness or external conformity of conduct to a disposition towards wise and compassionate action.

By neglecting the sentimental dimension of education in theory and practice, we allow that our aspirational default in education reverts to a kind of externally oriented *instrumental fitness,* an adaptation of human cognition and psychology to the imperative of efficient functioning in established institutions that does nothing to

---

[5] See, for example, the view of Joseph Ratzinger: "No doubt, the two main partners in the correlationality [of reason and faith] are Christian belief and Western secular rationality. This can and must be said without false eurocentrism" (Ratzinger, in Habermas & Ratzinger 2018, p. 57, own trans.).

that prized faculty of "critical thinking" because it leaves the critical thinker victim to the vicissitudes of their untrained minds.

As long as civility is understood as mere external nonviolence or politesse, we hope in vain to close the doors on incivility that are always ajar. Under conditions of the civil society's inherent fragility (see Chap. 2 by Meyer), even minor differences of ethnic or racial membership can appear as intrusions on the individual's private sovereignty and bring in their tow an opening to overt incivility.

Exterior pacification without a corresponding interior moral development is inherently unstable. Rather than producing a sustainable form of peaceful self-governance, it produces prosperous, but restless, self-reliant, but anxious individuals whose jealousies are aroused by otherness and whose abiding dissatisfaction with their condition is tenuously held in check by a habit of merely continent self-coercion. This is the person who will be an easy prey for demagogues and authoritarians who promise the kind of purification in the external world that we have been unable or unwilling to cultivate in our interior.

References

Ames, R. T. (2016). On teaching and learning (Xueji 學記): Setting the root in Confucian education. In X. Di & H. McEwan (Eds.), *Chinese philosophy on teaching and learning: Xueji* (學記) *in the twenty-first century* (pp. 21–38). Albany, NY: SUNY Press.

Aristotle. (1999). *Nicomachean ethics* (T. Irwin, Transl.). Indianapolis: Hackett.

Bhikkhu Anālayo. (2003). *Satipaṭṭhāna: The direct path to realization.* Birmingham: Windhorse.

Bhikkhu Bodhi. (2000). *The connected discourses of the Buddha: A translation of the Saṃyutta Nīkāya.* Sommerville: Wisdom.

Bhikkhu Bodhi. (2011). What does mindfulness really mean? A canonical perspective. *Contemporary Buddhism, 12,* 19–39. https://doi.org/10.1080/14639947.2011.564813

Burnyeat, M. F. (1980). Aristotle on learning to be good. In A. Oksenberg Rorty (Ed.), *Essays on Aristotle's ethics* (pp. 69–92). Philosophical Traditions: Vol. 2. Berkeley, CA: University of California Press.

Carr, D. (2018). Virtue ethics and education. In N. E. Snow (Ed.), *The Oxford handbook of virtue* (pp. 640–658). New York, NY: Oxford University Press. https://doi.org/10.1093/oxfordhb/9780199385195.013.10

Dalai Lama. (1999). *Ethics for the new millennium.* New York: Riverhead.

Duckworth, A. (2016). *Grit: The power of passion and perseverance.* New York: Scribner.

Dunne, J. (1997). *Back to the rough ground: Practical judgment and the lure of technique.* Notre Dame, IN: University of Notre Dame Press. (Original work published 1993). https://doi.org/10.2307/j.ctvpj7dg7

Dunne, J., & Hogan, P. (Eds.). (2004). *Education and practice: Upholding the integrity of teaching and learning.* Malden: Blackwell.

Edelglass, W. (2017). Buddhism, happiness, and the science of meditation. In D. L. MacMahan & E. Braun (Eds), *Meditation, Buddhism, and science* (pp. 62–83). New York, NY: Oxford University Press. https://doi.org/10.1093/oso/9780190495794.003.0004

Einstein, A. (1938). 1938 Albert Einstein's commencement address. Retrieved from http://swat150.swarthmore.edu/1938-albert-einsteins-commencement-address.html

Elster, J. (Ed.). (1986). *The multiple self.* Cambridge, UK: Cambridge University Press.

Ergas, O. (2017). *Reconstructing 'education' through mindful attention: Positioning the mind at the center of curriculum and pedagogy.* London: Macmillan. https://doi.org/10.1057/978-1-137-58782-4

Gethin, R. (2011). On some definitions of mindfulness. *Contemporary Buddhism, 12,* 263–279. https://doi.org/10.1080/14639947.2011.564843

Goldin, P. R. (2018). Xunzi. In E. N. Zalta (Ed.), *The Stanford encyclopedia of philosophy* (Fall 2018 edition). Retrieved from https://plato.stanford.edu/archives/fall2018/entries/xunzi.

Habermas, J., & Ratzinger, J. (2018). *Dialektik der Säkularisierung: Über Vernunft und Religion* [Dialectics of secularization: About reason and religion]. Freiburg: Herder.

Hadot, P. (1995). *Philosophy as a way of life* (A. I. Davidson, Ed., with an introduction by A. I. Davidson). Malden: Blackwell.

Haidt, J. (2006). *The happiness hypothesis: Finding modern truth in ancient wisdom.* New York: Basic.

Hirschman, A. O. (1977). *The passions and the interests: Political arguments for capitalism before its triumph.* Princeton, NJ: Princeton University Press.

Jacobs, J. (2001). *Choosing character: Responsibility for virtue and vice.* Ithaca, NY: Cornell University Press. Retrieved from https://www.jstor.org/stable/10.7591/j.ctv75d1zg

Jacobs, J. (2012). Theory, practice, and specialization: The case for the humanities. *Arts and Humanities in Higher Education, 11,* 206–223. https://doi.org/10.1177/1474022212441771

Kirkland, R. (2004). *Taoism: The enduring tradition.* New York: Routledge.

Kosman, L. A. (1980). Being properly affected: Virtues and feelings in Aristotle's ethics. In A. Oksenberg Rorty (Ed.), *Essays on Aristotle's ethics* (pp. 103–116). Berkeley, CA: University of California Press.

Kristjánsson, K. (2015). *Aristotelian character education.* Routledge Research in Education. Abingdon: Routledge. https://doi.org/10.4324/9781315752747

Lai, C. (2016). The ideas of "educating" and "learning" in Confucian thought. In X. Di & H. McEwan (Eds.), *Chinese philosophy on teaching and learning: Xueji in the twenty-first century* (pp. 77–96). Albany, NY: SUNY Press.

MacIntyre, A. (1984). *After virtue: A study in moral theory* (2nd ed.). Notre Dame, IN: University of Notre Dame Press.

Mariotti, S. (2020). Zen and the art of democracy: Contemplative practice as ordinary political theory. *Political Theory, 48,* 469–495. https://doi.org/10.1177/0090591719887224

Meyer, H.-D. (2022). The dialectic of civil and uncivil society—Fragility, fault lines, and countervailing forces. In L. Suarsana, H.-D. Meyer, & J. Glückler (Eds.), *Knowledge and civil society* (pp. 19–42). Knowledge and Space: Vol. 17. Cham: Springer. https://doi.org/10.1007/978-3-030-71147-4_2

Meyer, H.-D., & Benavot, A. (Eds.). (2013). *PISA, power, and policy: The emergence of global educational governance.* Oxford Studies in Comparative Education: Vol. 23. Oxford: Symposium. https://doi.org/10.15730/books.85

North, H. (2019). *Sophrosyne: Self-knowledge and self-restraint in Greek literature.* St. Augustine: Sophron. (Original work published 1966)

Oksenberg Rorty, A. (1980). Akrasia and pleasure: Nicomachean ethics book 7. In A. Oksenberg Rorty (Ed.), *Essays on Aristotle's ethics* (pp. 267–284). Berkeley, CA: University of California Press.

Olendzki, A. (2009). Mindfulness and meditation. In F. Didonna (Ed.), *Clinical handbook of mindfulness* (pp. 37–44). New York: Springer. https://doi.org/10.1007/978-0-387-09593-6_3

Peters, M. A. (2020). Educational philosophies of self-cultivation: Chinese humanism. https://doi.org/10.1080/00131857.2020.1811679

Pieper, J. (1998). *Leisure: The basis of culture.* South Bend: St. Augustine's. (Original work published 1952)

Rorty, R. (1998). Human rights, rationality, and sentimentality. In R. Rorty (Ed.), *Truth and progress* (pp. 167–185). Philosophical Papers: Vol. 3. Cambridge, UK: Cambridge University Press. https://doi.org/10.1017/CBO9780511625404.010

Sanderse, W. (2015). An Aristotelian model of moral development. *Journal of Philosophy of Education, 49,* 382–398. https://doi.org/10.1111/1467-9752.12109

Seligman, M. E. P., Ernst, R. M., Gillham, J., Reivich, K., & Linkins, M. (2009). Positive education: Positive psychology and classroom interventions. *Oxford Review of Education, 35,* 293–311. https://doi.org/10.1080/03054980902934563

Simon, H. (1957). *Models of man.* New York: John Wiley.

Slingerland, E. G. (2014). *Trying not to try: The art and science of spontaneity.* New York: Crown.

Slingerland, E. G. (2015). The situationist critique and early Confucian virtue ethics. In N. E. Snow (Ed.), *Cultivating virtue: Perspectives from philosophy, theology, and psychology* (pp. 135–170). Oxford, UK: Oxford University Press. https://doi.org/10.1093/acprof:oso/9780199967421.003.0007

Smith, T. W. (2001). *Revaluing ethics: Aristotle's dialectical pedagogy.* Albany, NY: SUNY Press.

Snow, N. E. (Ed.). (2015). *Cultivating virtue: Perspectives from philosophy, theology, and psychology.* Oxford, UK: Oxford University Press. https://doi.org/10.1093/acprof:oso/9780199967421.001.0001

Steel, S. (2014). *The pursuit of wisdom and happiness in education: Historical sources and contemplative practices.* Albany, NY: SUNY Press.

Sternberg, R. J. (1990). Wisdom and it's relations to intelligence and creativity. In R. J. Sternberg (Ed.), *Wisdom: Its nature, origins, and development* (pp. 142–159). Cambridge, UK: Cambridge University Press. https://doi.org/10.1017/CBO9781139173704.008

Sternberg, R. J. (2001). Why schools should teach for wisdom: The balance theory of wisdom in educational settings. *Educational Psychologist, 36,* 227–245. https://doi.org/10.1207/S15326985EP3604_2

Sternberg, R. J., Reznitskaya, A., & Jarvin, L. (2007). Teaching for wisdom: What matters is not just what students know, but how they use it. *The London Review of Education, 5*(2), 143–158. https://doi.org/10.1080/14748460701440830

Vélez de Cea, J. A. (2013). *The Buddha and religious diversity.* Routledge Studies in Asian Religion and Philosophy: Vol. 6. Abingdon: Routledge. https://doi.org/10.4324/9780203072639

Zajonc, A. (2009). *Meditation as contemplative inquiry: When knowing becomes love.* Great Barrington: Lindisfarne.

The Klaus Tschira Foundation

The Klaus Tschira Foundation was created in 1995 by the physicist Klaus Tschira (1940–2015). It is one of Europe's largest privately funded non-profit foundations. The foundation promotes the advancement of natural sciences, mathematics, and computer science and strives to raise appreciation of these fields. The focal points of the foundation are "Natural Sciences—Right from the Beginning," "Research," and "Science Communication." The involvement of the Klaus Tschira Foundation begins in kindergartens and continues in primary and secondary schools, universities, and research facilities. The foundation champions new methods in the transfer of scientific knowledge, and supports both the development and intelligible presentation of research findings. The Klaus Tschira Foundation pursues its objectives by conducting projects of its own but also awards subsidies after approval of applications. To foster and sustain work on selected topics, the foundation has also founded its own affiliates. Klaus Tschira's commitment to this objective was honored in 1999 with the "Deutscher Stifterpreis," the award conferred by the National Association of German Foundations.

The Klaus Tschira Foundation is located in Heidelberg and has its head office in the Villa Bosch, once the residence of Carl Bosch, a Nobel laureate in chemistry.

www.klaus-tschira-stiftung.de

© The Author(s) 2022

J. Glückler et al. (eds.), *Knowledge and Civil Society*, Knowledge and Space 17, https://doi.org/10.1007/978-3-030-71147-4

Fig. 1 Participants of the symposium "Knowledge and Civil Society" at the Studio Villa Bosch in Heidelberg, Germany. © Johannes Glückler, Heidelberg

Fig. 2 Villa Bosch, the head office of the Klaus Tschira Foundation, Heidelberg, Germany. © Peter Meusburger, Heidelberg

Index

A

Adult education centers, 86, 89
Aga Khan Foundation (AKF),
    213–222, 224–226
Agenda-setting, 3, 114, 239–243, 246
Agent of change, 43–55
Agriculture, 77, 81, 84–86, 88, 91, 94–96, 98
Aidland, 209, 213
Alternative economic practices, 131, 132,
    136, 142
Americas, 23, 25, 43, 50, 51, 54, 60–62, 65,
    112, 281, 289
Anti-displacement, 265, 266, 270
Aristotle, 28, 296–298
Association
    LandFrauen (*see* LandFrauen association)
    voluntary, 83, 111–115, 126
    women's (*see* Women's association)
Authenticity, 9, 209–229
Authorities, 29, 67, 193, 209–229, 237, 238,
    240, 249, 278, 281, 283, 285

B

Basic Law, 239–241, 243, 244, 246, 247
Beijing, 235, 239, 240, 242–247
Benevolent activities, 8, 179, 180, 183, 184,
    187, 200
Berlin Wall, 5, 25, 50
Biocultural diversity, 213, 218, 221–223
Böckenförde, 7, 34–37
Bosnia, 291
Bristol, 8, 152–160, 162–165, 170–172
Buddha, 302
Business firms, 189, 190, 194–196, 198–201

C

California, 60, 62–64, 67–69
Cape Town, 8, 152, 153, 155, 158, 160–162,
    166–171, 173, 275
Centralization, 28, 134, 139
China, 48, 243, 244, 246, 248, 249
Christensen Fund, 213, 218, 221–225, 227
Civic network, *see* Network, civic
Civic organization
    transient, 131–142, 151–153, 155,
    158, 169
Civic participation, 111, 256
Civic pluralism, 25
Civic sectors, 8, 180, 182, 183, 200
Civic space, 45, 46
Civil disobedience, 236, 240, 242, 246, 248
Civility, 5, 10, 20, 21, 27, 30–32, 37, 38, 149,
    150, 305, 306
Civil referendum, 236, 239, 240, 243, 244,
    247, 248
Civil society
    agents of, 20, 47, 51, 100
    contextualization of, 97
    development-focused, 9, 209, 211,
    213, 214
    fault lines of, 22
    German, 46, 50, 80–82, 214
    global, 151, 154, 170, 212, 214, 256
    local, 3, 4, 9, 55, 77, 82, 96, 97, 100, 131,
    153, 170, 209–229, 255, 260, 265
    normative dimension of, 30, 31
    silos of, 259
    structural dimension of, 30
    value-based approach of, 52
Civil society knowledge, 10, 209–229

J. Glückler et al. (eds.), *Knowledge and Civil Society*, Knowledge and Space 17,
https://doi.org/10.1007/978-3-030-71147-4

Civil society mobilization, 65
Civil society organization, *see* Organization, civil society
Civil society practices, 9, 10, 100, 257
Civil society space, 6
Climate-change adaption, 220
Clubs, 8, 49, 58, 77, 80, 83–95, 97–101, 110, 131, 185, 188–190, 196
Cognitive skill, 291
Collaborative engagement, 201
Collaborative philanthropy, *see* Philanthropy, collaborative
Collective social action, 80
Colonialism, 228, 285
Communities of practice, 79, 98
Community
    epistemic, 215, 221, 225, 260, 262
    rural, 100
    social justice, 278, 282, 286
Community boards, 268, 269
Community currencies, 132, 135, 136
Community forestry, 218, 219, 227
Community participation, 220, 227
Confucius, 302
Connectivity, 69, 99, 135, 137, 139, 182–184, 191–196, 201
Constitutional reforms, 9, 239–243, 245, 246
Contextualization, 80, 84–86, 97, 100
Cooperations, 3, 4, 26, 29, 31, 68, 78, 80, 86, 87, 90–92, 96–99, 101, 133, 134, 152, 163, 164, 166–168, 183–185, 189, 190, 193–195, 200, 201, 212, 265, 305
Corona pandemic, 90–91, 93, 98
Corporate citizenship, 181
Corporate social responsibility (CSR), 181, 195, 199
Counter-expertise, 238, 242, 247
Countervailing forces, 19–39
COVID-19, 43, 44
Cultural infrastructure, 77, 87
Culture
    wisdom, 304

D
Dalai Lama, 302
Daoist, 293–295
Deliberation, 3, 4, 6, 60, 236, 239–241, 243, 246–248, 264, 276, 278, 286, 287
Democracy
    crisis of, 45, 53
    deliberative, 6, 241
    discursive, 45

liberal, 6, 22, 25, 32
    representative, 6, 44, 48, 158, 265
    schools of, 4, 111–113
    western, 32, 39, 44, 238, 242
Democracy movement, *see* Movement, democracy
Democratic despotism, 25–29
Democratic functions, 6
Democratization, 6
Development
    global/international, 9, 211, 212, 214, 218, 223, 256
Development organization, *see* Organization, development
Development practices, 3, 65, 77, 79, 82, 149, 201, 209–213, 217, 219–221, 227
Digitalization, 3, 10, 90, 94, 97
Donations, 49, 180, 184–187, 189–193, 196–200

E
Education
    higher, 3, 4, 84, 158, 242, 276
    privatization of, 4
Effects
    associative, 27, 29–31
    dissociative, 20, 29–31
Einstein, A., 291–294, 305
Embeddedness, 3, 79, 87, 88, 97–99, 153, 162
Embodied mind, 10, 291–306
Embodied virtue, 38
EMF radiation, 66, 67, 69
EMF risk organization, *see* Organization, EMF risk
Empowerment, 79, 82, 90, 95, 97, 261
Epistemic activism, 255, 257, 265, 271
Epistemic community, *see* Community, epistemic
Epistemic politics, 265–270
Epistemic unity, 260–265
Ethnographic interviewing, 212
Europe, 23, 24, 36, 43, 48, 50, 51, 65, 66, 68, 269, 281, 289

F
Fault-line
    moral, 38
    political, 38
    socio-economic, 38
Foods, 90, 91, 136, 137, 139, 149–173, 254, 255, 262, 263, 270, 300

Forest conservation, 213, 218
Foundations, v, 3, 20, 30, 32, 36, 46, 47, 50,
        64, 70, 109, 116, 136, 179–181, 185,
        187–191, 193–196, 198–201, 210, 213,
        218–222, 224–226, 254, 256–258,
        276, 294
Fragilities, 5, 6, 19–39, 303, 306

G
Genealogy
    alternative, 253, 255
    mainstream, 253, 255
Generational challenge, 281
Generational conflict, 281
Genetically modified food (GM food), 155,
        156, 158–163, 165, 167, 170, 172, 173
German LandFrauen, 77–102
Germany
    southern, 8, 135
Giving
    charitable, 111, 115, 118, 179–181,
        187, 201
    connectivity of, 180, 186
    financial, 46, 179, 180, 198, 238
    geography of, 8, 179–201
    practices of, 9, 201
Giving circles, 7, 109–126
Glasgow, 8, 152–155, 158–160, 162,
        165–167, 170–172
Global coalition, 305
Globalization, 3, 20, 25, 39, 53, 54, 158, 172
Governance
    regional, 3, 44, 180, 198
Government
    limited, 22, 248
Government policies, 35, 111, 117, 120, 123,
        125, 126
Grassroots, 61–64, 69, 109, 111, 171, 211,
        218, 219, 221–225, 254, 271

H
Habermas, 2, 3, 34–37, 45, 49, 101, 150, 241
Heart-mind, 295, 301–306
Heilbronn-Franconia, 8, 180, 184, 185,
        187–189, 192, 193, 195–197, 200, 201
Hong Kong, 9, 10, 235–249
Hot and cold cognition, 294–296, 299, 301

I
Iconic turn, 53–55

Incivility, 5, 10, 20, 21, 31, 38, 39, 306
Individualism, 26–28, 33, 35, 38
Industrial aristocracy, 28
Industrial transitions, 7, 58–61, 69, 70
Inequality
    social, 5, 19, 170
Information gap, 243
Inner cultivation, 293–296
Innovation
    social, 3, 43, 53, 77–80, 82, 96, 97,
        101, 102
Innovation processes, 3, 79
Innovation systems, 3
Institutional frames, 2, 77, 85, 86,
        89–93, 97, 101
Institutional structure, 86
Institutions, 2–4, 19, 20, 23, 26, 35, 45–47,
        51–53, 64, 77–102, 111, 133, 150, 196,
        210, 211, 218, 221, 226, 228, 255, 265,
        266, 278, 283, 286, 303, 305
Interest representation, 77, 94, 100
Intermediality, 5, 6
Intermediaries, 47, 48, 83, 100, 185, 193–195,
        217, 224, 265
International development, 3, 90, 209, 210,
        213, 217, 223, 228

K
Kenya, 9, 90, 213, 218–219, 222, 223
Knowledge
    alternative, 9, 235–249, 257
    counter-, 70, 238
    diffusion of, 101
    everyday, 90, 238, 247, 259
    exchange of, 78
    expert, 4, 9, 96, 209–212, 214–220,
        222–228, 238, 239, 247
    global, 3, 4, 9, 209–211, 214–219, 222,
        223, 226–228, 238, 275
    indigenous, 211, 213, 218, 221–228, 257
    local, 8, 63, 78, 89–91, 95, 96, 99, 101,
        209, 215–225, 227, 228, 237, 264
    reinterpretation of, 297
    reproduction of, 2
    traditional, 91, 211, 221–223, 226, 239
Knowledge communities, 79
Knowledge creation, 1, 3, 10, 79, 200, 238
Knowledge dissemination, 10, 89
Knowledge network, *see* Network, knowledge
Knowledge production, 3
Knowledge transfers, 77, 211, 226
Kyrgyzstan, 9, 213, 214, 216–217

L

LandFrauen associations, 78, 82, 84, 87, 91, 94, 96, 100

LandFrauen organization, 8, 77–102, *see* Organization, LandFrauen

LEADER initiatives, 82

Learning

    adult, 4

    cognition-centered, 292

    intellectual, 293

Legitimacy, 44, 50, 55, 98, 153, 183, 199, 210, 211, 215, 219, 222, 223, 226, 228, 255, 264, 268, 276, 281–283

Leitkultur, 36

Lobbies, 3, 81, 100, 267

Lobbying, 81, 100, 267

M

Market

    tamed, 38

    untamed, 21, 29

Martin Luther King Jr, 282, 284

Mass organization, *see* Organization, mass

Media, 10, 48, 52, 55, 62, 84, 85, 90, 187, 189, 193, 235, 239–241, 243, 246–249, 254, 265, 266, 269, 283

Media analysis, 8, 180, 185, 186, 189, 191

Mindfulness, 294, 299–301, 303

Mobilizations, 5, 6, 9, 58–65, 68, 70, 82, 95, 97, 100, 154, 236, 239, 248, 278, 279

Modern state, 46

Montesquieu, 19, 22–24, 27

Moral entropy, 34

Movement

    democracy, 59, 61, 238, 241, 244, 245, 248, 265, 275

    #FeesMustFall, 9, 275–279, 282, 284–289

    local, 235, 265, 268, 269, 289

    Occupy Central with Love and Peace (OCLP), 236, 239–241, 243, 244, 246–248

    place-based, 265–267, 271

    #RhodesMustFall, 275, 276

    social, 9, 58, 69, 110, 236–240, 246, 247, 254, 265, 271, 275, 276, 278, 285, 288

    social justice, 275–289

Movement of Justice in El Barrio, 266–268, 270

Multiple-method approach, 187

N

Nation states, 7, 20, 43, 45, 215

Network

    anti-smart-meter, 60, 62–64

    civic, 8, 142, 150–152, 158, 163, 165–167, 169, 170, 192, 195

    ego-, 135

    knowledge, 8, 61, 67, 93, 96, 99, 101, 134, 210, 213, 217, 218, 259

    local, 97–99, 132, 135, 152, 156, 163, 170, 182, 201, 244

    organizational, 8, 97, 99, 101, 132, 134, 149, 151, 152, 156, 171, 181, 193, 195

    personal, 139, 171, 195, 201, 213

    regional, 182, 200, 201, 218

    social, 8, 26, 99, 101, 109, 132–135, 142, 150, 151, 156, 158, 160, 161, 164, 165, 170, 171, 181, 185, 192, 201, 259

    theory of, 133

Network alliance, 163–169

Network analysis, 8, 132, 134–140, 142, 150, 185, 192, 200, 259

Network governance, 201

Network of cooperation, 191–196

Network of issues, 156–162, 165, 170, 171

Nongovernmental actors, 4

Nonknowledge, 61

Nonprofit

    organization (*see* Organization, nonprofit)

    sector (*see* Sector, nonprofit)

Nonracialism, 284, 285

O

Organization

    civic (*see* Civic organization)

    civil society, 23, 48, 58, 212, 214, 253, 254

    development, 160, 212

    EMF risk, 61, 65–69

    LandFrauen, 85

    mass, 286

    nonprofit, 58, 269

    privacy, 61, 63–65, 69

    voluntary, 23, 48

Organizational alliances, 151

Organizational fields, 8, 102, 183

P

Pakt Zukunft, 195, 196

Participation

    civic, 29, 109–126, 253, 256, 261

    political, 62, 109–126, 256

Participatory development, 219, 220

Participatory observation, 84

Patrons, 179, 187, 189, 190, 201

Personal growth, 48
Personal network, *see* Network, personal
Personal relations, 194, 200, 201
Philanthropic commitment, 181, 188, 189,
    198, 199
Philanthropic engagement, 180, 181, 186, 200
Philanthropic field, 8, 9, 97, 98, 179–201
Philanthropy
    collaborative, 7, 109–126, 201
    new, 111, 181, 200
Philosophies, 46, 293, 294, 297, 302, 303
PISA, 294, 305
Plato, 28, 29, 47, 302
Pluralism
    civic (*see* Civic pluralism)
    thick, 25
Poland, 5, 184
Political activities, 3, 4, 84, 95, 97, 101, 111,
    113, 118, 120, 123–126
Political agenda-setting, 3, 114, 239–243, 246
Political cleavages, 152–154
Political discourses, 1, 47, 48
Political ethics, 288, 299
Privacy engineering, 65, 70
Privacy implementation, 64
Privacy organization, *see* Organization, privacy
Privacy technology, 64
Private sector, *see* Sector, private
Protestant ethic, 299
Protests, 9, 48, 49, 62, 151, 153, 154,
    225, 235, 236, 239, 241, 245, 253, 259,
    266, 268, 270, 275–284, 288, 289
Proximities, 63, 79, 134, 153, 183, 200
Public agenda setting, 239, 240, 246
Public attentions, 9, 239–241, 246
Public sector, *see* Sector, public
Public sphere, 2–5, 20, 26–30, 43, 45, 49,
    51–53, 101, 238, 241, 264, 292

Q
Qualitative content analysis, 83
Qualitative interviews, 82, 185, 194
Qualitative data, 119

R
Reform coalition, 260–265
Regional analysis, 185
Regional development, 8, 79–82, 89,
    179, 201
Regional field, 185, 189
Regional governance, *see* Governance,
    regional

Regional network, *see* Network, regional
Regional stakeholders, 195, 201
Relation
    social, 6, 7, 113, 162
Relational approaches, 149–151, 170,
    171, 271
Relational events, 271
Relational geography, 133
Relational practices, 271
Relational thinking, 132–134, 142
Religion, 22, 32, 33, 35–38, 43, 49, 191
Repertoires of action, 153
Representation of interests, 3, 101
Richard Rorty, 291
Rural areas, 8, 77, 80, 82, 84–86, 88–101
Rural infrastructures, 88, 100

S
Science
    undone, 61, 62, 65, 67, 68, 70
Sector
    civic (*see* Civic sector)
    nonprofit, 46, 47, 181, 183
    private, 25, 47, 48, 53, 183, 189
    public, 25, 47, 48, 111, 115, 183, 189, 201
    third, 7, 8, 30, 47, 181, 183, 189, 201
Selection effect, 113
Self-cultivation, 293, 303
Self-generating mind, 301
Sense-making, 3, 255, 257, 259, 265, 267, 268
Shared cognitive system, 237, 248
Silent majority, 242, 243
Smart cities, 7, 57–70
Smart grids, 57, 60, 65, 70
Smart meters, 7, 57, 58, 60–68, 70
Social capital, 81, 87, 113, 182
Social change, 7, 8, 10, 43, 45, 49, 51, 53, 54,
    80, 82–84, 96–102, 109, 115, 256,
    277, 282
Social divisions, 153, 154
Social infrastructure, 85
Social innovation, *see* Innovation, social
Social integration, 34, 87, 92
Socialization effect, 113
Social justice community, *see* Community,
    social justice
Social justice movement, *see* Movement,
    social justice
Social justice outcomes, 279, 284, 285, 288
Social media, 51, 94, 236, 239, 242, 243, 248
Social mobilization, 9, 275, 277–279
Social movement, *see* Movement, social
Social outcomes, 278, 288

Social practice, 2, 3, 10, 34, 79, 80, 142
Social proximity, 99
Social relation, *see* Relation, social
Societal challenges, 3, 77, 80, 90–91, 100
Societal change, 43, 45, 58, 59, 70, 77, 78, 82, 84–93, 96–101
Societal developments, 7, 45, 47, 82, 101, 200
Society
    bourgeois, 6, 20, 21
    crisis of, 7
    gilded, 6, 19–21
    uncivil, 6, 21
Sociotechnical transition, 59
Socrates, 47
Solidarity, 36, 37, 49, 79, 115, 131, 134, 165, 169, 183, 195, 242, 244, 263, 264, 266, 267, 270, 288
Somatic power, 301, 303
Sophrosyne, 293, 296–298, 301, 302
South Africa, 9, 152, 153, 275, 276, 281, 287–289
Soviet Union, 5, 24
Student activists, 280
Sustainability, 38, 52, 90, 155, 173, 283

T
Teaching, 86, 111, 136, 220, 243, 281, 292, 300, 302, 304
Technological change, 60
Technological systems, 57–59, 67
Technological transition, 65
Technologies, 3, 7, 57–70, 90, 137, 158, 172, 219, 261, 295
Third sector, *see* Sector, third
Time banks, 8, 131, 132, 134–137, 139–142
Tocqueville, 6, 7, 19, 21–29, 32–37, 39, 49, 112
Togetherness, 87, 88
Tradition
    Greek philosophical, 302
    moral, 30, 32, 37, 248, 304
    wisdom, 305

Transformations, 21, 46, 48, 53, 79, 82, 111, 113, 185, 227, 275, 296
Trust, 23, 44, 51–53, 112, 115, 150, 195, 212, 213, 218, 220, 244, 246, 265, 288
Tyranny, 23, 26, 28–29, 33, 303

U
Umbrella Movement, 9, 235, 236, 239, 246, 248
United Kingdom (UK), 110, 111, 114–126, 132, 152–155, 159, 160, 162, 163, 169, 170, 269
United States (US), 21, 23, 24, 28, 29, 60, 61, 63, 64, 66, 67, 70, 110, 111, 114–125, 131, 154, 253–272, 285, 292
Universal suffrage
    international standards of, 241, 244, 246, 248
Unlearning, 237
Urban collective action, 5, 45, 46, 150–152, 154, 158, 165, 170, 171, 282
Urban ecologies, 155

V
Violence
    political, 281–283, 292
    structural, 261, 280, 281
Voluntary association, *see* Association, voluntary
Voluntary groups, 110, 123
Voluntary organization, *see* Organization, voluntary
Volunteering, 111, 116–122, 125, 126, 183

W
Waso Trustland, 213, 218, 223
Welfare state, 24, 25, 115
Western conception, 301
Women's association, 5

Printed by Printforce, United Kingdom